The Land Tracts

of

The Battlefield of South Mountain

other material by the author

The Braddock Expedition and Fox's Gap in Maryland
(published in 1995 by Family Line Publications, Westminster, Maryland)

The Land Tracts of the Battlefield of South Mountain - Long Version
(copies at the Washington County Free Library, Hagerstown, and the Maryland State Archives)

Kodak Photo CD-Rom Disc - Fox's Gap in Maryland
(copy in the Western Maryland Room, Washington County Free Library, Hagerstown)

The Land Tracts of the Battlefield of South Mountain

Including Many Other Tracts Near the Area from Land Records of Frederick County, Washington County and the Maryland Archives

Curtis L. Older

HERITAGE BOOKS
2008

HERITAGE BOOKS
AN IMPRINT OF HERITAGE BOOKS, INC.

Books, CDs, and more—Worldwide

For our listing of thousands of titles see our website
at
www.HeritageBooks.com

Published 2008 by
HERITAGE BOOKS, INC.
Publishing Division
100 Railroad Ave. #104
Westminster, Maryland 21157

Copyright © 1999 Curtis L. Older

Other books by the author:
The Braddock Expedition and Fox's Gap in Maryland

All rights reserved. No part of this book may be reproduced or transmitted in any form or by any means, electronic or mechanical, including photocopying, recording or by any information storage and retrieval system without written permission from the author, except for the inclusion of brief quotations in a review.

International Standard Book Number: 978-1-58549-066-0

In Memory Of

Mavis Lorene Older

Contents

Preface and Acknowledgments	ix
Introduction	x
How To Use This Book	xiii
A Note on Footnotes and Standard Spelling and Abbreviations Used in This Book	xiv
Part I: Early Tracts, Roads, and Mountain Gaps	1
Author's Master Road Map and Author's Master Tract Map	3
Master and Sub-Master Tract Drawings	7
Early Roads and Gaps	30
Part II: Tables	62
Maps	63
Contiguous Land Tracts	70
Additional Land Tract Information	76
Unplotted Land Records in the Vicinity of the Battlefield	86
Wives Identified in Land Tract Records	95
Part III: Individual Plotted Land Records	97
Maryland Hall of Records (MdHR) - Plotted Tracts	98
Frederick County Land Records (FCLR) - Plotted Tracts	139
Washington County Land Records (WCLR) - Plotted Tracts	192
Part IV: Historic Sites:	205
The Reno Monument	206
The Fox Inn	211
The Reno School along the Old Sharpsburg Road	214
The War Correspondents Memorial Arch at Crampton's Gap	215
The Mountain House at Turner's Gap	217
The Dahlgren Memorial Chapel at Turner's Gap	222
The Moses Chapline Senior Cemetery	226
Part V: Supplemental Material	230
Occupations of Residents along the Old Sharpsburg Road in the 1700s	231
Kodak Photo CD-Rom Disc - "Fox's Gap in Maryland"	233
Biographical Listing of Some Early Land Owners of the Area	235
Bibliography	241
Index	244
About the Author	259

Preface and Acknowledgments

The motivation for undertaking this work was my desire to identify and locate the land tracts owned by some of my ancestors in Fox's Gap. This area is at the crest of the Blue Ridge, along the Old Sharpsburg Road between Middletown and Sharpsburg, Maryland. *The Fox Genealogy* by Daniel Gebhart Fox, published in 1924, indicated Frederick Fox and some of his in-laws were landowners near Fox's Gap in the 1700s.

The area of Fox's Gap is best known for its Civil War history. Lesser known is its role in the Braddock Expedition of 1755. A brief study of the Braddock Expedition led me to seek the answer to the following question: Did the participants in the Braddock Expedition use Crampton's, Fox's, Orr's, or Turner's Gap to travel from Frederick Town to Ft. Cumberland? The gaps constituted the primary routes that Braddock and his men might use. These routes are all within the area that became the Battlefield of South Mountain on September 14, 1862.

My objectives included identifying the earliest roads and tracing several of the historic sites on the battlefield from the earliest tract owner through the years to the current owner. Several of these historic sites, such as the Reno Monument and the War Correspondents Memorial Arch, often appear on current published maps of the area.

The methodology employed to identify land tracts in the battlefield area began with obtaining survey or patent records for the tracts listed in *The Fox Genealogy* for Frederick Fox and his father-in-law, Bartholomew Booker. I initially plotted these tracts on paper using protractor and pencil but quickly moved to my computer for assistance. Next, I sought to identify contiguous tracts, obtain survey or patent records for those tracts, and then plot them on the computer. At the same time, I obtained copies of deeds related to the Reno Monument and worked backward to identify previous owners of the tracts. I applied the same technique to the Mountain House at Turner's Gap and to the Fox Inn. I was surprised to find the Fox Inn still standing in 1993. Seven years after I began the project in 1991, I had collected about 400 land records for tracts in the area of the battlefield.

Material from the Tracey Collection in the Historical Society of Carroll County was invaluable in identifying many tracts. In *Western Maryland Genealogy* I learned of Robert H. Fox of Cincinnati, Ohio, who told me about the Tracey Collection. At an early point in time, Robert sent me information he had that described the tract of Grim's Fancy. The Grim's Fancy survey mentioned John Fox's house and the road to Swearingen's Ferry. The correspondence indicated that material existed in the Tracey Collection that I should review.

In my book, *The Braddock Expedition and Fox's Gap in Maryland*, published in 1995, I used master tract drawings created from many of the land records I identified and plotted up to that time. I also used records of Frederick County court minutes, original writings of participants in the Braddock Expedition, genealogical records, and other contemporary sources of material that could be used to substantiate the events of the Braddock Expedition.

This book is an abbreviated version of *The Land Tracts of Fox's Gap, including material on Crampton's, Orr's, and Turner's Gap*, also known as *The Land Tracts of the Battlefield of South Mountain - Long Version*. The long version is about 1,000 pages in length and copies are at the Washington County Free Library in Hagerstown, Maryland, and in the Maryland Archives, Annapolis, Maryland. Both this book and its Long Version are part of my attempt to preserve the work expended in researching the land tracts. By using these books, other researchers may, to some extent, avoid having to retrace my steps.

My research success would not have been possible without the assistance of Susanne Flowers of Frederick, Maryland. Susanne worked in the office of the Clerk of the Circuit Court for 16 years before retiring in 1990. Her efforts went far beyond the call of duty. She deserves credit for documenting many of the land tracts mentioned in this book. She also provided materials that led me to sources of information that otherwise were unknown to me.

Those who provided assistance in my research of the battlefield area or assisted in the preparation of this book include Doug Bast, Director of the Boonsborough Museum of History, Boonsboro, Maryland; Donna Valley Russell, editor of *Western Maryland Genealogy*; Jay Graybeal of the Historical Society of Carroll County, Westminster, Maryland; Kathy Crosby of Charlotte, North Carolina, and my daughter, Rachael Lynn Older. Any errors, oversights, or omissions are entirely mine.

Introduction

The Old Sharpsburg Road, from Middletown, Maryland, through Sharpsburg to Shepherdstown, Virginia [now West Virginia], crossed South Mountain at Fox's Gap. The route of this road exists today, as it has for over 250 years, but is known by a number of names along its path. Heading east from Sharpsburg to just north of Middletown its names are Geeting Road, Dog Street Road, Reno Monument Road, and Marker Road in that order. This road played a role in historic events with worldwide significance. Two of these events were the Braddock Expedition of 1755 and the Battle of South Mountain on September 14, 1862.

The Battle of South Mountain began at Fox's Gap about 9:00 Sunday morning, September 14, 1862. United States Major General Jesse Lee Reno and Confederate General Samuel Garland died at Fox's Gap during the battle.

I believe the Battle of South Mountain is one of the most overlooked and underrated battles of the Civil War. I also believe the battle was a Union victory, not a standoff or an indecisive battle some authors believe it to have been. Two newspaper accounts at the time of the battle support my view. "The most complete victory of the war was gained yesterday. We stormed and took the rebel Gibraltar. Braver and more desperate fighting was never before seen on the continent."[1] "At one point in a mud road to the left of the turnpike, nearly four hundred bodies are strewn thickly over less than an acre of ground, all of them in the unmistakable Rebel garb."[2]

The Battle of Antietam occurred three days after the Battle of South Mountain. The Battlefield of Antietam is approximately five miles west of Fox's Gap. Antietam was the single bloodiest day in American history, with over 23,000 casualties within a 24-hour period.

In writing the history of a battle I suggest three principles to follow: 1) know the order of battle, 2) visit the battlefield, and 3) do not form a preconceived idea of the battle and then go about collecting information to support the preconceived idea or theory.

U. S. Presidents George Washington, Abraham Lincoln, Rutherford B. Hayes, and William McKinley all came to Fox's Gap as the result of military missions. Many other famous Americans were associated with the Battle of South Mountain in 1862 and the Braddock Expedition of 1755. George McClellan, the Democratic Party's candidate for President in 1864, was the Commander of the Union Army at the battle of South Mountain. McClellan had on his staff at the battle a young officer named George Armstrong Custer.

Anyone interested in the land tracts of the Battlefield of South Mountain should see the Tracey Collection at the Historical Society of Carroll County in Westminster, Maryland. This collection contains much valuable material on the early land tracts of western Maryland.

A map prepared for some Frederick County Land Records is in the Frederick County Library in Frederick, Maryland. "In 1966, Dr. H. Hanford Hopkins of Baltimore arranged for Joseph W. Urner of Frederick, an architect, to draw a large map (scale 3:2 inches = 1 mile) of the area of Frederick County . . . each original land grant is named and numbered, another set of numbers refers to colonial homes standing in 1966. These numbers are coordinated with the Tracey Collection cards and copy of the map is at the Burr Artz Library, Frederick."[3]

Readers should be mindful that Washington County was part of Frederick County until 1776. Frederick County was part of Prince Georges County until 1748. The Frederick County/Washington County line runs along the crest of the Blue Ridge and through the mountain gaps. It may cause frustration at times in digging out land records because sometimes land records are needed from both counties.

Any researcher must be aware that it is entirely possible for more than one land tract or more than one individual to have the name you are researching. In the 1700s, many families named children after the parents or grandparents.

Following are some of the sources of information that I recommend the reader keep in mind:

1. Records in the <u>Tracey Collection at the Historical Society of Carroll County</u> are an invaluable source of information that should be used when researching land tracts in western Maryland.

2. The <u>Maryland Archives</u> has many materials that can assist you. The following books at the Maryland Archives are useful in tracing owners of tracts in the early 1800s. Owners of tracts appear in these books along with the related tract

names:
Frederick County, years of 1819-1868. Location: S 1736-1, 50,096-14, 1/28/1/6

Washington County, early 1800s, Location: 50,096-24-2, 1/28/1/16 MSA S 1388-2

3. *Pioneers of Old Monocacy* by Grace L. Tracey and John P. Dern is one useful reference book that cites many land tract records and provides related history. However, this book, like most of that ilk, is not foolproof.

4. Newspaper abstracts, such as those found in *The Maryland Gazette 1727-1761 Genealogical and Historical Abstracts* by Karen Mauer Green, may prove significant in your research. A good index to newspaper abstracts may make finding information faster and easier.

5. Maps substantiate the old saying that a picture is worth a thousand words. Numerous early maps exist of the area of the battlefield. Early Pennsylvania and Virginia maps also may be useful in researching Maryland roads.

6. People who are knowledgeable of the area can provide valuable assitance. Seek out these individuals and don't assume there is not someone out there who can help you find the answers to your questions.

7. Journals, diaries, and writings of participants in the events, i.e. George Washington, the Braddock Expedition journals, civil war letters, and diaries, if contemporary, can provide valuable insight.

8. Genealogy books and related materials may provide information that can be found nowhere else. Some excellent examples include: *Jacob Fluck of Middletown, Frederick County, Maryland, and his Flook and Fluke Descendants* by Patricia Abelard Andersen; *Chaplines from Maryland and Virginia* by Maria J. Liggett Dare; *The Fox Genealogy including the Metherd, Benner, and Leiter Descendants* by Daniel Gebhart Fox; *The Dulanys of Maryland* by Aubrey C. Land; and *From Mill Wheel to Plowshare* by Julia A. Drake and James R. Orndorff.

9. Closely related to genealogy sources are wills and administration accounts. These records should not be overlooked as a source of information by the researcher.

10. Court minutes may be an important supplement to the land records. One useful source of court minutes is *This Was the Life excerpts from the judgment records of Frederick County, Md. 1748-1765* by Millard M. Rice. Another sourse is *Minutes and Proceedings of Washington County Court held in Elizabethtown, 1776-1810* by Gerald Sword. Court minutes also may be obtained from the Maryland Archives.

11. Court cases can help clarify land transactions. An excellent example is the case of Joseph Chapline Jr versus William W. Chapline and Jacob Smith. The case was fought over a tract called Exchange. The court records mention Frederick Fox. The case appears in Maryland Archives Chancery Records at B 49 - 243 under Frederick Fox.

12. Local area histories are useful if they rely on original source materials and cite references for that material. An excellent example is an article in the Maryland Genealogical Society Bulletin entitled, "Coming Home: The Deardorff Family in Burkittsville, Frederick County, Maryland, 1779-1803" by Timothy Reese.

13. Histories such as *History of Maryland* by James McSherry; *History of Western Maryland* by J. Thomas Scharf; and *History of Washington County, Maryland* by T. J. C. Williams and Folger McKinsey are helpful in obtaining a panorama of information about the area. These authors are not always accurate; however, and often they do not cite sources of the information they present.

14. The Frederick, Washington, and Carroll County Historical Societies may have some helpful information, also.

15. Historical accounts in Pennsylvania and Virginia may provide insight into early Maryland events.

16. Land Tract Indexes should be investigated. A Washington County, Maryland, Land Patent Index does exist; a copy is at the Washington County Court House. The index gives the following: name of tract, surveyed for, date, acreage, book, and page. This index appears in alphabetical order by tract name.

The Maryland Archives has a list that shows patent records held by the archives by description, MSA number, MdHR number, and location for related years. An example follows:

Dates	Description	MSA No.
1748-1750	BY & GS 3, pp. 1-347	S 11-86
1750-1762	BY & GS 3, pp. 348-731	S 11-87

MdHR No.	Location
17,404-1	1/23/2/40
17,404-2	1/23/2/41

The Maryland Archives has two card index systems a researcher may use to find land patent information. One card index uses land tract names as the key search words. Another land tract card index uses the names of individuals who patented tracts as the key search words.

17. <u>Various organizations</u> such as the Central Maryland Heritage Leauge, Inc., with headquarters in Middletown, and the Association for the Preservation of Civil War Sites, Inc., with headquarters in Hagerstown, may provide valuable assistance to a researcher. The National Park Service or the Potomac Appalachian Trail Club, with headquarters in Vienna, Virginia, may be a source of information. Also, the Sons or Daughters of the American Revolution, Civil War societies, Civil War round table groups, and others with an interest in history, genealogy, or related areas.

Never underestimate what you can dig out of old records. More information on the past probably exists than you imagine. Don't assume that you cannot find some record that will help you solve the question you are researching. Most research is time consuming and expensive.

An important research principle to follow is to seek original source documents related to an issue. Stories passed down as local lore are often inaccurate to some degree. A researcher should use sources and accounts contemporary with the events being studied. Second-hand, non-contemporary accounts often change to a material degree some of the facts and circumstances surrounding the point being researched.

You must have correct data to create an accurate history. My own experience has led me to keep researching an issue until I am convinced that additional research would only lead me to more information that would support my conclusions and agree with my findings.

Footnotes - Introduction

[1] Chicago Tribune, probably Monday, September 22, 1862, The Eighth Illinois Cavalry at Boonsboro. Correspondence N. Y. Tribune. Boonsboro, Md, Sept. 15, 1862.

[2] Washington Post, front page, upper right column, September 18, 1865, The Battlefield.

[3] Source not known.

How to Use this Book

I urge the user of this book to read the Preface and Introduction to learn how to obtain the most benefit from the material presented. The reader should assume that errors exist in a book of this nature. Reference should be made to the original source document at the Maryland Hall of Records, Frederick County Courthouse, or Washington County Courthouse to obtain the most authoritative record.

The earliest land tracts in Maryland history were given names and most of them typically were of an irregular shape. The unit of measure for these early tracts was the perch; one perch equals 16.5 feet.

Many early tracts have lines that overlap contiguous tracts. Some of these errors are due to the surveyor, the one who wrote down the survey record, or to my ability to plot the tract according to the actual record. Some tract names humorously reflect these errors, i.e., We Could Not Agree and Long Dispute.

The Author's Master Road Map and Author's Master Tract Map (shown on pages three and five) display the area of the Battlefield of South Mountain and the surrounding portion of Western Maryland. Reviewing each of these maps is a good place to begin one's understanding of the material presented in this book. The maps provide the reader with an overall view of the location of towns, the course of the roads, and the location of historic sites within the area with which the reader should become familiar.

The Author's Master Road Map shows the primary roads and landmarks in the area encompassing Williamsport, Sharpsburg, Burkittsville, Middletown, Boonsboro, and Hagerstown. The Author's Master Tract Map shows the same roads and towns as the Author's Master Road Map, but shows the location of many of the tracts plotted by the author in relationship to the roads and towns.

Users of this book should review the Master Tract Drawings to identify areas of the battlefield in which they may have an interest. Sub-Master Tract Drawings give a more detailed view of a smaller area than do the Master Drawings. Reference to the various Tables allows the reader to identify more detailed information about an individual tract or area.

Individual plotted land tracts appear under three categories: Maryland Hall of Records (MdHR), Frederick County Land Records (FCLR), and Washington County Land Records (WCLR). The Index at the back of the book lists plotted tracts, archived reference numbers for tracts, individuals mentioned in the book, and other entries. The Index provides the related page number(s) where the item listed in the Index appears in the book.

Tables included in the book allow the reader to identify contiguous tracts, provide information in addition to that given with the individual tract drawing, identify land tracts in the area of the battlefield that the author did not plot, describe maps to which the reader may wish to refer, and identify wives mentioned in land tract records.

Land tract records in the Maryland Hall of Records (MdHR) section appear in alphabetical order by tract name. The MdHR reference number appears with each tract, the date of survey or patent, the name of the person in whom the survey or patent was made, and the number of acres in the tract. Frederick County Land Records (FCLR) appear in sequence by the Frederick County reference number under which the land record may be found at the Frederick County Court House. Many of the FCLR tracts included in this book consist of parts of more than one original tract.

Washington County Land Records (WCLR) appear in sequence by the Washington County reference number under which the land record may be found at the Washington County Court House. Like the FCLR tracts, many of the WCLR tracts included in this book consist of parts of more than one original tract.

Working with the earliest tracts and even later tracts can be as much an art as a science. Later deeds may contain corrections to earlier surveys for "variation in the magnetic needle." Later land tract records often help clarify earlier tracts; therefore, tracts may best be studied by evaluation over a period of time. The safest approach to obtain accuracy is to continue to gather information until you are convinced further research will only result in obtaining additional material to support your conclusion.

The plotted tracts that appear in this book have the north side of the tract closest to the top of each page and the south side of each tract is correspondingly closest to the bottom of each page. The orientation is confirmed by the following sign on some drawings: **N ^**

A Note on Footnotes

Footnotes appear at the end of each section of the text to which they relate.

In citing works in the footnotes, works frequently cited have been identified by the following abbreviations.

FCLR	Frederick County Land Records
MdHR	Maryland Hall of Records (State Archives), Annapolis, Maryland
MSA	Maryland State Archives (Annapolis)
WCLR	Washington County Land Records

Standard Spelling and Abbreviations Used in This Book

As Used in This Book	As May Appear in Source Documents
ac	acres
Add	Addition
afsd	aforesaid
and	&
Antietam	Andiatum
beginning	begining
bound	bd
Chapline	Chaplin, Chaplain
Conococheague	Conochiege
Curry's	Curries, Carey's
draft	draught
Dulany	Dulaney
marked	markd, markt
Monocacy	Monocicee
Mt.	Mount
parcel	parcell
part	pt
ps	pr, per, pers, perches
Potomac	Patomack
reversed	reverst
Rsy, rsy	Resurvey, resurvey
running	runing
said	sd
Shaff (Casper)	Shaaff, Shaaf
Shanandore	Shannadore
Sharpsburg	Sharpsburgh
the, that	ye
wagon	waggon

Part I

Early Tracts, Roads, and Mountain Gaps

Author's Master Road Map
Author's Master Tract Map
Master Tract Drawings
Sub-Master Tract Drawings
Early Roads and Gaps

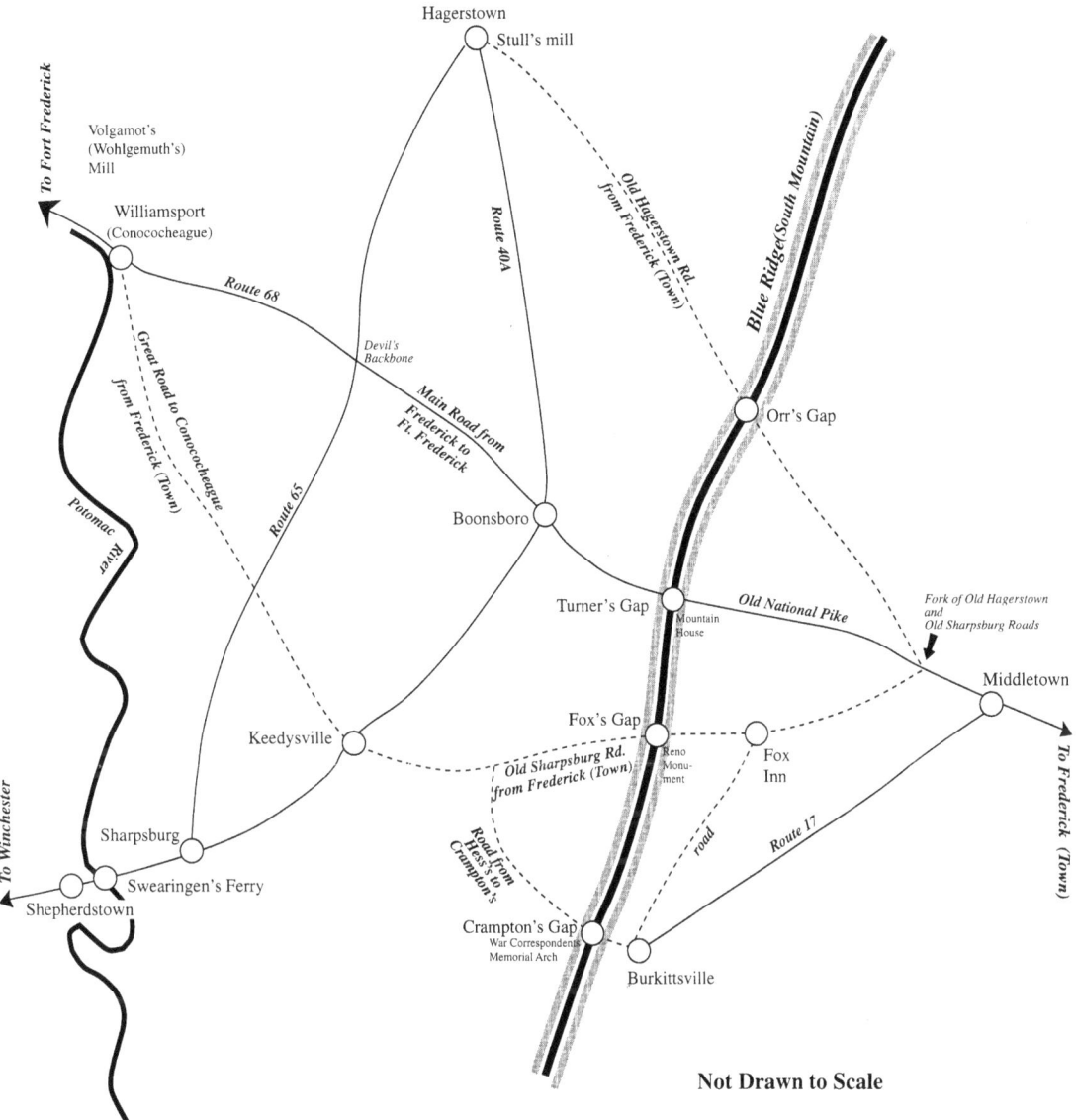

Author's Master Road Map

- **Battlefield of South Mountain** - includes the areas of Turner's, Fox's, and Crampton's Gaps
- **Key landmarks on the Battlefield of South Mountain** - Mountain House at Turner's Gap, Reno Monument at Fox's Gap, and War Correspondents Memorial Arch at Crampton's Gap

Points Along the Roads

- **Old Sharpsburg Road** – Frederick, Middletown, Fox's Gap, Sharpsburg
- **Old Hagerstown Road** – Frederick, Middletown, Orr's Gap, Hagerstown
- **Great Road to Conococheague** – Frederick, Middletown, Fox's Gap, Keedysville, Williamsport
- **Main Road from Frederick to Fort Frederick** – Frederick, Middletown, Turner's Gap, Boonsboro, Devil's Back Bone, Williamsport, Fort Frederick
- **Old National Pike** – Frederick, Middletown, Turner's Gap, Boonsboro, Hagerstown
- **Great Philadelphia Wagon Road** – Winchester, Shepherdstown, Sharpsburg, Fox's Gap, Middletown, Frederick, Philadelphia
- **Route 40A** – Frederick, Middletown, Turner's Gap, Boonsboro, Hagerstown
- **Road from Frederick Town to Swearingen's Ferry** – Frederick, Middletown, Fox's Gap, Sharpsburg, Shepherdstown

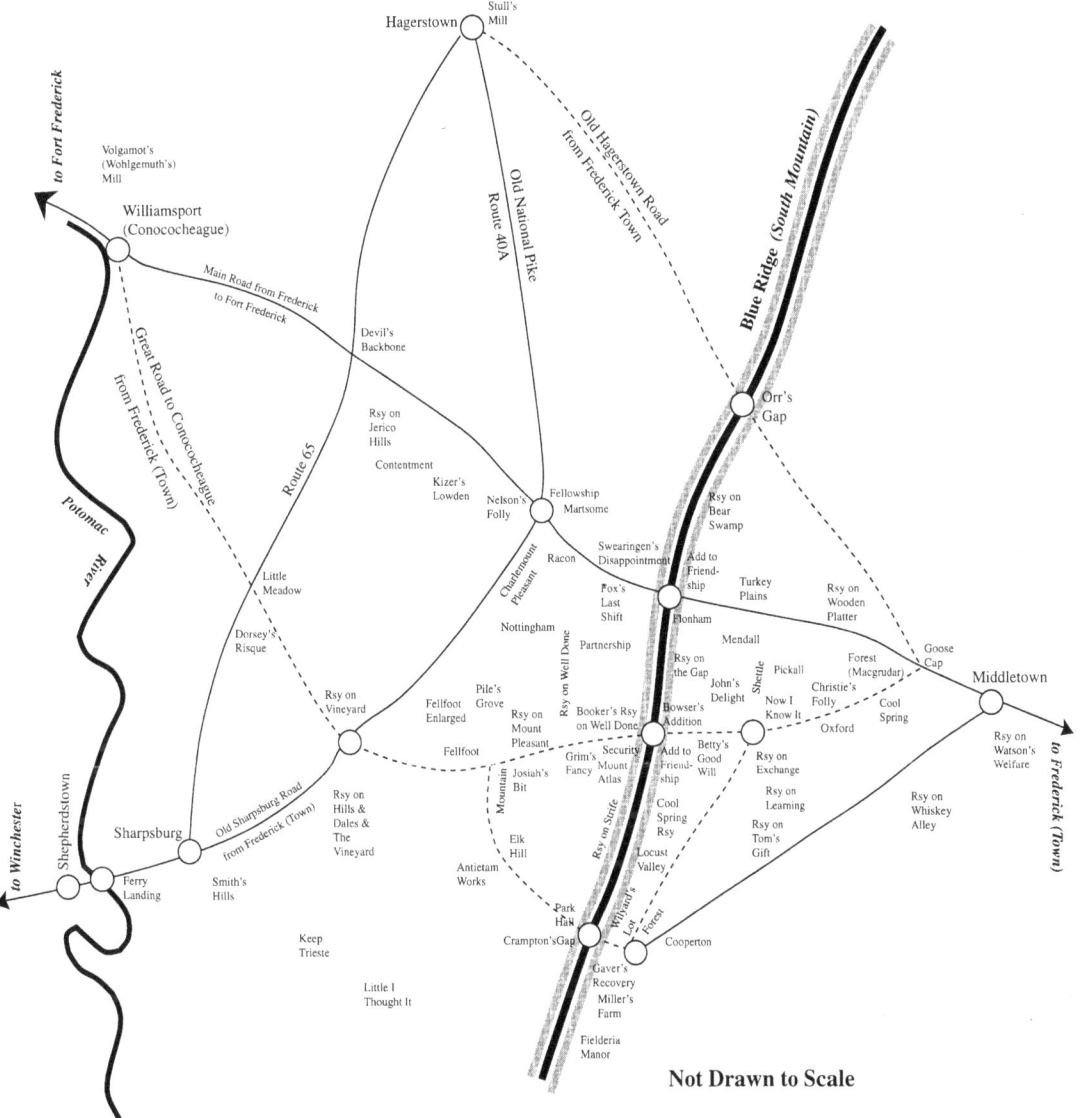

Author's Master Tract Map

1. This map is identical to the Author's Master Road Map on page three as far as the lines that show roads, towns, the Potomac River, the Blue Ridge, Swearingen's Ferry, or other locations. Comparison of the Author's Master Tract Map with the Author's Master Road Map should give the reader the ability to identify the approximate location of those tracts shown on the Author's Master Tract Map.

2. The location of tracts is only approximate on this map. Please refer to Master and Sub-Master drawings for the detail of a tract and its surrounding tracts. Only selected tracts appear on the above map.

3. Sub-Master Tract Drawings that appear on the following pages include: Fellfoot Enlarged Master; Resurvey on Hills and Dales and (The) Vineyard Master; Resurvey on (The) Gap Master; Resurvey on Well Done Master; Contentment Master; Resurvey on Oxford Area; West of Fox's Gap all the way to Crampton's Gap; Gaver's Recovery Master #1; Gaver's Recovery Master #2; Cost's Content Master; Tracts Surrounding the Mountain House at Turner's Gap; The Fox Inn Area - Selected Tracts; and Pile's Grove Master.

Master Tract Drawings

	Page
From Fox's Gap Southeast along the Old Sharpsburg Road	8
From Fox's Gap South towards Crampton's Gap	9
The Area North and South of Crampton's Gap	10
The West Side of Crampton's Gap	11
Tracts near the Fox Inn and along the Old Sharpsburg Road	12
The Old Sharpsburg Road from the Fox Inn to the Old Hagerstown Road	13
1792 Road from Fox's Gap West through Fellfoot Tract	14
South and East of the Fox Inn	15

From Fox's Gap Southeast along the Old Sharpsburg Road

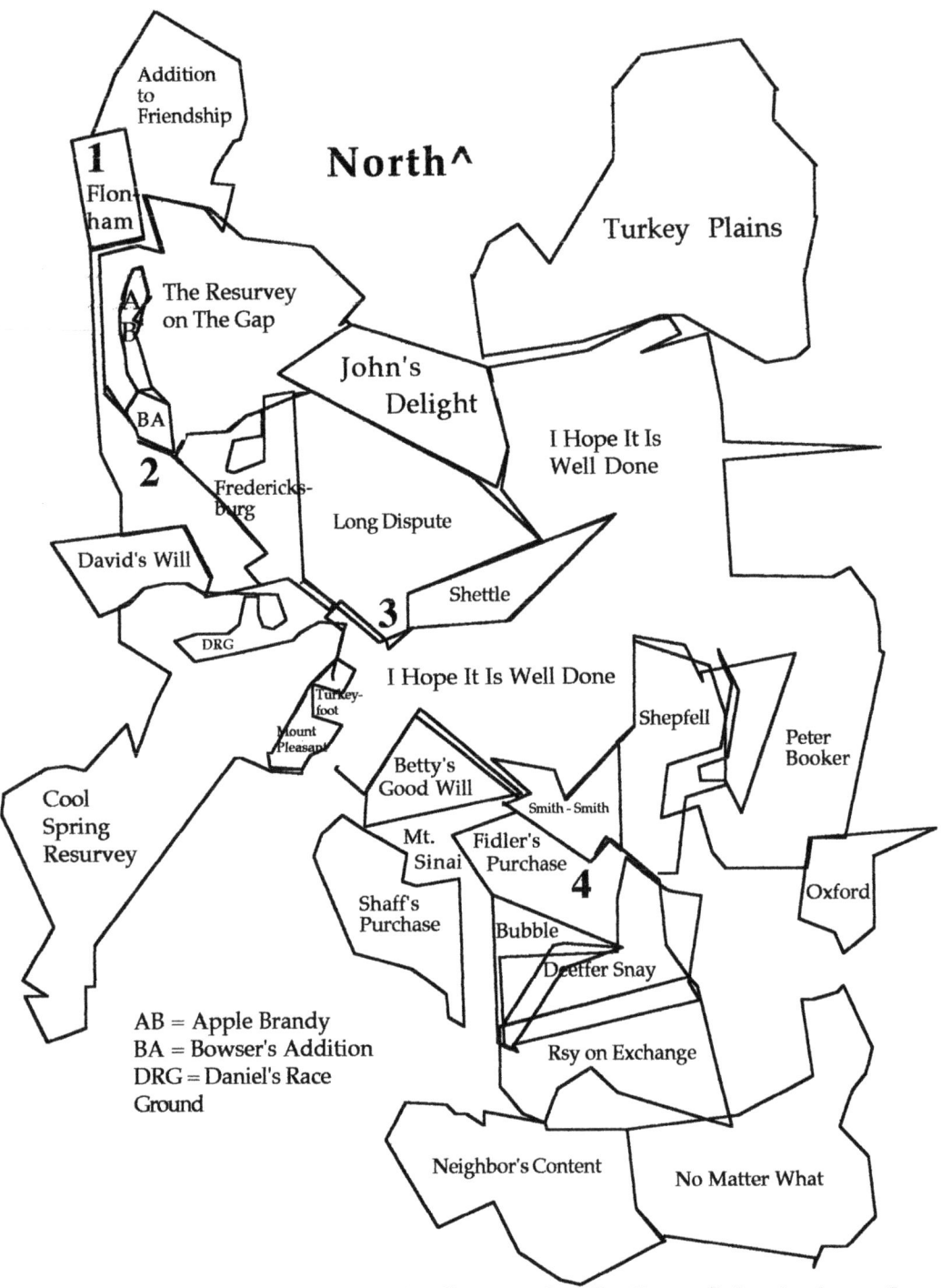

1. The Mountain House at Turner's Gap
2. The Reno Monument at Fox's Gap
3. The Reno School along the road
4. The Fox Inn along the road

These tracts lie on the east side of South Mountain in Frederick County.

From Fox's Gap South towards Crampton's Gap

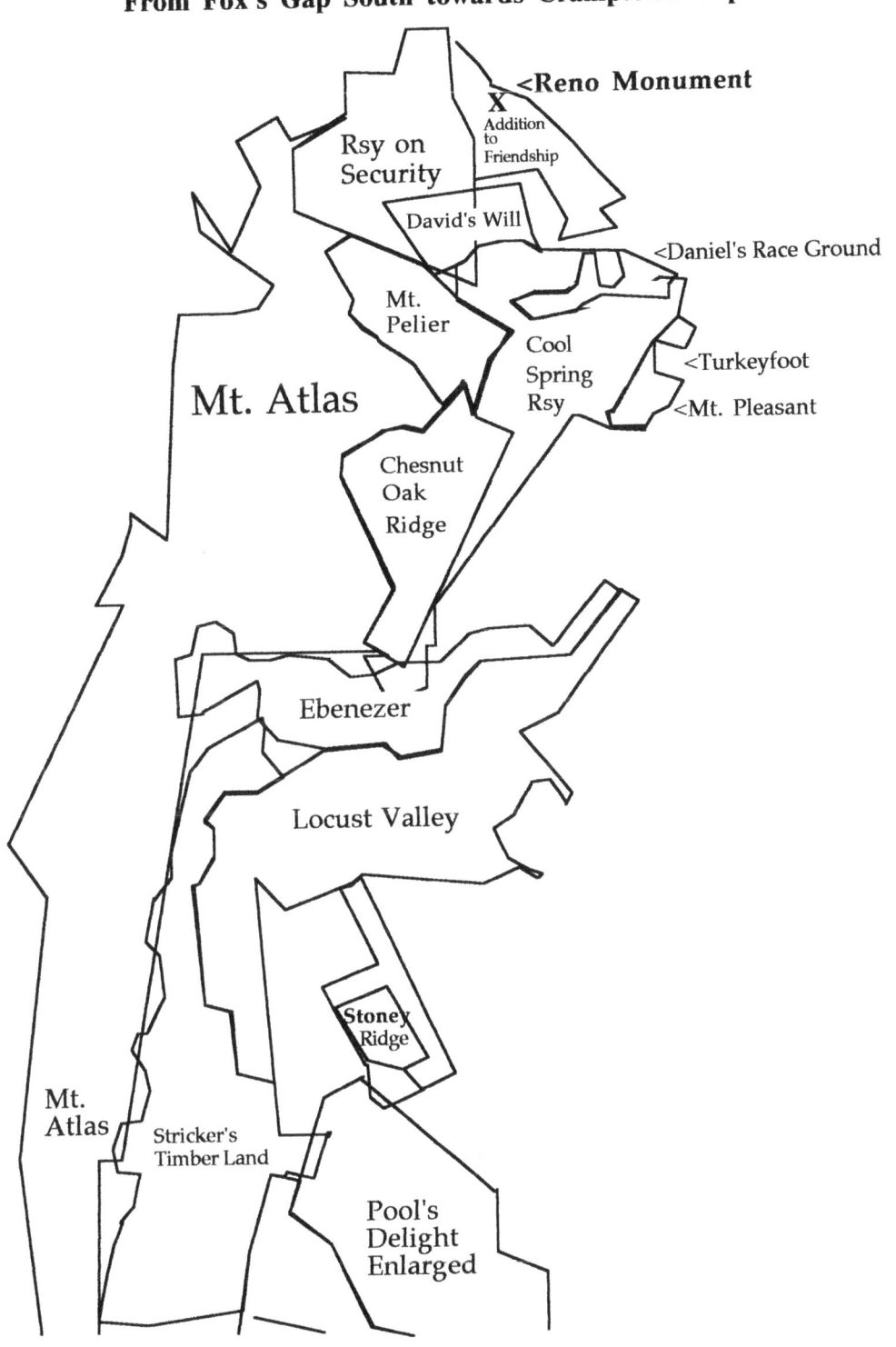

These tracts lie along or near the Blue Ridge.

The Area North and South of Crampton's Gap

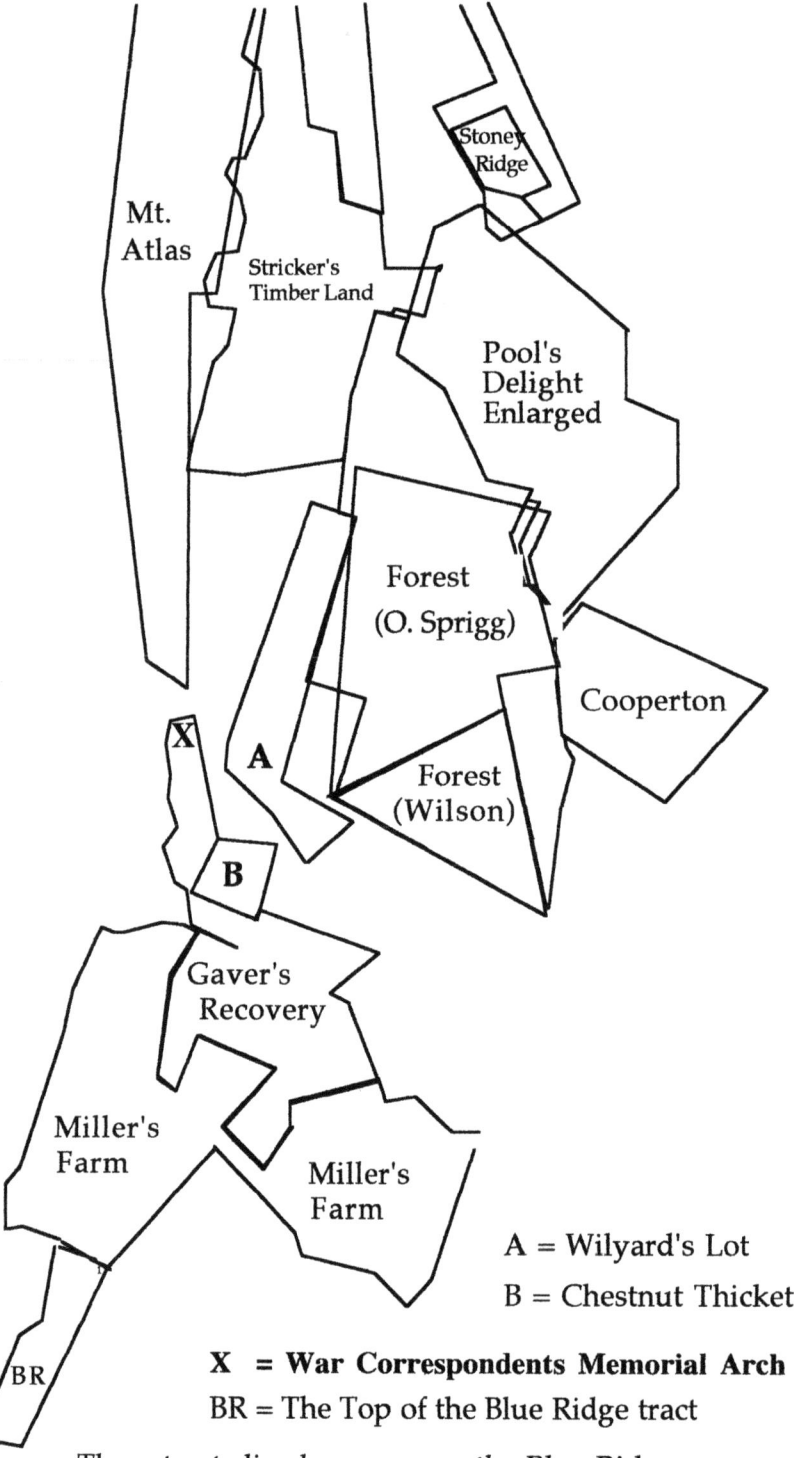

A = Wilyard's Lot
B = Chestnut Thicket
X = War Correspondents Memorial Arch
BR = The Top of the Blue Ridge tract

These tracts lie along or near the Blue Ridge.

The West Side of Crampton's Gap

1. Antietam Works
2. Elk Hill
3. Park Hall
4. Strife
5. Mt. Atlas
6. Robinett to Huffer (Park Hall)
7. Peddicord to Crampton (Park Hall)
8. Shelton to Crampton (Park Hall)
9. Burrell's Disappointment
10. I Hope It Is So
11. Badham's Refuse
12. Anderson to Grims

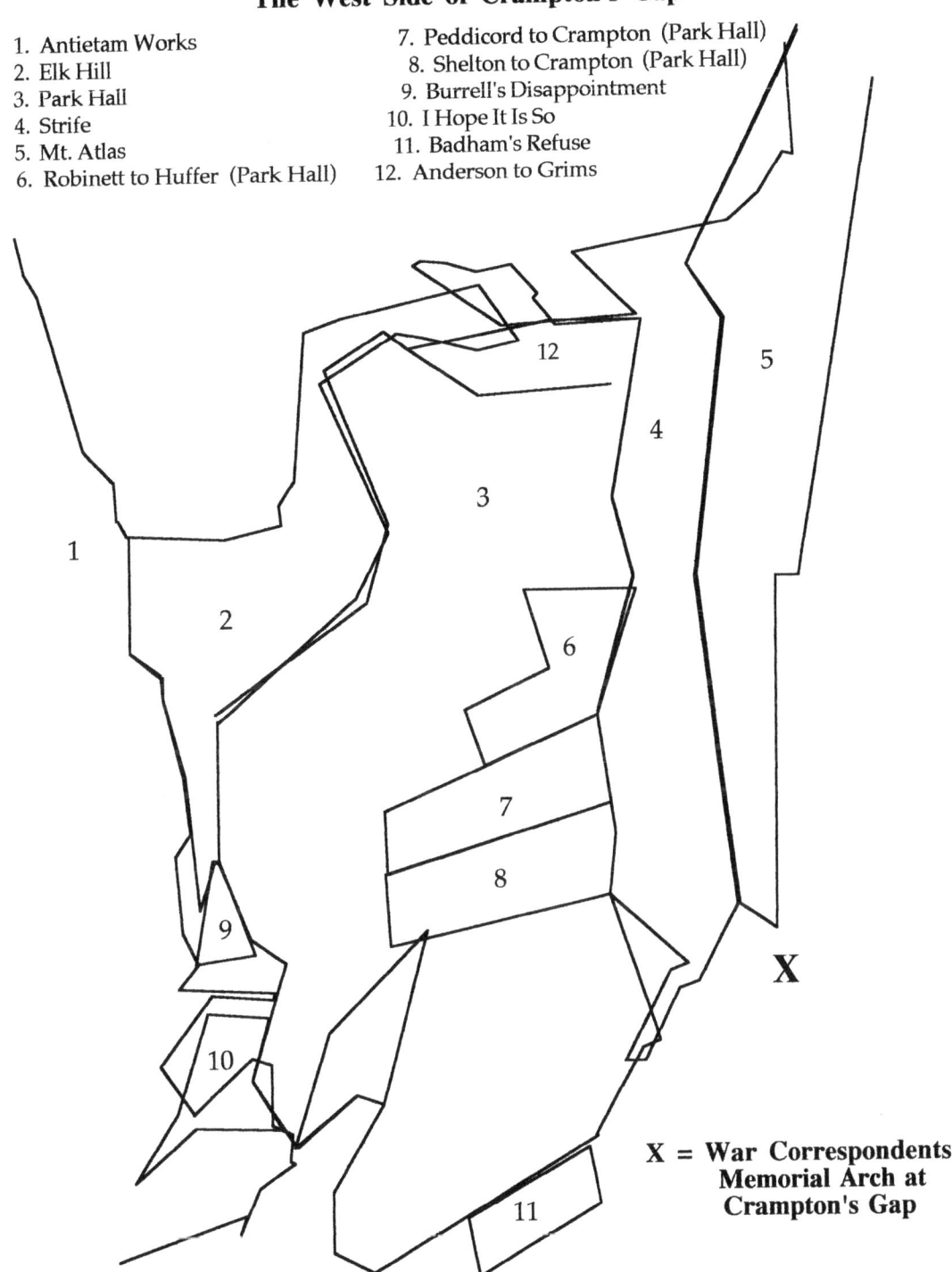

X = War Correspondents Memorial Arch at Crampton's Gap

These tracts are on the west side of South Mountain.

Tracts near the Fox Inn and along the Old Sharpsburg Road - East Side of Fox's Gap

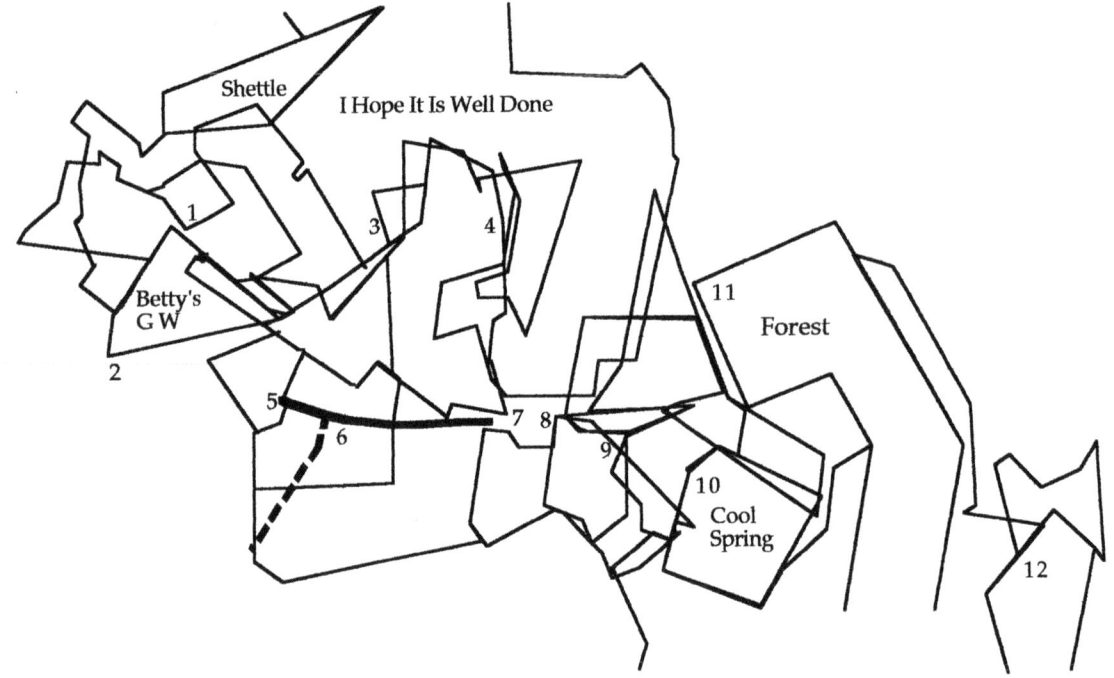

Points 1, 5, 6, 7, 8, 9, and 12 are along the Old Sharpburg Road, in part shown as the heavy black line. The dotted line is the road from the Fox Inn to Burkittsville.

1. Beginning Tree - Bartholomew Booker to Frederick Fox, FCLR, WR-7, 4 Apr 1787, "at a stone near the Main Road that leads from Middle Town to Sharpsburg."
2. Beginning Tree - Betty's Good Will, Robert Evans, MdHR, BC & GS 4, pp. 195-196, 16 Oct 1747, ". . . at the foot of Shanandore Mountain near the wagon road that goes from Teague's Ferry to Monocacy Town."
3. 50 perches along the Main Road to Boonsboro - Michael Miller to Jacob Smith, FCLR, WR-32-225, recorded 30 Dec 1807, "to the middle of the main road leading to Boonsboro."
4. Beginning Tree - Bartholomew Booker to Michel Shepfell, Resurvey on Mendall, FCLR, F-1077, 100 Acres, 6 Jun 1760, "road from Bartholomew Booker's to Peter Beaver's."
5. Vincent Sanner to Samuel Ausherman, FCLR, CM-1-582. Point 5 is on Old Sharpsburg Road.
6. The Fox Inn - Stanley F. Young to Richard B. and Helen B. Rudy, FCLR, Liber 605, page 469, 25 Sep 1958.
7. End of Line 5 - Now I Know It, Jacob Smith, FCLR, THO-1-220, 17 Dec 1802, "to a stone marked 38 in the main road planted at the end of the 38th line of said lands."
8. Beginning Tree - Oxford, James Wardrop, MdHR BY & GS 5, p. 594, 23 Jul 1751, ". . . about ten or fifteen yards of the main road that leads through Frederick Town by Robert Evans and on the north side of the said road."
9. Along Main Road - We Could Not Agree, FCLR, THO-1-188, resurveyed 18 Jul 1800, "to the middle of the main road and down it."
10. Beginning Tree - The Cool Spring, James Wardrop, MdHR, BY & GS 5, pp. 608-609, 17 May 1750, "beginning at a bounded white oak standing on the top of a hill about two hundred yards from the wagon road that leads through Frederick Town and about a mile from John Burger's."
11. Beginning Tree - Forest, John Magrudar, MdHR, AM 1, pp. 365-366, 2 Oct 1733, "about half mile above the wagon road that goes from Conestoga to Opequon crosses a creek called Catoctin Creek which falls into Potomac River about six miles above Monocacy."
12. Approximate fork of the Old Sharpsburg and Old Hagerstown Roads at the mouth of Mill Creek on the Catoctin Creek - Goose Cap, FCLR, WR-8-632, Richard Butler to Jacob Fulwiler.

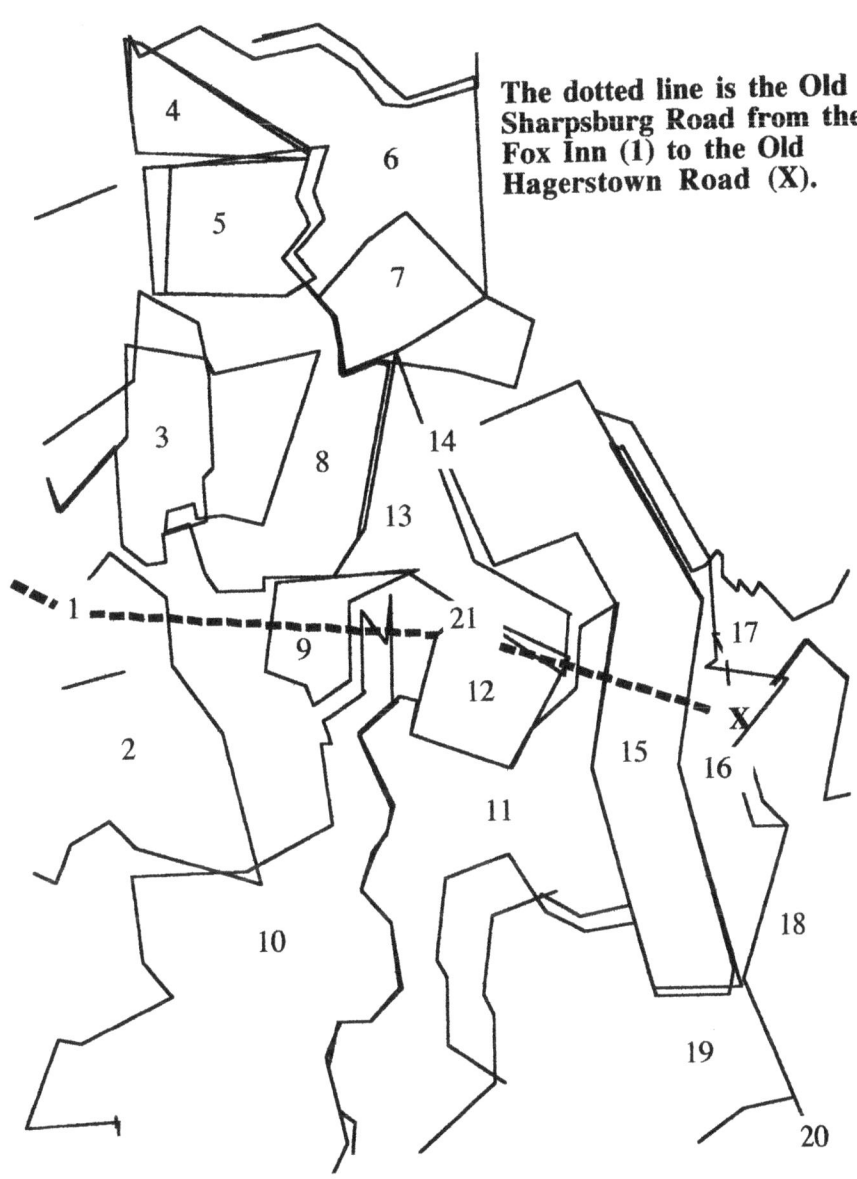

The dotted line is the Old Sharpsburg Road from the Fox Inn (1) to the Old Hagerstown Road (X).

1. The Fox Inn - on (The) Exchange, surveyed 1742
2. Rsy on Exchange - patented 1754
3. Smith Sr. to Jr., 1795 - I Hope It Is Well Done
4. Booker to Yeaste, 1760 - Rsy on Mendal l
5. Booker to Everhart, 1760 - Rsy on Mendal l
6. Booker to Koogle, 1791 - Rsy on Wooden Platter
7. Wooden Platter - surveyed 1742
8. Pickall of Booker - patented 1764
9. Oxford - surveyed for Wardrop in 1750
10. Rsy on Learning etc. - resurveyed 1765
11. Rsy on Tom's Gift - patented 1764
12. Cool Spring - surveyed for Wardrop in 1750
13. Christie's Folly - Smith to Beaver, 1755
14. Beginning tree of (The) Forest (Magrudar)
15. The Forest (Macgrudar) - surveyed 2 Oct 1733
16. Rsy on Whiskey Alley - 12 May 1762
17. Goose Cap - Fink to Welch, 1771
18. Rsy on Watson's Welfare - Joseph Chapline, 1752
19. Rsy on Whiskey Alley
20. Beginning tree of Watson's Welfare
21. Beginning tree of Cool Spring - James Wardrop
X = Fork of the Roads

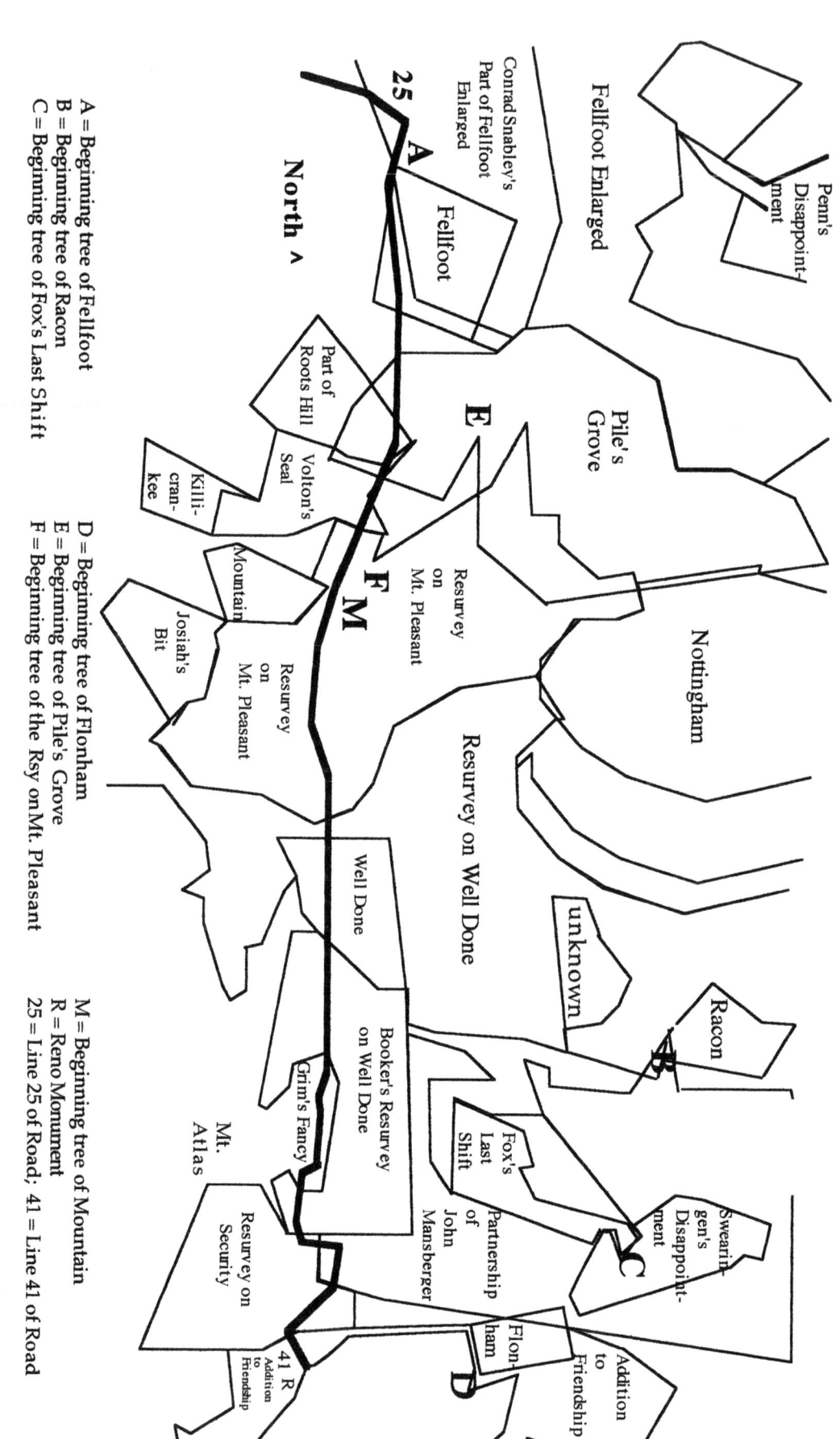

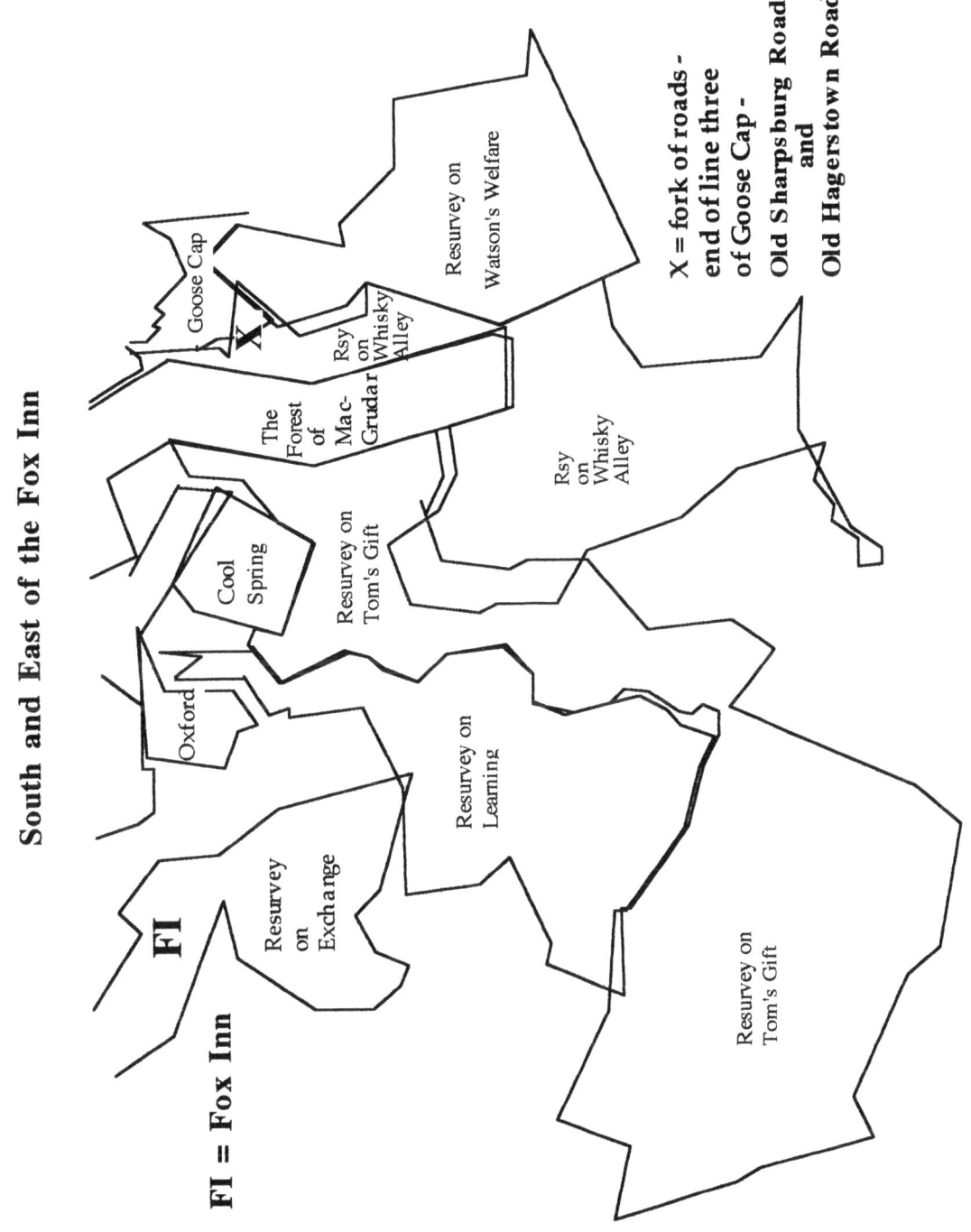

Sub-Master Tract Drawings

	Page
Fellfoot Enlarged Master	17
Resurvey on Hills and Dales and (The) Vineyard Master	18
Resurvey on (The) Gap Master	19
Resurvey on Well Done Master	20
Contentment Master	21
Resurvey on Oxford Area	22
West of Fox's Gap all the way to Crampton's Gap	23
Gaver's Recovery Master #1	24
Gaver's Recovery Master #2	25
Cost's Content Master	26
Tracts Surrounding the Mountain House at Turner's Gap	27
The Fox Inn Area - Selected Tracts	28
Pile's Grove Master	29

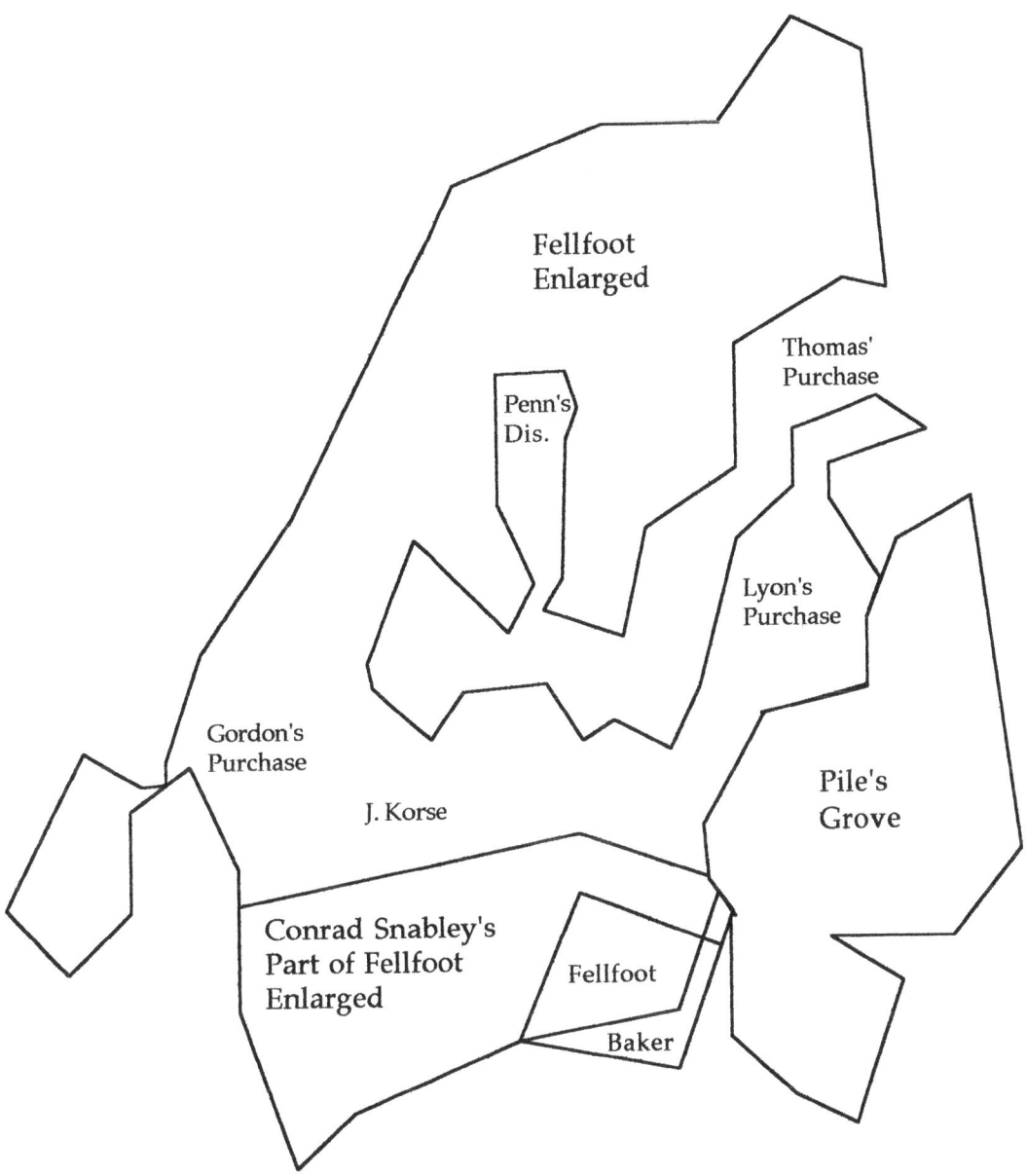

Fellfoot Enlarged Master

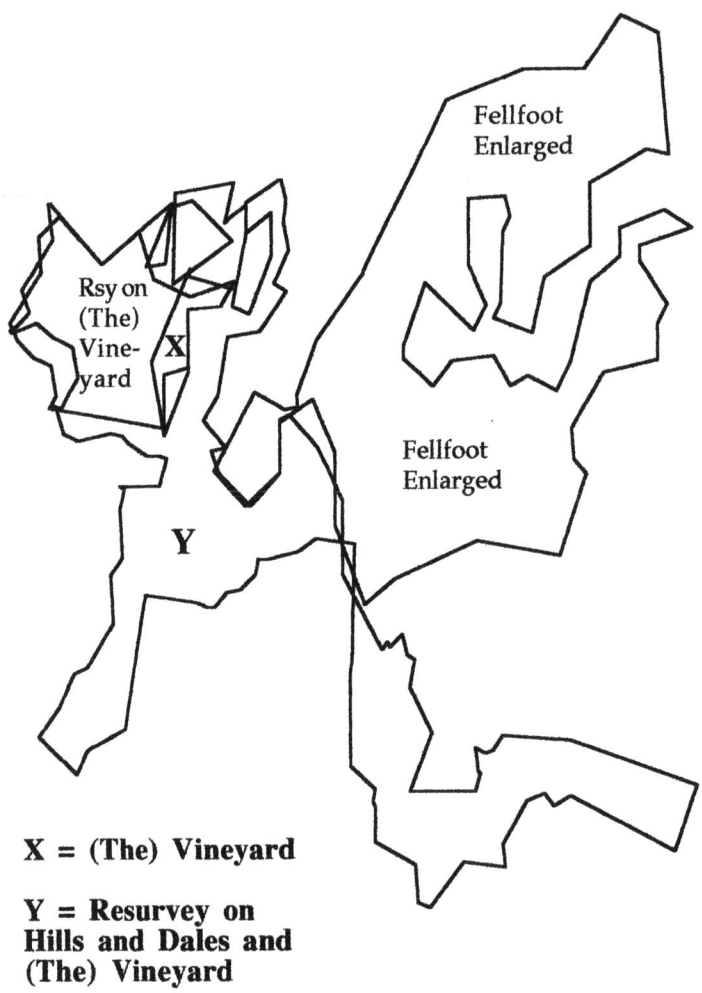

Resurvey on Hills and Dales and (The) Vineyard Master

Overlay of Tracts in the Resurvey on (The) Gap, Apple Brandy, and Bowser's Addition

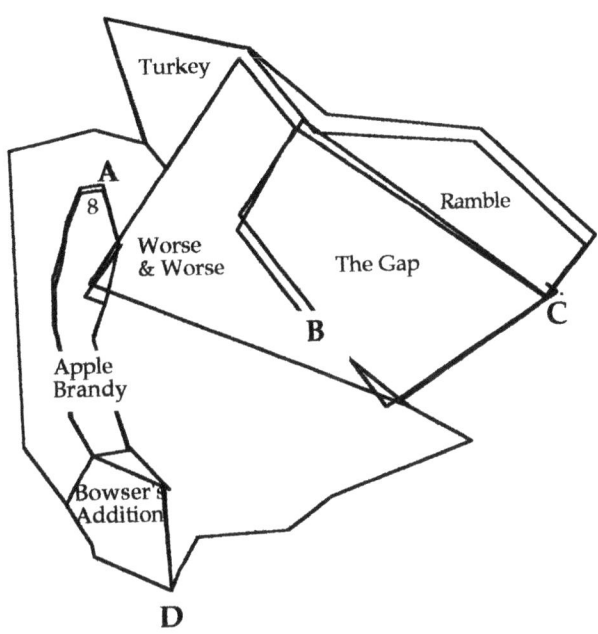

A = End of line 8 of Apple Brandy
B = Beginning tree of Worse and Worse
C = Beginning tree of The Gap and Turkey Ramble
D = Beginning tree of Bowser's Addition

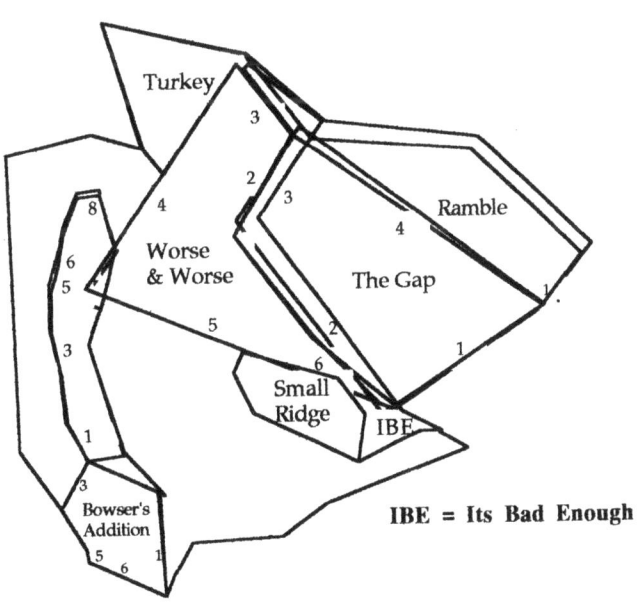

IBE = Its Bad Enough

Resurvey on (The) Gap Master

19

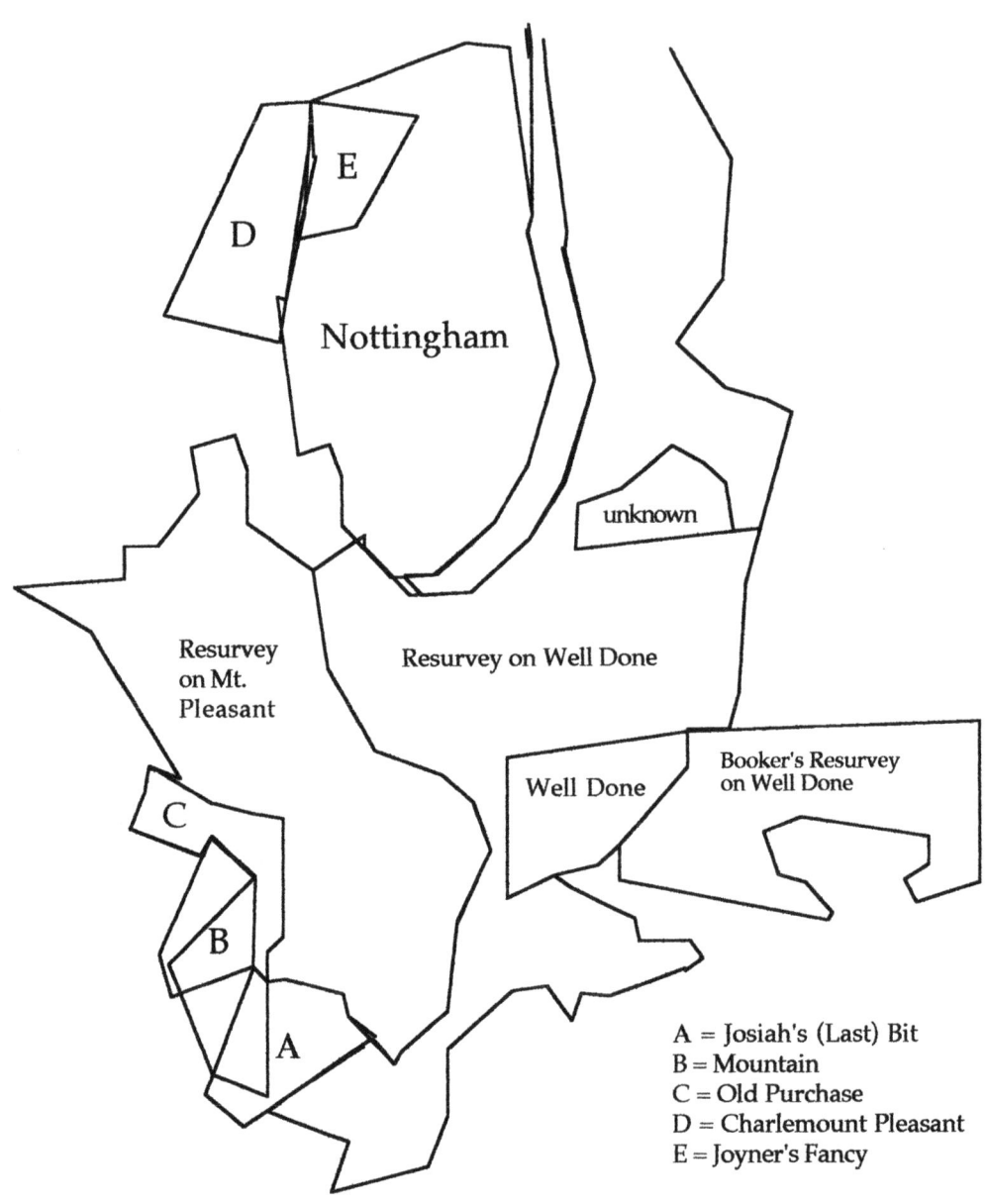

Resurvey on Well Done Master

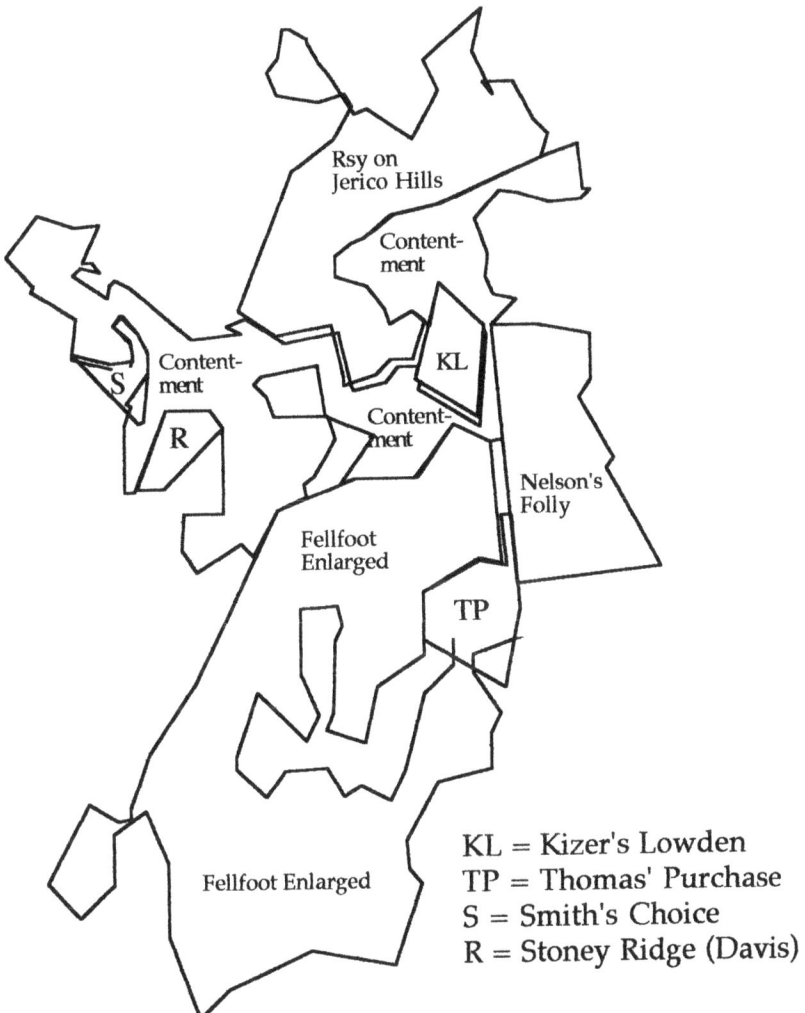

Contentment Master

The Resurvey on Oxford Area

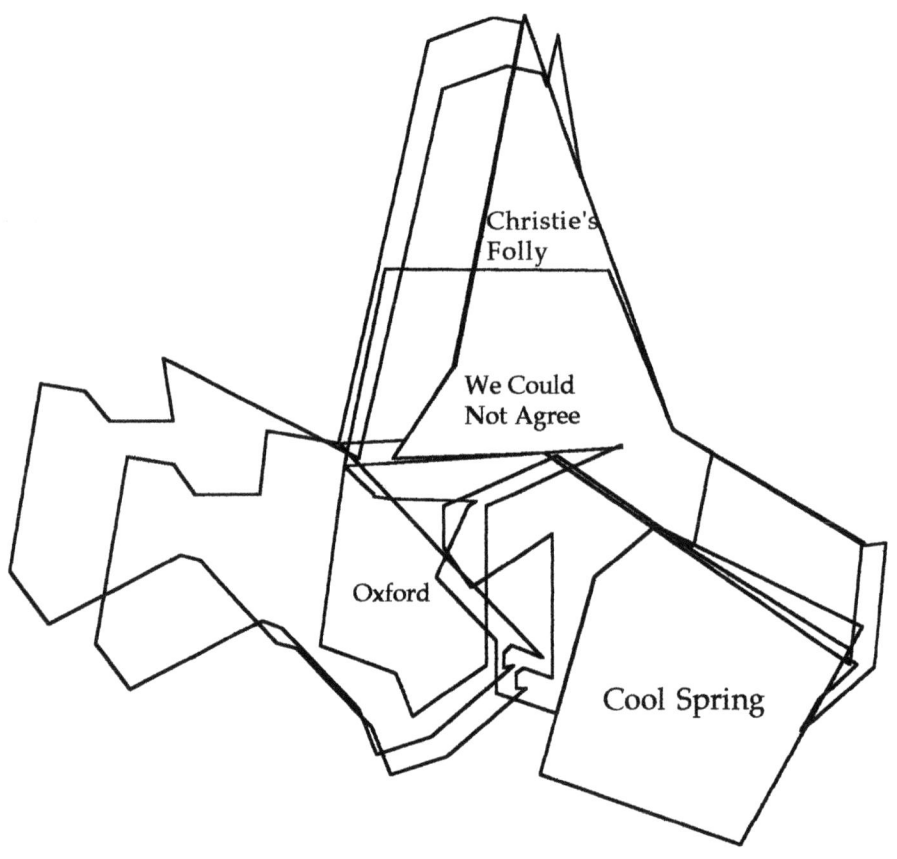

1. Resurvey on Oxford - Peter Beaver, MdHR, BC & GS 50, pp. 173-175, 5 Jun 1775, 24 Nov 1774, 252 and 1/2 acres.
2. (The) Cool Spring - James Wardrop, survey, MdHR, BY & GS 5, pp. 608-609, 17 May 1750, 75 acres.
3. We Could Not Agree - FCLR, THO 1-188, resurveyed 18 Jul 1800, 119 and 1/2 acres.
4. Oxford - Philip Marshall and Jacob Young, FCLR, WR-6-135, recorded 28 Sep 1785, 100 acres.
5. Christie's Folly - Richard Smith, MdHR, BC & GS 1, pp. 173-4, surveyed 17 Oct 1750, 200 acres.
6. Oxford - James Wardrop, survey, MdHR, BY & GS 5, p. 594, 23 Jul 1751, 54 acres.

These tracts are an excellent example of overlapping property lines due to survey errors.

West of Fox's Gap all the way to Crampton's Gap

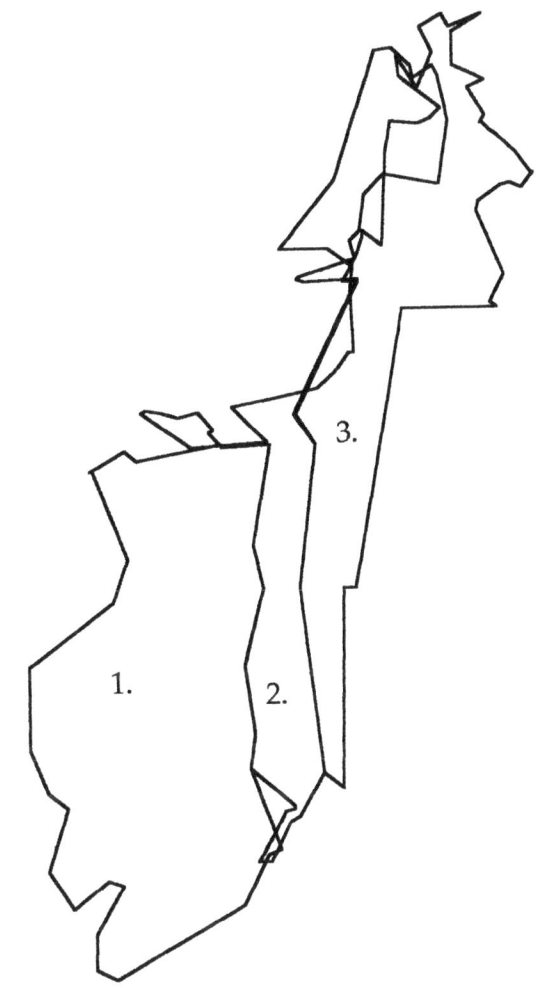

Park Hall, Resurvey on Strife, and Mount Atlas.

1. Park Hall - MdHR, AM #1, 236-7, SR 7472, 9 Apr 1731, William Parks.
2. Resurvey on Strife - MdHR, BC & GS #41 pp. 259-261, SR 7748, 902 acres, patented 19 Nov 1770.
3. Mt. Atlas - MdHR, IC M, 470-471, John Booth and Jonas Hogmire, patent, 1798.

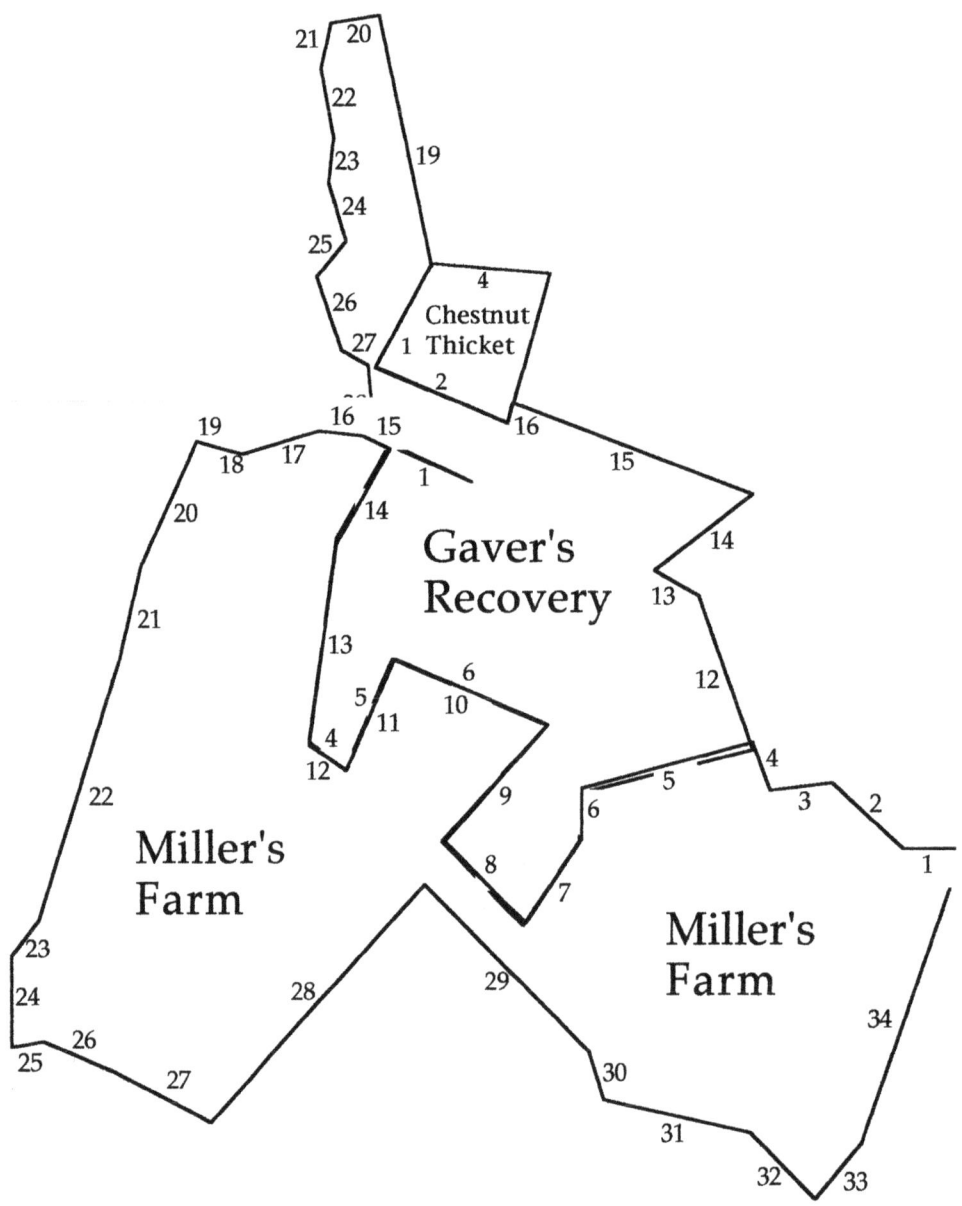

Gaver's Recovery Master #1

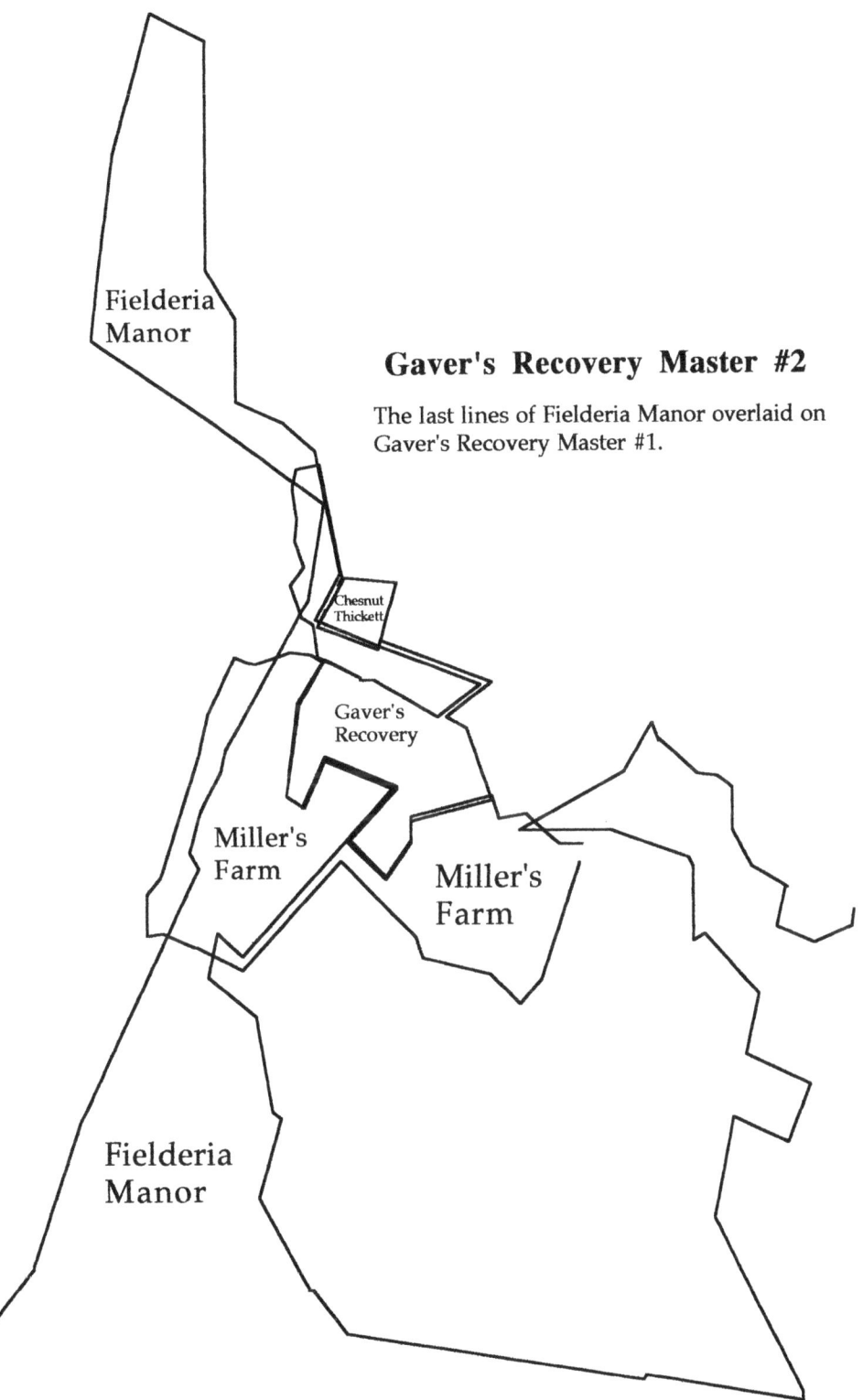

Gaver's Recovery Master #2

The last lines of Fielderia Manor overlaid on Gaver's Recovery Master #1.

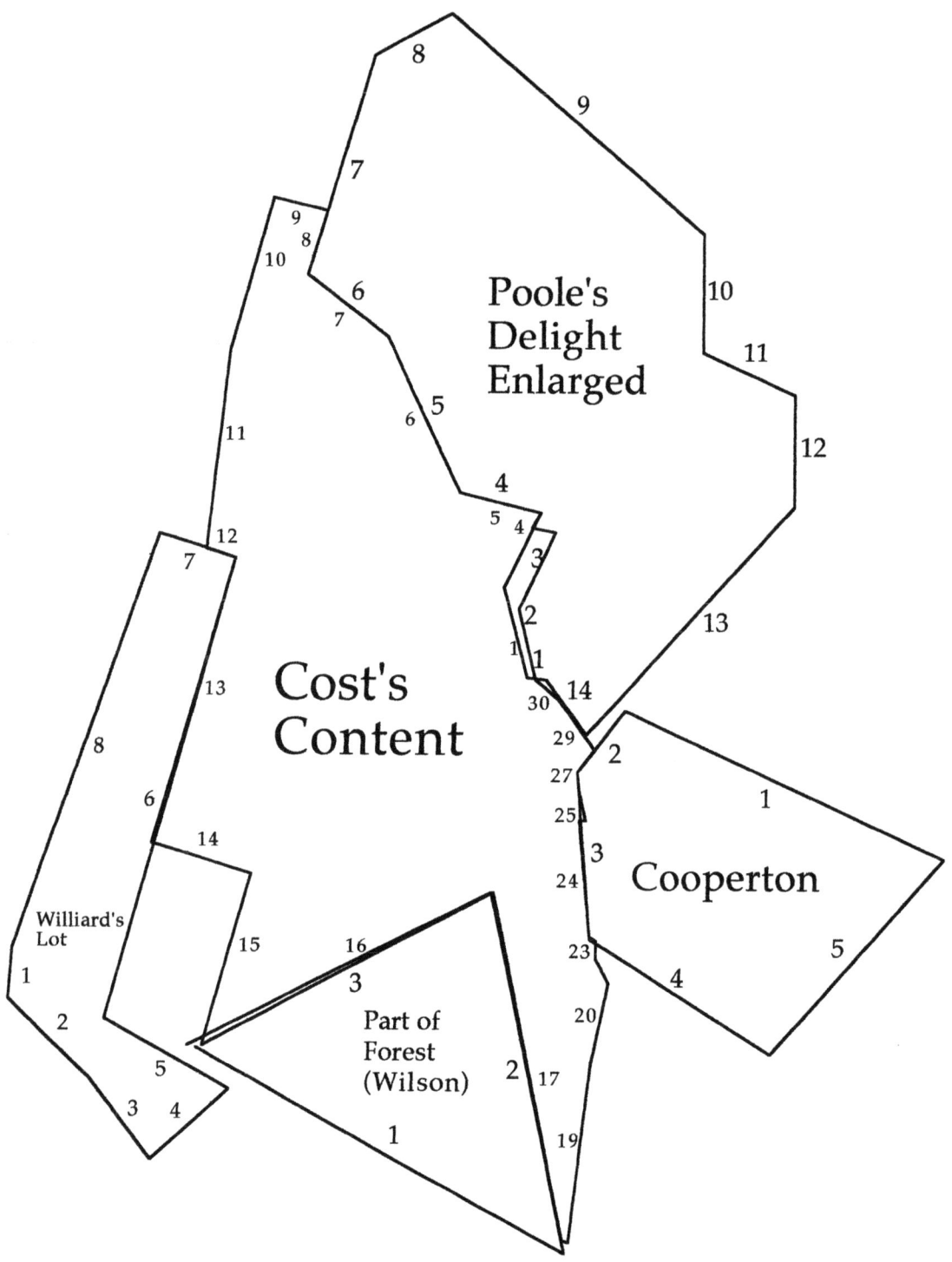

Cost's Content Master

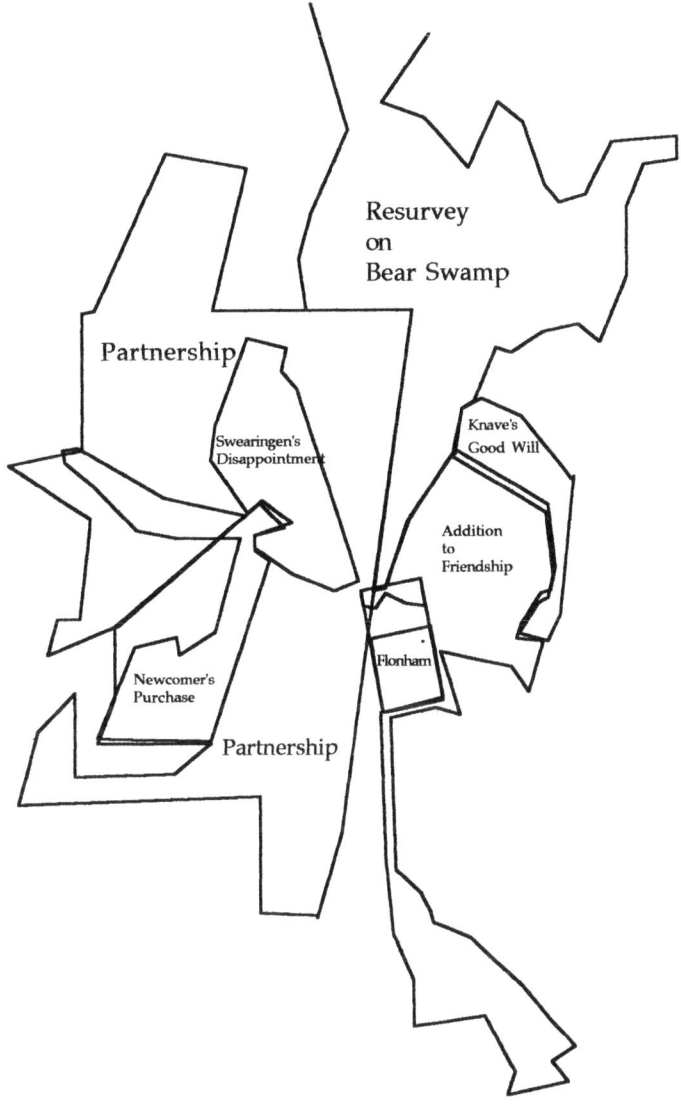

Tracts surrounding the Mountain House at Turner's Gap

The Fox Inn Area - Selected Tracts

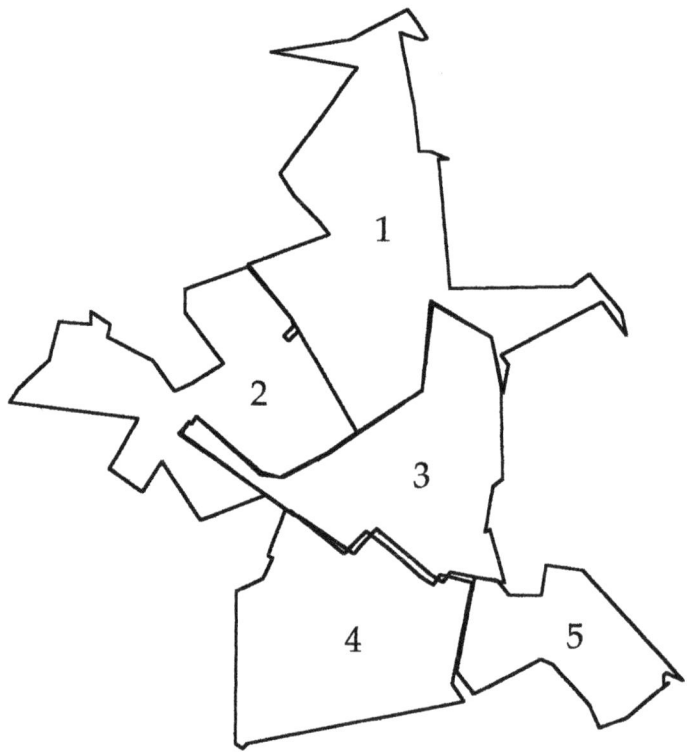

1. **Bartholomew Booker Estate**, FCLR, WR-12, 358-364, recorded 19 Apr 1794, 304 acres, ". . . beginning at a bounded white oak tree bounded tree of a tract of land called John's Delight and running thence by and with the Main Road South 38 degrees East 24 perches". Newspaper notice: "on road from Frederick Town to Williamsport and Hagerstown".

2. Frederick Fox to Henry Ascherman, FCLR, WR 32-63, 1807, recorded 14 Oct 1807, 199 and 1/2 acres, **part of I Hope It Is Well Done, Shettle, Exchange, Pegging Awl, Turkey Foot, Mount Pleasant and Peter's Neglect**. "Beginning at stone planted near the main road leading to Sharpsburg and the beginning of Daniel Booker's land."

3. **Now I Know It**, Jacob Smith, FCLR, THO-1-220, recorded 17 Dec 1802, 178 and 1/2 acres.

4. Vincent Sanner to Samuel Ausherman, FCLR, CM-1-582, recorded 14 Apr 1868, 194 and 1/2 acres, **part of Fidler's Purchase, Resurvey on Exchange, Bubble, and Deeffer Snay**. Line 17: "North 22 degrees East 20 perches into the Old Sharpsburg Road."

5. Philip Marshall and Jacob Young, FCLR, WR-6-135, recorded 28 Sep 1785, 100 acres.

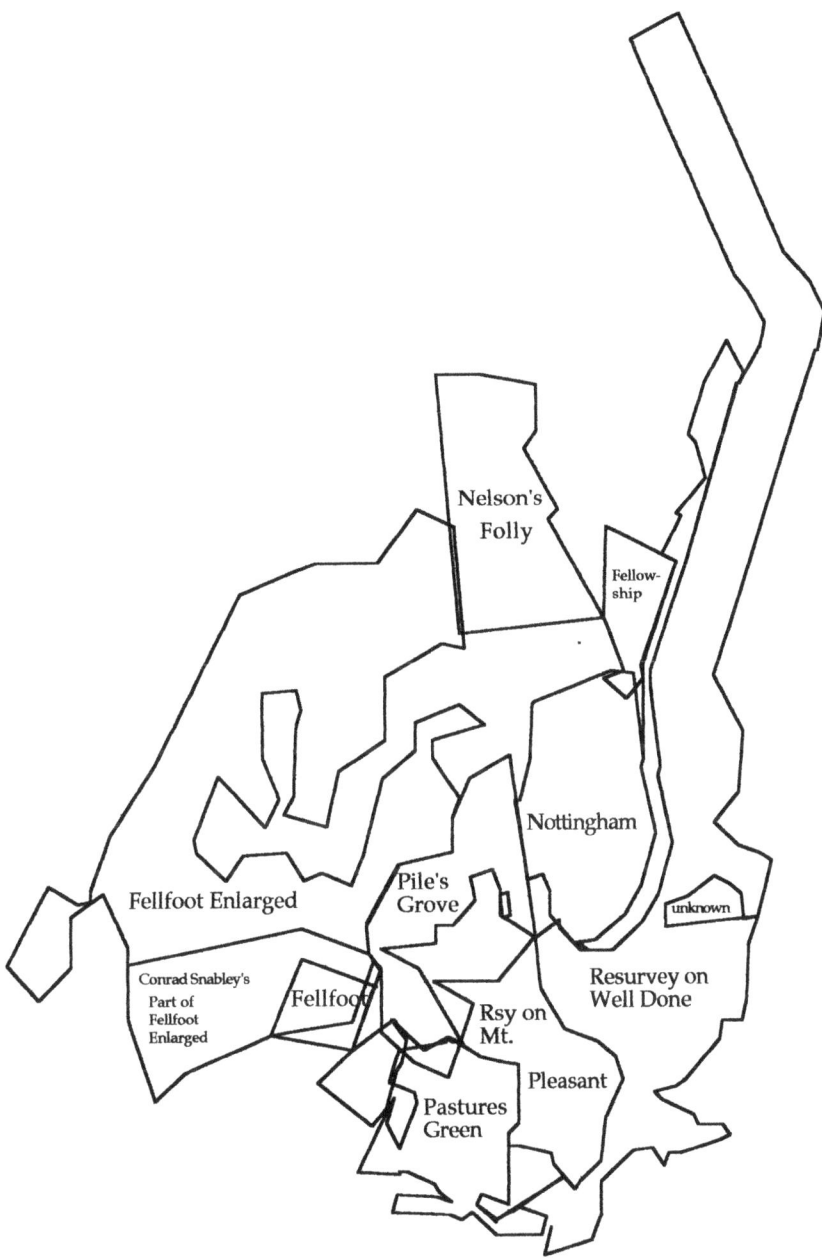

Pile's Grove Master

Early Roads and Gaps

	Page
The Road from Swearingen's Ferry to Fox's Gap	31
The Road from Williamsport to Turner's Gap	33
Overlay of Tracts at Turner's or Curry's Gap and Fox's Gap	35
The Main Road from Frederick Town to Fort Frederick through Turner's or Curry's Gap	37
The Fork of the Turnpike Road with the Old Sharpsburg Road before 1830	38
Fox's Gap	40
The Land Tract Records of the Old Sharpsburg Road from Frederick Town	41
The Great Road from Frederick Town to Conococheague (Williamsport)	43
Crampton's Gap	44
Turner's or Curry's Gap	45
The Main Road from Frederick Town to Fort Frederick	46
The 1781 Frederick County Court Minutes	49
The Turnpike Road Through Turner's Gap (The Old National Pike)	51
Orr's Gap and the Old Hagerstown Road to Frederick Town	53
Footnotes - Early Roads and Gaps	56

Early Roads and Gaps

The Road from Swearingen's Ferry to Fox's Gap

Maryland State Archives, Special Collections (MSA Map Collection) 507 "Road from Swearingen's Ferry on the Potomac River through Sharpsburg to the top of the South Mountain at Fox's Gap." [MSA G1427-507, B5-1-3]

The following text is taken directly from the map in the Maryland Archives. The reader will have to get a copy of the original map at the Maryland Archives in order to view the dotted lines referred to below.

The old road shown by plain lines and is the distance of 11 1/4 miles - 56 pchs.
The alternations made by the commissioners is shown by dotted lines, and the road by them laid out is represented by lines numbered from 1 to 41 Difference 71 perches.
Note: The courses and boundaries above mentioned are to be taken for the middle of the road.

Washington County Sect.
By virtue of dower invested in an act of the assembly for the purpose we hereby certify that we laid out the road from Swearingen's Ferry on Potomac River through Sharpsburg to the top of the South Mountain in Fox's Gap agreeable to the courses and distances above expressed = As witness our hands and seals this 13th day of August 1792.
        William Good (seal)
        Jacob   (seal)
        Christopher (seal)

Beginning at the bank of the Potomac River at the said Ferry and running:

Crse No.	North South	Degrees East or West	Length
1	N	80 East	12 ps opposite the ferry house
2	S	49 East	56 ps to a post
3	S	62 East	62 ps to a post
4	N	44 East	43 ps to a marked poplar
5	N	62 East	264 ps to a marked white oak sapling
6	N	41 1/2 East	360 ps to a bounded white oak tree
7	N	69 1/2 East	320 ps to the square in Sharpsburg - still continuing the course
8	N	69 1/2 East	110 ps to a post
9	N	60 East	64 ps to a marked locust sapling
10	N	69 1/2 East	112 ps to a marked hickory sapling
11	S	76 East	20 ps to a marked white oak tree
12	N	65 East	84 ps to a marked apple tree
13	N	85 East	16 ps
14	S	54 East	14 ps to Orendorff's Bridge
15	S	77 East	8 ps
16	N	19 East	23 ps
17	N	3 West	26 ps to a bounded black oak
18	N	73 East	40 ps to a post
19	S	85 East	76 ps to a bounded Spanish oak
20	S	88 East	68 ps to a post
21	N	58 East	260 ps to a bounded black oak sapling
22	N	16 East	74 ps to a post
23	N	35 East	54 ps to a marked red oak & locust sapling
24	S	73 East	72 ps to a post
25	N	83 1/2 East	120 ps to a walnut tree at Conrad Snavely's house
26	S	89 1/2 East	161 ps to a bounded black oak sapling
27	S	66 1/2 East	170 ps to a post near a marked black oak sapling

Early Roads and Gaps

Crse No.	North South	Degrees East or West	Length
28	S	74 East	71 ps to a post
29	S	85 East	84 ps to a post
30	N	69 East	62 ps to a post
31		E - - - - - - - - -	324 perches to interesect the old road near top of Domer's Hill
32	S	69 1/2 East	30 ps along the old road
33	N	83 East	20 ps
34	S	86 1/2 East	54 ps
35	S	28 East	20 ps
36	S	84 East	50 ps
37	N	77 East	22 ps
38	N	5 1/2 East	44 ps
39	[estimate - not given on the map - South 81 East 40-45 ps]		
40[1]	S	44 East	70 ps
41	N	60 East	41 perches to a stone set up in the road on the top of the mountain at the county line.

The following drawing was made by the author from the preceding listing of lines.

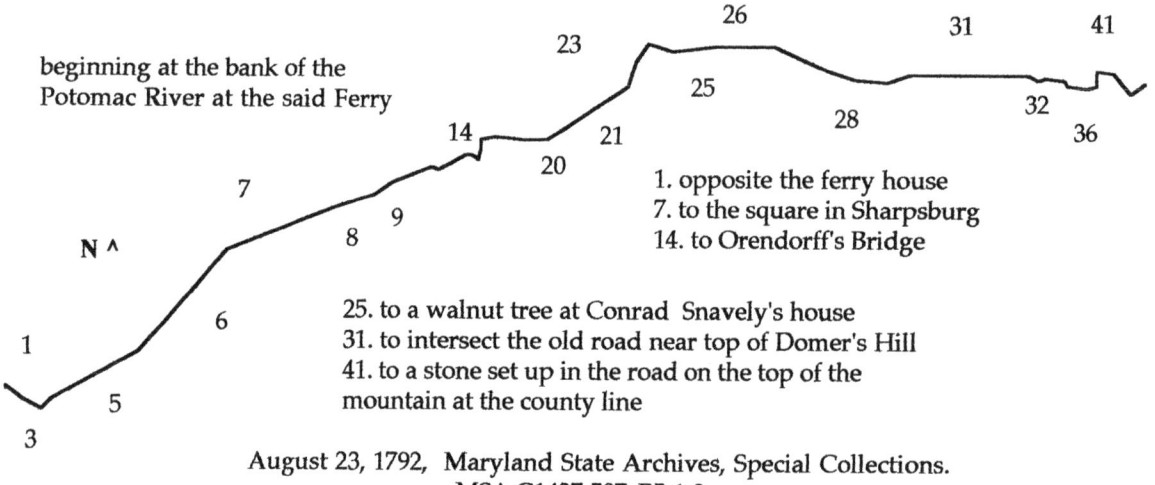

August 23, 1792, Maryland State Archives, Special Collections. MSA G1427-507, B5-1-3.

Two drawings of the road appear on this map, representing two measurement scales. The uppermost drawing is shown with the following indication: Scale 100P. The lower drawing is shown with the following indication: Scale 1/62,500 topographical map size.

The map identifies the following points along the road: Swearingen's Ferry on the Potomac River (starting point); the square in Sharpsburg (end of line 7); Orendorff's Bridge over the Antietam (end of line 15); Smith's shop (end of line 20); Jacob Russell (end of line 21); top of Red Hill (end of line 23); Conrad Snavely (end of line 25); Samuel Baker's (end of line 26); old road near top of Tomer's (or Domer's) Hill (line 31); Andrew Bash (end of line 36); top of the South Mountain at Fox's Gap (end of line 41).

Early Roads and Gaps

The Road from Williamsport to Turner's Gap in the South Mountain

Special Collections (Maps) No. 504 Road from Williamsport to Turner's Gap, 1791 [MdHR 1427-504, B5-1-3]

The following text is taken directly from the map in the Maryland Archives. The map also identifies the intersection of the road from Williamsport to Turner's Gap and the road from Funkstown to Turner's Gap. It also shows the road from Shafer's Mill to Turner's Gap.

Persuant to an act entitled an act to straighten and amend the several roads, recorded October 17th 1791 to wit.

The plat and courses of the road leading from Williamsport to Turner's Gap in the South Mountain. Beginning for the said road at the south end of Artisans Street at Williamsport and running thence through Otho Holland Williams' land.

Line No.	North South	Degrees East or West	Length
1	S	5 East	15 perches
2	S	60 East	135
3	S	56 East	170
4	S	69 East	198 through Ringold's Manor
5	N	86 East	60
6	S	85 East	66
7	S	58 East	232 to the mouth of Ringold's Quarter Lane then through said plantation
8	S	50 East	506
9	S	42 East	315 to Iagnatious Simms his house
10	S	68 East	16
11	S	52 East	50
12	S	61 East	34
13	S	60 East	74
14	S	52 East	96
15	S	58 East	236
16	S	15 East	40
17	S	45 East	40 ps to Booth's Bridge on Antietam Creek
18	S	6 East	24
19	S	62 West	44
20	S	52 East	22
21	S	72 East	44 to Beaver Creek
22	S	68 East	64
23	S	72 East	86
24	S	78 1/2 East	168 through Michael Taylor's land
25	S	58 East	96
26	S	45 East	74 through John Ringer's Land
27	S	72 East	48
28	S	78 East	122
29	S	40 East	32
30	S	53 East	26
31	S	59 East	28
32	S	49 East	54
33	S	70 East	72 through Scott's land
34	S	41 East	146
35	S	31 East	96
36	S	29 East	80

Early Roads and Gaps

Line No.	North South	Degrees East or West	Length
37	S	20 East	140 through Boon's land
38	S	9 East	100
39	S	35 East	66 to Booke's tavern and from thence through Aulabaugh's land and Summer's land
40	S	53 East	322 into the old road in Turner's Gap then up through the gap
41	S	58 East	14
42	S	32 East	22
43	S	54 East	20
44	S	57 East	68
45	S	86 East	48
46	S	70 East	128 ps to where it is supposed to intersect Frederick County line on the top of the mountain

Explanation	miles
Red line shows the straight course	13 & 27 ps
dotted line shows the new road and measures	14 miles
black lines show the old road measures	14 1/2 & 40 ps

new road shows and measures one half miles short & forty perches by a scale of 100 equal perches in the inch.

Commissioners   Wm VanLear (seal)
Jonas Hogmire (seal)
Conrad Nicodemus (seal)

The following drawing was made by the author from the preceding listing of lines.

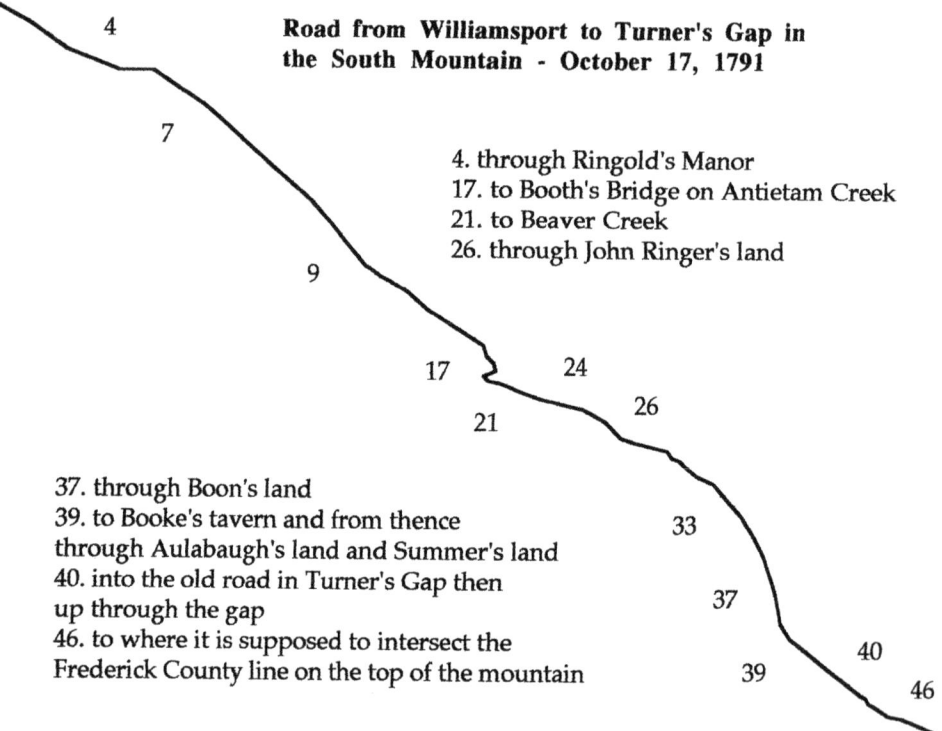

Road from Williamsport to Turner's Gap in the South Mountain - October 17, 1791

4. through Ringold's Manor
17. to Booth's Bridge on Antietam Creek
21. to Beaver Creek
26. through John Ringer's land

37. through Boon's land
39. to Booke's tavern and from thence through Aulabaugh's land and Summer's land
40. into the old road in Turner's Gap then up through the gap
46. to where it is supposed to intersect the Frederick County line on the top of the mountain

Overlay of Tracts at Turner's or Curry's Gap and Fox's Gap

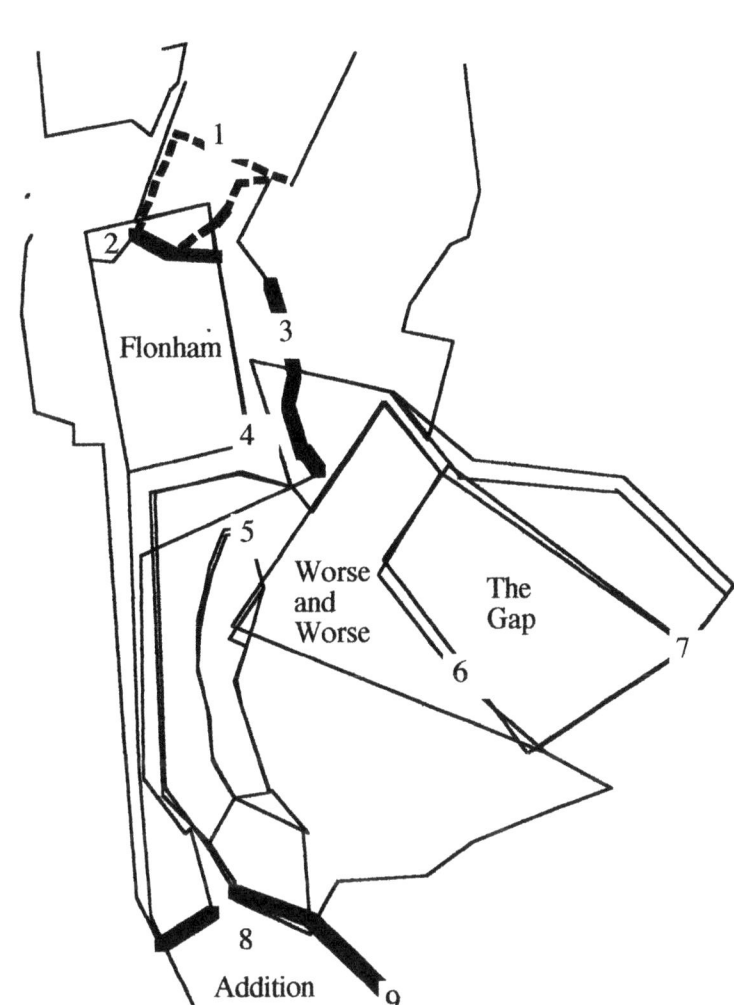

1. 10 acres around the Chapel at Turner's Gap - bold dotted line - these 10 acres were excepted from the transfer from St. Mary's Academy of Notre Dame, Indiana, to Charles M. Hewitt - recorded 1925
2. The Mountain House at Turner's Gap - 5 acres of Flonham - Henry Miller - recorded 1825
3. **The turnpike road - 1800s - bold solid line**
4. The beginning tree of Flonham - Philip Jacob Schafer - surveyed 1770
5. The end of line eight of Apple Brandy - "to the main road" - Jacob Fulwiler - surveyed 1791
6. The beginning tree of Worse and Worse - John Teem (Team) - surveyed 1766
7. The beginning tree of The Gap - Joseph Chapline Sr. - surveyed 1761
8. The Reno Monument at Fox's Gap - Addition to Friendship - Frederick Fox - surveyed 1797
9. **The road through Fox's Gap - bold solid line**

Early Roads and Gaps

Following Page - tracts identified:

V	Daniel's Race Ground (1793)
DW	David's Will (1763)
F	Flonham (1770)
FLS	Fox's Last Shift (1764)
FB	Fredericksburg (1792)
G	(The) Gap (1761)
GF	Grim's Fancy (1764)
JD	John's Delight (1750)
R	Racon (1762)
RCS	Resurvey on Cool Spring (1801)
RWD	Resurvey on Well Done (1764)
S	Shettle (1744)
SD	Shidler's Dispute (1760)
SW	Swearingen's Disappointment (1782)
W	Worse and Worse (1766)

Following Page - beginning trees identified:

1	Racon - south side of a road (1762)
2	Fox's Last Shift - on the north side of the main country road (1764)
C	Flonham - on the right hand side of the main road (1770)
4	Worse and Worse - south side of road (1766)
5	Pickall - by the side of the main road (1764)
5	John's Delight (1750 - no road mentioned)
5	Shidler's Dispute, Long Dispute, 1791 Booker Estate - along the main country road
H	(The) Gap (warrant in 1750, patent in 1761 - no road mentioned)
K	Bowser's Addition - at Fox's Gap (1763) - near the top of the South Mountain on the side of the main road from Frederick Town to Sharpsburg

Following Page - points on road:

3	End of line 8 of Apple Brandy, 1791 - "to the main road"
5	Shidler's Dispute, Long Dispute, 1791 Booker Estate - "with the main road," and Pickall, patented in 1764 - "by the side of the main road"

Dotted Line - Main Road from Frederick Town to Ft. Frederick
Solid Line - the Old Sharpsburg Road through Fox's Gap

The Main Road from Frederick Town to Ft. Frederick through Turner's or Curry's Gap

Dotted Bold Line - Main Road from Frederick Town to Fort Frederick through Turner's or Curry's Gap
Solid Bold Line - the Old Sharpsburg Road through Fox's Gap

Early Roads and Gaps

The Fork of the Turnpike with the Old Sharpsburg Road before 1830 or 1840

Following page:

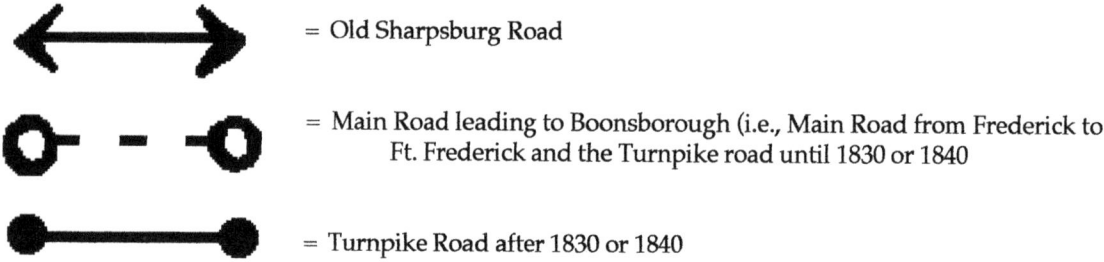

= Old Sharpsburg Road

= Main Road leading to Boonsborough (i.e., Main Road from Frederick to Ft. Frederick and the Turnpike road until 1830 or 1840

= Turnpike Road after 1830 or 1840

Tract 1 = FCLR, DSB-1, 398, George Routzahn to W. Koogle, recorded 22 Apr 1867. Line 4 goes to the middle of the turnpike thence, line 5, along said road 84 perches (1300+ feet), containing sixteen and a quarter acres, being part of Pickall, part of the Resurvey on Mendall, part of I Hope It Is Well Done, and part of Shettle.

Tract 2 = FCLR, DSB-1-397, Mary Sheffer to John W. Koogle, recorded 22 May 1867. Line 4 went to the middle of the turnpike road, line 5 went along the road for 58 perches (900+ feet), containing 23 acres, being part of the Resurvey on Mendall, part of Pickall, part of I Hope It Is Well Done, part of Shettle, and part of Martitany.

Tract 3 = FCLR, WR-32-225, Michael Miller to Jacob Smith, I Hope It Is Well Done, recorded 30 Dec 1807. Line 1 went to the middle of the main road leading to Boonsborough and with said road. Line 2, was 50 perches. The tract contained ten and one eighth acres.

Tract 4 = FCLR, WR-36-85, Michael Miller to Jacob Smith, recorded 26 Dec 1809, containing 112 and a half acres of land more or less excepting thereout ten and one eight acres heretofore conveyed the said Jacob Smith.

The drawing shows land records related to the area north and east of the Fox Inn. The Tract 1 deed between Koogle and Routzahn in 1867 indicates 84 perches were along the turnpike at that time. The Tract 3 deed between Miller and Smith indicates 50 perches were along the Main Road to Boonsboro in December 1807. The Main Road to Boonsboro should have been along the same route as the Main Road from Frederick to Ft. Frederick. The route of the turnpike, built in the early 1800s, also probably followed the same route. The Tract 3 deed supports the conclusion that the Main Road from Frederick to Ft. Frederick through Turner's Gap met the Old Sharpsburg Road a short distance east of the Fox Inn at one time, as shown on the 1808 Varle Map.

Early Roads and Gaps

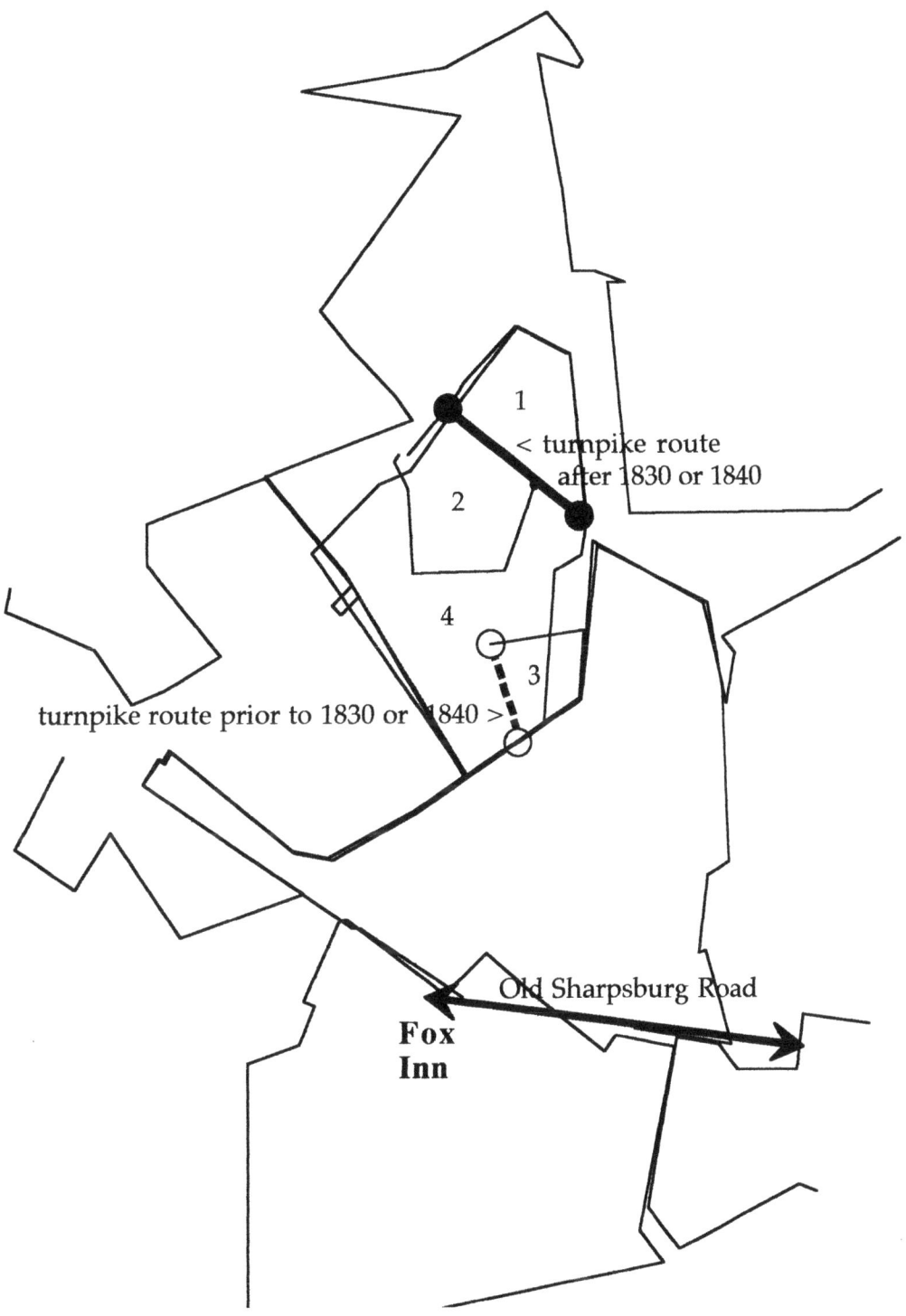

The Fork of the Turnpike with the Old Sharpsburg Road before 1830 or 1840

Early Roads and Gaps

Fox's Gap

Fox's Gap includes the area in the immediate vicinity of the Reno Monument.[1] Bowser's Addition,[1] surveyed in 1763, is contiguous to the north side of the Wise Tract[2] of Civil War fame. The ten acres of Bowser's Addition was "by the side of the wagon road leading from Sharpsburg to Frederick Town and on top of South Mountain." The Bowser's Addition tract offers proof the road through Fox's Gap crossed the mountain at the same point in 1763 as it does today.

The Reno Monument stands on a 40-foot square portion of the Wise Tract.[3] The Wise tract is part of Addition to Friendship, which was patented by Frederick Fox in 1805[4] and consisted of 202 acres. Approximately 65 acres were at Fox's Gap on the south side of the road and approximately 125 acres were on the east and north sides of Turner's Gap. The remaining 12 acres or so ran from Fox's Gap to Turner's Gap, connecting the two larger sections.

A deed from Susan Miller et al. to John Miller for 13 and 1/4 acres, recorded in 1845, included Bowser's Addition and 3 and 1/4 acres of Addition to Friendship.[5] The Wise Tract (i. e., John Wise to Jonas Gross) consists of only 4 and 3/4 acres. The Miller deed and Wise deed both include the two courses, "with said road, East 7 perches" and "North 86 degrees East, 16 perches." Lines 6 and 7 of the Miller - Miller deed are the same as lines 1 and 2 of the Wise - Gross deed.

Frederick Fox's 1792 survey for Fredericksburg identifies lines 8, 9, and 10, a total of 144 perches or 2376 feet, along "the main road."[6] Line 10 went "to the bounded tree of a tract of land called Bowser's Addition." Fredericksburg was on the east side of Fox's Gap and primarily on the north side of the road. Also in the vicinity of Fox' Gap are David's Will[7] of David Bowser and the Cool Spring Resurvey[8] in 1801 of Samuel Shoup. The Shoup tract is not a resurvey on the Cool Spring patented by James Wardrop in 1750.

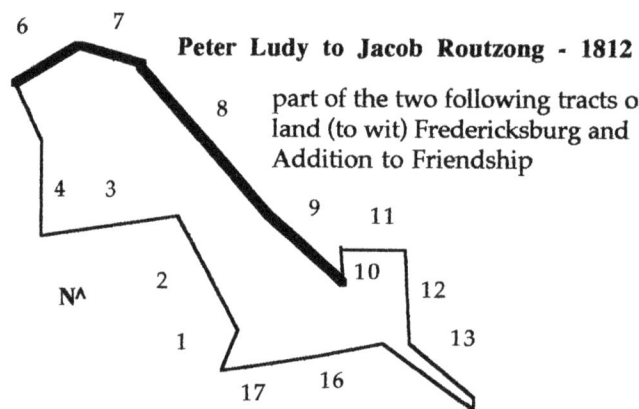

Peter Ludy to Jacob Routzong - 1812
part of the two following tracts of land (to wit) Fredericksburg and Addition to Friendship

Line 6 ran North 60 degrees East 35 perches to the top of the mountain in the said road then with it three following courses
Line 7 ran South 75 degrees East 31 perches to the bounded tree of a tract of land called Bowser's Addition
Line 8 ran South 43 degrees East 88 perches
Line 9 ran South 35 degrees East 47 perches to the end of the seventh line of the aforesaid land called Fredericksburg
(Note: bold line is along road)

The deed for Grim's Fancy is the only proof John Fox lived in the vicinity of Fox's Gap. There are no land records for John Fox except for lots in Sharpsburg. A deed between John Fox of Frederick Town and Elias Bruner, farmer, recorded May 22, 1766, transferred lot #269 in Frederick Town "being the lot where the said John Fox now lives."[9] Daniel G. Fox refers to this deed in *The*

Fox Genealogy. John Fox acquired Lot #269 from Daniel Dulany269 from Daniel Dulany on May 16, 1764.[10] This author believes the John Fox of Frederick Town was not the same John Fox who lived at Fox's Gap. Church records of the period indicate there was a John George Fox and wife Christina at Frederick Town.[11]

John Fox must have lived at Fox's Gap before David Bowser arrived in the early 1760s; otherwise, the gap would be named Bowser's Gap. The will of John Fox, who died in 1784, indicates, "I give and Bequeath unto my beloved Wife Christina all that I do possess of during her Natural life . . ." Christina died August 6, 1812.[12]

The last line given on the *Map of the Road from Swearingen's Ferry to Fox's Gap* ends at the end of line 5 of Bowser's Addition.[13] Line 41 of the road was "North 60 degrees East 41 perches to a stone set up in the road on the top of the mountain at the county line." Line 6 of a deed from Peter Ludy to Jacob Routzong contained the following line: "North 60 degrees East 35 perches to the top of the mountain in the said road."[14] This deed was for part of Addition to Friendship and Fredericksburg.

Line 6 of the Ludy-Routzong deed ends at the end of line 5 of Bowser's Addition. Line 7 of the Ludy-Routzong deed went "to the bounded tree of a tract of land called Bowser's Addition."

The road from Frederick Town through Fox's Gap to Shepherdstown, later called the Old Sharpsburg Road, was traveled by General Braddock, George Washington, and Maryland Governor Sharp on May 2, 1755. They were on their way from Frederick Town to Ft. Cumberland. They passed through Fox's Gap, took Swearingen's Ferry across the Potomac, and traveled on to Winchester and Ft. Cumberland.

Dunbar's Regiment, also part of the Braddock Expedition of 1755, passed through Fox's Gap on their way from Frederick Town to Conococheague (Williamsport). They took the Great Road to Conococheague from Frederick Town. This route also passed through Fox's Gap. Near Keedysville, the route of this road left the road to Shepherdstown and passed through Bakersville and on to Conococheague.

The road from Shepherdstown through Sharpsburg and Fox's Gap played an important role in the American Revolution. An article by Paul David Nelson makes the following statement on page 186, "In fact, some historians say that the region gave a disproportionately high amount of its substance to the cause. Large quantities of supplies for America's armies came from Berkeley and Frederick counties (in Virginia) and were funnelled through Mecklenburg (present-day Shepherdstown) on the Potomac River."[15]

The Land Tract Records of the Old Sharpsburg Road from Frederick Town

Land tracts in western Maryland during the 1700s and early 1800s were given names and many early land tracts ran afoul of contiguous tracts. Plotting some of these early tracts is sometimes as much an art as a science. It is often the land tracts of the early 1800s that clarify the location of earlier surveys. Deeds for later transfers of some tracts indicate the level of precision of the earlier survey measurements required an "allowance for variation of the magnetic needle," sometimes up to two degrees. The unit of measure for these early tracts was the "perch." One perch is 16.5 feet or equal to one pole.

A number of land tracts on the west side of Fox's Gap support the road through Fox's Gap to Shepherdstown before 1755. Historical Society of Carroll County records indicate a "1744 Virginia court record shows that a road was opened in 1744 from Shepherds Ferry to the Bullskin." George Washington owned land on the Bullskin and the name of Washington appears on the Fry and Jefferson Map of 1755 near the Bullskin in Virginia, west of Shepherdstown.

Smith's Hills had its "beginning at a bounded white oak standing on the side of a hill, within a quarter mile of a wagon road that crosses the Antietam Creek."[16] This tract is near the Lower (or Burnside) Bridge near Sharpsburg. Fellfoot was "about ten perches from a road commonly called the wagon road."[17] The bounded white oak that was the beginning tree of Mountain was "near the road that leads from Monocacy to Teagues Ferry."[18] Teagues Ferry must have been at Shepherdstown. Teagues Creek meets the Potomac there today.

Early Roads and Gaps

Mt. Pleasant was "within 30 poles of the wagon road that goes from Shepherd's ford to the Monocacy."[20] The beginning tree of Pile's Grove was "about half a mile above a road commonly called the wagon road."[21]

The land tracts mentioned in the 1762 will of Moses Chapline Sr. are near several of the above mentioned tracts. The Resurvey on Mt. Pleasant began "at the end of the 4th line of the original."[22] Josiah's Bit had its "beginning at the end of the twelfth line of the second Resurvey on Mt. Pleasant laid out for said Chapline and the end of the second line of a tract of land called Mountain."[23]

Three later tracts in the same area, Old Purchase,[24] Pastures Green,[25] and Miller's Hills,[26] identify the road during the late 1700s and early 1800s. Lines 6, 7, 8, and 9 of Old Purchase identify 142 perches (2,343 feet) along "the wagon road that leads to Frederick Town." Old Purchase began "at the end of the second line of a tract called Mountain."

The Pastures Green survey mentions a number of the above tracts. Pastures Green encompassed the Old Purchase tract. Line 31 of Pastures Green went "to the wagon road twenty feet north of a stone standing in said line." Miller's Hills had its "beginning for the outlines of the whole at the end of the 2nd line of a tract of land called Piles Grove." Line 19 of Miller's Hills went to "the main road leading from Fox's Gap to Sharpsburg." The distance from the beginning tree to the road in 1813 was about 1/2 mile.

Security began at a tree "standing on the north side of the South Mountain and about two hundred yards from the main road leading from Frederick Town to Sharpsburg on the south side thereof."[27] The Resurvey of Security is adjacent to Addition to Friendship on the west side of Fox's Gap.[28] Ferry Landing was "on the bank of the Potomac near Swearingen's Ferry."[29] This tract is near the present Rumsey Bridge at Shepherdstown.

Conrad Snavely owned most of the southern portion of Fellfoot Enlarged.[30] Line 25 from the 1792 map of the road ended at Conrad Snavely's house. This reference point agrees with the route of the road identified in the Fellfoot patent.

Also on the west side of Fox's Gap is Mt. Atlas.[31] This patent, consisting of one large tract and two smaller tracts, is contiguous to the Resurvey on Security, Booker's Resurvey on Well Done,[32] and Grim's Fancy, among others.

Four tracts laid out prior to 1755 on the east side of Fox's Gap support the road through Fox's Gap from the area that became Middletown. The Forest began "at a bounded hickory standing about half a mile above the wagon road that goes from Conestoga to Opequon crosses a creek called Catoctin Creek which falls into Potomac River about six miles above Monocacy."[33] This tract begins about 1/2 mile above the bridge over the Catoctin Creek just north of Middletown. The Forest was adjacent the south side of a tract named Wooden Platter.

The 1794 *Dennis Griffith Map of Maryland* shows the route of the road from Conestoga to Opequon. The road began at Conestoga, Pennsylvania, near Lancaster. It passed through York, Pennsylvania, and Taneytown, Woodsborough, Frederick Town, Middletown, Fox's Gap, and Sharpsburg in Maryland. It crossed the Potomac at Shepherdstown and went on to Opequon, located about five miles southwest of Winchester, Virginia. This route also was known as the German Monocacy Road. Tracey and Dern, page 51 of *Pioneers of Old Monocacy*, are incorrect when they indicate the "Road to Opequon" went through Turner's Gap. The road actually went through Fox's Gap. The Old Sharpsburg Road was part of the road from Conestoga to Opequon.

The road from Conestoga to Opequon was the same road as the Great Philadelphia Wagon Road. The *Frye and Jefferson Map* identifies the Great Philadelphia Wagon Road in Virginia. The road crossed the Potomac at Shepherdstown.

The Post Map identifies the Great Philadelphia Wagon Road from Philadelphia to the Maryland line north of Taneytown, Maryland. It is probably the Monocacy Road that is shown on the map as the "Great Philadelphia Wagon Road."[34]

The Great Philadelphia Wagon Road through Fox's Gap was not the same road as the Great Wagon Road to Philadelphia through Conococheague (Williamsport). The Great Wagon Road to Philadelphia, also shown on the 1755 Frye and Jefferson Map, went from Winchester through Conococheague and southern Pennsylvania to Philadelphia.

Oxford, surveyed for James Wardrop in 1750, had its "beginning at a bounded black oak standing at the head of a valley that falls into a branch called John Crisles Spring Branch and about ten or fifteen yards of the main road that leads through Frederick Town by Robert Evans and on the north side of the said road."[35] This tract began about 1,000 feet east of the Fox Inn.

Wardrop's Cool Spring was near the east side of Oxford. It was surveyed for James Wardrop in 1750 and began "at a bounded white oak standing on the top of a hill about two hundred yards from the wagon road that leads through Frederick Town and about a mile from John Burger's house."[36]

Betty's Good Will, surveyed for Robert Evans in 1727, had its "beginning at a bounded white oak standing at the foot of Shanandore Mountain near the wagon road that goes from Teagues Ferry to Monocacy Town."[37] The 1727 date is the earliest date the author found in his research of the land records of western Maryland:

> . . . whereas Robert Evans of Frederick County had on the twentieth day of October seventeen hundred and twenty seven surveyed & laid out for him a tract or parcel of land called Betty's Good Will lying and being formerly in Prince Georges but now in Frederick County containing fifty acres by virtue of so much part of an assignment of a warrant for three hundred acres from John Mills who was assignee of Daniel Oneal by renewment the twenty second day of April seventeen hundred and forty seven but before the said Evans laid out our grant thereon he did on the fourth day of May seventeen hundred and forty nine assign over all his right title and interest thereto unto Edward Grimes . . .[38]

Various deeds identify the route of the Old Sharpsburg Road between Fox's Gap and the Catoctin Creek after 1755. A 1787 deed for part of I Hope It Is Well Done had its "beginning for said part at a stone near the main road that leads from Middle Town to Sharpsburg."[39] This point is about 500 feet north of Betty's Good Will.

A deed from Vincent Sanner to Samuel Asherman in 1869, consisting of Part of the Resurvey on Exchange, Bubble, and Deeffer Snay,[40] included "Line 17, North 22 degrees East 20 perches into the Old Sharpsburg Road." This point is just west of the Fox Inn.

A Resurvey called Now I Know It consisted of portions of Betty's Good Will, the Resurvey on Mendall, the Resurvey on Learning, and I Hope It Is Well Done. The Now I Know It survey mentions Exchange, the Resurvey on Exchange, Pickall, and Pegging Awl.[41] It included "Line 5, South 16 degrees East 46 perches to a stone marked 38 in the main road." This point is just east of the Fox Inn.

The Great Road from Frederick Town to Conococheague (Williamsport)

A land tract near Keedysville identifies a road to Conococheague by the year 1740. This route is along the current road between Keedysville and Williamsport through Bakersville. The Vineyard had its "beginning at a bounded red oak standing on the west side of Antietam Creek within ten poles of Conococheague Road crosses the said creek."[42] The beginning tree of The Vineyard apparently is within 10 poles or perches of the Upper (Hitt) Bridge over the Antietam, just northwest of Keedysville.[43] The author has not researched this point conclusively.

The Vineyard is northwest of Fellfoot Enlarged. The tract became part of the Resurvey on The Vineyard[44] and The Resurvey on Hills and Dales and the Vineyard.[45] William Steuart assigned the Resurvey on The Vineyard to Benjamin Tasker Sr and Benjamin Tasker Jr on March 12, 1754.

A map drawn by Arthur Tracey in the Tracey Collection indicates that the route through Fox's Gap to Conococheague was a "public road in 1733." Arthur G. Tracey is documented at the Maryland Archives in G 1456-1073 0/10/7/74. Tracey (not Arthur) and Dern indicate, "The first roads of present-day Frederick County to be made 'public roads' were identified in Prince Georges County Court of November 1733."[46]

Material in the Tracey Collection also gives the following: "Nov. Court 1743 Overseer of road Monocacy to Conococheague - Robert Owings." Apparently there were two Robert Owings. One settled at Conewago and one at South Mountain.

Early Roads and Gaps

Tracey and Dern mention: "One final resident who arrived in the upper Potomac area before 1743 should be noted. He was Robert Owings, who in that year was appointed overseer of the road from 'Monocacy to Conococheague' the road over Crampton's Gap."[47] The road through Crampton's Gap was not the main route to Conococheauge (Williamsport) from Frederick Town. Various authors are mistaken in their contention that Crampton's Gap was on any wagon road before 1768.

The following passages, from the August Court of 1755, give proof the Great Road to Conococheague passed through or near the property of a Richard Smith and a James Christie:

> Richard Smith's petition for a license to operate his tavern "on the Great Road leading to Conococheague" is also granted.[48]

> James Christie states that he lives "on the Great Road that leads from Frederick Town to Conococheague" and asks for a license to keep a public house there. All these petitions are granted.[49]

Richard Smith owned a tract named Christie's Folly which was near the Fox Inn along the road through Fox's Gap. However, James Christie is not on record as owning any land tract. These two court records appear to eliminate Orr's Gap and Crampton's Gap from possessing the Great Road to Conococheague. They support the conclusion that the Great Road to Conococheauge from Frederick Town went through Fox's Gap and passed through Bakersville on its way to Conococheague.

Richard Smith transferred part of Christie's Folly to Peter Beaver. See FCLR, E-753, recorded June 19, 1755. The deed included the following: "between Richard Smith of Frederick County in the Province of Maryland Innholder of the one part and Peter Beaver of the same county and province aforesaid of the other part . . . all that tract or parcel of land called part of Christie's Folly situate lying and being in the county aforesaid being part of a tract of land called Christie's Folly patented in that name of the aforesaid Richard Smith." Christie's Folly began at the beginning tree of Capt. Samuel Magruder's land, The Forest.

During the Braddock Expedition of 1755, Dunbar's Regiment stopped at "one Walker's" the first night out of Frederick Town on their way to Conococheague (Williamsport). The Tracey Collection contains two cards that identify a land tract of a Thomas Walker on the route of the Conococheague Road near Bakersville.

Dorsey's Risque had its beginning "at the beginning of a tract belonging to Thos. Walner (Walker)."[50] This tract was surveyed for Edward Dorsey in 1754. Little Meadow of Thomas Walker was on the "wagon road that goes to Stull's Mill."[51] This was the road from Sharpsburg to Hagerstown which crossed the Conococheague Road from Frederick Town near these two tracts.

The following appears in the minutes of the August Court of 1764:

> A petition by sundry inhabitants of the County states that "there is a great want and need of a bridge to be made on the new road leading to Swearingen's Ferry and to the mouth of Conococheague over Catoctin Creek between Samuel Magruder's and Philip Fink's as there has several people in great danger and almost lost at said fording these last freshes [freshets]." They ask that such a bridge be built.
>
> The Court orders that Messrs. Joseph Smith and Peter Bainbridge agree with workmen to build a bridge over Catoctin Creek near Samuel Magruder's.[52]

These court minutes give clear evidence that one road over the Catoctin Creek north of Middletown led both to Swearingen's Ferry and to Conococheague. The Great Road to Conococheague from Frederick Town went through Fox's Gap.

Roads and Gaps

Crampton's Gap

"Thomas Crampton was born on the ocean in 1735, where his father had just died. Crampton came to Pleasant Valley before 1759. He aided in building a road through the wilderness which led from the old pack horse ford below Shepherdstown, through Crampton's Gap, and on to Frederick Town."[53]

A 1761 deed from John Shelton to Thomas Crampton was for "part of a tract of land called Parks Hall beginning at a marked white oak standing near the old Indian road."[54] An "Indian road" is not the same as a wagon road. Land records indicate the route through Crampton's Gap was just a horse trail in 1768. It is doubtful the road through Crampton's Gap became a wagon road until many years later.

Two land records eliminate, in the author's opinion, Crampton's Gap as a wagon road at the time of the Braddock Expedition in 1755. Stoney Ridge, between Crampton's and Fox's Gaps according to Tracey Collection records, surveyed July 29, 1768, was "between the bridal road gap and the main road gap that leads from Sharpsburg to Frederick."[55] The Stoney Ridge tract is indeed between Fox's Gap and Crampton's Gap. Fox's Gap was the main road gap, as documented by the Grim's Fancy land record. The author believes the words *bridal road*, or bridle road, mean horse trail.

Wilyard's Lot,[56] surveyed December 31, 1765, was "at the foot of the Blue Ridge Mountain where the bridal road crosses said Mountain about 2 or 3 perches north of said road." Dr. Tracey placed this tract about 1/2 mile east of Crampton's Gap.

The Forest, patented or surveyed in 1734, was "on the north side of the Conococheague Road near the Shenandoah Mountain." The location of this tract is near the east side of Crampton's Gap. Part of the tract is very near the War Correspondents Memorial Arch.

The horse trail through Crampton's Gap to Conococheague met the wagon road through Fox's Gap to Shepherdstown, just south of Keedysville, near Jacob Hess's Mill and home. The route through Fox's Gap was the shortest of the two routes from Frederick Town to the Keedysville area.

Crampton's Gap was not the primary route used to travel from Frederick Town to Swearingen's Ferry or Conococheague, either by horse or wagon. The main road from Frederick Town to the Sharpsburg area and to Conococheague, prior to 1756, was through Fox's Gap, not Crampton's. Travelers through Crampton's Gap from Frederick Town probably went on to the area that became Harper's Ferry or perhaps the area at the mouth of the Antietam Creek on the Potomac.

Turner's or Curry's Gap

The Main Road from Frederick Town to Ft. Frederick passed through Turner's or Curry's Gap. It is likely there was a horse trail through the area of Turner's or Curry's Gap prior to the creation of the main road. The turnpike road, built in the early 1800s, crossed South Mountain about a quarter mile north of where the Main Road from Frederick to Ft. Frederick crossed the mountain. This was probably done to make an easier grade over the mountain. The Main Road from Frederick to Ft. Frederick crossed the mountain about three fourths of a mile north of Fox's Gap and a quarter mile south of the present gap and the Mountain House.

The route of the turnpike road, built in the early 1800s, followed the roadbed of the main road from Frederick Town to Ft. Frederick except on the immediate near east side of the Mountain House at Turner's or Curry's Gap. The portion of the turnpike road coming up the mountain on the near east side of the Mountain House lies north of the roadbed of the main road from Frederick to Ft. Frederick.

Robert Turner patented Nelson's Folly, at the present site of Boonsboro, in 1750.[57] It is possible to trace lots in the town of Boonsboro to the Nelson's Folly tract.[58] Turner was "made overseer of roads in Antietam Hundred" in 1748.[59] The earliest mention of Robert Turner, 1745, appears in a survey of Charlemount Pleasant for Samuel Ogle Esqr.[60] "Beginning at a bounded Black Oak standing on a small hill to the eastward of a spring that falls in Little Antietam about half a mile to the southward of Robert Turner's."

Nelson's Folly ran north and west from the

present site of Boonsboro.[61] Related land records indicate Robert Turner did not live at Turner's Gap. Jacob's Brune had its "beginning at a bounded black oak standing on the east side of a tract of land called Lannafield near the foot of the South Mountain and on the west side thereof about one half a mile from Robert Turner's House."[62]

Martsome, at Mousetown, began "at a bounded white oak standing by the side of a branch falling from the end of the Short Hill Mountain down to Robert Turner's plantation being a draft of Little Antietam."[63] There does not appear to be another Turner, other than Robert, for whom to name Turner's Gap.

Turner's Gap, today, includes the area in the immediate vicinity of the Mountain House, now The Old South Mountain Inn. The 1791 map of the *Road Leading from Williamsport to Turner's Gap in the South Mountain* identifies almost one mile of road on the west side of the mountain as being "up through the gap." This part of the Main Road on the west side of the mountain may have came near the present Mountain House, perhaps within a tenth of a mile or less.

The route of the Main Road from Frederick to Ft. Frederick passed over the mountain about a quarter mile directly south of the Mountain House. Since the Mountain House is on the bed of the turnpike, built in the early 1800s, the house might only date to sometime after the creation of the turnpike. However, the author does not rule out the possibility the Mountain House may date to before the creation of the turnpike. It seems possible the house could have been built sometime after 1770, when the Flonham tract was surveyed, but before the creation of the turnpike.

Byron L. Williams, the author of *The Old South Mountain Inn, An Informal History,* was able to trace records from the present owners of the Mountain House, Russell and Judy Schwartz, back to the 1830s or 40s and the estate of Henry Miller. He was unable to trace land records for Robert Turner and his Nelson's Folly tract to the present owners of the Mountain House. He could not do this because Nelson's Folly is well over one mile from The Old South Mountain Inn at Turner's Gap.

The Mountain House at Turner's Gap stands on the south side of the Old National Pike and on the northern portion of a tract named Flonham. A portion of the ten acres that surround the Dahlgren Chapel, across the road from the Mountain House, is part of Addition to Friendship, patented by Frederick Fox in 1805.

The Main Road from Frederick Town to Fort Frederick

The earliest road from Frederick Town to the area that became Williamsport, passing through the general vicinity of Turner's Gap, was the main road from Frederick Town to Ft. Frederick. In 1756, Governor Sharp supervised the construction of Ft. Frederick which is on the Potomac, about 15 miles west of Williamsport.

The name of the main road from Frederick Town to Ft. Frederick describes both why it was built and when it was built. On May 14, 1756, the Maryland Assembly passed the Supply Bill. "An Act for granting a Supply of Forty Thousand Pounds for his Majesty's Service and striking Thirty Four Thousand and Fifteen Pounds Six Shillings thereof, in Bills of Credit, and raising a Fund for sinking the same."[64] The bill authorized the building of Ft. Frederick near the North Mountain.

The bill allowed for the construction of one fort and up to four block-houses. The bill did not explicitly appropriate funds for the construction of a road to the fort, as indicated by the State Roads Commission quote that follows. However, the creation of a road to the fort does seem to be implicit in the act and an allowable expenditure under it:

> Following Braddock's ill-fated campaign, bands of Indians terrorized all Western Maryland and at least one group rampaged within 30 miles of Baltimore. The Maryland Legislature in 1755 took immediate action and appropriated money to build a huge stone fort and a road leading to it, twelve miles west of Williamsport. Called Fort Frederick, this massive edifice is still standing and is enshrined as a state park on the Potomac, south of present-day Clear Spring on U.S. 40 in Washington County. The road they built, leading to it from the east, can be identified as the

course of State Routes 68 and 56.[65]

Later, the State Roads Commission indicates the following:

> Thus the French and Indian War advanced the opening of Western Maryland by many years. This new road, (connecting Ft. Frederick and Ft. Cumberland) together with Braddock's Road (through Turner's Gap connecting Frederick Town and Ft. Frederick), both war measures, gave a direct if extremely rough connection between Baltimore, Annapolis and the far western parts of the province.[66]

Excerpts from the Supply Bill of 1756 follow:

> And be it Enacted, That the said Sum of Forty Thousand Pounds be laid out and applied in Manner following, that is to say, in building and constructing one Fort, and any Number not exceeding four Block-Houses, on the Western Frontiers of this Province, accommodating and paying Workmen employed therein, in paying, arming and victualling, in Bounty-Money for enlisting, cloathing common Soldiers, transporting and conveying any Number not exceeding Two Hundred Men (Officers included), that shall be kept in Garrison in the same, and all other Necessaryies for the Support and Maintenance of the said Garrison, such Sum or Sums of Money as shall be necessary; not exceeding Eleven Thousand Pounds, including the Commissions of the Agents herein after appointed . . . Mr. William Murdock, Mr. James Dick, and Mr. Daniel Wolstenholme, shall be and are hereby appointed Agents . . . for the purchasing and procuring all such Tools, Cloaths, Provisions, Arms, and other Warlike Stores, and transporting and conveying the same, as shall be necessary and requite for the Officers and Soldiers in Garrison, in the said Fort and Block-Houses, to be built on such convenient Places on or near and not beyond the North-Mountain, and in such Form as his Excellency Horatio Sharpe, Esq; or the Governor or Commander in Chief, for the Time being, shall direct and appoint, and for the Payment of the Workmen, and the said Officers and Soldiers, that shall be in the same, or any others, that shall be enlisted or raised by Virtue of this Act for any Expedition, and for cloathing, providing for and arming the same, and for purchasing and contracting for any necessary Stores for his Majesty's Service for the Purposes in this Act mentioned.[67]

The new route crossed the South Mountain at Turner's or Curry's Gap. Frederick County court records support the creation of this road in the late 1750s. The following Frederick County Court Minutes are from records in the Tracey Collection:

> Nov. Court 1759: Road - The new road that goes through Curry's Gap.
> Nov. Court 1759: The new road from Curry's Gap to Beaver Creek.
> Nov. Court 1760: The new road that goes through Curry's Gap (East Side) to Beaver Ck.
> Nov. Court 1761: The new road that goes through Curry's Gap (East Side) to Beaver Ck.

A note on the card in the Tracey Collection indicates this route was along Old US 40, the route of the Old National Pike through Turner's Gap. This is contradictory to other material by Arthur Tracey in the Tracey Collection that indicates Curry's Gap became Fox's Gap. Land records indicate Curry's Gap did not become Fox's Gap.

The following appear in *This Was the Life* by Millard M. Rice:

> Sundry inhabitants of the County, who are unnamed, petition the Court that they "conceive a better and nigher road might be made to Fort Frederick for the road to begin out of the road now leading thereto between the Mountains through Curry's Gap by Robert Turner's and by Joseph Holmes, by Dr. Neal's and so into the road by Joseph Volgamot's." The Court appointed Capt. Moses Chapline, Mr. James Smith and Mr. Joseph Tomlinson to lay out the road.[68]

Joseph Smith and Moses Chapline,

Early Roads and Gaps

who had been appointed by the Court to view a road desired through a gap in the Mountains called Curry's Gap, state that this road "is a better way from Frederick Town to Fort Frederick than any yet carried across said Mountain."[69]

> ... the new road that goes through Curry's Gap: John George Arnold Jr ...[70]

The first statement above indicates the new road to Ft. Frederick was to lead out of the current road to the fort.

Land tract records indicate that there was a route through Turner's or Curry's Gap only after the 1750s. "The Main Road from Frederick Town to Ft. Frederick" appears in deeds for Pickall, Worse and Worse, Flonham, Fox's Last Shift, Kizer's Lowden, and Smithsburg.

Pickall, patented in 1764, began at "the beginning tree of a tract of land called John's Delight patented by James Wardrop which tree is a white oak standing by the side of the main road that leads from Frederick Town to Fort Frederick."[71] John's Delight, patented in 1750, began "at a bounded white oak standing about thirty feet from a small run called Curry's Branch nigh the foot of Shanandore Mountain near Curry's Gap."[72] This record is the earliest found by the author that mentions Curry's Gap.

The patent for John's Delight does not state the beginning tree of the tract was along a road in 1750. However, five later tracts that began at the beginning tree of John's Delight identify the beginning tree as being along a main road. The Pickall patent, Shidler's Dispute deeds of 1760[73] and 1767,[74] the Long Dispute[75] deed of 1767, and the 304 acre tract of the Bartholomew Booker Estate[76] in 1792[77] refer to "the main road." Both Shidler's Dispute deeds mention Curry's Gap.

The following newspaper notice appeared after Bartholomew Booker's death:

> 101. FTM Aug 28 1792/Margaret Booker, Frederick Fox, exec, to sell farm, late the prop of Bartholomew Booker, decd, 304 a., on road from Fred Town to Williamsport, and Hager's Town, about 3 miles above Middletown.[78]

The notice indicates a single road by Bartholomew Booker's land led to both Williamsport and Hagerstown in 1792.

Worse and Worse, surveyed for John Teem on February 7, 1766, had its "beginning at a bounded white oak standing on the east side of the South Mountain and on the south side of the main road that leads from Frederick Town to Fort Frederick about forty perches from the said John Teems dwelling house."[79] The Worse and Worse tract eliminates Fox's Gap from possessing the main road from Frederick Town to Ft. Frederick.

A tract named Its Bad Enough began "at a bounded white oak tree the beginning of a tract of land called Worse and Worse."[80] Its Bad Enough, a very narrow tract of 14 and 3/4 acres, was between the Worse and Worse tract and a tract called The Gap. The beginning of The Gap was "at the end of the third line of Wardrop's land called Curry's Old Place."[81] A deed from John Team to Joseph Chapline for The Gap, recorded December 27, 1766, had its "beginning at the end of the third line of Wardrop's land called Carey's Old Place."[82] Perhaps Curry was Carey or Cary.

The tracts of It's Bad Enough, Worse and Worse, The Gap, and Turkey Ramble became part of the Resurvey on The Gap.[83] The Resurvey on The Gap was on the east side of South Mountain and ran from Fox's Gap to just south of Turner's Gap.

The Flonham tract, surveyed August 27, 1770, had its "beginning at a bounded white oak standing about a perch from the head of a spring on the south side of the Shanandore Mountain on the right hand of the main road leading from Frederick Town to Fort Frederick."[84] The Flonham tract is of rectangular shape. The Flonham survey in 1770 makes no mention of any buildings or appurtenances.

Fox's Last Shift was west of Flonham but extended farther north. It had its "beginning at a bounded white oak tree standing on the north side of the main country road that leads from Frederick Town to Fort Frederick in the South Mountain."[85] A deed in the early 1800s indicates the turnpike road crossed this tract.[86]

A resurvey on Fox's Last Shift, called Newcomer's Purchase, is interesting.[87] Newcomer's Purchase, surveyed January 5, 1786, added 29 acres to the original 72 acres of Fox's Last Shift. The road to Williamsport, on the west side of Turner's Gap, appears to pass through these 29 acres.

Partnership of John Mansberger encompassed 685 acres in 1795.[88] It surrounded the tracts of Fox's Last Shift, Newcomber's Purchase, and Swearingen's Disappointment.

The most interesting aspect of the tract named Fox's Last Shift is its name. No one named Fox owned the tract. This author feels the name derived from the fact a new route between Conococheague and Frederick Town came about in the late 1750s. The new road went through Turner's or Curry's Gap and Fox's Last Shift. This route was the main road from Frederick Town to Ft. Frederick.

The 1791 map of the *Road Leading from Williamsport to Turner's Gap in the South Mountain* shows the road crossing the Antietam near the mouth of Beaver Creek. The area where the road crosses Beaver Creek is called the Devil's Backbone and is near Delemere. Beaver Creek, identified in the 1759-61 court minutes previously cited, must have meant the mouth of Beaver Creek on the Antietam Creek.

Susanne Flowers cites a large picture at the Washington County Court House in Hagerstown that shows the Devil's Backbone Bridge over Little Beaver Creek on Maryland Highway 68. The picture's title reads, incorrectly, the bridge, built in 1824, was the "spot where Braddock and his Redcoats crossed the Little Beaver in 1755."

Braddock, Washington, and Governor Sharp crossed the Antietam east of Sharpsburg on the Old Sharpsburg Road. Dunbar's Regiment crossed the Antietam near the Upper (Hitt) Bridge near Keedysville. The road through the Devil's Backbone and over Beaver Creak was part of the Main Road from Frederick to Ft. Frederick, built after 1755.

Farther west of Fox's Last Shift, Racon had its "beginning at a bounded white oak standing on the south side of a road near the south mountain."[89] Raccoon was a resurvey on Racon.[90] The resurvey was for 253 acres and began at the beginning tree of the original tract.

Kizer's Lowden lies northwest of Boonsboro. The tract had its "beginning at a bounded white oak standing on the north side of the main road leading from Frederick Town to Ft. Frederick between Robert Turner's plantation and Antietam Creek and by the side of a road that leads from Isaac Houser's to Chapline's Mill."[91] This is consistent with a route from the Boonsboro area to Williamsport.

The road from Ft. Frederick to Ft. Cumberland, now Cumberland, Maryland, was approved under Article XCV of an act that appropriated 250 pounds for building "a good wagon road" from Ft. Frederick to Ft. Cumberland.[92]

The 1781 Frederick County Court Minutes

Frederick court minutes from 1781 appear below:

> ... from the forks of the roads where the Sharpsburg Road leads out of Braddock's Road to the top of South Mountain, being the direct road from Frederick passing Robert Turner's old place to Fort Frederick.[93]

The court minutes contain at least five elements: 1) the road from Frederick to Ft. Frederick; 2) the location of Robert Turner's old place; 3) the "forks of the roads"; 4) the Sharpsburg Road and the Braddock Road met; and 5) the year, 1781. Elements four and five present statements of fact and need no further clarification. The first three elements require additional information for clarification. The court minutes do not tell us where Robert Turner lived, the course of the road, or where the roads forked.

Court minutes in 1748 33 years earlier, indicate, "Road that leads out from John Georges that leads via Robt. Evans to top of Shenandoah."[94] This author believes these court minutes refer to the fork in the road just north of Middletown and very near the Catoctin Creek. John George's Road was the same as the road from Frederick Town to Stull's Mill [the Old Hagerstown Road]. The road by Robert Evans was the same as the route of the Old Sharpsburg Road from Frederick Town through Fox's Gap to Shepherdstown.

John George Arnold owned land near Orr's Gap. Tracts near Orr's Gap owned by John George Arnold include Ram's Horn[95] and Hog Yard.[96] However, a John George Arnold owned land near

Early Roads and Gaps

Conococheague, according to the Ash Swamp land record of February 19, 1739.[97]

Robert Evans[98] lived along the Old Sharpsburg Road.[99] His name also is associated with the Cuckhold's Horns[100] tract, probably near Orr's Gap. However, Evans assigned his interest to Henry Rhodes who received the patent for the Cuckhold's Horns tract. Early records tie Robert Evans to the Old Sharpsburg Road:

> Beginning in 1741 and for several years thereafter, Mark and Thomas Whitaker were overseers for the road from "Shenandoah Mountain to Catoctin Mountain." Thomas Whitaker petitioned the March Court of 1745: "Having been appointed overseer of the main road and having marked and distinguished the Potomac Ferry [now Shepherdstown] Road extending to the city of Annapolis and several other remarkable places . . . to acquaint your honorable worships that a certain Robert Evans hath stopped the said road and will not suffer travelers to pass nor the road to extend through the enclosure as it formerly went but tumbles logs into the road and hath turned the road where it is mortally impossible to make it good. Pray further instructions..."[101]

The above records indicate the road through Fox's Gap was "the main road" and that it was extended to the city of Annapolis by Whitaker before 1745. The extension of the road to the city of Annapolis was approved in 1739 by the Maryland Assembly:

> Phillip Lee Esqr from the upper house delivers Mr. Speaker a petition of the inhabitants about monoccacy and about the mountains on Potomack River on the back part of Virginia. A petition of the inhabitants at and about Monocacy Creek. A petition of the inhabitants to the northward of the Blue Ridge alias Shenandore Mountain, by which petition the several petitioners pray a road may be cleared through the country from the city of Annapolis for the more easy carriage of their grain provisions and other commodities which petitions by the Upper House are endorsed recommended to a consideration of the Lower House.[102]

Thomas Whitaker transferred a tract named Prevention to Nicholas Fink in 1750. Prevention had its "beginning at a bounded white oak standing at the mouth of a run called Mill Run that falls into Catoctin Creek."[103] The fork of the Old Sharpsburg Road and the Old Hagerstown Road is just southeast of the mouth of Mill Creek on the Catoctin Creek (see the 1808 Varle Map). This juncture is just north of Middletown.

The fork of the roads is near the end of line three of a 66 acre tract, part of Goose Cap, from Nicholas Fink to Thomas Welch in 1771. "Beginning at a bounded Sycamore tree standing on the north west side of Mill Creek and about two perches from the said Creek." Line two went "South 29 degrees east 24 perches to the Great Road that leads from Frederick Town to Hagers Town then by and with the said road the two following courses."[104]

An 1832 deed from John Stemple et ux to George Baltzell[105] included portions of the tracts of The Forest, the Resurvey on Watson's Welfare,[106] Smithfield, Whiskey Alley,[107] Goose Cap, What Nots, and I Wish There Was More.[108] Jacob Keefour deeded 50 acres of the Resurvey on Whiskey Alley to the "Trustees of the German Reformed Lutheran and Calvinist Congregations in and about Middletown" in 1783.[109]

Watson's Welfare had its "beginning at a bounded hickory tree standing on the east side of Catoctin Creek a draft of Potomac near a mile below the Great Road that leads from John Stull's Mill to the mouth of Monocacy."[110] This author concludes that "near a mile below the Great Road that leads from John Stull's Mill to the mouth of Monocacy" meant one mile below the forks of the Old Sharpsburg and Old Hagerstown Roads (i.e., the roads through Fox's and Orr's Gaps).

The fork in the road identified by the 1781 court minutes was at the Catoctin Creek just north of Middletown, where the Old Sharpsburg Road met the Old Hagerstown Road. Middletown is about one mile south of the fork of the Old Sharpsburg and Old Hagerstown Roads. Millard M. Rice, in *New Facts and Old Famililes*, presents what is probably the most accurate history of the founding of Middletown.[111] His work includes land tract analysis and material on the Great Road to Conococheague.

Some might argue that the forks in the roads mentioned in the 1781 Court Minutes was where the main road from Frederick Town to Ft. Frederick, through Turner's or Curry's Gap, met the Old Sharpsburg Road. This point, shown on the 1808 Varle Map just east of "Ringer," was between the Fox Inn and the bridge over the Catoctin Creek just north of Middletown. The intersection of these roads also appears on an 1840 map in the Tracey Collection. This fork in the roads was "by Casper Shaffs" in 1768.

Bartholomew Booker lived along the Main Road from Frederick Town to Ft. Frederick. Bartholomew Booker was "overseer of road from the top of Catoctin Mtn. that leads to Robert Turner's and to the top of South Mtn. from where the road forks by Casper Shaff's to the top of South Mtn" in 1768.[112] The beginning tree of the Bartholomew Booker Estate in 1791 was along the Main Road from Frederick Town to Ft. Frederick. Casper Shaff owned Oxford, just east of the Fox Inn. The fork in the road at Casper Shaff's was where the roads through Fox's Gap and Turner's or Curry's Gap met in 1768.

Peter Beaver acquired Oxford from Casper Shaff on October 18, 1769. A portion of the Resurvey on Mendall from Jacob Smith Sr. to Bartholomew Booker, January 15, 1772, began "near a road that leads from Bartholomew Booker's to Peter Beaver's."[113]

A 1760 deed from Bartholomew Booker to Michael Shepfell, for the same property as above, began "at a bounded red oak standing by the head of a little spring and near a road that leads from Bartholomew Booker's to Peter Beaver's."[114] This material supports the conclusion the road from Frederick to Ft. Frederick met the road through Fox's Gap in the area between the Fox Inn and the Catoctin Creek at one time, as shown on the 1808 Varle Map.

The 1781 Frederick Court Minutes indicate the road from Frederick Town to Ft. Frederick went by Robert Turner's Old Place. Robert Turner did not live at Turner's Gap. He lived near the present site of Boonsboro.[115] The 1781 court minutes represent an accurate statement related to the roads in 1781. The 1781 Court Minutes refer to two roads built at different times. The road through Fox's Gap dates to before the Braddock Expedition of 1755, whereas the road through Turner's or Curry's Gap dates only from after the Braddock Expedition in 1755.

The Turnpike Road through Turner's Gap (The Old National Pike)

The state of Maryland passed a law in November 1804 approving three turnpike companies. One of these three, the Baltimore and Frederick Town Turnpike Company, was to construct a turnpike from Baltimore through Frederick Town and Middletown to Boonsborough (Boonsboro). Subscriptions for stock were taken in March, 1805. In April of that year, a law passed providing for the extension of the turnpike road to Williamsport and Hagerstown from Boonsboro:[116]

> Sec. 11. . . . and be it enacted, That the said roads shall be made in, over, and upon the beds of the present roads, as laid out and confirmed by the commissioners of review, and the several acts of Assembly relating to the same, and also upon every extension of the said roads as established by this law: Provided always, That, should it appear, on a resurvey of any part of the extension of said roads by sworn surveyors, that a considerable saving in distance would thence arise to the public, and in expense to the company or companies, that in all such cases it shall be lawful to depart from the tract of the road so originally laid down, and improve the shorter and less expensive route: Provided, also, That, in all such deviations, the road shall not be diverted or taken from any town or village through which it now passsses . . .[117]

> Sec. 17. . . . it shall in no place rise or fall more than will form an angle of four degrees, with a horizontal line, except over the Catoctin and South Mountains, where it may rise or fall to an angle of six degrees, with a horizontal line . . .[118]

> . . . and although the law authorizing this road admits of six degrees

over the South Mountain, still, as the same force will propel so much greater a load on a four degree hill than the same force would on an angle of six degrees, we shall rather submit to some loss of distance than exceed four degrees to the termination of the road.[119]

Election of a president, eight managers, and a treasurer was held on May 13, 1805, by the Baltimore and Frederick Town Turnpike Company. Notices for the letting of work appeared in late May. An advertisement in June sought to hire a manager of turnpike construction. The following newspaper notice ran October 2, 1805, and for a number of weeks thereafter:

> Advertisement
> I will sell a tract of land containing 105 acres in Washington County lying on the main road leading from Williamsport to Frederick Town and about two miles from Boonsborough - on this land are 2 never failing springs of excellent water, well calculated for a distillery - there is a dwelling house and out houses on the premises, also between two and three hundred bearing apple trees also a number of peach and cherry trees, - as the turnpike road is generally expected to pass on the present road, and near the dwelling house, presume it will make this property very valuable to a purchaser.
> Peter Summers
> living on the premises.[120]

John Summers patented Raccoon in August 1770. As shown on the 1791 map of the *Road Leading from Williamsport to Turner's Gap in the South Mountain,* the course of the old road was just south of Summers' house. The new route was just north of Summers' house.

The report of the president and managers of the Baltimore and Frederick Town Turnpike Company on October 9, 1805, said ten miles through Baltimore County were to be completed by April 1, 1806, and three miles in Anne Arundel County were to be completed by August 1806.

A January 2, 1807, notice by the turnpike company stated sufficient money had been raised to complete the road at least as far as Boonsboro. A notice on August 22, 1807, stated a Mr. Herbaugh had been hired by the company to oversee the building of a bridge over Monocacy, consisting of five arches of thirty feet each.[121]

Lewis Wampler, Secretary of the Baltimore and Frederick Town Turnpike Co., sent Governor Edward Lloyd a letter, dated January 28, 1811, requesting the appointment of a committee to inspect and approve ten miles, three furlongs, and twelve perches of the turnpike completed to Boonsboro. Fifty miles already had been approved from Baltimore. The Governor nominated John Schley, Stephen Stoner, and Lawrence Bringle on February 15. The three nominees sent a report to the Governor, indicating the road had been done in a workmanlike manner as far as Boonsboro on March 11, 1811.[122]

The road through Turner's Gap was destined to become part of a national road to the western part of the nation. The House of Representatives of the United States approved a bill on March 27, 1806, previously passed in the Senate, for the construction of a road from Cumberland, Maryland, to Ohio.

Discussion of the route of the road appears in articles in January and February 1807 in the *Maryland Herald and Hagerstown Weekly*. A January 13 article, discussing the route of the proposed road, mentions Braddock's Road and Dunbar's Run.

Five early land tracts lie in the vicinity of Turner's Gap.[123] These tracts are Addition to Friendship, Flonham, Partnership of John Mansberger, Resurvey on Bear Swamp, and Swearingen's Disappointment.

The beginning tree of Flonham indicates the route of the turnpike road on the immediate near east side of the Mountain House was not the same route as the Main Road from Frederick to Ft. Frederick in that immediate area. The bounded tree of Flonham is about 1/4 mile south, southeast of the Mountain House. Two deeds in the 1800s substantiate the turnpike road was on the right hand side of the bounded tree of Flonham.

A deed from Susan Miller et al. to Daniel Beagley states the turnpike crossed the fourth line of Flonham at 84 purchases north of the beginning tree.[124] This tract is along the south and east sides of Flonham and consists entirely of land from the Addition to Friendship tract.

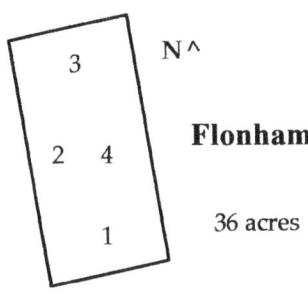

Flonham

36 acres

A deed from George Baltzell to Henry Miller[125] included two tracts of land. The first tract was 75 1/2 acres of Addition to Friendship lying south of the turnpike road. The second tract consisted of 114 acres of Addition to Friendship lying north of the turnpike road. Lines 14, 15, and 16 of the second tract are along the turnpike.

A tract named Apple Brandy gives adequate proof that the turnpike road on the immediate near east side of Turner's Gap did not lie on the roadbed of the Main Road from Frederick Town to Fort Frederick. The beginning tree of Apple Brandy of Jacob Fulwiler was "a bounded Spanish oak near the top of the south mountain."[126] This tree is near the end of the second line of Bowser's Addition.

Line 8 of Apple Brandy went "to the main road." The end of line eight is approximately 600 feet south of the beginning tree of Flonham. The beginning tree of Flonham was on the right-hand side of the point in the road identified in the Apple Brandy tract.

The Apple Brandy deed substantiates the Main Road from Frederick to Ft. Frederick was south of the turnpike on the near east side of the Mountain House. Line 20 of the Resurvey on The Gap, which is the same as line 8 of Apple Brandy, does not read "to the main road," but only "to the fourth line of Worse and Worse."[127]

The turnpike road through Turner's Gap ran in a southerly direction on the near east side of the mountain. At its closest point, the turnpike was approximately 460 feet from the beginning tree of Flonham. The turnpike road at Turner's Gap runs about 24 perches south of, and mostly parallel to, the north, or third, line of Flonham.

The following information can be obtained from the deed from Phillip Sheffer to Henry Miller. The turnpike crosses the fourth line of Flonham 23 1/2 perches below the northeast corner of the tract and 82 1/2 perches north of the beginning tree of Flonham. Line 4 of 18 perches and line 5 of 20 3/4 perches were "by and in the middle of" the turnpike. Line 5 ended at the fourth or last line of Flonham. Line 6 went 23 1/2 perches with and to the end of line three of Flonham. The fourth, or last, line of Flonham was 108 perches.[128]

The turnpike continued almost due east at least 15 4/10 perches into Addition to Friendship. Line 6 of the Smith-Dahlgren deed went "to the middle of the aforesaid turnpike and with it." Lines 7 and 8 of this deed are the same as lines 4 and 5 of the Shaffer-Miller deed. Line 9 went "15 4/10 perches to a stake on the south side of said turnpike thence leaving it."[129] Part two of the Baltzell-Miller deed started at the end of the third line of Flonham.[130]

The end of line 12 of St. Mary's Academy of Notre Dame to Charles M. Hewitt was "to the middle of the state road leading from Frederick to Hagerstown" and line 15 was "to a white oak tree on the east side of the state road above mentioned."[131] Lines 13 and 14 probably were along the road. Deeds for Susan Miller et al. to Daniel Beagley[132] and John W. Derr et al. to Adam Koogle[133] place the turnpike and state road on the right-hand side of the beginning tree of Flonham.

Henry Miller acquired 67 acres that were part of Addition to Frendship and part of Fredericksburg under a writ of Fieri Facia from John Routzah.[134] Henry Miller acquired most of Addition to Friendship from the heirs of Joseph Swearingen.[135] George Baltzell, attorney, was Miller's agent for this acquisition. Swearingen acquired Addition to Friendship from Frederick Fox in 1807.[136] Frederick Fox patented Addition to Friendship May 27, 1805.[137] Joseph Swearingen was one of three individuals appointed by law in 1805 to take subscriptions for stock in the turnpike company at Middletown.[138]

Henry Miller acquired 5 acres of Flonham from Philip Jacob Shafer.[139] Shafer, or perhaps his father of the same name, acquired the patent to Flonham. A Philip Jacob Shafer was a witness to the will of Bartholomew Booker.[140]

Randolph Abott Shotwell, a Confederate soldier in the Battle of South Mountain, was a North Carolina newspaper editor after the war.

Roads and Gaps

The following statement about Turner's Gap appears in *The Papers of Randolph Abbot Shotwell*. "The present turnpike through the Gap is of modern construction; prior to it, the Gap was not used."[141]

Land records for Fox's Last Shift, Racon, and Raccoon, support the road through Turner's Gap on the west side of the mountain in the early 1760s. The 1791 map of the *Road Leading from Williamsport to Turner's Gap in the South Mountain* supports the use of the route on the west side of Turner's Gap prior to the creation of the turnpike, as does the advertisement by Peter Summers in 1805. The author has not determined precisely where the end of the last line of the 1791 map of the road meets the Frederick County line, but it appears to be in the vicinity of the Old South Mountain Inn at Turner's Gap.

Orr's Gap and the Old Hagerstown Road to Frederick Town

Jonathan Hager Sr. founded Hagerstown in 1762.[142] He died accidentally on November 6, 1775, at his new saw mill, where he was supervising the preparation of timber for building a German Reformed Church in Hagerstown.

One of the earliest roads in western Maryland connected the areas that became Frederick Town, Middletown, and Hagerstown.[143] In the 1740s this was the road from Monocacy to Stull's Mill. The road from Monocacy to John Stull's mill was made a public road by the November Court of 1739.

John Stull built his mill on Whiskey, located where the Hagerstown power plant now stands.[144] The road crossed South Mountain through Orr's Gap, about three miles north of Fox's Gap and about two miles north of Turner's Gap. This route became the Old Hagerstown Road from Frederick Town. Today Interstate 70 and Route 40 cross the Blue Ridge at Orr's Gap.

Just north of Middletown, before crossing the Catoctin Creek, a sign today identifies the Old Hagerstown Road branching off to the right and passing through Orr's Gap. The 1808 Varle Map agrees with the currently posted sign. It indicates the road through Orr's Gap met the road through Fox's Gap at the Catoctin Creek just north of Middletown.

Some records indicate the road branching off the Old National Pike near Bolivar and passing through Orr's Gap by way of the Mount Tabor Church, also was known as the Old Hagerstown Road. Daniel Harvey Hill Jr indicates a gap called Hamburg Pass was on the Old Hagerstown Road. "North of the main turnpike about two miles was another gap known as Hamburg Pass. The road to this pass branches off from the National Road at Bolivar, sweeps north by Mount Tabor Church. It is generally known as the Old Hagerstown Road."[145]

The road from Frederick Town to Stull's Mill, near the area that became Hagerstown, was a wagon road by the time of the Braddock Expedition in 1755. Land records for Barron Hill (June 23, 1752), Mt. Pleasant (Aug. 24, 1747), John's Lot (Aug. 1, 1754), Terms Stool (May 13, 1745), and Gaming Alley (Aug. 27, 1744) support this conclusion. Gaming Alley was "on the great road that leads from Stull's Mill to the Monocacy."

Dr. Tracey labeled Orr's Gap as Braddock's Gap on the map he created of the early roads in western Maryland. Dr. Tracey probably relied upon the 1808 Varle Map or the 1791 map of the *Road from Elizabethtown [Hagerstown] to Newcomber's Mill and Frederick County Line* as his reference. An 1840 Maryland map in the Tracey Collection also shows Braddock's Gap at the location of Orr's Gap.

A map, dated April 5, 1791, of the *Road from Elizabethtown to Newcomber's Mill and Frederick County Line* is in the Maryland Archives.[146] This map identifies Orr's Gap as Braddock's Gap. Conrad Hogmire, Daniel Winder, and an unknown individual signed this map. It shows John Orr's house about one mile northwest of the gap in South Mountain. *Stull's* appears near a bridge, about one mile from the Market House in Elizabethtown [Hagerstown]. The map includes the courses of the route similar to a land tract record. However, these measurements are difficult to read. For this reason, the map is not included in this book.

Charles Varle, engineer, offered to publish by subscription a map of Washington County together with a plan of Hagerstown in the July 22, 1807, *Maryland Herald and Hagerstown*

Weekly.[147] The Varle Map of 1808 shows Braddock's Gap on the Old Hagerstown Road from Frederick Town. Varle shows Fox's Gap and Turner's Gap on his map as well. The Varle Map identifies the Fox Inn, labeled as "Ringer." George Fox sold the Fox Inn to John Ringer in 1807. The map makes no note of an inn or other landmark at Turner's Gap.

A road from the area of Stull's Mill (Hagerstown) to Conococheague (Williamsport) existed by 1755. A tract named Contentment, in 1742, was "90 perches from a wagon road that goes from Bumgardner's Mill to Feltygrove's." This tract is between Hagerstown and Williamsport, according to records in the Tracey Collection.

Jeffery Wyand cites the first session of the new Frederick County Court in March 1749. ". . . the road that Leads from Volgamot's to Stull's." Wyand states, "Volgamot's or Wohlgemuth's mill was not far above modern Williamsport."[148] Orr's Gap, therefore, was a viable route for the wagons of the Braddock Expedition and for Dunbar's Regiment to use to reach Conococheague from Frederick Town.

The following letter gives a possible explanation why Orr's Gap received the label of *Braddock's Gap:*

> I am also to inform your Excellency that one William Roberts (who is esteemed a Man of Credit) was with us Yesterday, and says he came through the South Mountain Thursday last, this side of which he saw four Houses burnt about four Miles from Major Ogles and that a Messenger came to him yesterday morning to give him an Account that four men were killed the same day he came through Mountain and at the same Gap he pass'd which is not above Sixty five Miles from this Place.[149]

Perhaps the gap to which the letter refers was Orr's Gap. The Orr family did not live at the gap but about one mile north. The label of Orr's Gap, for this reason, probably was not strong.

An analogy seems appropriate at this point. Many streets across America have the name Washington. However, it is obvious George Washington never came near most of them. The same idea applies to Orr's Gap. General Braddock did not go through Orr's Gap to reach Swearingen's Ferry on May 2, 1755.

General Braddock, Washington, and Governor Sharp took the road through Fox's Gap from Frederick Town to Swearingen's Ferry on May 2, 1755. Dunbar's Regiment, in late April 1755, took the Great Conococheague Road from Frederick Town, through Fox's Gap and Bakersville, to Conococheague.

Early Roads and Gaps

Footnotes - Early Roads and Gaps

[1] There is no course number 39 indicated on this map. The author believes this missing line in the written description of the road should be south, about 81 degrees east, about 40 to 45 perches.

[2] MdHR, 17,448, 1-23-4-2, Bowser's Addition, surveyed April 10, 1765, 10 acres. MSA, BC & GS #37, 138-9.

[3] FCLR, BGF-6-216, Joel Keller to John Wise, recorded Oct. 17, 1860, "part of the same land which the said Joel Keller obtained from Susan Miller, John W. Derr, Elizabeth Derr and others heirs at law of the late Henry Miller deceased by deed dated the 7th day of May 1844." Also, FCLR, WIP-9-149, John W. Wise et ux to Jonas Gross, recorded Apr. 5, 1889, 4 3/4 acres. ". . . which is more particularly described in a deed from Joel Keller and wife to the said John Wise and Matilda Wise, dated on the seventh day of May in the year eighteen hundred and fifty eight . . . "

[4] FCLR, WIP-11, folios 8, 9 and 10, Jonas Gross to Society of the Burnside Expedition, Nov. 23, 1889, 40 feet square.

[5] MdHR, 17,478, 1-23-4-34, Frederick Fox, patent for Addition to Friendship, May 27, 1805, 202 acres. MSA, IC #P, 672-3.

[6] FCLR, WBT-1-100, Susan Miller et al. to John Miller, recorded Apr. 1, 1845, 13 and 1/4 acres. Bowser's Addition and part of Addition to Friendship.

[7] FCLR, HGO-1-156, Frederick Fox, survey for Fredericksburg, July 6, 1792, 75 acres.

[8] MdHR, 17,438, 1-23-3-38, David Bowser, patent for David's Will, Dec. 24, 1763, 49 acres. MSA, BC & GS, 396.

[9] FCLR, THO-1-194, Samuel Shoup, resurvey called The Cool Spring, Jan. 18, 1801, 266 1/2 acres. This is a resurvey of The Case Is At End.

[10] FCLR, K-499-500, John Fox to Elias Bruner, Lot #269 in Frederick Town, May 22, 1766.

[11] FCLR, J-504-5, Daniel Dulany to John Fox, Lot #269 in Frederick Town, June 2, 1764.

[12] Frederick S. Weiser, ed., *Evangelical Reformed Church, Frederick, Frederick County, 1746-1789, Maryland German Church Records* Vol. 5, (Manchester, Md.: Noodle-Doosey Press, 1987), 23. "Christina, dau. of Philipp and Elisabetha Casper, b. 20 Oct. 1766, bp. 19 Dec. 1766. Sponsors: Johann Georg and Christina Fux [sic]."

[13] Letter, dated "Aug 9, 1812," from "Sharpsburg," that was "received and forwarded from Lebanon, Warren County, Ohio, Sept. 8, 1812, addressed to Msrs. Fredric(k) and Michael Fox, Franklin Township, Warren Co. Ohio," from Jacob Reel. Robert H. Fox of Cincinnati, Ohio, provided the author with a copy of this letter.

[14] Maryland State Archives, Special Collections, G1427-507, B5-1-3, Road from Swearingen's Ferry on the Potomac River Through Sharpsburg to the Top of the South Mountain at Fox's Gap, Aug. 13, 1792.

[15] FCLR, WR-42-550, Peter Ludy to Jacob Routzong, recorded July 9, 1812, 68 acres. Part of Addition to Friendship and part of Fredericksburg.

[16] Paul David Nelson. "Lee, Gates, Stephen and Morgan: Revolutionary War Generals of the Lower Shenandoah Valley." *West Virginia History*. 37 (1976): 185-200. Nelson places all four, Charles Lee, Horatio Gates, Daniel Morgan, and Adam Stephen, in the Braddock Expedition. See page 186 for Stephen, page 187 for Morgan, page 187 for Gates, and page 188 for Lee. All four lived within a 15 square mile area in the lower Shenandoah Valley at the outset of the American Revolution. This area includes present-day Jefferson County, West Virginia, and Frederick County, Virginia.

[17] MdHR, 17,396, 1-23-2-30, James Smith, patent for Smith's Hills, Dec. 27, 1739, 208 acres. MSA, PT #1, 261-3.

[18] MdHR, 17,388, 1-23-2-20, Thomas Swearingen, patent for Fellfoot, Nov. 10, 1737, 115 acres. MSA, EI #2, 623-4.

[19] MdHR, 17,400, 1-23-2-34, Joseph Chapline, patent for Mountain, Apr. 9, 1745, 50 acres.

[20] MdHR, 17,395-2, 1-23-2-29, Mount Pleasant, surveyed Mar. 11, 1744/5. MSA, LG #E, 559-60.

[21] MdHR, 17, 388, 1-23-2-20, Richard Sprigg, survey for Piles's Grove, Aug. 14, 1736, 560 acres. MSA, EI #5, 106.

22 FCLR, BD-1-535, Moses Chapline Jr to John Cary and Christopher Edelen, Resurvey on Mt. Pleasant and Josiah's (Last) Bit, Oct. 18, 1775, 471 and 50 acres, except Old Purchase of 77 acres. Also see MdHR, 17,410, 1-23-3-4. The Resurvey on Mt. Pleasant, surveyed Oct. 23, 1751. MSA, GS #1, 101-2.

23 [near to MdHR, 17,438, 1-23-3-38], Moses Chapline, his certificate for Josiah's (Last) Bit, patented to William Good, April 20, 1786, 67 acres. MSA, IC #B, 481.

24 FCLR, BD-1, Moses Chapline Jr to William Good, May 18, 1775, Old Purchase, 77 acres.

25 MdHR, 17,465, 1-23-4-19, William Good, survey for Pastures Green, Dec. 11, 1784, 290 acres. MSA, IC #B, 480-1.

26 MdHR, 17,490, 1-23-5-3, John Miller, survey for Miller's Hills, Dec. 4, 1813, 180 acres. MSA, IB #G, 303-4.

27 MdHR, 17,476, 1-23-4-32, Jacob Hess, survey for Security, May 10, 1791, 85 acres. MSA, IC #N, 6-7.

28 Jacob Hess, resurvey for Security, Sept. 11, 1792, 175 acres.

29 Patent date of May 2, 1782.

30 WCLR, G-7, 621-6, Jacob Hess et al., survey for Fellfoot Enlarged, March 19, 1792, 2100 acres.

31 MdHR, 17,745, 1-23-4-31, John Booth and Jonas Hogmire, patent for Mt. Atlas, 1798, MSA, S11 IC #M, 470-1.

32 MdHR, 17,458, 1-23-4-12, Philip Booker, survey for Booker's Resurvey on Well Done, Apr. 2, 1772, 332 acres. MSA, BC & GS #47, 39-40.

33 MdHR, 17,386, 1-23-2-18, John Magrudar, survey for The Forest, Oct. 2, 1733, 300 acres. MSA, AM #1, 365-6. Also see, MdHR, 17,390, 1-23-2-22, John Magrudar, patent for The Forest, Apr. 9, 1734, 300 acres. MSA, EI 4, 60-1.

34 Maryland Geological Survey, *Report on the Highways of Maryland* (Baltimore: The Johns Hopkins Press, 1899), 128. See John Gibson, ed., *History of York Co., Pennsylvania* (Baltimore: Genealogical Publishing Company, 1975), 514. This book discusses the Post Map of New England, New York, New Jersey, and Pennsylvania, by Moll, dated 1730.

35 MdHR, 17,406-3, 1-23-2-44, James Wardrop, survey for Oxford, July 23, 1751, 54 acres. MSA, BY & GS #5, 594.

36 MdHR, 17,406-3, 1-23-2-44, James Wardrop, survey for The Cool Spring, July 23, 1751, 75 acres. MSA, BY & GS #5, 608-9.

37 MdHR, 17,415, 1-23-3-9, Robert Evans, survey for Betty's GoodWill, Oct. 16, 1747, 50 acres. MSA, BC & GS 4, 195-6.

38 MdHR, 17,415, 1-23-3-9, Edward Grimes, patent for Betty's GoodWill, Sept. 29, 1754. MSA, GS #2, 12-3. The Grimes patent gives a survey date of Oct. 20, 1727, in the name of Robert Evans.

39 FCLR, WR-7, Bartholomew Booker to Frederick Fox, April 4, 1787, 92 acres. Part of I Hope It Is Well Done and Pegging Awl.

40 FCLR, CM-1-582, Vincent Sanner to Samuel Ausherman, recorded April 14, 1868, 194 1/2 acres. Part of Fidler's Purchase, part of the Resurvey on Exchange, part of Bubble, and Deeffer Snay.

41 FCLR, THO-1-220, Jacob Smith Jr, resurvey called Now I Know It, Dec. 17, 1802, 198 acres.

42 MdHR, 17,405-1, 1-23-2-42, William Steuart, patent for The Vineyard, Oct. 10, 1750, 154 acres; warrant of George Steuart, The Vineyard, April 7, 1739, 154 acres. MSA, BC & GS #4, 181-3; See William Hand Browne, ed., *The Correspondence of Governor Horatio Sharpe, 1753-1771.* Archives of Maryland. (Baltimore: Maryland Historical Society, 1888-1911), 6:16. Perhaps Dr. George Stewart and his brother, William, who are mentioned in a letter from Lord Glencairn to Horatio Sharpe (HS), Dec. 24, 1753.

43 See Otto B. Smith to Daniel R. Berry, transferred between 1867 and 1869, on the west side of the Antietam Creek and the south side of the stone bridge on the road from Keedysville to Bakersville, next to Jacob Hammond's, Jos. Hoffman's, Daniel Miller's, and Dr. Kennedy's.

44 MdHR, 17,412, 1-23-3-6, William Stewart's assignment and Benjamin Tasker Sr.'s patent for the Resurvey of The Vineyard, Sept. 10, 1752, 506 acres. MSA, BC & GS #1, 164.

Early Roads and Gaps

[45] MdHR, 17,456, 1-23-4-10, Joseph Chapline, Resurvey on Hills and Dales and The Vineyard, Nov. 9, 1771, 2,256 acres. MSA, BC & GS #45, 22-5.

[46] Grace L. Tracey and John P. Dern, *Pioneers of Old Monocacy* (Baltimore: Genealogical Publishing Company, 1987), 54-5.

[47] Tracey and Dern, *Pioneers of Old Monocacy*, 98.

[48] Millard M. Rice, *This Was the Life excerpts from the judgment records of Frederick County, Md. 1748-1765* (Redwood City, California: Monocacy Book Company, 1979), 166.

[49] Rice, *This Was the Life*, 166.

[50] MSA, BC & GS 1-355, Edward Dorsey, Dorsey's Risque, Dec. 14, 1754, 158 acres.

[51] Little Meadow, Thomas Walker, Sept. 26, 1756, 200 acres.

[52] Rice, *This Was the Life*, 258.

[53] Thomas J. C. Williams, *History of Washington County, Maryland* 2 vol. (Baltimore: Regional Publishing Company, 1968), 1:27-8.

[54] FCLR, G-287, John Shelton to Thomas Crampton, recorded Nov. 18, 1761, 101 and 1/2 acres.

[55] MdHR, 17,448, 1-23-4-2, Stoney Ridge, surveyed July 29, 1768. MSA, BC & GS #37, 144-5.

[56] MdHR, 17,458, 1-23-4-12, Wilyard's Lot, surveyed Dec. 31, 1765. MSA, BC & GS #30, 259-61.

[57] WCLR, B, 336-8, Robert Turner, patent for Nelson's Folly, recorded March 5, 1750, 500 acres. ". . . according to the certificate of survey thereof taken and returned into our land office bearing date the fourth day of June seventeen hundred and thirty four..."

[58] Land tract analysis by the author and material supplied by Doug Bast of the Boonsborough Museum of History.

[59] Tracey Collection records in the Historical Society of Carroll County.

[60] MdHR, 17,420, 1-23-3-14, Samuel Ogle, survey for Charlemount Pleasant, January 1, 1745, 100 acres.

[61] MSA, B, pp. 336-8, Robert Turner, patent for Nelsons Folly, March 5, 1750. The certificate of survey date was June 4, 1734.

[62] MdHR, 17,465, 1-23-4-19, Henry Poulis, survey of Jacob's Broom, March 27, 1772. MSA, IC #B, 301.

[63] MdHR, 17,456, 1-23-4-10, Peter Baker, survey for Martsome, May 26, 1763. MSA, BC & GS #45, 27.

[64] Archives of Maryland, Proceedings and Acts of the General Assembly, 1755-1756, May 14, 1756, 52:480-521, Chapter 5, 1756. MSA, SC 2908, MdHR, 2764.

[65] State Roads Commisision of Maryland, *A History of Road Building in Maryland* (n. p, 1958), 16.

[66] State Roads Commisision of Maryland, *A History of Road Building in Maryland*, 17.

[67] *Archives of Maryland*, Proceedings and Acts of the General Assembly, 1755-1756, May 14, 1756, 52:487-8.

[68] Rice, *This Was the Life*, 186.

[69] Rice, *This Was the Life*, 189.

[70] Rice, *This Was the Life*, 200.

[71] MdHR, 17,441, 1-23-3-41, Bartholomew Booker, patent for Pickall, Feb. 22, 1764, 1224 acres. MSA, BC & GS #30, 214-6.

[72] MdHR, 17,406, 1-23-2-44, James Wardrop, patent for John's Delight, May 17, 1750, 104 acres. MSA, BY & GS #5, 59.

[73] FCLR, F-1064, Bartholomew Booker to George Shidler, June 25, 1760, 100 acres. Shidler's Dispute, being part of Mendall, and a tract called Small All.

[74] FCLR, L-69, George Shidler to Bartholomew Booker, Oct. 15, 1767, 100 acres. Shidler's Dispute, being part of Mendall, and a tract called Small All.

75 FCLR, L-71, Bartholomew Booker to George Shidler, Oct. 15, 1767, 200 acres. Long Dispute, being all of Shidler's Dispute and part of Pickall.

76 FCLR, WR-12, 358-64, Frederick Fox and Margaret Booker to John Routzahn, April 19, 1794, 304 acres. Part of five tracts of land: the Resurvey on Mendall, Pickall, I Hope It Is Well Done, Shettle, and Martitany.

77 Frederick County, Md., Register of Wills Records, GM-2-431, will of Bartholomew Booker, Oct. 21, 1791.

78 F. Edward Wright, *Western Maryland Newspaper Abstracts 1786-1798* (Silver Spring, Md.: Family Line Publications, 1985), 1:14.

79 MdHR, 17,448, 1-23-4-2, John Teem, survey for Worse and Worse, Feb. 7, 1766, 41 1/2 acres. MSA, BC & GS #37, 218-9. Also see FCLR, P-632, John Team to Adam Coil, recorded Mar. 22, 1773.

80 FCLR, THO 1, Henry Beagley, survey for Its Bad Enough, June 8, 1795, 14 3/4 acres.

81 MdHR, 17,435, 1-23-3-35, Joseph Chapline, survey for The Gap, Mar. 29, 1761, 50 acres. MSA, BC & GS #24, 270.

82 FCLR, K-917, Joseph Chapline to John Team, The Gap, Jan. 9, 1767, 50 acres.

83 MdHR, 17,476, 1-23-4-32, Henry Beakley, Resurvey on The Gap, May 1, 1798, 219 1/2 acres. MSA, IC #N, 467-8.

84 MdHR, 17,458, 1-23-4-12, Philip Jacob Shafer, survey for Flonham, Aug. 27, 1770, 36 acres. MSA, BC & BS #47, 496-7. MdHR, 17,455, 1-23-4-9, Philip Jacob Shafer, patent for Flonham, April 20, 1774, 36 acres. MSA, BC & GS #44, 439-40.

85 MdHR, 17,438, 1-23-3-38, Robert Smith, survey for Fox's Last Shift, Oct. 5, 1764, 72 acres. MSA, BC & GS #27, 311.

86 WCLR, Elias Butter to Philip Laypole, Aug. 23, 1824, for 142 perches of Fox's Last Shift. This deed indicates a number of lots were laid out for a town on this tract of land.

87 MdHR, 17,472, 1-23-4-28, John Mansberger, resurvey of Fox's Last Shift called Newcomer's Purchase, Jan. 5, 1786, 101 acres. MSA IC #1, 713.

88 MdHR, 17,473, 1-23-4-29, John Mansberger, resurvey of Newcomer's Purchase called Partnership, Aug. 20, 1794, 685 acres. MSA, IC #K, 343-4.

89 MdHR, 17,430-1, 1-23-3-26, Jacob Hessing, survey for Racon, Apr. 10, 1762, 50 acres. MSA, BC & GS #19, 310-1.

90 MdHR, 17,456, 1-23-4-10, John Summer, patent for Raccoon, Aug. 27, 1770, 253 acres. MSA, BC & GS #45, 10-1.

91 MdHR, 17,443, 1-23-3-43, John Summer, patent for Kizer's Lowden, May 26, 1763, 110 acres. MSA, BC & GS #22, 89-90. Probably adjacent to Contentment and Resurvey on Jerrico Hills. See MdHR, 17,441, 1-23-3-41, survey for Contentment, Aug. 20, 1764. MSA, BC & GS, 259-61.

92 *Archives of Maryland*, Article XCV, 58:543.

93 Byron L. Williams, *The Old South Mountain Inn*, (Shippensburg, Pa.: Beidel Printing House, Inc., 1990), 70.

94 Tracey Collection records in the Historical Society of Carroll County, Westminster, Maryland.

95 MdHR, 17,395-1, 1-23-2-28, Daniel Dulany Esqr., survey of Ram's Horn, April 14, 1744, 600 acres. MSA, LG #E, 346-8. See Rice, New Facts and Old Families, 114-5, for the plotting of the Rams Horn tract, Interstate 70, U.S. 40, and the old Hagerstown Road.

96 MdHR, 17,395-2, 1-23-2-29, Daniel Dulany Esqr., survey of Hogyard, Oct. 7, 1742, 100 acres. MSA, LG #E, 397.

97 Tracey Collection records in the Historical Society of Carroll County.

98 Frederick County, Maryland, Robert Evans Administration Account, B-2-169, July 6, 1771.

99 MdHR, 17,415, 1-23-3-9, Robert Evans, survey of Betty's Good Will, Oct. 20, 1727, 50 acres. MSA, BC & GS 4, 195-6.

100 MdHR, 17, 412-2, 1-23-2-37, Robert Evans, survey of Cuckhold's Horns, Oct. 14, 1747, 150 acres. MSA, BY & GS #1, 611-2.

101 Tracey and Dern, *Pioneers of Old Monocacy*, 245.

Early Roads and Gaps

[102] *Maryland Archives*, Acts of Assembly, 1737-1740, 19:220, 307, and 308. "Saturday Morning May 12th 1739."

[103] FCLR, B-172, Thomas Whitaker to Nicholas Fink, Prevention, May 19, 1750, 50 acres.

[104] FCLR, O-540, Nicholas Fink to Thomas Welch, Goose Cap, recorded Sept. 2, 1771, 66 acres. See MdHR, 17,456, 1-23-4-10, survey of Goose Cap, Oct. 10, 1770. MSA, BC & GS #45.

[105] FCLR, JS-39-260, John Stemple et ux to George Baltzell, recorded July 5, 1832, 273 1/2 acres.

[106] MdHR, 17,408, 1-23-3-1, Joseph Chapline, patent for the Resurvey on Watson's Welfare, July 28, 1752. MSA, Y & S #7, 192.

[107] MdHR, 17,443, 1-23-3-43, Philip Keywhaughvor, Resurvey on Whiskey Alley, May 12, 1762. MSA, BC & GS #32, 480-3.

[108] See Tracey and Dern, *Pioneers of Old Monacacy*, 245. They mention Prevention, Forest, and Wooden Platter. See MdHR, 17, 412-2, 1-23-2-37, Resurvey on Wooden Platter, surveyed Sept. 1, 1748, MSA, BY & GS #1, 604-5. Also, MdHR, 17,412, 1-23-3-6, Resurvey on Prevention, surveyed May 10, 1752, MSA, BC & GS #1, 155.

[109] FCLR, WR-4-179, Jacob Keefour to Members et al. Aug. 20, 1783.

[110] MdHR, 17,394, 1-23-2-27, Ewen McDonald, patent for Watson's Welfare, August 27, 1744, 100 acres. MSA, LG #C, 56-7.

[111] Millard M. Rice, *New Facts and Old Families*, 137-48. Also see, George C. Rhoderick Jr, The Early History of Middletown, Maryland, Middletown Valley Historical Society.

[112] Tracey Collection records.

[113] FCLR, N-560, Bartholomew Booker to Jacob Smith, recorded Jan. 23, 1772, 100 acres.

[114] FCLR, F-1077, Bartholomew Booker to Michel Shepfell, part of the Resurvey on Mendall, June 6, 1760, 100 acres.

[115] The surveys for Kizer's Lowden, Jacob's Broom, and Marstone mention the location of Robert Turner's plantation.

[116] The reader may find the following article of interest. "The Old National Pike," Harper's New Monthly Magazine, Vol. LIX, 1879.

[117] *Laws, Documents and Judicial Decisions, Relating to The Baltimore and Fredericktown, York and Reisterstown, Cumberland and Boonsborough Turnpike Road Companies* (Baltimore: John D. Toy, 1841).

[118] *American State Papers: Miscellaneous* 1:901-7.

[119] *American State Papers: Miscellaneous* 1:909. "Answers to the queries respecting artifical roads, so far as relate to the Baltimore and Fredericktown Turnpike Road, by Jona. Ellicott."

[120] *Maryland Herald and Hagerstown Weekly*, 1805-1809, MSA Special Collections, M 8099.

[121] *Maryland Herald and Hagerstown Weekly*, 1805-1809, MSA Special Collections, M 8099.

[122] MdHR, 19,999-059-006 1/8/5/48, 59/3, 4, and 6. MSA, S 1005-7887.

[123] WCLR, 74-264, George F. Smith to Madeleine Dahlgren, Apr. 19, 1876, 60 acres. Part of Addition to Friendship, part of Partnership, part of Swearingen's Disappointment, and part of Flonham.

[124] FCLR, WBT-10-143, Susan Miller et al. to Daniel Beagley, Apr. 21, 1849, 14 acres. Part of Addition to Friendship.

[125] FCLR, JS-39-264-8, George Baltzell to Henry Miller, Apr. 1, 1833, 189 1/2 acres. Part of Addition to Friendship.

[126] MdHR, 17,487-1, 1-23-4-44, Jacob Fulwiler, survey for Apple Brandy, Oct. 31, 1791, 14 acres. MSA, IC F, 307. Patented to John R. Magruder, May 8, 1815.

[127] MdHR, 17,476, 1-23-4-32, Henry Beagley, Resurvey on The Gap, July 16, 1798, 219 1/2 acres. MSA, IC #N, 467-8.

[128] FCLR, JS-25-372, Philip Sheffer to Henry Miller, July 6, 1826, 5+ acres. Part of Flonham.

129 WCLR, 74-264, George F. Smith to Madeleine Dahlgren, Apr. 19, 1876, 60 acres. Part of Addition to Friendship, part of Partnership, part of Swearingen's Disappointment, and part of Flonham.

130 FCLR, JS-39-264-8, George Baltzell to Henry Miller, July 5, 1832, 189 1/2 acres. Part of Addition to Friendship.

131 WCLR, 172-524, "St. Mary's Academy" of Notre Dame to Otho Hewitt, Charles M. Hewitt, and Robert W. Hewitt, recorded Sept. 11, 1925.

132 FCLR, WBT-10-143, Susan Miller et al. to Daniel Beagley, May 7, 1844, 14+ acres. Part of Addition to Friendship.

133 FCLR, BFG-5-516, John W. Derr et al. to Adam Koogle, Mar. 16, 1854, 25 1/10 acres. Part of Addition to Friendship.

134 FCLR, JS-38-194, Jacob Routzah to Henry Miller, recorded Feb. 18, 1832, 67 acres. Part of Addition to Friendship and part of Fredericksburg. Also see FCLR, JS-30-58-61, Jacob Routzong to George Routzong, recorded Aug. 8, 1828.

135 FCLR, JS-39-264-8, George Baltzell Atty. to Henry Miller, May 31, 1832, 189 1/2 acres. Part of Addition to Friendship. Baltzell was attorney for the heirs of Joseph Swearingen.

136 FCLR, WR-32-26-8, Frederick Fox to Joseph Swearingen, Sept. 21, 1807, 202 acres of Addition to Friendship and 30 acres of Fredericksburg.

137 MdHR, 17,478, 1-23-4-34, Frederick Fox, patent of Addition to Friendship, May, 9, 1797, 202 acres. MSA, IC #P 672-3.

138 *American State Papers: Miscellaneous* 1:738; *Laws, Documents and Judicial Decisions, relating to the Baltimore and Fredericktown, York and Reisterstown, Cumberland and Boonsborough Turnpike Road Companies.* (Baltimore: John D. Toy, 1841).

139 FCLR, JS-25-372, Philip Sheffer to Henry Miller, July 6, 1826, 5+ acres. Part of Flonham.

140 MdHR, 17,458, 1-23-4-12, Philip Jacob Shafer, survey for Flonham, Aug. 27, 1770, 36 acres. MSA, BC & BS #47, 496-7.

141 J. G. de Roulhac Hamilton, ed., *The Papers of Randolph Abbot Shotwell* (Raleigh: N. C. Historical Commission, 1929), 1:305-71.

142 Dieter Cunz, *The Maryland Germans, a History* (Princeton: Princeton University Press, 1948), 81-3.

143 Drake and Orndorff, *From Mill Wheel to Plow Share*, 41.

144 Tracey and Dern, *Pioneers of Old Monocacy*, 55-6.

145 Daniel Harvey Hill Jr, *Bethel to Sharpsburg* 2 vols. (Raleigh: Edwards & Broughton Co., 1926), 1:366.

146 MdHR, G 1427 508, Road from Elizabethtown to Newcomber's Mill and Frederick County Line, April 5, 1791. WCLR G. f. 549.

147 MSA Special Collections, *Maryland Herald and Hagerstown Weekly*, July 22, 1807. Microfilm M 8099, 1805-1809.

148 Jeffrey A. Wyand, *Maryland Historical Magazine*, Vol. 67, No. 3, Fall, 1972, 303-4.

149 John Hall to HS, from Baltimore Town, Sept. 5, 1756, *Correspondence*, 6:479.

Part II

Tables

	Page
Maps	63
Contiguous Land Tracts	70
Additional Land Tract Information	76
Unplotted Land Records in the Vicinity of the Battlefields (South Mountain and Antietam)	86
Wives Identified in Land Tract Records	95

Maps

The following maps appear on pages 62 through 65:

1. 1995 Map of Frederick to Hagerstown area

2. The Battlefield Area in 1993

3. Old Sharpsburg Road in area of The Fox Inn in 1993

4. The Old Sharpsburg Road from Spoolsville through Fox's Gap - 1993

5. Boonsboro Area - 1993

6. Crampton's Gap Area - 1993

7. From Fox's Gap to Crampton's Gap - 1993

Note - map 1 above is under copyright of the Maryland Dept. of Transportation; maps 2 through 7 are under copyright of DeLorme Mapping.

The following is a chronological listing of maps that may be useful in the research of the Battlefield of South Mountain area:

The Great Conestoga Road. See Papers Read before the Lancaster County Historical Society, June 5, 1908, Vol. XII. No. 6. The Great Conestoga Road by H. Frank Eshleman Esq., page 215. A map included in the booklet identifies the earliest roads west from Philadelphia.

Post Map of New England, New York, New Jersey, and Pennsylvania, by Moll, dated 1730. It is probably the Monocacy Road that is shown on the map as the "Great Philadelphia Wagon Road." This map supports, in Pennsylvania to the Maryland line, the road from Conestoga to Opequon through Fox's Gap. This road also was known as the Great Philadelphia Wagon Road (to Winchester via Fox's Gap in Maryland). It was not the same road as the Great Wagon Road to Philadelphia (from Winchester through Conococheague).

The Winslow Map of 1736. Library of Congress, Benj. Winslow. "A Plan of the upper Part of Patomack River called Cohongoroot Survey'd in the year 1736. Geography & Map Div. Collection contains a reproduction, the original map is owned by Enoch Pratt Free Library of Baltimore, MD. [U.S. Potomac River (reg.). . 1736 . . Winslow]. "Messrs. Wm. May, Robert Brook, --- Winslow, and --- Savage appointed surveyors in 1736. The party which performed this work consisted of the four surveyors with thirteen assistants, six of them chain-carriers, employed at three shillings per day. Among the names employed to describe features of Maryland territory may be noticed the following variations from present usage: Monokasy [Monocacy], Kittokton [Catoctin], Conigochego [Conococheague]."[1]

Maps

See the William and Mary College Quarterly Historical Magazine, Vol. 18, Second Series, April, 1938, No. 2, for an article on the "Maps of the First Survey of the Potomac River, 1736-37." Also see Library of Congress: Robert Brooke. A plan of Patomack River, from the mouth of Sherrendo, down to Chapawamsick/surveyed in the year 1737. Scale ca. 1:160,000 ms. 57 x 43 cm. Present sheet covers from Little Falls to south. Northern sheet missing. pen-and ink on tracing paper [3792.P6 1737.B7 Vault].

The "Mayo" Map of 1736-7. See the Winslow Map of 1736.

Fry and Jefferson Map of 1751, 1755, and 1775. "The most important map of the Middle British Colonies published during the second half of the eighteenth century was the result of the joint labors of Professor Joshua Fry and Mr. Peter Jefferson. It is probable that the information represented on the map indicates the highest degree of knowledge of the country attainable at that time. The map apparently was completed in the year 1749, although it is dated 1751. The Maryland portion of the sheet does not adequately represent the high character of the map, since there is little indicated besides names and a few roads on the Maryland portion, while Virginia streams and roads are carefully delineated with their names attached. The roads are only such as were main thoroughfares connecting different portions of Virginia with Philadelphia."[2] Library of Congress: Fry, Joshua. A map of the inhabited part of Virginia . . . G3880 1751 .F7 (Negative No. 2802) [1755 ed].

Lewis Evans. See Henry M. Stevens, Lewis Evans, His Map of the British Middle Colonies in America, A Comparative Account of 18 Different Editions Published between 1755 and 1814 (London: n.p., 1920). Also see Walter Klinefelter, Lewis Evans and His Maps (Philadelphia: American Philosophical Society, 1971).

Col. Thomas Cresap's Map of the Sources of the Potomac. June, 1754. This map appears in the Archives of Maryland, Correspondence of Gov. Horatio Sharpe, 6:72. The map shows "Conegocheig" along the course of the Potomac River.

Map accompanying the agreement between Lord Baltimore and T. & R. Penn. Pennsylvania Archives, 1760-1766, Volume 4.

Road from Elizabethtown [Hagerstown] to Newcomber's Mill and Frederick County Line. April 5, 1791. Maryland State Archives, Special Collections. MdHR G 1427 508 Maps.

Road from Swearingen's Ferry on the Potomac River Through Sharpsburg to the Top of the South Mountain at Fox's Gap. August 23, 1792. This map was recorded at one time in Washingon County Land Records, G, p. 867. Maryland State Archives, Special Collections. MdHR G 1427 507, B5-1-3.

Road from Williamsport to Turner's Gap in South Mountain. Recorded October 17, 1791. This map was recorded at one time in Washington County Land Records, G, p. 533. Maryland State Archives, Special Collections. MdHR G 1427 504, B5-1-3.

1794 Dennis Griffith Map of Maryland. Drawn by Dennis Griffith, a Philadelphian, and copyrighted June 20, 1794. "Map of the State of Maryland Laid down from an actual Survey of all the principal Waters, public Roads, and Divisions of the Counties therein; describing the Situation of the Cities, Towns, Villages, Houses of Worship and other public Buildings, Furnaces, Forges, Mills, and other remarkable Places."[3] Library of Congress: [G3840 1794.G72 Vault] Scale a:308,000. size 134 x 79 1/2 cm.

1808 Varle Map. The map shows Braddock's Gap at the location where today Interstate 70 and Main Route 40 pass over South Mountain. The map shows the name Ringer at the location of the Fox Inn. Library of Congress: A map of Frederick and Washington Counties, State of Maryland. 1808, by Charles Varle; engraved, Francis Shallus, Phila. G3843.F7 1808 .V3 1983. 84-691291.

Maps

1809 Map of Frederick, Berkeley, and Jefferson Counties in the state of Virginia. Executed AD 1809 by Charles Varle Engineer & Geographer. Engraved by Benjamin Jones Philadelphia. Berkeley County Historical Society.

Bond Map. Frederick County, Maryland. Prepared under the direction of Lieut. Col. J. N. Macomb, Chf. Topl. Engr. for the use of Maj. Gen. G. B. McClellan, Commanding US Army. Drawn from I. Bond's map by E. Hergesheimer. Based on Isaac Bond's map of Frederick County, Maryland, published 1858. Library of Congress G3843 .F7 1861 .H4

Battle-Fields of South Mountain. South Mountain, Md. September 14, 1862. The Official Military Atlas of the Civil War, Plate XXVII, 3. This map accompanies the report of Maj. Gen. Geo. B. McClellan, U.S. Army. See the Official Records, Series 1, Vol. XIX, Part 1, page 36. This map shows the Old Sharpsburg Road from the "forks of the roads" at the Catoctin Creek to Moses Chapline Sr's homestead, indicated as "G. Shiffler" on the map.

Antietam. The Official Military Atlas of the Civil War, Plate XXIX, 2. Prepared by Bvt. Brig. Gen. N. Michler, Major of Engineers. Compiled and drawn by Major F. Weyss. Assisted by F. Theilkuhl, J. Strass, and G. Thompson. This map shows the Old Sharpsburg Road from Moses Chapline Sr's homestead, indicated as "G. Shiffler" on the map, through Springvale, Porterstown, the square in Sharpsburg, and on to Shepherdstown.

Map of the Battle-Fields of Harper's Ferry and Antietam. September 13 to 17, 1862. The Official Military Atlas of the Civil War, Plate XXIX, 1. Prepared by S. Howell Brown, 1st Lt. Engineer Troops. This map shows the Old Sharpsburg Road from Shepherdstown and Swearingen's Ferry on the Potomac through Sharpsburg, Porterstown, and east towards Fox's Gap.

Footnotes - Maps

[1] Edward Bennett Mathews, *The Maps and Map-Makers of Maryland* (Baltimore: The Johns Hopkins University Press, October, 1898), 388-90.
[2] Mathews, *Maps and Map-Makers of Maryland*, 391.
[3] Mathews, *Maps and Map-Makers of Maryland*, 398.

1995 Map of Western Maryland - Maryland Department of Transportation base map copyright - State Highway Administration

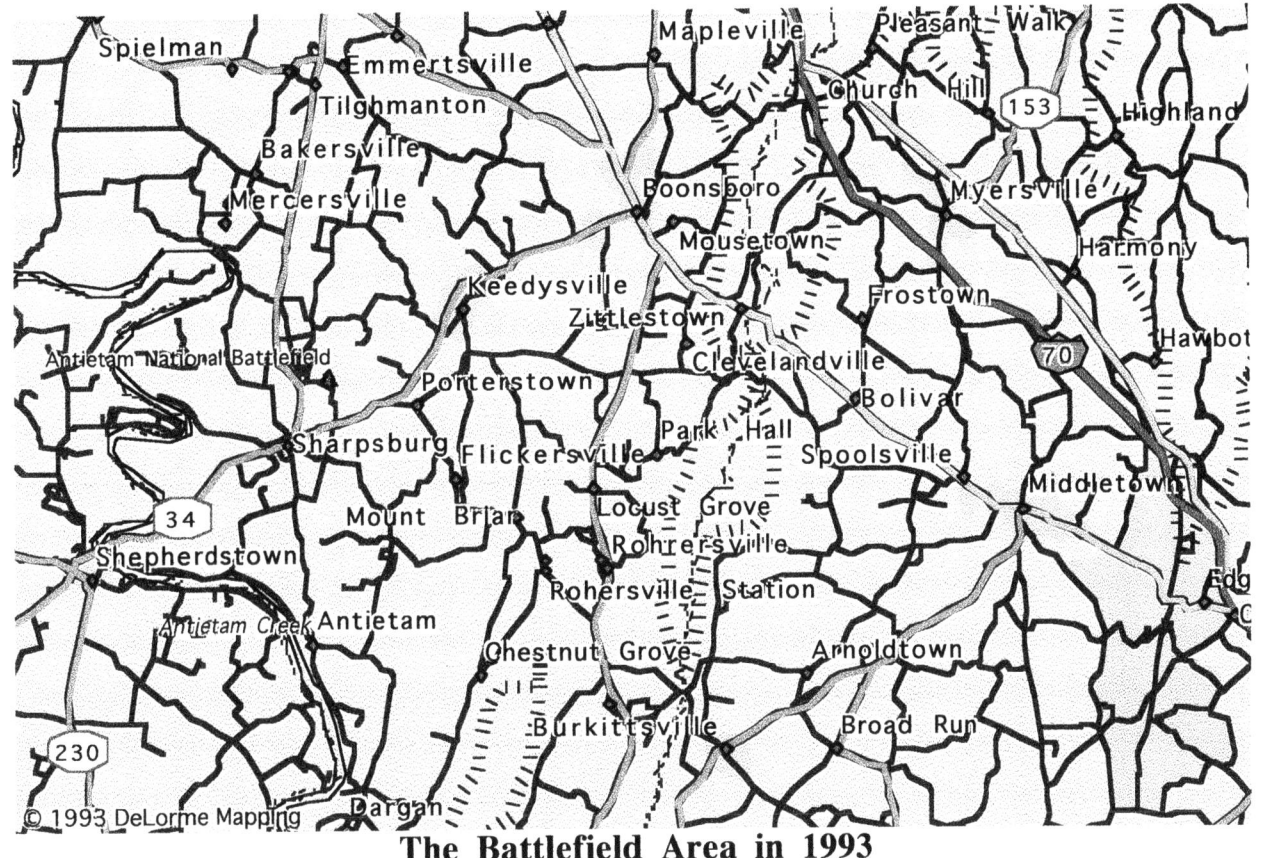
The Battlefield Area in 1993

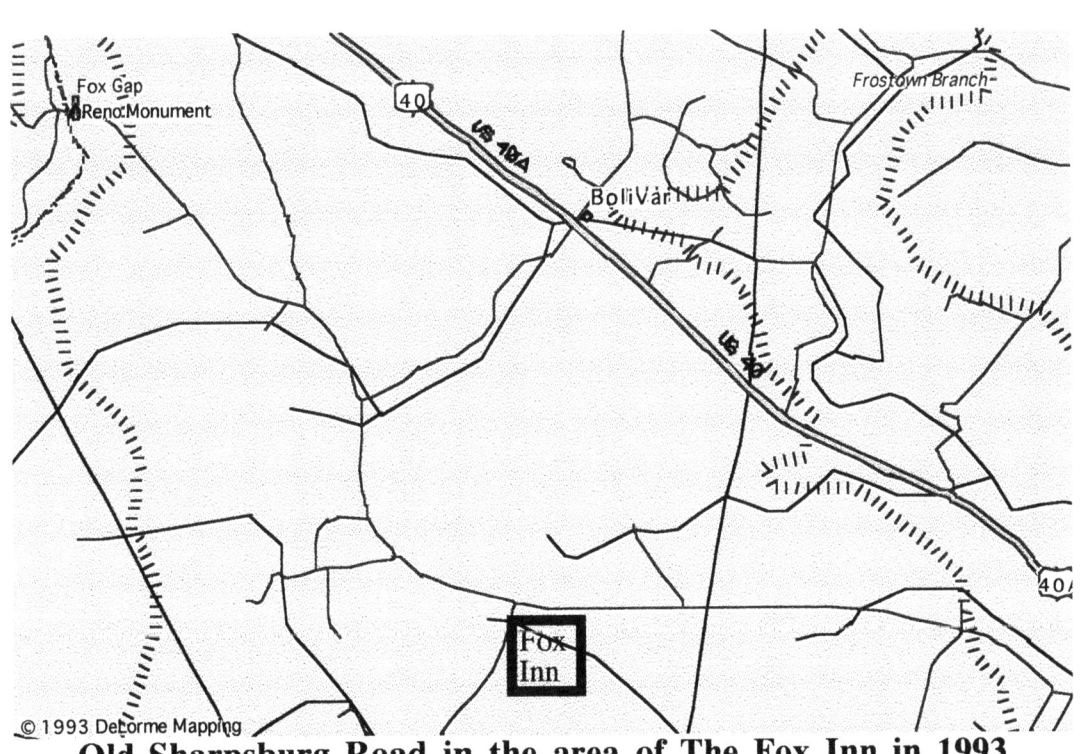
Old Sharpsburg Road in the area of The Fox Inn in 1993

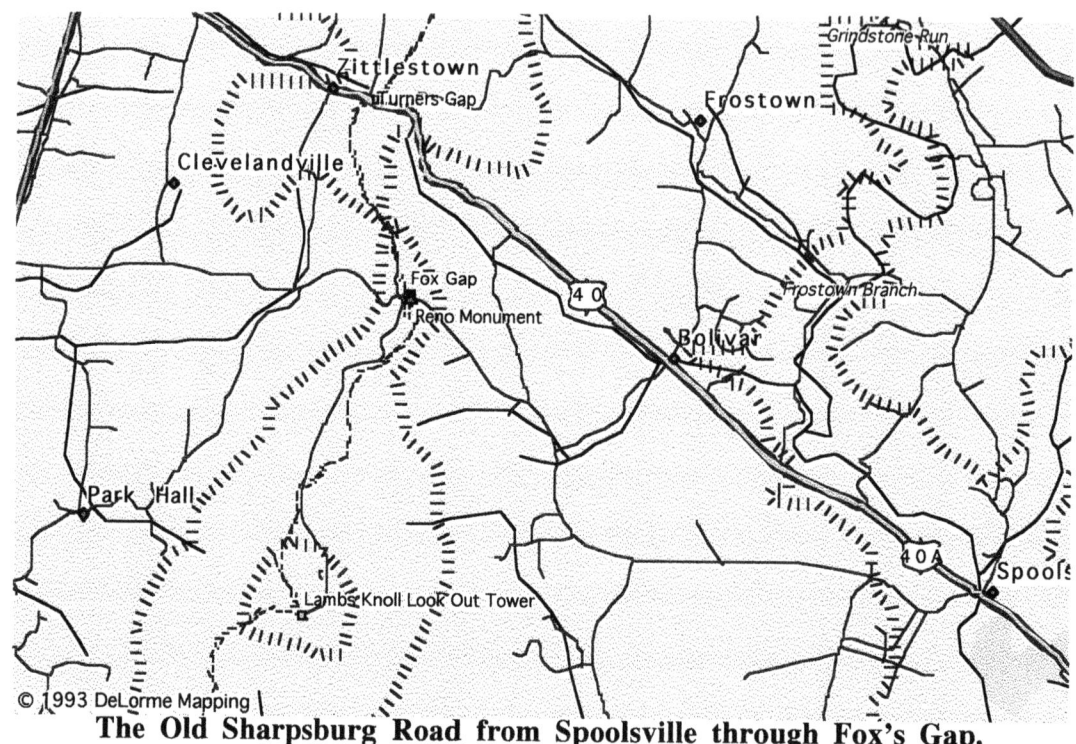
The Old Sharpsburg Road from Spoolsville through Fox's Gap.

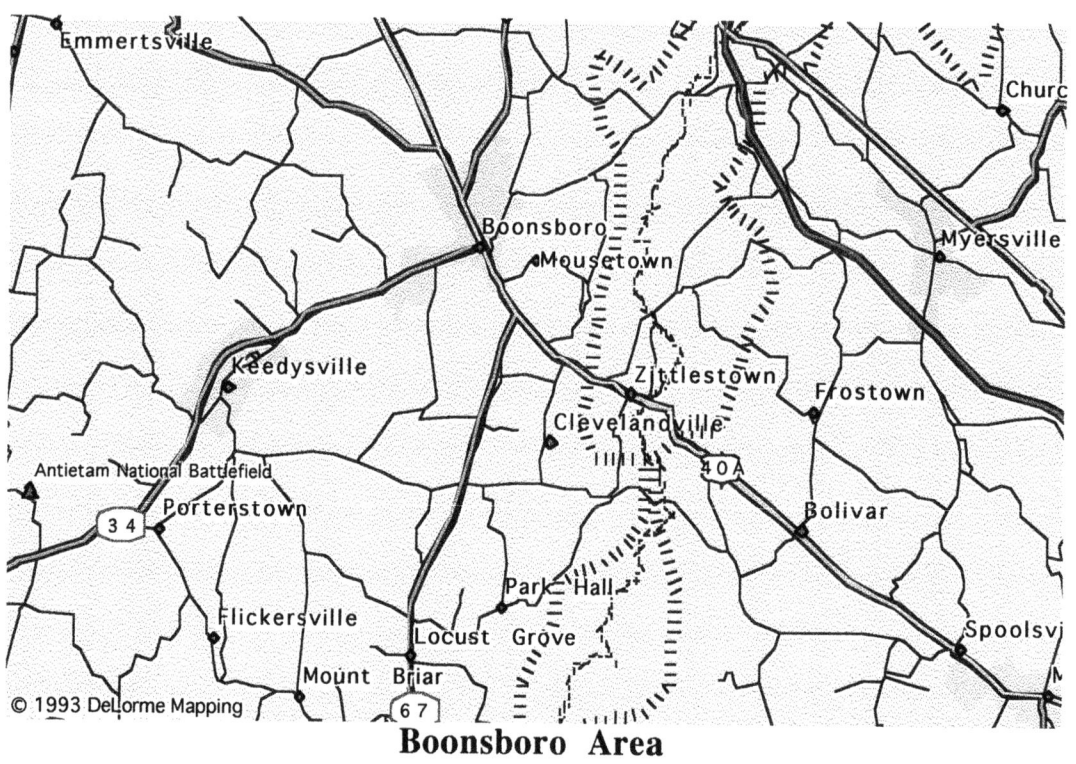
Boonsboro Area

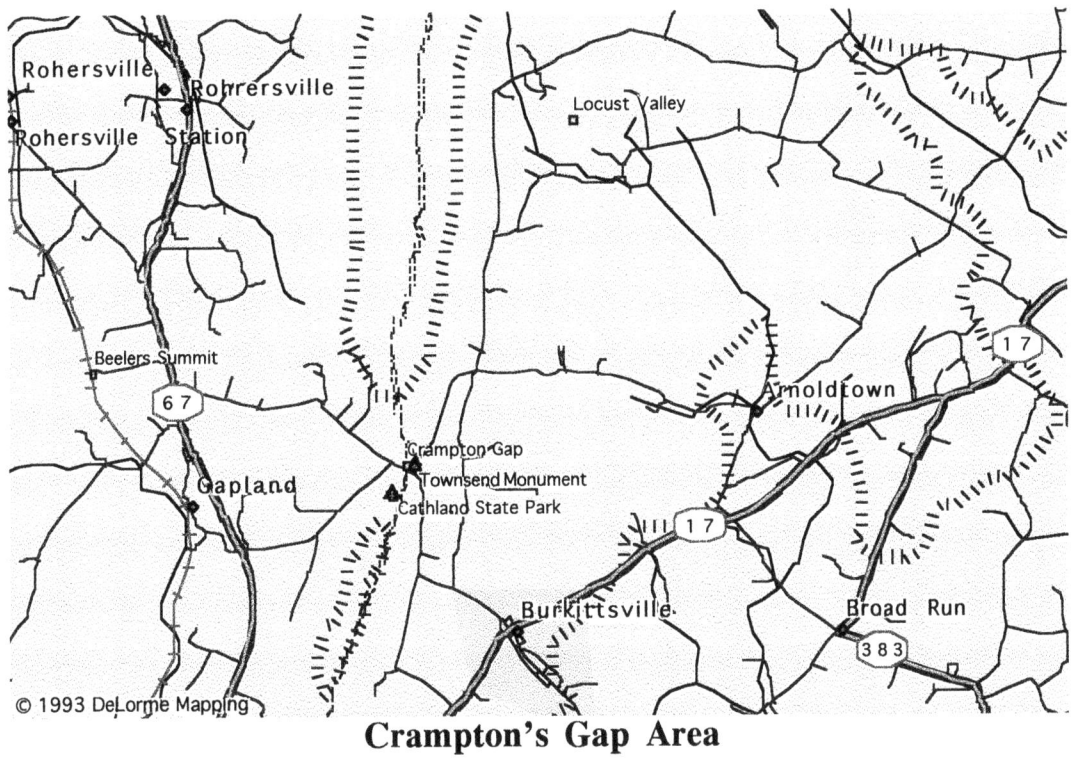
Crampton's Gap Area

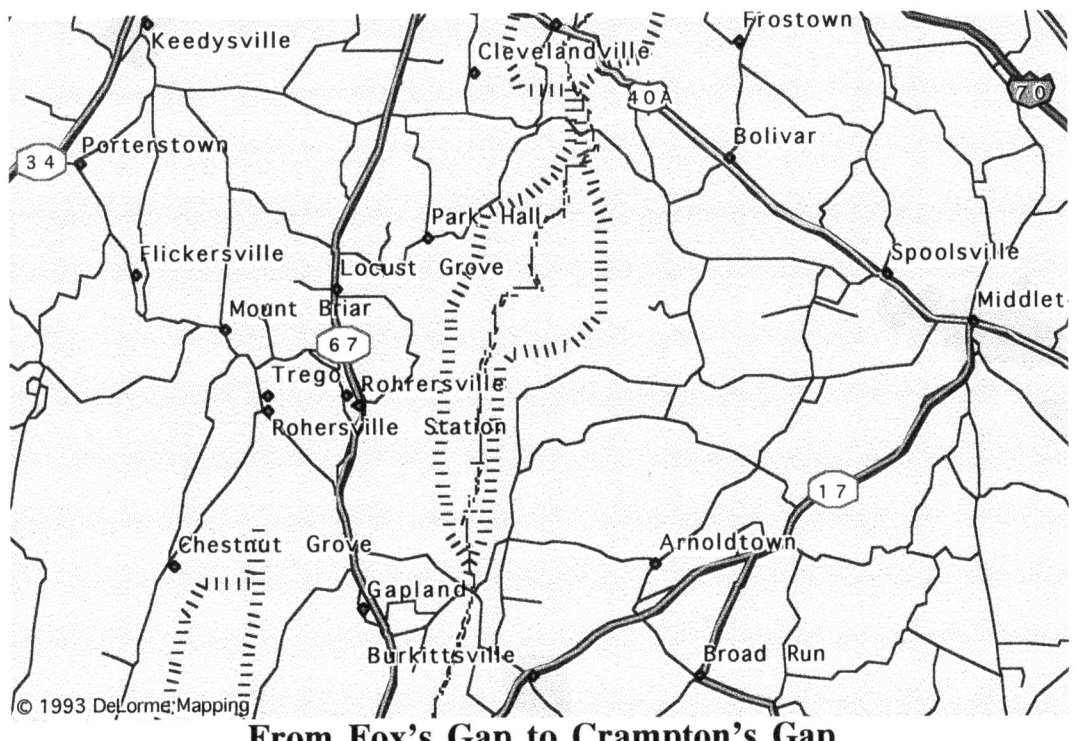
From Fox's Gap to Crampton's Gap

Contiguous Land Tracts

Tract names in the far left column appear in alphabetical order. This listing does not include all of the plotted tracts that appear in this book. The listing for each tract name may not include all contiguous tracts. In some cases the location of a tract is given and not the contiguous tracts.

Tract Name	Contiguous Tracts
Adam's Expense	Little Good, Pickall, Quaker's Mistake, Adam's Hill, Shoemaker's Tricks, Rsy on Bear Swamp, Rsy on Martitany, Add to Deep Hole
Add to Friendship	Flonham, David's Will, Rsy on the Gap, Partnership, Knave's Good Will, Friendship, Rsy on Security, Turkey Ramble, Bowser's Addition
Add to Learning	Learning, Rsy on Learning
Add to Little Worth	Knave's Ill Will, Martitany, Add to Crephole, Nothing Hardly, Little Worth
Add to Miller's Purchase	Miller's Purchase
Add to Penn's Disappointment	Penn's Disappointment, Fellfoot Enlarged
Add to Raccoon	Raccoon, Racon
Add to Tom's Gift	Tom's Gift
Alexandria	Forest of Needwood.
Antietam Bottom	Pell Mell, Antietam Hills, Fengs Landing Enlarged, Antietam Works, Add to Hisband, Rsy on Part of Antietam Bottom
Apple Brandy (Flook)	Rsy on Tom's Gift, Rsy on Whiskey Alley, Rsy on Blooming Month of May
Apple Brandy (Fulwiler)	Bowser's Addition, Rsy on the Gap, Worse and Worse
Ashbough	Boonsboro area.
Bad Enough	Rsy on Add to Pile's Delight
Badham's Refuse	Park Hall
Baker's Purchase	Fellfoot Enlarged
Beall's Chance	Near Boonsboro.
Beam's Purchase	Pile's Grove, (The) Grove, Fellfoot Enlarged
Bear Swamp Forest	Rsy on Bear Swamp Forest
Betty's Good Will	I Hope It Is Well Done, Pickall, (The) Exchange, Mt. Sinai, Shaff's Purchase, Now I Know It, Mendall, Water Enough, Rsy on Exchange, Rsy on Mendall
Biegley's Displeasure	Tick Neck, Good Luck, (The) Breeches, Pleasant Meadow
Bird's Bill	Lucky Hit, Partnership (Mansberger)
Blooming Month of May	Rsy on Learning, Add to Learning and Part of the Rsy on Learning, Rsy on Tom's Gift, Part of the Rsy on Part of Tom's Gift
Blooming Plains	Pile's Grove, Rsy on Well Done, Exchange (Good), Not Much, Rsy on Mt. Pleasant
Bloomsbury	Chesnut Oak Ridge, Mt. Atlas, Cool Spring Rsy, Mt. Pelier
Booker's Purchase	Little Good, Add to Little Good
Boston	Potomac River, Antietam Bottom, Dutch Loss, Moors Delight, Little I Thought It, Mill Place, Hunting the Hare, Saturn, Pough, Turkey Hill, Stoney Glade, Rsy on Stoney Glade, Prospect, Rsy on Hills and Dales, Elk Hill, Inverness, Hogg's Delight
Bowser's Addition	North side of the Wise tract and Reno Monument at Fox's Gap. Rsy on the Gap, Add to Friendship, Apple Brandy (Fulwiler)
Brayface (Bray-face)	Rsy on Oxford, Pickall, We Could Not Agree
Breeches	Biegley's Displeasure, Rsy on Trembling, Nazareth, Tick Neck, Rsy on Hard to Find, Tuckett, Poole's Delight Enlarged, Small Expense
Bubble (Boble)	Exchange, Deeffer Snay, Mt. Sinai
Burrell's Disappointment	Park Hall, Elk Hill, Antietam Works
Chapline's Ill Will	Kizer's Lowden, Contentment

Tract Name	Contiguous Tracts
Charlemount Pleasant	Nottingham, Beall's Chance, Fellfoot Enlarged, Rsy on the Grove, Beam's Purchase
Chestnut Oak Ridge	Mt. Atlas, Cool Spring Rsy (Shoup), Ebenezer
Chestnut Thicket	Gaver's Recovery, Wilyard's Lot
Christie's Folly	Forest (Macgrudar), Part of the Rsy on Oxford, Cool Spring (Wardrop)
Contentment	Smith's Choice, Fellfoot Enlarged, Rsy on Jerico Hills, Chapline's Ill Will, Rsy on Content, Jerico
(The) Cool Spring (Wardrop)	Rsy on Oxford, Rsy on Tom's Gift
Cool Spring Rsy (Shoup)	Mt. Pleasant (Fox), Daniel's Race Ground, David's Will, Mt. Atlas
Cooperton	Cost's Content, Poole's Delight Enlarged, Forest (Sprigg)
Cornucopia	Rsy on Well Done, Fellowship, Lannafield, Nottingham, Ashbough, Jacob's Broom (Brune)
Cost's Content	Poole's Delight Enlarged, Cooperton, Forest (Sprigg), Wilyard's Lot, Stricker's Timber Land
Cuckold's Horns	Ram's Horn, Pickall, Quaker's Mistake
Curry's Old Place	Between Fox's and Turner's (Curry's) Gap.
Daniel's Race Ground	Cool Spring Rsy (Shoup), Turkeyfoot, Fredericksburg
Dawson's Purchase	East side of Crampton's Gap.
David's Will	Add to Friendship, Cool Spring Rsy (Shoup), Rsy on Security
Deeffer Snay	Bubble (Boble), Rsy on Exchange, Rsy on Learning
Discontent	Probably near Slusser's Choice.
Dorsey's Risque	Add to Loss and Gain, Add to Dorsey's Risque, Little Meadow Resurveyed, Little Meadow
Ebenezer	Locust Valley, Stricker's Timberland, Mt. Atlas
Elk Hill	Park Hall, Antietam Works
Elzwick's Dwelling	Sharpsburg to Keedysville area.
(The) Exchange (Dulany)	Now I Know It, Betty's Good Will, Mt. Sinai, Bubble (Boble)
Fellfoot	Fellfoot Enlarged, Roots Hill, Paul's Travels
Fellfoot Enlarged	Rsy on Hills and Dales and (The) Vineyard, Contentment, Fellfoot, Thomas's Purchase, Lyon's Purchase, Baker's Purchase, Penn's Disappointment
Fellowship	Beall's Chance, Cornucopia, Jacob's Broom (Brune), Nottingham, Nelson's Folly
Ferry Landing	"On the bank of the Potomac near Swearingen's Ferry." Near the Rumsey Bridge over the Potomac at Shepherdstown.
Fidler's Purchase	Bubble (Boble), Exchange, Rsy on Exchange, Deeffer Snay
Fielderia Manor	Cut Knee, Add to Hazzard Thicket, Fertile Meadows, Sweed's March, Confusion Amended, Mountain Side, Grim's Delight, Top of the Blue Ridge, Gaver's Recovery
Flohnam	Add to Friendship, Partnership, Rsy on Bear Swamp
Flook's Content	Rsy on Oxford
Forest (Macgrudar)	Rsy on Oxford, Rsy on Tom's Gift, Rsy on Whiskey Alley, Wooden Platter, Rsy on Watson's Welfare
Forest (Sprigg)	Cooperton, Poole's Delight Enlarged, Cost's Content, Wilyard's Lot
Forest of Needwood	Alexandria. Southeast of Crampton's Gap.
Fox's Last Shift	Partnership, Swearingen's Disappointment, Newcomer's Purchase
Fredericksburg	Add to Friendship, Long Dispute, Pickall, Rsy on the Gap, Bowser's Addition
Friendship (Fox)	Add to Friendship, Fredericksburg, Bowser's Addition
(The) Gap	Rsy on the Gap, Turkey Ramble, Worse and Worse, It's Bad Enough, John's Delight, Curry's Old Place
Gaver's Recovery	Miller's Farm, Chesnut Thicket

Contiguous Land Tracts

Tract Name	**Contiguous Tracts**
Good Hope	Rsy on Hills and Dales and (The) Vineyard, Fellfoot Enlarged, Antietam Finished
Good Intent	Park Hall, I Have Got It At Last, Little I Thought It, Keep Trieste
Goose Bill	Rsy on Prevention, Prevention
Goose Cap	Rsy on Watson's Welfare, Rsy on Whiskey Alley
Gordon's Purchase	Fellfoot Enlarged
Grim's Fancy	Mt. Atlas, Booker's Rsy on Well Done, Rsy on Security
(The) Grove	Pile's Grove
Hard to Find	(The) Meadow, Rsy on Hard to Find. East of Crampton's Gap.
Hickory Tavern	Keedysville to Sharpsburg area.
Hills and Dales	Keedysville to Sharpsburg area.
Hogyard	Orr's Gap area.
Honesty Best When Looked To	Crampton's Gap area.
Horse Neck	Confusion, Cost's Content, Honesty Best When Looked To, Second Long Looked For, Confusion Amended
I Have Got It At Last	Park Hall, Good Intent, Keep Trieste
I Hope It Is So	Crampton's Gap area.
I Hope It Is Well Done	Shettle, Turkey Plains, Johns' Delight, Oxford, Betty's Good Will, Turkeyfoot, Rsy on Mendall, Pickall
Inverness	Burrell's Disappointment
It's Bad Enough	(The) Gap, Rsy on the Gap, Worse and Worse, Turkey Ramble, John's Delight, Small Ridge, Pickall
Ive's Folly	Slusser's Choice, Smith's Choice, Stoney Ridge (Davis), Discontent, Rsy on Content, Contentment, Dear Bought
Jacob's Broom (Brune)	Lannafield
Jerico Hills	Rsy on Jerico Hills
John's Delight	(The) Gap, I Hope It Is Well Done, Long Dispute, Turkey Plains, Shidler's Dispute
Joseph's Tricks	Nottingham
Josiah's (Last) Bit	Old Purchase, Rsy on Mt. Pleasant, Mountain, Rsy on Well Done, Pastures Green
Joyner's Fancy	Nottingham
Keep Trieste	West of Crampton's Gap.
Kelly's Purchase	Fellfoot Enlarged, Rsy on Hills and Dales, Rsy on Elzwick's Dwelling
Kemp's Long Meadow	East of Crampton's Gap.
Killicrankee	Volton's Seal, Mountain, Josiah's (Last) Bit, Part of Roots Hill
King Cole	Antietam Works
Kizer's Lowden	Chapline's Ill Will, Contentment, Rsy on Jerico Hills
Knave's Good Will	Add to Friendship, Turkey Plains, Bear Swamp Forest, Adam Knave's Land, Neiff's Ill Will, Little Worth
Lannafield	Jacob's Broom (Brune)
Learning	Rsy on Learning, Add to Learning, and Part of the Rsy on Learning, (The) Exchange, Rsy on Exchange
Little Meadow	Dorsey's Risque, Add to Loss and Gain, Garigg's Delight
Locust Valley	Ebenezer, Mt. Atlas, Chesnut Oak Ridge, Stoney Ridge
Long Dispute (Ended)	Betty's Good Will, Fredericksburg, John's Delight, Shettle, Shidler's Dispute, Pickall, Rsy on the Gap
Loving Brother	Youngest Brother
Lucky Hit	Bird's Bill
Lyon's Purchase	Rsy on (The) Grove, Fellfoot Enlarged, Pile's Grove

Contiguous Land Tracts

Tract Name	Contiguous Tracts
Martitany	Add to Little Worth, Little Worth, Knave's Good Will, Knave's Ill Will, Add to Crephole, Nothing Hardly
Mankine	See Tracey and Dern. "Near the main road."
Martsome	At Mousetown near Boonsboro.
Maryland	Rsy on Maryland, Rsy on Grim's Delight, (The) Mountain Side
Mary's Cowpen	Pile's Grove, Nottingham, Rsy on Mt. Pleasant
Middletown	Youngest Brother, Rsy on Exchange, Widow's Design, Loving Brother, Rsy on Learning
Miller's Farm	Near the east side of Crampton's Gap.
Miller's Hills	Pile's Grove, Volton's Seal, Rsy on Roots Hills, Volton's Retreat, Pastures Green
Miller's Purchase	Near east side of Crampton's Gap.
Mendall (Mindall)	Rsy on Mendall, Pickall
Morgan's Delight	Add to Phillip's Chance, Strife, Rsy on Well Done
Mt. Atlas	Grim's Fancy, Mt. Pelier, Ebenezer, Stricker's Timberland, Rsy on (The) Seven Mountains, Partnership, Add to Friendship, Reeder's Delight, Rsy on Strife, Chesnut Oak Ridge, Rsy on Security, Booker's Rsy on Well Done, Add to Phillip's Chance, Rsy on Well Done (M. Chapline)
Mt. Pelier	Mt. Atlas
Mt. Pleasant (M. Chapline)	Rsy on Mt. Pleasant
Mt. Pleasant (Fox)	Turkeyfoot, Cool Spring Rsy (Shoup), I Hope It Is Well Done, Pickall
Mt. Sinai	Now I Know It, Betty's Good Will
Mountain (Baley)	Old Purchase, Josiah's (Last) Bit, Volton's Seal, Killicrankee, Rsy on Mt. Pleasant, Pastures Green, Rsy on Well Done, Old Purchase
Mountain (Gaver)	Gaver's Recovery, Fielderia Manor, Miller's Farm
Nazareth (Nazarih)	East of Crampton's Gap.
Neighbor's Content	Youngest Brother, Rsy on Exchange, Widow's Design, Loving Brother, Rsy on Learning, Middletown
Nelson's Folly	Chapline's Ill Will, Thomas's Purchase, Fellfoot Enlarged, Contentment, Beall's Chance, Contentment, Arrow Point, Fellowship, Security, Rsy on Grove, Grove
Newcomer's Purchase	Fox's Last Shift, Partnership, Swearingen's Disappointment
No Matter What	Rsy on Learning, Add to Learning, and Part of the Rsy on Learning
Not Much	Blooming Plains
Nottingham	Cornucopia, Joyner's Fancy, Charlemount Pleasant, Mary's Cow Pen, Beall's Chance, Pile's Grove, Rsy on Mt. Pleasant, Fellowship
Now I Know It	Rsy on Learning, Mendall, I Hope It Is Well Done, Pickall, Pegging Awl, Betty's Good Will, Exchange, Rsy on Exchange, Mt. Sinai
Old Purchase	Rsy on Mt. Pleasant, Josiah's (Last) Bit, Mountain
Oxford	Rsy on Oxford, Forest (Macgrudar), Pickall, I Hope It Is Well Done, Cool Spring, Rsy on Learning, Christie's Folly
Park Hall	Stife, Elk Hill, I Hope It Is So
Partnership (Mansberger)	Fox's Last Shift, Swearingen's Disappointment, Booker's Rsy on Well Done, Raccoon, Boon's Purchase, Remnant, Rsy on Well Done, Bird Bill, Showman's Purchase, Security, Stony Point, Vineyard, Lucky Bit, Rsy on Well Done
Partnership (Wardrop)	Volton's Seal, Rsy on Hills and Dales and Vineyard, Josiah's (Last) Bit, Come By Chance, Killicrankee, Corea, Nova Zembia
Pastures Green	Pile's Grove, Mountain, Come by Chance, Josiah's Bit, Killicrankee, Rsy on Mt. Pleasant
Paul's Travels	Fellfoot
Penn's Disappointment	Fellfoot Enlarged

Contiguous Land Tracts

Tract Name	**Contiguous Tracts**
Peter's Neglect	I Hope It Is Well Done, Mt. Pleasant (Fox)
Pickall	John's Delight, Shidler's Dispute, Long Dispute, Shettle, Fredericksburg, Now I Know It, Mendall, Small All, Oxford, Rsy on Oxford, Ram's Horn
Pegging Awl	Now I Know It, Betty's Good Will
Pile's Grove	Fellfoot Enlarged, Lyon's Purchase, Rsy on Mt. Pleasant, Rsy on Roots Hill, Volton's Seal, Knavery Detected, Mary's Cow Pen, Miller's Hills, Volton's Retreat, Blooming Plains, Not Much, Come By Chance, Nottingham, Pastures Green, Beam's Purchase
Poole's Delight Enlarged	Poole's Delight, Cost's Content, Tucket, (The) Forest (Sprigg), Cooperton, Rsy on Stricker's Timber Land, Michael's Luck, (The) Breeches
Prevention	Rsy on Prevention
Raccoon	Racon
Racon	Raccoon
Ram's Horn	Pickall
Roots Hill	Fellfoot, Fellfoot Enlarged
Rsy on Bear Swamp	Partnership, Add to Friendship, Flonham, Knave's Good Will
Rsy on Bear Swamp Forest	Shank's Trouble Ended, Adam's Expense, Rsy on Part of Rodenpelier's Ramble, Quaker's Tricks, Shoemaker's Tricks
Rsy on Biegley's Displeasure	Tick Neck, Tuckett, Pleasant Meadow, Nazareth, Rsy on Hard to Find, (The) Barrells, Rsy on Mason's Folly, Rsy on Trembling, Rsy of Tom's Gift, Spurgeon's Folly
Rsy on Dawson's Purchase	Dawson's Purchase
Rsy on Dearbought	Dearbought
Rsy on Exchange (Shaff)	Exhange, Bubble (Boble), Now I Know It, Fidler's Purchase, Deeffer Snay
Rsy on Grim's Delight	Fielderia Manor
Rsy on the Grove	Grove, Pile's Grove
Rsy on Hills and Dales and (The) Vineyard	Ward Spring, Rsy on the Vineyard, Rsy on Elzwick's Dwelling, Hills and Dales, Smith's Purchase, Rsy on Dearbought
Rsy on John's Delight	John's Delight, (The) Gap
Rsy on Learning	Learning
Rsy on Learning, Add to Learning, and Part of the Rsy on Learning	Learning, Now I Know It
Rsy on Mason's Folly	East of Crampton's Gap.
Rsy on Mendall (Mindall)	Mendall, Shidler's Dispute, Long Dispute, Shepfell's Purchase
Rsy on Mt. Pleasant (M. Chapline)	Mary's Cow Pen
Rsy on Nelson's Folly	Nelson's Folly
Rsy on Nottingham	Nottingham
Rsy on Oxford	Forest (Macgrudar), Oxford, We Could Not Agree
Rsy on Ram's Horn	Ram's Horn
Rsy on Roots Hill	Fellfoot Enlarged, Pile's Grove, Roots Hill
Rsy on Security	Security, David's Will, Grim's Fancy, Mt. Atlas, Add to Friendship
Rsy on Stoney Ridge	Stoney Ridge
Rsy on the Gap	John's Delight, (The) Gap, Apple Brandy (Fulwiler), Bowser's Addition, Worse and Worse, Its Bad Enough, Turkey Ramble, Add to Friendship, Pickall, Friendship (Fox)
Rsy on the Grove	(The) Grove
Rsy on the Seven Mountains	(The) Seven Mountains, Mont Serado, Morgan's Delight
Rsy on the Vineyard	(The) Vineyard, Rsy on Hills and Dales and the Vineyard
Rsy on Tom's Gift	Tom's Gift
Rsy on Trembling	Trembling
Rsy on Watson's Welfare	Watson's Welfare

Tract Name	Contiguous Tracts
Rsy on Well Done (Booker)	Rsy on Well Done (Chapline), Grim's Fancy, Well Done
Rsy on Well Done (Chapline)	Rsy on Mt. Pleasant, Booker's Rsy on Well Done, Cornucopia
Rsy on Whiskey Alley	Whiskey Alley
Rsy on Wooden Platter	Wooden Platter
Security	Rsy on Security, David's Will, Grim's Fancy, Mt. Atlas, Add to Friendship, Booker's Rsy on Well Done
Shaff's Purchase	Betty's Good Will
Shettle	Pickall, Long Dispute, I Hope It Is Well Done, Rsy on Mendall,
Shidler's Dispute	Long Dispute, John's Delight
Showman's Forest	Valley Mills, Boston, Antietam Works, Elk Hill, Little I Thought It, (The) Three Brothers, Rsy on Hills and Dales and Vineyard, Keedy's Chance.
Showman's Purchase	Partnership (Mansberger), Help to Dearbought
Small All	Rsy on Mendall
Small Ridge	Rsy on the Gap, It's Bad Enough, Worse and Worse
Smith's Hills	Near Burnside Bridge. Rsy on Smith's Hills.
Smithsburg	On the east side of Antietam Creek a small distance from the wagon road leading to Ft. Frederick.
Smithsfield	On the wagon road.
Slusser's Choice	Dearbought, Stoney Ridge (Davis), Ive's Folly, Discontent, Rsy on Content, Contentment
Spurgeon's Folly	Biegley's Displeasure. East side of Crampton's Gap.
Stoney Ridge (Davis)	North of Keedysville.
Stoney Ridge (Keepheart)	Locust Valley, Poole's Delight. Between Fox's and Crampton's Gaps.
Strife	Mt. Atlas, Park Hall
Striker's Timberland Enlarged	Near Crampton's Gap.
Swearingen's Disappointment	Partnership (Mansberger), Fox's Last Shift
Thomas's Purchase	Fellfoot Enlarged, (The) Grove, Nelson's Folly
Three Springs	Mt. Pleasant, Rsy on Three Springs
Tick Neck	Biegley's Displeasure
Timber and Stone	Park Hall, King Cole
Tom's Gift	Rsy on Tom's Gift
Top of the Blue Ridge	Miller's Farm, Miller's Purchase, Fielderia Manor
Tuckett	Biegley's Displeasure
Turkey Ramble	(The) Gap, Worse and Worse, Add to Friendship, Its Bad Enough, Rsy on (The) Gap
Turkeyfoot	Mt. Pleasant, I Hope It Is Well Done
Turkey Plains	John's Delight, I Hope It Is Well Done, Pickall, Mendall
(The) Uncle's Gift	Rsy on Uncle's Gift, Stoney Ridge.
(The) Vineyard	Rsy on (The) Vineyard, Rsy on Hills and Dales and (The) Vineyard
Volton's (Vulton's) Seal(e)	Killicrankee, Rsy on Mt. Pleasant, Part of Roots Hill
Ward Springs	Keedysville area.
Water Enough	Betty's Good Will, Boot and Strap, Joseph's Tricks
Watson's Welfare	Rsy on Watson's Welfare
We Could Not Agree	Rsy on Oxford, Christie's Folly
Well Done	Booker's Rsy on Well Done, Rsy on Well Done (M. Chapline)
What Not	Fork of Sharpsburg and Hagerstown roads north of Middletown.
Whiskey Alley	West of Middletown.
(The) Wooden Platter	Rsy on Wooden Platter, (The) Forest (Macgrudar)
Worse and Worse	Turkey Ramble, (The) Gap, It's Bad Enough, Apple Brandy (Fulwiler), Rsy on (The) Gap
Wilyard's Lot	Cost's Content
Youngest Brother	Learning, Rsy on Learning

Additional Land Tract Information

Tract names in the far left column appear in alphabetical order. Additional information may include tract location, historic sites located on the tract, interesting history related to the tract, information about the lines of the tract, or other related tract information. The author did not plot all tracts that appear in this listing. This listing does not include all of the plotted tracts that appear in this book. The following abbreviations appear frequently in this section: Rsy = Resurvey; Add = Addition; ac = acres; ps = perches

Tract Name	Key Tract Information
Add to Friendship	The Reno Monument stands on this tract. The Wise log cabin of Civil War fame stood on this tract. The tract runs from south of Fox's Gap to north of Turner's Gap. Also see Friendship (Fox), Unpatented Certificate #228, MdHR.
Add to Learning	Probably a quarter mile or more south of the Fox Inn.
Add to Penn's Disappointment	Northeast of Keedysville. See Fellfoot Enlarged Sub-Master.
Add to Raccoon	Northwest of Turner's Gap towards Boonsboro.
Add to Tom's Gift	Robert Evans lived along the Old Sharpsburg Road east of Fox's Gap. He assigned away his interest he held in tracts outside that area.
Alexandria	Near Forest of Needwood, south of Crampton's Gap.
Antietam Bottom	Beginning by the side of the Potomac River near Samuel Taylor's Ferry. Near the mouth of the Antietam Creek on the Potomac River.
Antietam Works	Courses 110 through 118 and 130 through 135 are along the wagon road from Hess's Mill (just east of Keedysville on the Old Sharpsburg Road) to Thomas Crampton's (Gap). See the 1794 Dennis Griffith Map.
Apple Brandy (Flook)	To rsy Part of the Rsy on Tom's Gift and Part of the Rsy on Part of Tom's Gift. Southeast of the Fox Inn.
Apple Brandy (Fulwiler)	Surveyed 31 Oct 1791. Line 8 went to the main road. The point on the Main Road from Frederick to Fort Frederick indicates the road was not the same route as the turnpike road built in the early 1800s in the area on the near east side of Turner's Gap. Midway between the Mountain House and the Reno Monument.
Ashbough	Near Lannafield and to the right hand of the road leading from Stull's Mill (Hagerstown area) to Robert Turner's (Boonsboro area).
Bad Enough	Beginning at the end of 60 ps in the 71st line of Col. Edward Sprigg's Rsy on the Add to Pile's Delight.
Badham's Refuse	South of Crampton's Gap.
Baker's Purchase	Samuel Baker's part of Fellfoot Enlarged. East of Keedysville.
Beall's Chance	Near Boonsboro.
Beam's Purchase	To rsy part of a tract called Pile's Grove with liberty given on 4 Aug 1786 to include part of Fellfoot Enlarged and part of Grove. East of Keedysville.
Bear Swamp Forest	Line 6 went to the end of the 29th line of Partnership; line 7 to the 3rd line of Flonham; line 10 to the end of the 7th line of Knave's Good Will; line 13 to the end of the 3rd line of Little Worth. The correct name is George Darr, not Starr. North of Turner's Gap.
Betty's Good Will	Surveyed for Robert Evans in 1727. The 1727 date is the earliest date the author found in his research of the land records of western Maryland. West of the Fox Inn along the Old Sharpsburg Road. Robert Evans lived along the Old Sharpsburg Road east of Fox's Gap. He assigned away any interest he held in tracts outside that area.
Biegley's Displeasure	To Christian Harshman of Frederick County 3 Jun 1791 to rsy Good Luck on 16 Dec 1788 granted Christian Harshman 174 ac; 26 1/2 ac part of

Additional Land Tract Information

Tract Name	**Key Tract Information**
	The Breeches on 8 Aug 1770 granted Abraham Lemaster for 56 ac; and 1/2 ac part of Pleasant Meadow on 17 Oct 1787 resurveyed for John Jacob Young for 2222 ac. The tract was contiguous to the Rsy on Tom's Gift. Line 4 went to a stone on the 12th line of the Rsy on Mason's Folly then with sd line reversed as the same was surveyed by the state of Maryland in the year 1781. Perhaps the state laid out a road in 1781. Line 7 went to a stone at the end of 46 1/2 ps on the given line of Tick Neck. Another line went to a stone at the end of 6 ps on the 23rd line of Pleasant Meadow.
Bird's Bill	Adjacent Lucky Hit. West side of Fox's Gap.
Blooming Month of May	To Jno Flook of Frederick County 14 May 1792 to rsy the following tracts: part of the Rsy on Learning, Add to Learning, and part of the Resy on Learning on 20 May 1765 resurveyed for Jacob Flook for 476 ac; part of the Rsy on Tom's Gift, in 2 parcels, on 21 May 1764 granted Joseph Chapline for 526 1/2 ac and part of the Rsy on Part of Tom's Gift on 15 Oct 1770 granted Joseph Chapline for 526 1/4 ac. Line 3 went to a stone at the end of 36 ps on the 1st line of 150 ac, Part of the Rsy on Tom's Gift, formerly conveyed by Henry Balzer to Leonard Starrum.
Blooming Plains	A rsy of part of the Rsy on Mount Pleasant, part of the Rsy on Well Done, part of Exchange, and part of Not Much.
Bloomsbury	Beginning about half a mile northeast of John Burger's house, between two mountains.
Booker's Purchase	Part of two tracts, Little Good and Add to Little Good.
Boston	A rsy of part of Little I Thought It, part of Keep Trieste, part of Dutch Loss, and Mill Place. Beginning at a stone marked A 1769 standing on the bank of Potomac River about 447 ps below the mouth of Antietam Creek and at the end of 89 ps on a line drawn north 16 degrees westerly from the most northerly corner of a tract called Benjanew Panry the said stone stands 2 ps distant from a marked or bounded walnut tree on a line north 67 degrees westerly and in the given line of the afsd part of Little I Thought It. Lines 1 to 7 next to Potomac River; lines 8 to 9 Antietam Bottom; lines 10 to 12 Dutch Loss; lines 14 to 18 Moor's Delight; lines 20 to 22 Dutch Loss; line 23 Antietam Bottom; lines 24 to 27 Little I Thought It; lines 28 to 29 Mill Place; lines 30 to 32 Little I Thought It; lines 33 to 35 Mill Place; lines 36 to 62 Little I Thought It; lines 63 to 80 Hunting The Hare; lines 81 to 82 Little I Though It; line 83 Saturn; lines 84 to 95 Pough 75 ac; lines 99 to 100 Saturn; lines 102 to 107 Turkey Hill; lines 108 to 123 Stoney Glade and Rsy on Stoney Glade; lines 124 to 126 Little I Thought It; lines 127 to 130 Prospect 54 ac; lines 131 to 141 Rsy on Hills and Dales; lines 153 to 168 Elk Hill 330 ac; lines 169 to 170 Inverness 100 ac; lines 171 to 185 Little I Thought It; lines 186 to 195 Hogg's Delight; lines 196 to 200 Little I Thought It.
Bowser's Addition	Land and premises open to public sale to the highest bidder. Henry Miller obtained the tract by virtue of a writ of Fieri Facia.
Brayface (Bray-face)	Part of the Rsy on Oxford. Line 2 went to the end of 76 ps on the given line of Pickall.
Breeches	East of Crampton's Gap.
Bubble (Boble)	South of the Fox Inn.
Burrell's Disappointment	Beginning at a bounded white oak standing on the east side of the Elk Ridge Mountain and near a spring called the Poplar Spring.
Chapline's Ill Will	Line 3 went to the end of 11 ps in the second line of Kizer's Lowden granted John Summers.

Additional Land Tract Information

Tract Name	**Key Tract Information**
Charlemount Pleasant	Surveyed for Samuel Ogle, Governor of Maryland, on 1 Jan 1745. One of the earliest tracts to mention Robert Turner.
Chestnut Oak Ridge	Beginning at a bounded Chesnut Oak tree standing about six ps from the 4th line of Joseph's Tricks and near the road leading to Lamb's improvement.
Chestnut Thicket	See FCLR, WR-6-169, Thomas and Fielder Gantt to Peter Gaver, Fielderia Manor, recorded 12 Nov 1785, 25 ac.
Christie's Folly	Just northeast of the Fox Inn. James Christie lived on the Great Road to Conococheague in 1755. Christie's Folly joined a tract called Smithfield. Richard Smith also operated a tavern on the Great Wagon Road to Conococheague in 1755.
Conococheague Manor	A massive tract running from the Potomac River near Shepherdstown, east to Keedysville, north to Hagerstown, west to Williamsport, and down the bank of the Potomac River to near Shepherdstown.
Contentment	Part of the Rsy on Content on 14 Jan 1760 granted Ralph Hickenbottom for 440 ac.
Cool Spring (Wardrop)	East of the Fox Inn.
Cool Spring Rsy (Shoup)	South of Fox's Gap. By virtue of a special warrant of rsy granted to Samuel Shoup of Frederick County 27 Dec 1800 to rsy Case Is At End on the 24 May 1797 granted Samuel Shoup for 152 ac.
Cooperton	Northeast of Crampton's Gap.
Cornucopia	Line 1 went to the 3rd line of a tract called Ashbough. Line 3 went to the 7th line of Fellowship. Line 27 went to the end of the 3rd line of Lannafield. Also adjacent Jacob's Broom and the Rsy on Well Done.
Cost's Content	Northeast of Crampton's Gap. A special warrant of rsy granted George Cost of Frederick Cty 4 May 1789 to rsy the 5 following tracts: Long Looked For on 5 Oct 1764 granted John Tucket for 36 ac; Second Long Looked For on 15 Oct 1765 granted John Tucket for 12 ac; the Rsy on Forest, Part of Forest on 19 Jun 1771 granted George Cost for 175 ac, 105 ac part of The Forest on 10 Jun 1734 granted Osborn Sprigg for 285 ac; and 50 ac part of Wilyard's Lot on 16 Feb 1775 granted Devalt Wilyard for 100 ac.
Cuckold's Horns	Robert Evans assigned the tract to Henry Rhodes of Frederick County.
Curry's Old Place (Wardrop)	Between Fox's and Turner's Gaps on east side of mountain. Mentioned in John's Delight survey. No land record found.
Daniel's Race Ground	Southeast of Fox's Gap. Perhaps horse races were held near Fox's Gap. Line 19 went to the main road (the Old Sharpsburg Road).
Dawson's Purchase	Southeast of Crampton's Gap.
David's Will	This tract is adjacent the south side of Add to Friendship of Frederick Fox. See Bowser's Addition. David Bowser settled near Fox's Gap after John Fox.
Dearbought	Laid out for 100 ac 27 Jun 1749.
Deeffer Snay	Rsy of the following contiguous tracts: part of the Rsy on Exchange, part of the Rsy on Learning, and part of Bubble.
Delemere	Probably near the intersection of Beaver Creek and the road from Boonsboro to Williamsport. Devil's Backbone area.
Discontent	Line 1 went to the last line of Smith's Choice. Line 4 went to the end of 26 ps in the 9th line of Content.
Dorsey's Risque (Risk)	Near Little Meadow of Thomas Walker. The survey identifies the owner of the Little Meadow tract as Thomas Walker.
Ebenezer	Line 25 went to the end of the 30th line of Locust Valley resurveyed for Lawrence Oneal 1 Jun 1792 and with said land 8 courses.
Elk Hill	A rsy on Burrell's Disappointment.

Additional Land Tract Information

Tract Name	**Key Tract Information**
Elzwick's Dwelling	See Rsy on Hills and Dales and the Vineyard.
The Exchange (Dulany)	The Fox Inn stands on this tract. See the Joseph Chapline Jr. versus William William Chapline court case, Maryland Archives Chancery Records at B 49 - 243 under Frederick Fox.
Exchange (Evans)	The author was not able to determine the location of this tract.
Fellfoot	Along the Old Sharpsburg Road southeast of Keedysville.
Fellfoot Enlarged	Keedysville area.
Fellowship	Near Boonsboro.
Ferry Landing	On the bank of the Potomac near Swearingen's Ferry. Near the Rumsey Bridge over the Potomac at Shepherdstown.
Fidler's Purchase	South of the Fox Inn.
Fielderia Manor	To rsy the following contiguous tracts: Fielderia on 6 Sep 1763 granted Fielder Gannt for 8151 ac; 100 ac part of his Rsy on the Add to Hazel Thicket on 13 Oct 1753 granted Thomas Taylor for 436 ac; Cut Knee on 15 Apr 1750 granted George Frazer for 315 ac; 416 ac part of Wells's Invention on 10 Aug 1753 granted Robert Lamar for 2017 ac; Fertile Meadow on 5 Nov 1754 granted Fielder Gannt for 100 ac; and Sweed's March on 15 Aug 1753 granted Fielder Gannt for 300 ac.
Flonham	The turnpike did not follow the roadbed of the Main Road from Frederick Town to Fort Frederick in the area of the Mountain House. The end of line 8 of Apple Brandy (Fulwiler) went to the "main road" prior to the creation of the turnpike.
Flook's Content	Part of the Rsy on Oxford. East of the Fox Inn.
Forest (Macgrudar)	On the road from Conestoga to Opequon. The road began at Conestoga, Pennsylvania, near Lancaster. It passed through York, Pennsylvania, and Taneytown, Woodsborough, Frederick Town, Middletown, Fox's Gap, and Sharpsburg in Maryland. It crossed the Potomac at Shepherdstown and went on to Opequon, located about five miles southwest of Winchester, Virginia. See Eshleman, Esq., H. Frank. *Lancaster County Historical Society Papers*, "The Great Conestoga Road," Volume XII, No. 6 (June 5, 1908), pp. 215-232.
Forest (Sprigg)	Near Crampton's Gap, east side.
Forest of Needwood	Near Crampton's Gap, east side. Line 6 went to the end of 34 ps on the 1st line of Alexandria.
Fox's Last Shift	The turnpike road probably crossed this tract.
Fredericksburg	The area surrounded by this tract still appears on tax assessment maps.
Friendship (Fox)	Frederick Fox, 11 May 1795, to rsy 34 ac part of Fredericksburg on 13 Mar 1794 granted Frederick Fox for 75 ac. Unpatented Certificate #228, 231 1/2 ac, 8 Jun 1795.
(The) Gap	Between Fox's and Turner's Gaps on the east side of the mountain. There is no land record for James Wardrop's land called Curry's Old Place.
Gaver's Recovery	Part of the Rsy on Dawson's Purchase on 5 Oct 1752 granted Thomas Dawson for 215 and 3/4 ac; 89 ac part of I Got It At Last on 5 Nov 1754 granted Thomas Hawkins for 100 ac; (The) Mountain on 19 Oct 1760 granted Thomas Hawkins for 30 ac and 25 ac part of Fielderia Manor on 15 Jan 1772 granted Feilder Gannt for 10,471 and 1/4 ac. Line 5 went to a stone at the end of 75 and 1/2 ps on the 3rd line of I Got It At Last, also the end of the 2nd line of Peter Miller's rsy called Miller's Purchase. Line 14 went to a stone at the end of 119 and 1/2 ps on the 6th line of Adam Knouff's land called Honesty Best When Looked To. Line 18 went to the beginning of Chestnut Thicket.

Additional Land Tract Information

Tract Name	Key Tract Information
Good Hope	Adjoining the survey of Antietam Finished, Fellfoot Enlarged, and the Rsy on Hills, Dales and the Vineyard. Line 2 went to the 56th line of Fellfoot Enlarged.
Goose Bill	A rsy of the Rsy on Prevention. The Rsy of Prevention is not on record.
Goose Cap	At the fork of the Old Hagerstown and Old Sharpsburg Roads north of Middletown near the Catoctin Creek.
Gordon's Purchase	Ewen McDonald of Prince Georges County did set forth by his humble petition to his excellency Samuel Ogle Esqr Governor of Maryland the 26 Jun 1736 that persons had settled on our high lands on or near Antietam Creek without any right from us only under pretense that it was within the lines of the province of Pennsylvania.
Grim's Fancy	The only land record found to identify John Fox with Fox's Gap in Maryland. The survey places John Fox at Fox's Gap by 1763.
(The) Grove	Granted Joseph Chapline 23 Jun 1752 for 195 ac.
Hard to Find	Line 7 went to the end of the 18th line of the Rsy on Seth's Folly surveyed for George Scott.
Hickory Tavern	Part of a tract called Fellfoot Enlarged that belonged to Capt. Tobias Stansberry late of Baltimore County deceased.
Hogyard	John George Arnold of Prince Georges County, farmer.
Honesty Best When Looked To	East of Crampton's Gap.
Horse Neck	Assigned by Joseph Chapline to John Tucker, 10 Apr 1759.
I Have Got It At Last	See Miller's Farm. Also, FCLR, N-470, Daniel Arnold to Peter Miller, recorded 23 Nov 1770.
I Hope It Is So	Line 4 went to the end of the 72nd line of a tract called Little I Thought It.
I Hope It Is Well Done	A rsy on Pickall. Line 60 went to the beginning tree of a tract taken up by James Wardrop, also the beginning tree of Pickall. Line 43 is the same as line 3 of Betty's Good Will.
Inverness	A rsy of Burrell's Disappointment being in two distinct parts called Inverness on the east side of Elk Ridge Mountain near a spring called Poplar Spring at the beginning tree of Burrell's Disappointment.
It's Bad Enough	Line 3 went to the 8th line of a tract called Turkey Ramble. Line 5 went to the end of the 3rd line of a tract called The Gap. Line 8 went to the 12th line of a tract called Pickall. Line 10 went to the end of the 3rd line of a tract called Small Ridge. Line 12 went to the 5th line of Worse and Worse.
Ive's Folly	Line 3 went to the end of 64 ps and 1/2 perch on the 73rd line of Contentment granted Joseph Chapline.
Jacob's Broom (Brune)	The tract description helps identify the location of Robert Turner's house.
Jerico Hills	922 ac of land formerly surveyed by Robert Twigg.
John's Delight	The earliest survey found by the author that mentions Curry's Gap. The patent for John's Delight does not indicate the beginning tree of the tract was along a road in 1750. However, five later tracts that began at the beginning tree of John's Delight identify the beginning tree as being along a main road.
Josiah's (Last) Bit	Josiah was a son of Moses Chapline Sr. See the will of Moses Chapline Sr. Line 2 is the same as line 26 of Pastures Green.
Joyner's Fancy	West of Boonsboro.
Keep Trieste	Rsy of Badham's Refuse on 29 Sep 1762 granted Joseph Chapline.
Kelly's Purchase	Doctor George Steuart of Annapolis by petition to our agent for management of land affairs set forth that he had 4450 ac of land by virtue of an assignment from Samuel Ogle Esqr part of 5000 ac granted him by renewment 7 Mar 1732.

Additional Land Tract Information

Tract Name	Key Tract Information
Kemp's Long Meadow	East of Crampton's Gap.
Killicrankee	William Good was a son-in-law of Moses Chapline Sr.
King Cole	Northwest of Crampton's Gap. See the Antietam Works survey.
Kizer's Lowden	Located northwest of Boonsboro along the Williamsport-Boonsboro road.
Knave's Good Will	North of Turner's Gap.
Knavery Detected	A rsy of Good Luck on 27 Apr 1773 granted for 140 ac.
Lannafield	See Jacob's Broom (Brune) survey.
Learning	Part of an assignment of a warrant from Tobias Stansbury for 1000 ac granted Stansbury by renewment 14 Jan 1752 but on 11 Jul 1753 assigned over the land and premises therein mentioned unto Frederick Garrison.
Little I Thought It	Assignment to Samuell Beall Jr. for the Rsy on Rush Bottom, Joseph's Choice, and Bad Enough 8 Feb 1763, now called Little I Thought It, 24 May 1763. Line 138 went to the beginning of Bad Enough it being the end of 60 ps on the 71st line of the Rsy on Add to Pile's Delight.
Little Meadow	Near intesection of the road from the Sharpsburg area to the Hagerstown area and the road to Conococheague through Fox's Gap. Perhaps the location of "one Walker's" during the Braddock Expedition. There is some question regarding the name of the owner of this tract. It is probable the owner was Thomas Walker.
Locust Valley	Beginning at a large rock marked TVS standing near the head of a small spring and "in a gap of the South Mountain". This tract is very interesting and needs additional research. It indicates there was a gap in the mountain between Fox's and Crampton's Gaps.
Long Dispute (Ended)	The Reno School building is on this tract along the Old Sharpsburg Road.
Loving Brother	The patent mentions land and premises.
Lucky Hit	Adjacent Bird's Bill. West side of Fox's Gap.
Lyon's Purchase	Adjacent Pile's Grove. Line 3 went to Pile's Grove. Line 5 went to a piece of land laid out for Peter Barkmand.
Martitany	Northeast of Fox's Gap.
Mankine	See Tracey and Dern. Near the main road.
Martsome	Located at Mousetown near Boonsboro.
Maryland	See Rsy on Grim's Delight, Rsy on Maryland, and Mountain Side.
Mary's Cowpen	The patent mentions the tracts of Nottingham, Pile's Grove, and Rsy on Mt. Pleasant. A very small tract that helps locate three contiguous tracts.
Middletown	Southeast of the Fox Inn.
Miller's Farm	East side of Crampton's Gap.
Miller's Hills	To rsy the following lands: Volton's Seal, Volton's Retreat, and part of Pastures Green. Land record mentions Rsy on Roots Hill, main road from Fox's Gap to Sharpsburg, and Snyder's Mill. Pile's Grove and Miller's Hills records help prove the road through Fox's Gap back to 1734.
Miller's Purchase	Southeast of Crampton's Gap.
Mendall (Mindall)	Northeast of Fox's Gap.
Mt. Atlas	In three separate and distinct parts. Part one contiguous to Add to Friendship and Partnership for 19 and 1/2 ac. Beginning for the 3rd parcel at the end of the 4th line of Drunker Harbour. Mentions Rsy on Well Done of Moses Chapline. Third part has 5 and 1/4 ac. Second part of 1047 and 3/4 ac mentions tracts of Chestnut Oak, Add to Phillip's Chance, Grim's Fancy, Booker's Rsy on Well Done, Security, Mt. Pelier, Chestnut Oak Ridge, Rsy on Strife, Reeder's Delight, and Rsy on the Seven Mountains. To rsy a Rsy made for them by the name of Add to Partnership 21 Dec 1796.

Additional Land Tract Information

Tract Name	**Key Tract Information**
Mt. Pelier	Not very far south of Fox's Gap.
Mt. Pleasant (Fox)	Thomas Van Swearingen by an assignment 4 Apr 1791 transferred all his right, title, and interest in the certificate of the said land to Frederick Fox. The tract called Turkeyfoot is contiguous to lines 2, 3, and 4 of Mt. Pleasant.
Mt. Pleasant (M. Chapline)	One of the earliest tracts between Fox's Gap and Keedysville.
Mt. Sinai	West of the Fox Inn.
Mountain (Bailey)	Teague's Creek is at Shepherdstown, West Virginia. Shepherdstown probably was the site of Teague's Ferry. Monocacy probably meant the area that became Frederick, Maryland.
Mountain (Gaver)	At Crampton's Gap.
Nazareth (Nazarih)	East of Crampton's Gap.
Neighbor's Content	South of the Fox Inn.
Nelson's Folly	Line 40 of Contentment is the same as line 8 of Nelson's Folly. Arthur Nelson of Prince Georges County and George Nelson late of Annapolis had surveyed a tract called Nelson's Folly.
Newcomer's Purchase	A rsy on Fox's Last Shift. Line 10 went to the third line of the original. The turnpike might have passed through the banana-shaped portion of this tract.
No Matter What	Southeast of Fox's Gap.
Not Much	West side of Fox's Gap.
Nottingham	Line 1 went to the end of 10 ps on the 3rd line of Beall's Chance. Line 14 went to the 13th line of Pile's Grove of John Darnal Esquire. Line 15 went to the 4th line of Charlemount Pleasant. Line 16 went to the end of the 4th line of Charlemount Pleasant. Line 17 went to the end of the 2nd line of Joyner's Fancy.
Now I Know It	North of the Fox Inn.
Old Purchase	Southeast of Keedysville.
Oxford	Not far northeast of the Fox Inn.
Park Hall	An early deed indicates, "beginning near the old Indian road."
Partnership (Mansberger)	A rsy of Newcomer's Purchase that was a rsy of Fox's Last Shift. Line 16 went to the end of the 10th line of Lucky Bit. Line 17 went to the 7th line of Fox's Last Shift. Line 22 went to the end of the 3rd line of Bird's Bill. Line 26 went to the end of the 8th line of Security. Line 37 went to the end of the 1st line of Boon Forest. Line 32 went to the end of the 4th line of Raccoon. Line 31 went to the end of the 6th line of Stoney Point.
Pastures Green	A rsy of Mountain, Come by Chance, Killicrankee, Rsy on Mt. Pleasant, and Josiah's (Last) Bit. Line 5 went to the end of line 2 of Killicrankee. Line 10 went to the end of line 5 of Come by Chance. Line 20 went to a tract called Wood Stock. Line 25 went to the end of the 2nd line of Josiah's (Last) Bit. Line 31 went to the wagon road 20 feet north of a stone standing in said line. Line 26 is the same as line 2 of Josiah's (Last) Bit. Lines 28 through 35 are the same as lines 3 through 9 of Old Purchase.
Paul's Travels	Near Keedysville.
Penn's Disappointment	Northwest of Keedysville.
Peter's Neglect	Line 11 went to the beginning of Mt. Pleasant (Fox).
Phillip's Choice	Not Located.
Pickall	The patent for John's Delight does not indicate the beginning tree of the tract was along a road in 1750. However, five later tracts that began at the beginning tree of John's Delight identify the beginning tree as being along a main road. The Pickall patent, Shidler's Dispute deeds of 1760 and 1767, the Long Dispute deed of 1767, and the 304 acre tract of the

Additional Land Tract Information

Tract Name	Key Tract Information
	Bartholomew Booker Estate in 1792 refer to "the main road." Both Shidler's Dispute deeds mention Curry's Gap. To rsy part of 2 contiguous tracts 146 ac part of a Mendall on 21 Dec 1758 granted for 546 ac under new rent and 1/4 of an acre part of Small All on 24 Jun 1759 granted Bartholomew Booker for 25 ac. "I also find that the other tract called Small All has been all conveyed to a certain George Shidler but about 1/4 of an acre which quarter lays in the first original and I have added 3 pieces of contiguous vacancy containing 1020 ac." Lines 41 and 42 are contiguous to lines 6 and 7 of Christie's Folly. Line 44 is the same as line 39 of the Rsy on Oxford.
Pegging Awl (Piging Aul)	Part of Now I Know It
Pile's Grove	The distance from the beginning tree to the road in 1813 was about 1/2 mile. See Pastures Green and Blooming Plains.
Poole's Delight Enlarged	Ashbury Sutton of Norfolk in the Colony of Virginia to rsy Poole's Delight laid out for 100 ac 11 May 1750.
Prevention	See Tracey and Dern discussion of this tract.
Raccoon	Northwest of Turner's Gap.
Racon	Northwest of Turner's Gap. The road referred to in the land record must have been main road from Frederick to Fort Frederick.
Ram's Horn	East of Fox's Gap.
Roots Hill	Near Keedysville.
Rsy on Bear Swamp	North of Turner's Gap.
Rsy on Bear Swamp Forest	North of Turner's Gap.
Rsy on Biegley's Displeasure	Northeast of Crampton's Gap.
Rsy on Chestnut Hill	Not located.
Rsy on Dawson's Purchase	East of Crampton's Gap.
Rsy on Dearbought	Mr. James Wardrop of Prince Georges County to Rsy Dearbought laid out for 100 ac 27 Jun 1749.
Rsy on Exchange (Shaff)	The Fox Inn stands on this tract. Joseph Chapline on 9 May 1754 assigned over all his claim in the certifice of rsy and the land and premises to Casper Shaff.
Rsy on Grim's Delight	South of Crampton's Gap along the crest of the Blue Ridge.
Rsy on the Grove	East of Keedysville.
Rsy on Hills and Dales and (The) Vineyard	See Hills and Dales, Ward Springs, Rsy on the Vineyard, Rsy on Elwick's Dwelling, and Smith's Purchase. Line 5 is the same as the 7th line of the Rsy on the Vineyard. Lines 96, 97, 98, and 99 are the same as lines 56, 55, 54, and 53 of Fellfoot Enlarged.
Rsy on John's Delight	Taken from the original record at the Maryland Historical Society. Containing 131 ac, surveyed 20 Apr 1766. Line 9 went to the end of 42 ps in the 4th line of the original.
Rsy on Learning	Southeast of the Fox Inn.
Rsy on Mason's Folly	East of Crampton's Gap.
Rsy on Mendall (Mindall)	Bolivar area.
Rsy on Mt. Pleasant (M. Chapline)	East of Keedysville.
Rsy on Nelson's Folly	West of Boonsboro.
Rsy on Nottingham	Southwest of Boonsboro.
Rsy on Oxford	To rsy Oxford, part of the Rsy on Learning, part of Christie's Folly, part of the Rsy on Learning, Add to Learning, and part of the Rsy on Learning, and part of Pickall. Line 1 went to the end of 13 ps on the 6th line of part of the Rsy on Learning. Line 7 went to the end of 12 ps on the 2nd line of Oxford.

Additional Land Tract Information

Tract Name	Key Tract Information
	Line 26 went to the end of 7 ps on the 4th course of part of Christie's Folly. Line 38 went to the end of the 4th line of part of Pickall. Lines 33 and 34 are the same as lines 1 and 2 of Smith to Beaver for part of Christie's Folly. Peter Beaver acquired 53 ac of Pickall from Bartholomew Booker on 15 Dec 1770.
Rsy on Ram's Horn	Near Orr's Gap, about two miles north of Turner's Gap.
Rsy on Roots Hill	A rsy of Roots Hills. Line 4 went to the end of 10 ps on the last line of Fellfoot Enlarged. Line 6 went to the end of the 1st line of Fellfoot Enlarged. Line 7 went to the end of the 4th line of Pile's Grove.
Rsy on Security	Line 8 went to the 6th line of Booker's Rsy on Well Done.
Rsy on Stoney Ridge	Probably north of Keedysville.
Rsy on The Seven Mountains	Beginning for the outlines thereof at the end of the 3rd line of the original. To rsy Seven Mountains on 10 Apr 1765 granted Michael Workman for 36 ac.
Rsy on The Gap	The record mentions the tracts of Add to Friendship, (The) Gap, Turkey Ramble, Bowser's Addition, Apple Brandy, Worse and Worse, Fredericksburg, and John's Delight. Lines 25 and 26 are the same as lines 12 and 13 of Apple Brandy. Line 36 is the same as line 4 of John's Delight. Line 28 is the same as line 1 of Bowser's Addition.
Rsy on The Grove	Northeast of Keedysville.
Rsy on The Vineyard	William Steuart assigned the land and premises to Benjamin Tasker Sr. and Benjamin Tasker Jr. Esqrs. on 12 Mar 1754.
Rsy on Tom's Gift	Tom's Gift on 16 Oct 1757 granted Robert Evans for 50 ac.
Rsy on Trembling (Trimbling)	James Spurgeon assigned to Michael Beigler 12 Jan 1761 to rsy Trembling.
Rsy on Watson's Welfare	A Rsy of Watson's Welfare. Assigned by Ewen McDonald to Joseph Chapline on 4 Mar 1760.
Rsy on Well Done (Chapline)	Moses Chapline Jr., eldest son and heir at law of Moses Chapline Sr., assigned all his interest to William Good. Lines 36 through 45 of the Rsy on Well Done are the same as lines 16 through 25 of Conucopia.
Rsy on Well Done (Booker)	Includes original tract named Well Done of Moses Chapline Sr. To rsy a tract called Well Done. Line 7 went to the beginning tree of Well Done.
Rsy on Whiskey Alley	Near Middletown.
Rsy on Wooden Platter	Line 12 went to a stone at a black oak stump "the proof of Bartholomew Booker 120 ps on the same line stands a stone near a spring the proof of Samuel Buzzard." The record gives the age of Bartholomew Booker.
Security	Just west of Fox's Gap.
Shaff's Purchase	Just west of the Fox Inn.
Shettle	Daniel Dulany assigns to Robert Marks on 18 Oct 1751. Near Bolivar.
Shidler's Dispute	East of Fox's Gap. Two early Shidler's Dispute deeds mention Curry's Gap.
Showman's Forest	Southwest of Fox's Gap.
Showman's Purchase	Charles Beatty of the territory of Columbia to rsy Help to Dearbought on 24 Feb 1797 granted him for 77 ac. Line 1 went to the 24th line of Partnership. Line 2 went to the end of the 1st line of Bird's Bill. Line 4 went to the beginning of Lucky Bit. Line 5 went to the end of the 42nd line of Partnership. Line 6 went to the end of the 72nd line of the Rsy on Well Done. The second parcel of the tract was not plotted.
Slusser's Choice	A rsy of Smith's Choice, Stoney Ridge, Ive's Folly, Discontent, part of Contentment, and part of the Rsy on Content. Line 1 went to the end of the 7th line of Chapline's deed to Ringer for part of Contentment. Line 6 went to a stone marked NP at the end of 28 ps in the 1st line of Stoney Ridge. Line 21 went to a marked stone in the 4th line of Dearbought. Line 17 went to a marked stone on the east bank of Antietam Creek.

Additional Land Tract Information

Tract Name	**Key Tract Information**
Small All	Joseph Chapline on 24 Jun 1760 assigned over his right to the certificate of survey and the land and premises to Bartholomew Booker.
Small Ridge	East of Fox's and Turner's Gap.
Smith's Choice	Discontent is adjacent this tract. North of Keedysville.
Smith's Hills	Near the Burnside (Lower) Bridge. Lines 9 and 10 of Smith's Hills may be part of lines 36 and 35 of the Rsy of Hills and Dales and (The) Vineyard.
Smithburg	Northwest of Boonsboro.
Smithfield	Northeast of the Fox Inn.
Spurgeon's Folly	Northeast of Crampton's Gap.
Stoney Ridge (Davis)	Contiguous to Slusser's Choice.
Stoney Ridge (Keepheart)	This tract is between Fox's and Crampton's Gaps. It is a key tract used to prove the road through Crampton's Gap was only a horse trail or bridal path until at least 1768.
Strife	To rsy a tract called the Rsy on Part of Parks Hall on 28 Jul 1766 granted Andrew Grim for 510 ac.
Striker's Timberland Enlarged	North of Crampton's Gap.
Swearingen's Disappointment	Just northwest of Turner's Gap.
Thomas's Purchase	Northeast of Keedysville.
Three Springs	North of Keedysville.
Timber and Stone	Northwest of Crampton's Gap.
Tick Neck	Northeast of Crampton's Gap.
Tom's Gift	Southeast of the Fox Inn.
Top of the Blue Ridge	South of Crampton's Gap.
Tuckett	Northeast of Crampton's Gap.
Turkeyfoot	Henry Collman assigned to Frederick Fox on 19 Mar 1788.
Turkey Ramble	The land record mentions the tracts of Turkey Ramble, The Gap, John's Delight, Pickall, Small Ridge, and Worse and Worse. Line 9 went to the end of the last line of The Land of Gap.
Turkey Plains	To rsy a tract called the Rsy on Add to Turkey Plains on 13 Nov 1756 granted for 450 ac. Line 18 went to the 6th line of Martitany.
Uncle's Gift	Near Forest of Needwood.
Vineyard	Near the Hitt (Upper) Bridge on the Antietam northeast of Sharpsburg.
Volton's Seal	Keedysville area.
Ward Springs	Keedysville area.
Water Enough	West of the Fox Inn.
Watson's Welfare	One mile below the road from Stull's Mill (Hagerstown) to Monocacy (Frederick Town). Assigned by Daniel Dulany to Ewen MacDaniel so that he might obtain a patent, 26 Jun 1747.
We Could Not Agree	Northeast of the Fox Inn.
Well Done	Part of Booker's Rsy on Well Done.
What Not	At the fork of the Old Sharpsburg and Old Hagerstown Roads north of Middletown.
Whiskey Alley	Near Middletown.
Wilyard's Lot	A key tract used to prove the road through Crampton's Gap was only a bridal road or horse trail until at least 1768.
(The) Wooden Platter	Daniel Dulany assigned to James Wardrop on 26 Mar 1748.
Worse and Worse	John Team (Teem) was one of the earliest settlers in the area just east of Fox's and Turner's Gaps.
Youngest Brother	Line 5 went to the end of the 6th line of part of Learning. Line 6 went to the end of 4 ps in the 1st line of part of the Rsy on Exchange.

Unplotted Land Records in the Vicinity of the Battlefields

The author did not plot the tracts listed below and on the following pages. They do not appear in this book. The tracts are in either Frederick County or Washington County and within a few miles of the Battlefields of South Mountain or Antietam.

The following reference books at the Maryland State Archives may help identify later owners of tracts in Frederick or Washington County:
Frederick County, 1819-1868. 50,096-14, 1/28/1/6, MSA S 1736-1
Washington County, 50,096-24-2, 1/28/1/16, MSA S 1388-2

Unplotted Maryland State Archives Land Records

Tract names in the far left column appear in alphabetical order.

Tract Name	Reference Number	In Name Of	Acres	Date
Adam's Expense	MdHR IC #K-268	Adam Roughtsong	357	10 Oct 1792
Add to Learning	MdHR BC & GS 30, 225-6	Jacob Flook		15 Nov 1766
Add to Miller's Purchase	MdHR ICK:285			
	MdHR ICG:542	Peter Miller	52 3/4	29 May 1795
Add to Raccoon	MdHR IC I, 285			
	MdHR IC G, 225	Joseph Chapline		
Antietam Bottom	MdHR EI 5, 510			
	MdHR LG B, 189	John Moore	300	4 Aug 1739
Baker's Purchase	WCLR G7, 621-626	Jacob Hess et al.	2,100	19 Mar 1792
Beall's Chance		George Beall	100	26 Nov 1738
Bird Bill	Probably near Partnership (Mansberger) and Lucky Hit.			
Boston	MdHR BC & GS #47,12-18	Dr. David Ross	8,025	25 Jul 1769
Conococheague Manor	Includes area from Potomac to Keedysville to Hagerstown to Williamsport.			
	MdHR EI 5, 580	Lord Baltimore	10,000+	
	MdHR BC & GS 37, 113	Thomas Ringgold		
	MdHR BC & GS 38, 72	John Morton Jordan		21 Nov 1770
Curry's Old Place	No record found. Between Fox's and Turner's (Curry's) Gap. Identified in deed for (The) Gap, 29 Mar 1761.			
Dearbought	MdHR Y & S 7, 196	James Wardrop	500	
	MdHR BY & GS 3, 484			
Delamere	Probably near Beaver Creek and the road from Boonsboro to Williamsport.			
	MdHR ICQ:724			
	MdHR ICS:293	John Booth	1,147	1806
Dorsey's Risque	MdHR BC & GS 2, 112-3,	Edward Dorsey	158	12 Dec 1754
Elzwick's Dwelling	MdHR LG E, 74	Dr. George Stewart		24 Oct 1739
		John Elzwick Survey		
Ferry Landing	On the bank of the Potomac near Swearingen's Ferry. Near the Rumsey Bridge on the Potomac at Shepherdstown.			2 May 1782
Fielderia Manor	MdHR BC & GS #47, fol. 1	Fielder Gant	10,471	18 May 1770
(Partially plotted)	MdHR BC & GS 19:451			15 Jan 1772
	MdHR BC & GS 17:467			
Friendship (Fox)	Forerunner to Add to Friendship of Frederick Fox at Fox's Gap.			
	Unpatented Certificate #228	Frederick Fox	231 1/2	8 Jun 1795

Tract Name	Reference Number	In Name Of	Acres	Date
Good Intent	Crampton's Gap area.			
	MdHR IC#K-354	Joseph Chapline	72 1/2	18 May 1795
Grove	Probably west, northwest of Fox's Gap; south, southwest of Boonsboro.			
	MdHR BY & GS 4, 229	Joseph Chapline		
	MdHR Y & S 7, 95			
Horse Neck	MdHR BC & GS 14-86	Joseph Chapline	86	28 Jul 1752
		John Tucker		1 May 1761
Inverness	West of Crampton's Gap.			
Josephs Tricks	MdHR ICK: 739	Phillip Melchor	21	1796
	MdHR ICM:61			
King Cole	Northwest of Crampton's Gap.			
Lannafield	See the Doug Bast drawing of Boonsboro tracts on *Fox's Gap in Maryland* Kodak Photo CD-Rom computer disc.			
Maryland	Southeast of Fox Inn.			
Middletown	See Neighbor's Content	Henry Leiter	180	25 Nov 1790
		John Leiter		
Morgan's Delight	MdHR IB #D-695	William Morgan	165	22 Dec 1815
Mount Pleasant	MdHR LG E, 559	Moses Chapline		11 Mar 1744
	MdHR LG C, 542	Moses Chapline		5 Feb 1745
Not Much		William Good	11	10 Dec 1784
Phillip's Choice	MdHR BC & GS 27, 406	Phillip Litzsinger	31	9 Apr 1765
Roots Hill	MdHR BY & GS 4, 606			
	MdHR BC & GS 4, 200			
Rsy on Bear Swamp	MdHR BC & GS #30-176	George Darr	223	7 Dec 1765
	MdHR BC & GS #33:6			5 Sep 1766
Rsy on Dawson's Purchase	MdHR Y & S 7:184	Thomas Dawson	215 3/4	1753
	MdHR BY & GS 3:463			
Rsy on (The) Grove	MdHR BC & GS 1, 306	Joseph Chapline	520	1754
	MdHR BC & GS 2, 162			
Rsy on Mendall	Various sales by Bartholomew Booker.			
Rsy on Mt. Pleasant	MdHR GS 1, 101	Moses Chapline	217	1753
(See Mt. Pleasant of	MdHR Y & S 6, 329	Moses Chapline	217	1757
Moses Chapline Sr)	MdHR BC & GS 9, 164	Moses Chapline	471	
	MdHR BC & GS 6, 327	Moses Chapline	471	
	MdHR IB #D-226	Jacob Snyder	198	25 Apr 1814
	Near Keedysville. A Rsy on Part of the Rsy on Mt. Pleasant 21 Jul 1757 by Moses Chapline for 471 acres; A Rsy on Part of the Rsy on Well Done 25 Oct 1774 by William Good for 1822 acres; A Rsy on Josiah's (Last) Bit 20 Apr 1786 by William Good for 67 acres; A Rsy on Remnant 16 Jun 1791 by Michael Fackler for 8 and 1/4 acres. Near Jacob Snyder's Mill. The Michael Fackler tract may contain the Moses Chapline Sr family cemetery. See Chapline genealogy book by Dare and *Drums Along the Antietam* by Schildt.			
Rsy on Nelson's Folly	MdHR BC & GS 27, 261	Robert Turner	575	25 Jun 1765
Rsy on Nottingham	See Henry Stoner to Henry Nyman, probably 1824 to 1827.			
Rsy on Rams Horn	See Frederick Main to Daniel Main, probably 1840.			
	Also see Abrm Doub to Enos Doub, probably 1840.			
Rsy on Seven Mountains		George Fidler	155	14 Nov 1771
				28 Nov 1787
Rsy on Stoney Ridge	Unpatented	Henry Loll	178 1/2	1763
Showman's Forest	MdHR IC 1:562	Charles Beatty	330 1/2	20 Mar 1793
	MdHR ICG:300	John Showman		17 Oct 1793

Unplotted Land Records - Maryland Archives

Tract Name	Reference Number	In Name Of	Acres	Date
Smithsburg	On the east side of Antietam Creek a small distance from the wagon road leading to Ft. Frederick.			12 Nov 1760
Smithsfield	On the wagon road.	John W. Smith	150	2 Dec 1739
Timber and Stone	Beginning at the beginning of Park Hall. Next to King Cole.			
	MdHR IC#B-61	Richard Henderson	53	4 Jun 1783
		Edmond Brice		
		David Horatio		1 Jul 1784
		Abraham Ross		
Tom's Gift		Robert Evans		16 Oct 1747
Tuckett	MdHR BC & GS 41:236	Joseph Chapline	130	1770
	MdHR BC & GS 38:424			
Water Enough	Near Betty's Good Will; Boot and Strap, 2 1/4 acres; and Joseph's Tricks, 21 acres.			
	MdHR BC & GS 47-500	Alexander Hanson	15	1 Jan 1772
	MdHR BC & GS 46-311			10 Sep 1773

Unplotted Frederick County Land Records

The following listing is by Frederick County Land Record reference number sequence, i.e. entries appear in the following order:
From A-1 to Z-9
From AA-1 to ZZ-9
From AAA-1 to ZZZ-9
From 1-1 to 9-9

B-48, Miles Foy to James Spurgeon, Trembling, recorded 29 Jun 1749, 120 acres.

B-671, Francis Foy to James Spurgeon, Trembling, recorded 23 Nov 1752, 120 acres.

F-826, Richard Richardson, Power of Attorney, recorded 24 Sep 1759, part of Park Hall. "Granted by Governor Samuel Ogle under Lord Baltimore by a Patent or Grant unto William Parks of the City of Annapolis in Ann Arundell Cty . . . and willed by said Parks to Eleanor, his daughter, wife of the aforesaid John Shelton"

I-199, Lodowick Kemp, Dearbought, surveyed in 1772, granted Lodowick Kemp 11 Sep 8_. "Beginning at the end of 37 perches on the 40th line of the Amendment and at a bounded stone about 14 perches northeast from a small run."

J-735, I Would Not, George Tucker to Michael Beaghler, recorded 27 Aug 1764, 25 acres.

J-937, Tiel Clenman to Casper Shaff, recorded 28 Nov 1764, 100 acres, Good Hik.

J-1400, John Burroughs to John Fox, recorded 18 Aug 1767. "John Burroughs, James Black, and James McCay do confess judgement unto John Fox for the sum of one pound two shillings _ sixpence Debt of two shillings and sixpence cost" (Author's Note: Perhaps this John Fox lived at Fox's Gap, but he might have been the John George Fox of Frederick Town who appears in Frederick church records.)

K-1-86, Joseph Sprigg to Thomas Taylor, recorded 20 March 1767, 360 acres, Piles Hall. "Beginning at a bounded white oak near Israel Friend's Mill Road and where the said road crosses a hill called Catoctin"

K-10, Forest, Joseph Spriggs to George Cost, recorded 4 Oct 1765, 85 acres.

K-499-500, John Fox to Elias Bruner, recorded 22 May 1766, 60 feet in breadth and 393 feet in length, Lot #269 in Frederick Town. (Author's Note: I do not believe the John Fox of this deed is the John Fox of Fox's Gap in Maryland. Perhaps he was John George Fox who appears in Frederick church records.)

K-504-5, Daniel Dulany to John Fox, recorded 2 Jun 1764, 60 feet in breadth and 393 feet in length, Lot #269 in Frederick Town. (Author's Note: I do not believe the John Fox of this deed is the John Fox of Fox's Gap in Maryland. Perhaps he was John George Fox who appears in Frederick church records.)

K-703, Joseph Chapline to John Fox (of Fox's Gap), recorded 23 Aug 1766, 103 feet in breadth and 206 in length, Lot #143 in Sharpsburg.

K-1217, Rsy on (The) Grove, Martin Lyon, 7 May 1766, and Michael Thomas, 23 Mar 1754.

K-1278, Henry Joel to John Fox (of Fox's Gap), recorded 2 Jun 1767, 20 perches in breadth and 40 perches in length, Out Lot to Lot #17 in Sharpsburg.

K-1279, Henry Joel to John Fox (of Fox's Gap), recorded 2 June 1767, 51 feet and 1/2 feet in breadth and 206 feet in length, the easternmost part of Lot #6 in Sharpsburg.

M-549, Robert Turner to John Cary and Jacob Young, Rsy on Nelson's Folly, recorded 14 Oct 1769, 575 acres.

N-57, Bartholomew Booker to Christian Kizer, 11 Apr 1770, 485 acres.

O-376, Add to Penn's Disappointment, George Beall Jr, 12 Jun 1771.

P-284, Edward Grimes to Jacob Smith, Betty's Good Will and part of the Rsy on Mendall, 29 July 1772, _ acres.

P-632, John Teem to Adam Coil, recorded 22 Mar 1773, 41 and 1/2 acres, Worse and Worse.

P-651, George Shidler to Henry Smith, Long Dispute, 22 Mar 1773, 200 acres.

S-157, Little Meadow, Thomas Walker to George Garrick, recorded 26 Apr 1773, 100 acres.

S-389, George Common to Philip Booker, recorded 28 Jun 1773, 100 acres, Grim's Fancy.

T-344, William Tucker to Mathias Ahalt, part of the Second Rsy on Black Acorn, 18 Aug 1773, 70 acres.

W-26-217, Conrad Young to Jacob Young, recorded 15 Nov 1804, 4 and 1/2 acres, Youngest Brother.

W-308, John Hall to Thomas Walters, Middle Plantation, recorded 20 Nov 1774, 102 acres. Now in Washington County, probably between Bakersville and Williamsport.

AF-9-91, Simon D. Routzahn to John H. Routzahn, recorded 2 Apr 1884, the Fox Inn property.

Unplotted Land Records of Frederick County

AF-11-311, John Mentzer and Martha E. Mentzer, his wife, to County School Commissioners of Frederick County, recorded 1865, 1 acre, the Reno School property.

CM-2-379, Daniel Beackley and Hannah Beackley, his wife, to William Jones, recorded 8 Oct 1868, 3/4 acre and 10 perches, part of Flonham.

CM-7-381, William M. Feaga, Collector, to David Arnold, recorded 13 Oct 1871, 16 acres.

ES-3-57, Tilghman Biser to Ezra Williard and William Carroll, recorded 13 Apr 1853.

ES-5-427, Henry Derr to Daniel Castle, recorded 16 Feb 1855, two parcels transferred.

ES-6-243, Daniel Castle to Lewis O. Wise, recorded 22 Jan 1855, 77 square perches.

HS-2-326, Daniel Shoemaker to John P. Flook, recorded 2 May 1836.

HS-3-77, Susan Magruder to Phillip Sheffer, recorded 5 Jul 1836, 65 square perches, the road from the Sharpsburg Road to Phillip Sheffer's farm.

JS-15-260-262, Jacob Baumgardner to Frederick Black (Mortgage), recorded 18 Mar 1822, 24 and 3/4 acres, Fredericksburg.

JS-31-439-440, Elizabeth McCrea to George Fisher, recorded 20 May 1829, 1 acre, also 1 and 1/4 acres and 12 square perches, part of Fredericksburg.

JS 38, 480-481, Peter Brengle, Sheriff to Henry Miller, Bowser's Addition, recorded 7 Apr 1832, 10 acres.

JS-41-223-225, George Fisher to John Nankivell, recorded 16 Jan 1833, 1 acre, also 1 and 1/4 acre and 12 square perches, part of Fredericksburg.

TG-3-298, Samuel Ausherman to Eli Routzahn, recorded 10 May 1875, 192 acres and 2 roods, excepting about two acres.

TG-3-396, John W. and Sarah E. Koogle to George P. Sheffer, recorded 1 Jun 1875, part of Flonham.

TG-5-194, Madeleine V. Dahlgren from George P. and Amanda D. Sheffer, recorded 25 Apr 1876, 8 and 3/4 acres, excepting one half acre, part of Flonham.

TT 818-819, George Shafer and Jonathan Shafer to Peter Zittle, recorded 22 Feb 1837.

WR-4-179, Jacob Keefour to Members and Trustees of the German Reformed Lutheran and Calvinist Congregations in and about Middle Town, recorded 30 Aug 1783, 50 acres, part of Whiskey Alley.

WR-6-133, Peter Smelser to Bartholomew Booker, recorded 27 Sep 1785, 5 acres, Rsy on Martitany.

WR-8-662, Henry Smith to Peter Hutzell, Long Dispute, 2 Oct 1789, 200 acres.

WR-10, Frederick Fox and Margaret Booker to Christian Kizer, recorded 24 May 1792, 74 acres, part of Pickall.

WR-10-306, Michael Heverly to Nicholas Ohr, recorded 6 Oct 1791, 21 acres, The Irregular Figure.

WR-13-13, George Darr to George Scott, recorded 17 Jan 1795, 213 acres, Part of the Rsy on Bear Swamp.

WR-15-311, Jacob Fluke to Philip Melchor, recorded 13 May 1797, 103 acres, Rsy on Learning, Add to Learning and part of the Rsy on Learning.

WR-18-206, Frederick Fox, 11 Apr 1799, MountSinai. Adjacent Betty's Good Will and Schaff's Purchase, west of the Fox Inn.

WR-19-206, Christian Benner to Frederick Fox, recorded 11 Apr 1799. Shaff's Purchase containing 93 acres and MountSinai containing 27 and 3/4 acres.

WR-22-477, Christian Benner, MountSinai, 17 Apr 1802.

WR-23-15, Exchange, Jacob Smith to Joseph Chapline, recorded 4 Jun 1802, 25 acres. (Author's Note: This tract was the subject of a court case. The court ultimately found in favor of Joseph Chapline Jr. The court case mentions Frederick Fox. See Maryland Archives Chancery Records at B 49 - 243 under Frederick Fox.)

WR-23-286, Joseph Chapline to Frederick Fox, recorded 9 Aug 1802, 25 acres. (Author's Note: This tract was the subject of a long court fight between Joseph Chapline Jr. and William William Chapline. The court finally ruled in favor of Joseph Chapline Jr. The court case mentions Frederick Fox. See Maryland Archives Chancery Records at B 49 - 243 under Frederick Fox.)

WR-25, Christian Routsawn (Routzong) to Conrad Miller, recorded 5 May 1807, 151 acres except 7 and 1/2 acres, Rsy on Mendal l.

WR-25-556, Frederick Fox to Conrad Miller, recorded 5 May 1804, 1/2 acre, I Hope It Is Well Done and Shettle.

WR-33-288, Jacob Smith to Isaac Fry, recorded 10 June 1808, 8 and 1/4 acres, I Hope It Is Well Done, Last Shift, and Rsy on Mend All.

BFG-6-569, Adam Hutzel to Ezra Warrenfeltz, recorded 1 Apr 1861, 162 and 1/2 acres and 17 perches, Long Dispute Ended.

BFG-6-680, Ezra Warrenfeltz to Wm J. Kepler, recorded 7 May 1861, 162 and 1/2 acres and 17 perches, Long Dispute Ended.

BGF-7-56, William J. Kepler and Anna M. Kepler, his wife, to John Mentzer and Martha E. Mentzer, his wife, recorded 30 Jun 1862, 3 acres and 66 perches. (Author's Note: This land became the Reno School site.)

HGO-1-506, The Rsy on Part of the Rsy on Drunkard's Not Mistaken, resurveyed 28 Oct 1789, 1 acre.

HGO-1-633, Discontentment, resurveyed 18 Mar 1793, 244 acres.

HGO-1-667, William Kouds, More Bad Than Good, resurveyed 18 Nov 1792, 265 acres.

THO-1, Survey for the Add to Little Worth, Christian Koogle, surveyed 2 May 1796, 82 and 1/4 acres.

THO-1-108, George Shoup, I Wish There Was More, resurveyed 27 Oct 1796, 136 acres.

THO-1-365, Abraham Miller, Miller's Purchase, surveyed 9 Dec 1814, 5 acres.

THO-1-365, Valentine Bowlus, Boot and Strap, surveyed 9 Nov 1814, 2 and 1/4 acres.

324-321, John Routzahn to Stanley F. Young, recorded 3 Apr 1918, 175 acres and 151 square perches.

Unplotted Land Records of Frederick County

362-314, St. Mary's Academy to Ulrica Dahlgren Pierce, recorded 4 May 1927, 10 acres.

368-32, Board of Education to George L. Miller, the Reno School property, recorded 25 Aug 1928, 1 acre.

388-316, Stanley F. Young and Charlotte O. L. Young, his wife, to H. Noel Haller and Mary Louise Haller, his wife, recorded 21 Aug 1933, 175 acres and 151 square perches.

388-317, Stanley F. Young to H. Noel Haller, recorded 21 Aug 1935, 175 acres, and 151 square perches.

421-320, George L. Miller to Everett Moser, the Reno School property, 12 Sep 1939, 1 acre.

433-241, Josiah Pierce to Vernon E. Hutzell, recorded 27 Jan 1942, 9+ acres around the Dahlgren Chapel.

438-345, Everett Moser to Murvil L. and Edna I. Toms, the Reno School property, 19 Apr 1943, 1 acre plus 5 acres.

722-403, Edna E. Hewitt to Roy G. and Iona M. Routzahn, recorded 28 Apr 1965, _ acres, the Dahlgren Chapel or immediate vicinity.

2114-0200, Iona M. Routzahn to Central Maryland Heritage League, Inc., made 14 July 1995, the Dahlgren Chapel or immediate vicinity.

2186-0781, Central Maryland Heritage League, Inc. to United States of America, 10 May 1996, the Dahlgren Chapel or immediate vicinity.

Frederick County Court Records, B-103, recorded 22 Nov 1749, Nehemiah Ogdon to Thomas Crampton, Deed of Gift.

Frederick County Circuit Court, No. 4789 Equity, Public Sales, Valuable Farming Land, the Fox Inn property.

Unplotted Washington County Land Records

The following listing is by Washington County Land Record reference number sequence, i.e. entries appear in the following order:
From A-1 to Z-9
From AA-1 to ZZ-9
From AAA-1 to ZZZ-9
From 1-1 to 9-9

A-368, Jacob Soufrank to Frederick Fox, Sharpsburg, half Lot #4, recorded 27 Nov 1778, 51 foot and 1/2 in breadth and 206 foot in length.

A-536, Frederick Fox to Philip Waggoner, Sharpsburg #55, recorded 29 Apr 1779, containing 20 perches in breadth and 40 perches in length.

C-510, Frederick Fox to Adam Deats, Sharpsburg, part of Lot #4, recorded 8 Nov 1783, containing 51 feet and an half foot in breadth and 206 feet in length.

D-579, Jacob Nafe to Frederick Fox, Sharpsburg, Lot #5, recorded 7 Dec 1785, containing 103 foot in breadth and 206 feet in length.

G-441, Frederick Fox to Jacob Houser, a Sharpsburg Lot, 14 Jul 1791.

G-442, 1791, Frederick Fox to Jacob House, Lot #6, Sharpsburg.

G-443 18 Jul 1791, Frederick Fox selling under the will of John Fox.

G-444 18 Jul 1791, Frederick Fox selling under the will of John Fox.

G-445 18 Jul 1791, Frederick Fox selling under the will of John Fox.

G-754, Joseph Shough to Christena Fox widow, Sharpsburg, Lot #145, recorded 25 Jun 1792, containing 103 feet in breadth and 206 feet in length.

H-601, Peter Conn to Frederick Fox, Sharpsburg, Lot #145, recorded 31 Mar 1794, containing 82 and 1/2 feet in breadth and beginning 31 feet back from front and from thence 200 feet back.

I-434, John Mansberger to John Booth and Jonas Hogmire, recorded 17 Dec 1795, 585 acres, Partnership, except 101 acres of Newcomer's Purchase.

P-583, Christena Fox to Jacob Reel, Sharpsburg Lot #145, recorded 14 Apr 1804, containing 51 and 1/2 feet in breadth and 103 feet in length.

W-285, Frederick Fox to Peter Ham, a Sharpsburg Lot, recorded 12 Sep 1810, containing 20 perches in breadth and 40 perches in length.

Liber 239, Folio 18, Charles M. Hewitt and Edna E. Hewitt, his wife, to Cecil W. Morgan and wife, recorded 3 Dec 1946, 10.9 acres. Beginning at a large stone in the south margin of said highway, said stone being 71.5 feet southeast from the northeast corner of the stone foundation of the dwelling located upon the parcel of land hereby conveyed, and running thence crossing the highway.

GG-29-878, Michael Easterday to Henry Miller, recorded 31 May 1884, 68 perches, part of Fox's Last Shift.

IN-19-727, Peter Showman to Edward L. Boteler, recorded 2 Apr 1867, 29 and 1/4 acres.

IN-8 53, 442-443, William Booth and Andrew Hogmire, Trustees, to Daniel Richard, recorded 2 Feb 1854, 12 and 1/2 acres, part of Partnership. Beginning at the end of the first line of Joseph Long's second part of Partnership and running thence with the second line of said part.

MM-33, 870, John Booth and Jonas Hogmire, Trustees, to Peter Gittle, recorded 21 Jan 1832, 1/2 acre, part of Partnership. Beginning for said small parcel of land at a stone planted on the north side of the turnpike road and running from thence.

UU-40, Henry Nyman to Henry Miller, recorded 9 May 1839, 8 acres and 18 perches, excepting a road one perch wide for the public, part of Swearingen's Disappointment. Beginning for the part hereby conveyed at a Persimon tree standing at the end of the fourth line of a deed from the said Nyman to Joseph Knox for part of the aforesaid tract of land and bearing date the 17th day of April 1839, and running thence with the 1st line of Swearingen's Disappointment.

WW-41, 521-523, John Booth and Jonas Hogmire to John Nicodemus, recorded 16 Sep 1840, 46 and 1/4 acres, part of Partnership. Beginning at a stone and a marked Chesnut Oak tree it being the end of the second line of the deed from Jonas Hogmire and John Booth to John Hess for 48 acres.

Unplotted Land Records of Washington County

GBO-81, 336, Joseph Ennis and Juliann Ennis, his wife, to Madeleine V. Dahlgren, recorded 8 Sep 1881, 6 and 1/2 acres. Beginning at the north corner of the whole tract now owned by the said M. V. Dahlgren.

GBO-100, 619, Mauche H. Meline to Madeleine V. Dahlgren, recorded 18 Jul 1893, 1 acre. Beginning at a point in the south boundary line of the turnpike road running between Boonsboro and Frederick and adjoining the land of said Madeline Vinton Dahlgren.

W-MC-KK 4 70, 347, John Booth and Jonas Hogmire Trustees to Peter Gittle, recorded 27 Jan 1872, 30 and 1/2 acres, part of Partnership. Beginning at the end of 80 perches reversed on the 29h line of said land called Partnership and reversing said 29th line.

W-MC-KK 4 70, 348, John Booth and Jonas Hogmire, Trustees, to Ephraim Geeting, recorded 29 Jan 1872, 10 and 1/2 acres and 13 perches, part of Partnership. On the south side of the Boonsboro and Sharpsburg turnpike beginning at a stone planted on the south margin of said road it being the beginning of the deed from Phillip Pry and wife to Joseph Snively bearing date _ May 1871 and running thence.

330-475, Charles M. Hewitt to Mitchell H. Dodson and Bette J. Dodson, his wife, recorded 2 Dec 1957, 3 and 7/10 acres, the Mountain House at Turner's Gap. Beginning at a large stone on the south margin of said highway, said stone being seventy-one and five-tenths (71.5) feet southeast from the northeast corner of the stone foundation of the dwelling now owned and occupied by Cecil W. Morgan and wife, said stone also being the beginning of the deed from Charles M. Hewitt and wife to Cecil W. Morgan and wife dated November 29, 1946, and recorded in Liber No. 239, folio 18, one of the land records of Washington County, and running thence.

Out Lot to Lot #1 in Sharpsburg, Maryland, Frederick Fox to Peter Ham, indenture made 12 Sep 1810. Obtained from Doug Bast of the Boonesborough Museum of History in Boonsboro, Maryland. This document identifies the Frederick Fox of the Fox's Gap area as the Frederick Fox of Warren County, Ohio, in 1810. Also see the letter from Jacob Reel of Sharpsburg to Michael and Frederick Fox of Warren County, Ohio, about the death of their mother Christiana Fox (on *Fox's Gap in Maryland* Kodak Photo CD-Rom computer disc). Tombstones in the Gebhart Cemetery in Miamisburg, Ohio, also tie members of the Frederick Fox family and their in-laws to Frederick County, Maryland.

Land Patent Liber 2, Folio 413, Valley Mills, resurveyed 4 Feb 1828, 88 and 3/8 acres. Beginning for the whole at a bounded white oak tree on the north side of a mill dam and running thence.

Liber E, Folio 677, George Fidler to Jesse Reeder, recorded 7 Dec 1787, 66 acres, part of the Resurvey on Seven Mountains. Seven Mountains lying and being in the county and state aforesaid begininning for said part at the end of 31 perches on the 1st line of said resurvey and running thence.

Liber AA, Folio 637, Caspar Snavely to William Cost, recorded 24 Oct 1815, 1 and 1/2 acres and 13 perches, part of Showman's Forrest. Beginning for said part at a stone planted at the end of a line of a tract called Elk Hill near Frederick Rohrer's merchant mill and running thence with the line of said Elk Hill.

Wives Identified in Land Records

The following listing is in alphabetical order by the last name of the husband.

Husband's Name	Wife's Name	Reference	
Arnold, David	Mary	FCLR	AF-9-541
Ascherman, Samuel	Malinda	FCLR	TG-3-298
Baley, John	Annabellah	FCLR	L-276
Beachley, Daniel	Hannah	FCLR	CM 2-379
Beachley, John W.	Marietta	FCLR	TG 9-427
Biser, Tilghman	Mary Ann	FCLR	ES 3-57
Booker, Bartholomew	Margaret	FCLR	WR 12, 358-364
Booker, Philip	Catherine	FCLR	S-389
Boteler, Edward L.	Prudence C.	FCLR	WR 23-286
Bottenberg, William	Christina	FCLR	WR 34-313
Chapline Jr, Joseph	Abigail	FCLR	WR 23-286
Chapline Sr, Joseph	Ruhamah	FCLR	F-211
Coffman, James W.	Mary	FCLR	WIP 9-148
Dodson, Mitchell H.	Bette J.	WCLR	330-475
Dorcas, William	Sarah	FCLR	TG 3-396
Ennis, Joseph	Julian	WCLR	GBO 81, 336
Everhart Jr, Jacob	Eliza	FCLR	JS 42-481
Flook, Jacob	Elizabeth	FCLR	WR-15-311
Fox, Frederick	Catharine	WCLR	A-536
Fox, Frederick	Susannah	FCLR	WR 32-28
Fox, John	Christiana	FCLR	K-499-500

(Signed by his mark "H". Lot #269 in Frederick Town. The author does not believe this John Fox was the John Fox of Fox's Gap. Perhaps John George Fox identified in Frederick church records.)

Husband's Name	Wife's Name	Reference	
Grim (Trim), Alexander	Barbara	FCLR	L-649
Haller, H. Noel	Mary Louise	FCLR	Liber 388 Page 317
Hawkins, Thomas	Elizabeth	FCLR	H-53
Hepburn, John	Mary	FCLR	N-57
Hewitt, Charles M.	Edna E.	FCLR	722-403
Hutzell, John	Elizabeth	WCLR	78-234
Joel, Henry	Anne	FCLR	K-1278
Jones, William H.	Catherine	FCLR	TG 8-651
Keephart, Joseph	Catherine	FCLR	WR 7-531
Kepler, William	Anna M.	FCLR	BGF-7-561
Kefauver, George H.	Maryl R.	FCLR	WIP 9-148
Koogle, John W.	Sarah E.	FCLR	TG 3-396
Layman, Ludwick	Elizabeth	FCLR	WR 12-56
Layman, Peter	Catherine	FCLR	WR 27-543
Ludy, Peter	Christiana	FCLR	WR 42-550
McEntire, John	Elizabeth	FCLR	F-548
Menter, John	Martha E.	FCLR	AR-11-311
Methard, George	Christina	FCLR	WR 31-478
Miller, George L.	Orpha M.	FCLR	368-32
Miller, Henry	Susan	FCLR	TG 12-434
Miller, Michael	Magdelena	FCLR	WR 36-85
Murdock, John	Harriet C.	WCLR	TG 12-435
Ringer, John	Sidney	FCLR	JS 42-481

Wives Identified in Land Records

Husband's Name	Wife's Name	Reference	
Ringer, Mathias	Susannah	FCLR	K-758
Robinett, George	Catherine	FCLR	H-448
Routzahn, Jacob	Christiana	FCLR	JS 30-58-61
Routzahn, Roy G.	Iona A.	FCLR	722-403
Rudy, Richard B.	Helen	FCLR	Liber 605 Page 469
Sanner, Vincent	Susan	FCLR	TG-3-298
Shaaf, Casper	Alice	FCLR	K-1373
Shafer, John	Catherine	WCLR	GG(29) 877-8
Sheffer (Shafer), George P.	Amanda D.	FCLR	TG 5-194
Sheffer (Shafer), Philip	Sarah	FCLR	JS 25-372
Slifer, William	Lydia Ann	FCLR	Liber WBT 10, Folio 361
Smith, Jacob	Elizabeth	FCLR	WR 33-288
Smith, Joseph	Easter	FC Wills	GME-2-651
Shidler, George	Margret	FCLR	L-69
Soufrank, Jacob	Augarty	WCLR	A-368
Swearingen, Joseph	Ruth	FCLR	WR 34-315
Teem (Team), John	Christina	FCLR	P-632
Widmeyer, William	Madelain	FCLR	WR 13-488
Wilson, Josiah	Jamima	FCLR	N-273
Wise, John W.	Lana	FCLR	WIP 9-148
Young, Jacob	Fanney	FCLR	WR 13-621
Young, Stanley F.	Charlotte O. L.	FCLR	Liber 388 Page 317

Part III

Individual Plotted Land Records

Land Records from the

Maryland Hall of Records

(MdHR)

Maryland State Archives

Surveys and Patents

Note: Frederick County was part of Prince Georges County until 1748. Washington County was part of Frederick County until 1776.

Maryland Hall of Records

The following are the plotted land tracts from records in the Maryland Archives Hall of Records in Annapolis, Maryland.

Addition to Friendship
Frederick Fox
IC P, 672-673
surveyed 9 May 1797
patented 27 May 1805
202 acres

Beginning at the end of the first line of a tract of land called David's Will.

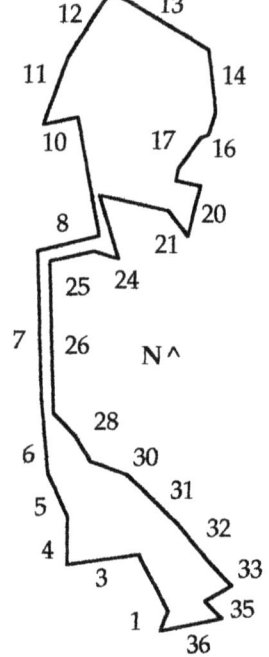

Addition to Tom's Gift
Robert Evans
GS 1, 209-211
surveyed 16 October 1747
50 acres

Beginning at a bounded white oak standing by the side of a little branch a draft of Catoctin Creek.

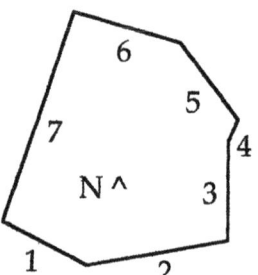

Apple Brandy
Jacob Fulwiler
D D, 75
surveyed 31 October 1791
14 acres

Beginning at a bounded Spanish oak near the top of the South Mountain.

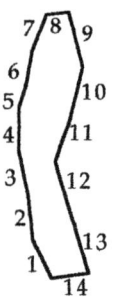

Apple Brandy
Barbara Flook
IC N, 191
resurveyed 2 December 1795
242 and 1/2 acres

Beginning for the outlines thereof at a stone planted at the end of the 25th line of a tract of land called the Rsy on Whiskey Alley.

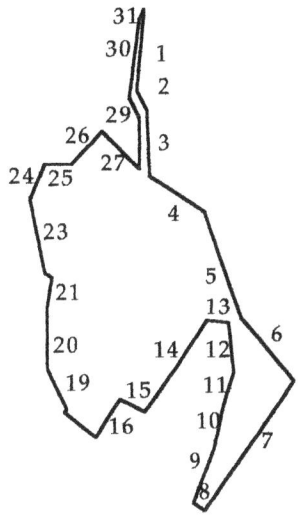

Ashbough
Tilghman Baker
BC & GS 47, 455
surveyed 18 January 1771
50 acres

Beginning at a bounded black oak standing on the north side of a hill to the south of a hollers near Lannafield and to the right hand of the road leading from Stull's Mill to Robert Turner's.

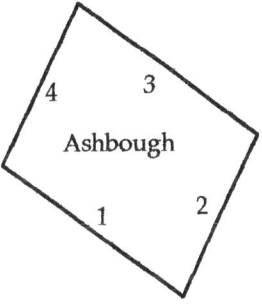

Bad Enough
Joseph Chapline
Y & S 6, 327-329
11 August 1753
136 acres

Beginning at the end of sixty perches in the seventy first line of Col. Edward Spriggs' Rsy on the Add to Pile's Delight.

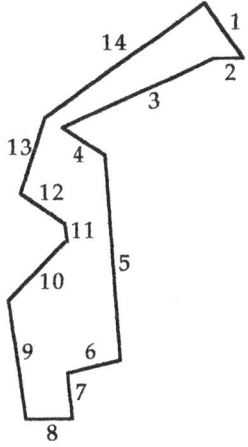

Badham's Refuse
Joseph Chapline
BC & GS 12, 92-3
surveyed 12 May 1759
50 acres

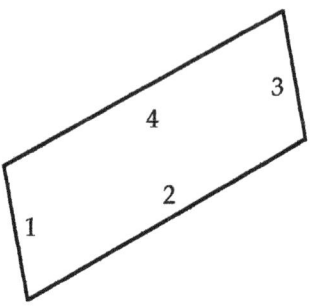

Beginning at a bounded white oak standing near the head of a little spring a draft of Travis Cabin Branch that falls into Potomac.

Burrell's Disappointment
James Williamson
BC & GS #1, 330
surveyed 15 February 1755
21 acres

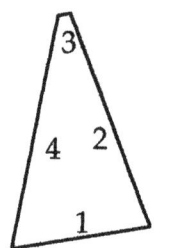

Beginning at a bounded white oak standing on the east side of the Elk Ridge Mountain and near a spring called the Poplar Spring.

Beam's Purchase
Jacob Beam
GGB 2, 141-142
resurveyed 9 September 1786
325 and 1/4 acres

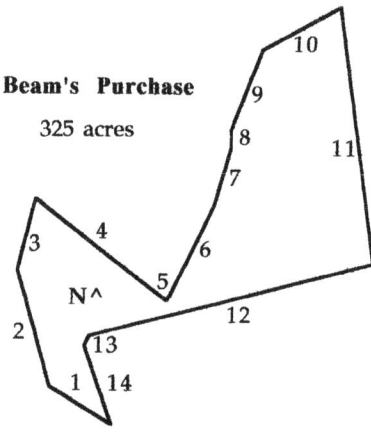

Beginning for the outlines of the whole by virtue of before mentioned warrant at the end of thirty eight perches on the south line of Pile's Grove where stands a stone marked I B it being the beginning of part of Pile's Grove one of the originals.

Betty's Good Will
Robert Evans
BC & GS 4, 195-196
surveyed 15 October 1747
50 acres

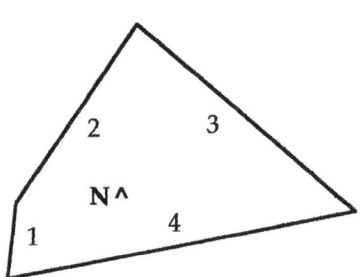

Beginning at a bounded white oak standing at the foot of Shanandore Mountain near the wagon road that goes from Teague's Ferry to Monocacy Town.

Blooming Plains
John Shuey
B D, 228-229
resurveyed 25 May 1813
patented 4 March 1815
318 and 1/2 acres

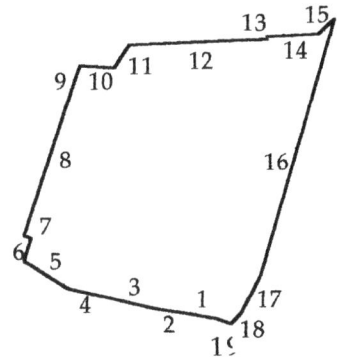

Beginning for the outlines of the rsy at a large stone marked BP set up on the south side of the road leading from Frederick Town through Fox's Gap in the South Mountain to Sharpsburg about a quarter of a mile to the westward of Jacob Snyder's house and running thence along said road.

Bloomsbury
James Wardrop
BY & GS 5, 607-609
surveyed 9 August 1750
104 acres

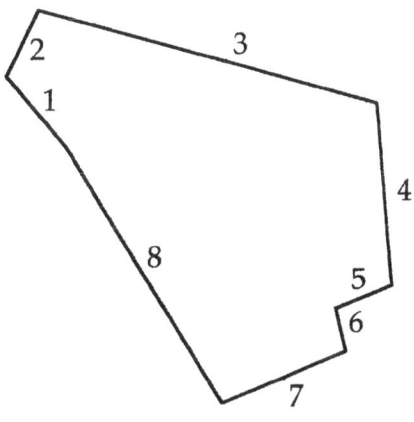

Beginning at a bounded white oak standing on the side of a hill about half a mile north east of John Burger's house between two mountains.

Chapline's Ill Will
Adam Fockler
IC B, 703-704
surveyed 15 March 1786
15 and 1/4 acres

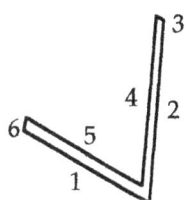

Beginning at the end of the eleventh course of a tract of land called Contentment granted to a certain Joseph Chapline the fifteenth day of September 1764.

Charlemount Pleasant
Samuel Ogle Esqr.
BC & GS 9, 405-406
surveyed 1 January 1745
100 acres

Beginning at a bounded black oak standing on a small hill to the eastward of a spring that falls in Little Antietam about half a mile to the southward of Robert Turner's.

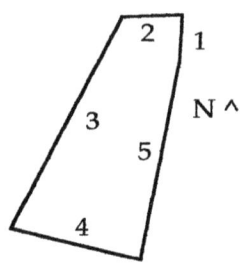

Christie's Folly
Richard Smith
BC & GS 1, 173-174
surveyed 17 October 1750
200 acres

Beginning at the beginning tree of Capt. Samuel Magruder's land running thence.

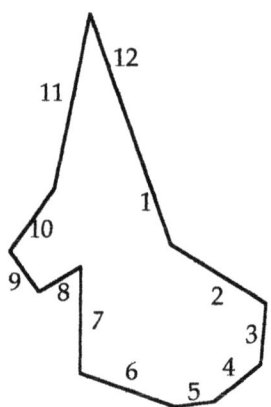

Contentment
Joseph Chapline
BC & GS 30, 259-261
Resurveyed 20 August 1764
1153 acres

Beginning at a bounded white oak it being the beginning tree of a tract of land called Jerico.

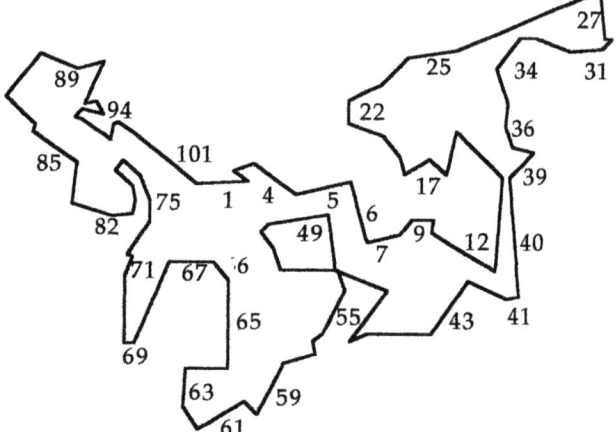

Cool Spring
James Wardrop
BY & GS 5, 608-609
surveyed 17 May 1750
75 acres

Beginning at a bounded white oak standing on the top of a hill about two hundred yards from the wagon road that leads through Frederick Town and about a mile from John Burger's.

Cornucopia
George Scott
IC I, 570-571
surveyed 12 March 1790
260 and 1/2 acres

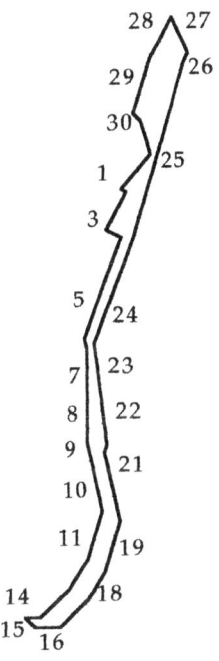

Beginning at a bounded black oak the beginning tree of a tract of land called Jacob's Broom surveyed for Henry Powlis.

Cuckold's Horns
Robert Evans
BY & GS 1, 611-612
surveyed 14 October 1747
150 acres

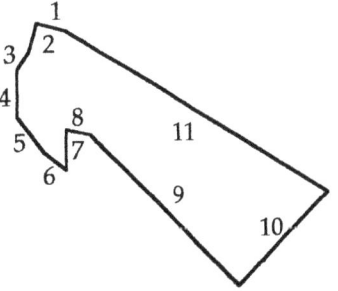

Beginning at the beginning tree of a tract of land called Ram's Horns.

Maryland Hall of Records

Daniel's Race Ground
Henry Ulrick
IC K, 288
surveyed 10 October 1792
25 acres

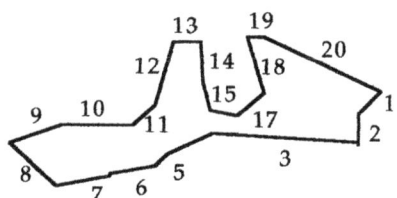

Beginning at a stone standing near the main road leading from Fox's towards Sharpsburg and near the end of the third line of a tract of land called Fredericksburg.

Dawson's Purchase
Thomas Dawson
LB #C, 196-8
surveyed 14 May 1741
140 acres

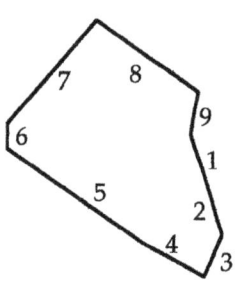

Beginning at a bounded white oak standing on the east side of the Blue Ridge on the south side of a small branch called the Cabin Branch which falls into Catoctin Creek about three hundred yards below the place called Phillip's Cabin.

David's Will
David Bowser
BC & GS 27, 396
surveyed 24 December 1763
49 acres

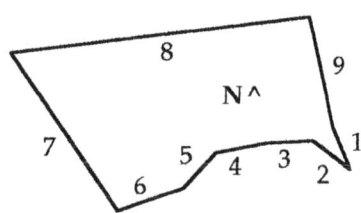

Beginning at a bounded white oak standing in the head of Grimes's Run on the east side of the South Mountain being a draft of Catoctin Creek.

Deeffer Snay
Adam Smeltzer
BC & GS 51, 252-253
resurveyed 27 December 1774
117 acres

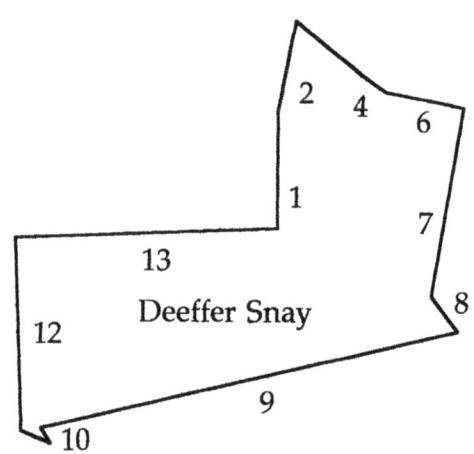

Beginning for the out lines thereof at a bounded black oak it being the beginning tree of a tract of land called the Rsy on Exchange and is also the beginning of the afsd part of the said Rsy on Exchange one of the originals.

Discontent
Peter Slusser
IC I, 99-100
surveyed 3 April 1796
4 and 1/2 acres

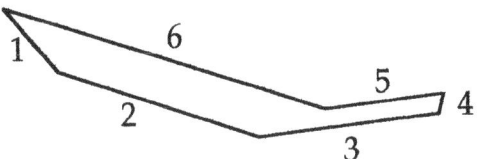

Beginning at the end of the seventh line of a tract of land called the Rsy on Content granted a certain Ralph Hickingbottom the 14th day of January 1760.

Dorsey's Risque
Edward Dorsey
BC & GS 2, 112-3
surveyed 12 December 1754
158 acres

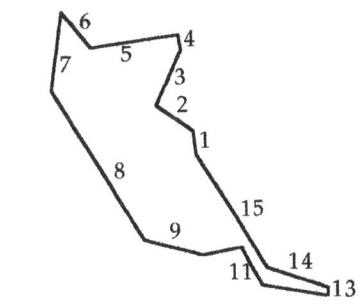

Beginning at a bounded hickory standing near a parcel of lime stone rocks and it being the beginning tree of a tract of land belonging to Thomas Walker.

Ebenezer
Christian Harsman
IC N, 188-189
surveyed 20 June 1790
120 acres

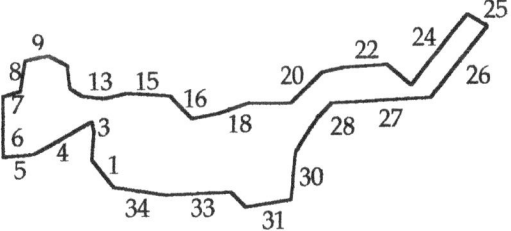

Beginning at a stone standing at the end of the twenty second line of that tract of land called the Rsy on Stricker's Timberland resurveyed for Andrew Arnold on the 4th June 1793 and running thence with said land.

Elk Hill
David Ross
BC & GS 14, 18-19
surveyed 17 March 1761
330 acres

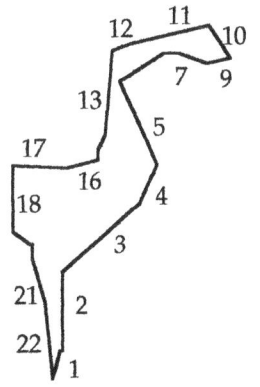

Beginning for the second part called Elk Hill at the end of the third line of the afsd land called Burrell's Disappointment.

(The) Exchange
Daniel Dulany
patented to Daniel and Walter Dulany
BC & GS 27, 578
surveyed 5 October 1742
100 acres

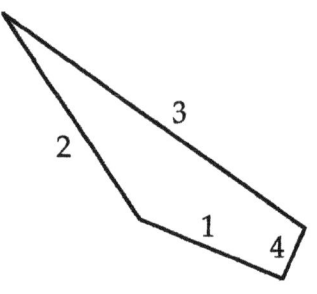

Beginning at a boundred oak standing by the side of a spring called Punch Spring it being a draft of Abrams Creek.

Exchange
Robert Evans
BY & GS 1, 610
surveyed 15 October 1747
50 acres

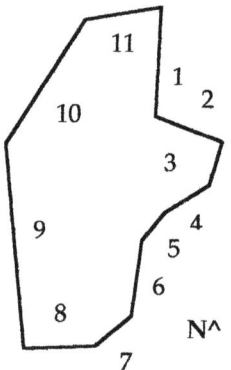

Beginning at a bounded Red Oak standing by the head of a little spring a draft of Catoctin Creek running thence.

Fellfoot
Thomas Swearingen
EI 2, 623-624
surveyed 12 June 1734
115 acres

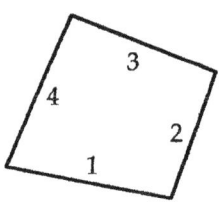

Beginning at a bounded white oak standing in the fork of Little Antietam about ten perches from a road commonly called the wagon road and running thence.

Fellowship
Doctor Charles Carroll of Annapolis
GS 1, 45-46
surveyed 17 July 1752
140 acres

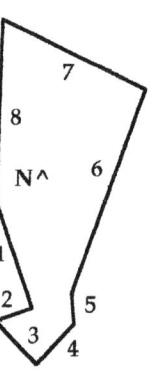

Beginning at a bounded white oak standing near Robert Turner's Spring which runs into Little Antietam it being also the bounded tree of a tract of land called Nelson's Folly belonging to said Turner.

Flonham
Philip Jacob Shafer
BC & GS 44, 439-440
patented 20 April 1774
36 acres

Beginning at a bounded white oak standing about a perch from the __ of a spring on the south side of the Shanandore Mountain on the right hand of the Main Road leading from Frederick Town to Fort Frederick.

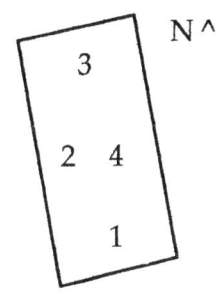

Forest
John Magrudar
AM 1, 365-366
examined and allowed 2 October 1733
300 acres

Beginning at a bounded hickory standing about half mile above the wagon road that goes from Conestoga to Opequon crosses a creek called Catoctin Creek which falls into Potomac River about six miles above Monocacy and running thence.

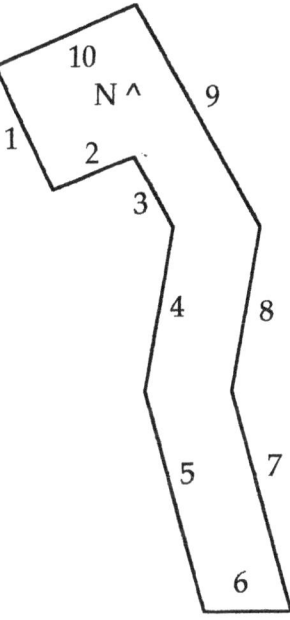

Forest
Osborn Sprigg
AM 1, 375-376
patented 10 June 1734
285 acres

Beginning at a bounded white oak standing near the head of a small branch on the north side of Conococheague Road near the Shanandore Mountains.

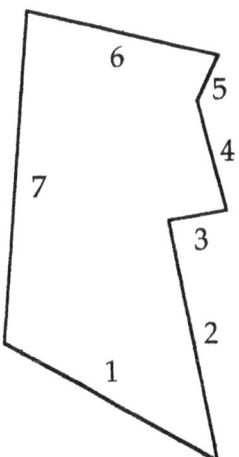

Maryland Hall of Records

Fox's Last Shift
Robert Smith
BC & GS 27, 331
examined and passed 5 October 1764
72 acres

Beginning at a bounded white oak tree standing on the north side of the main country road that leads from Frederick Town to Fort Frederick in the South Mountain.

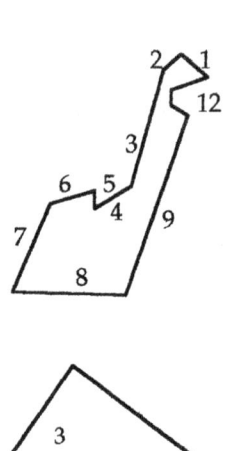

(The) Gap
Joseph Chapline
BC & GS 24, 270
surveyed 29 March 1761
50 acres

Beginning at the end of the third line of Wardrop's land called Curry's Old Place.

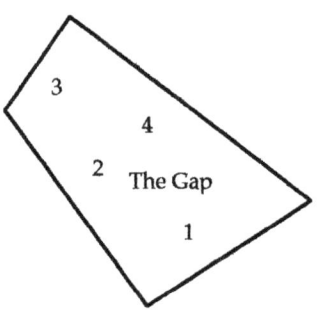

Gaver's Recovery
Peter Gaver
IC E 702-704
resurveyed 8 December 1789
197 acres

Beginning at a stone planted at the beginning of the Mountain one of the originals and marked BM 1789 and running thence with said land.

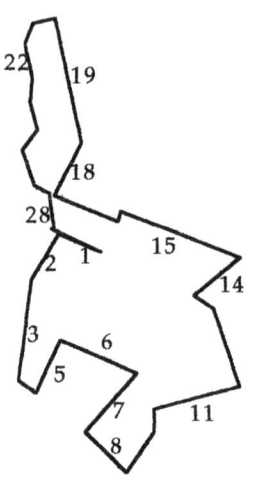

Good Hope
Joseph Chapline
IC I, 570-571
surveyed 10 February 1792
25 acres

Beginning at the end of the ninety first line of the Rsy of Hills Dales and the Vineyard and running thence.

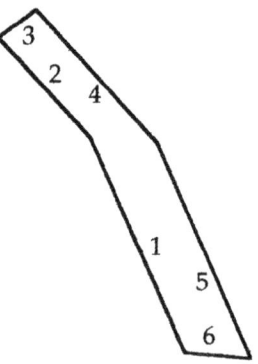

Nicholas Fink
BC & GS 27, 236-237
resurveyed 2 February 1764
478 acres

Beginning for the out lines of the whole by virtue of the before mentioned warrant at the original beginning tree.

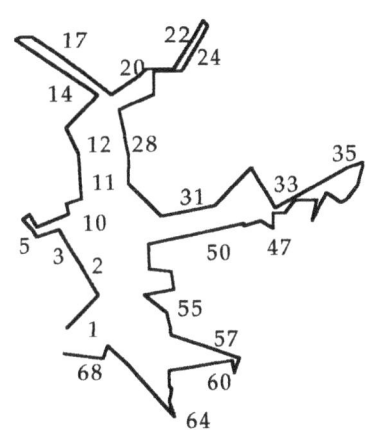

Gordon's Purchase
George Gordon
LG B, 1-2
24 October 1739
150 acres

Beginning at a bounded white oak standing on the stony knoll within one hundred yards of Little Antietam and by a place called the Middle Spring running thence.

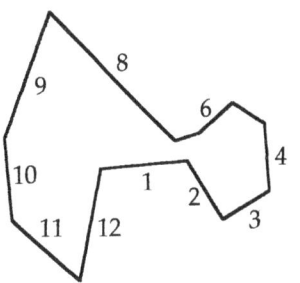

Grim's Fancy
Alexander Grim (Trim)
BC & GS 40, 114
surveyed 27 February 1764
50 acres

Beginning at a bounded black oak tree standing on the north side of the Main Road that leads from Frederick Town to Swearingen's Ferry and near to John Fox's house on the west side of the South Mountain.

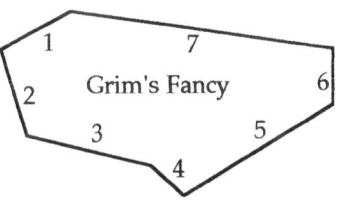

Hogyard
Daniel Dulany, Esq.
Patented to John George Arnold
LG E, 397
surveyed 7 October 1742
100 acres

Begining at a bounded white oak standing by parcel of rocks at the mouth of a branch called the Grindstone Branch a draft of Abrams Creek and running thence.

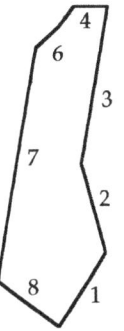

Horse Neck
John Tucker
BC & GS 14, 86-87
surveyed 28 July 1752
86 acres

Beginning at the end of the first line of a tract of land laid out for Osborn Sprigg conveyed to Thomas Wilson.

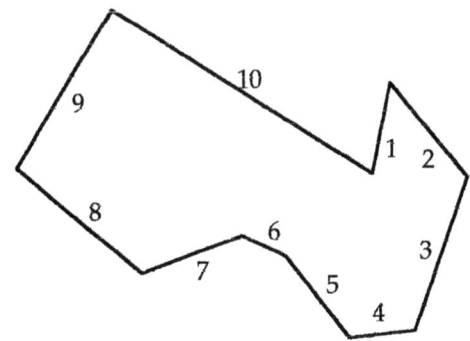

I Hope It Is Well Done
Bartholomew Booker
BC & GS 47, 31-33
resurveyed 1 January 1772
575 and 1/2 acres

Beginning tree of a tract of land called Mendall being also the beginning tree of a tract of land called the Rsy of Mendall.

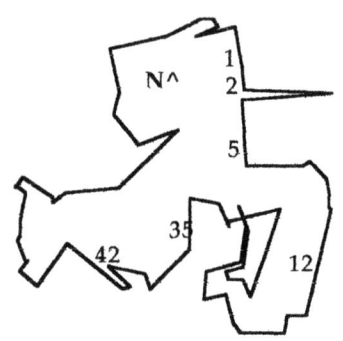

It's Bad Enough
Henry Peagley
IC L, 455
30 April 1798
14 and 1/4 acres

Beginning at a bounded white oak tree the beginning of a tract of land called Worse and Worse and running with it.

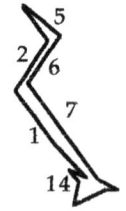

I Hope It Is So
Lodowick Keedy
IC H, 301
surveyed 2 October 1788
68 and 1/4 acres

Beginning at the end of twenty one perches in the ninth line of a tract called Park Hall.

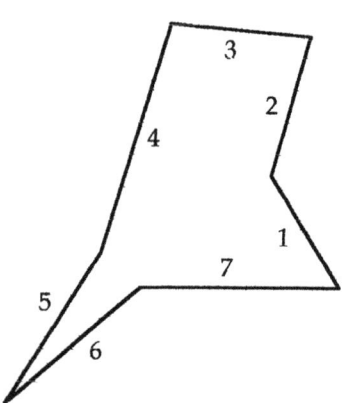

Ives Folly
Peter Slusser
IC I, 99-100
surveyed 3 April 1786
4 and 1/4 acres

Beginning at the end of thirty three perches in the fifth line of a tract of land called Smith's Choice granted a certain Daniel Dulany the 9th day of March 1752 and running thence with said land reversed.

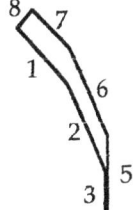

Knave's Good Will
Peter Smeltzer
IC A, 495
surveyed 16 October 1773
50 acres

Beginning at a bounded red oak standing on the edge of a hill and running thence.

Jacob's Broom (Brune)
Henry Poulis
IC B, 301
surveyed 27 March 1772
50 acres

Beginning at a bounded black oak standing on the east side of a tract of land called Lannafield near the foot of the South Mountain and on the west side thereof about half a mile from Robert Turner's House.

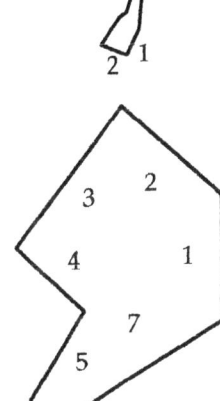

Jerico Hills
John Ridout
BC & GS 14, 19-21
surveyed 17 December 1760
922 acres

All that tract of land called Jerico Hills being the vacant land afsd lying and being in Frederick County.

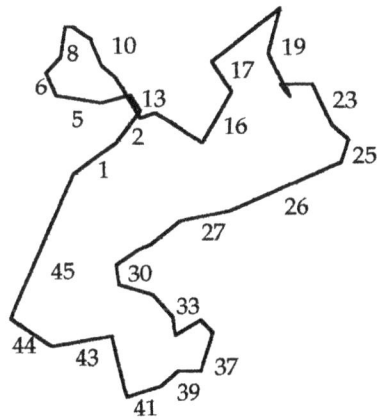

John's Delight
James Wardrop
BY & GS 5, 59
surveyed 17 May 1750
104 acres

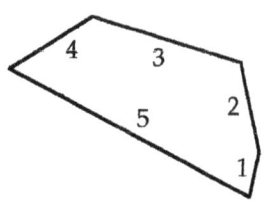

Beginning at a bounded white oak standing about thirty feet from a small run called Curry's Branch nigh the foot of Shanandore Mountain near Curry's Gap.

Josiah's (Last) Bit
Moses Chapline
patented to William Good
IC B, 480-481
20 April 1786
67 acres

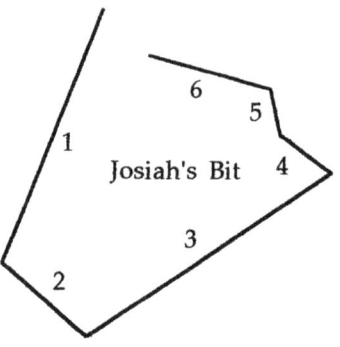

Beginning at the end of the twelfth line of the Second Rsy on Mount Pleasant laid out for said Chapline and the end of the second line of a tract of land called Mountain.

Kelly's Purchase
Thomas Kelly
BY & GS 4, 536-537
11 August 1753
256 acres

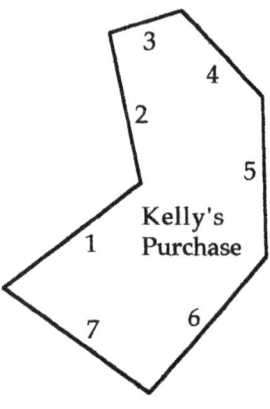

Beginning at a bounded black oak standing by the side of a valley near the head of Solomon Aldredge's Spring.

Killicrankee
William Good
BC & GS 41, 473
surveyed 30 August? 1770
36 acres

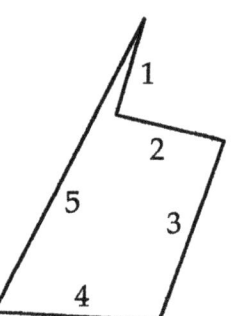

Beginning at the end of the seventh line of a tract of land called Volton's Seal.

Kizer's Lowden
John Summers
BC & GS 22, 89-90
surveyed 26 May 1763
110 acres

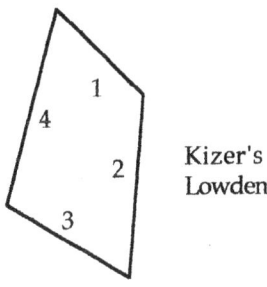
Kizer's Lowden

Beginning at a bounded white oak standing on the north side of the main road leading from Frederick Town to Fort Frederick between Robert Turner's plantation and Antietam Creek and by the side of a road that leads from Isaac Houser's to Chapline's Mill.

Learning
Frederick Garrison
BY & GS 4, 467-468
11 August 1753
50 acres

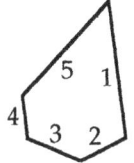

Beginning at a bounded white oak standing at the south east corner of a tract of land laid out for the said Chapline called the Exchange.

Little Meadow
Thomas Walker
BC & GS 5, 163-164
surveyed 21 December 1739
200 acres

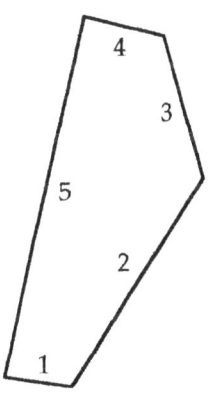

Beginning at a bounded hickory standing by the side of a meadow being a draft of Potomac River and within 30 poles of the wagon road that goes from Stull's Mill.

Loving Brother
George Sultiner
BY & GS 3, 427-428
surveyed 22 February 1752
100 acres

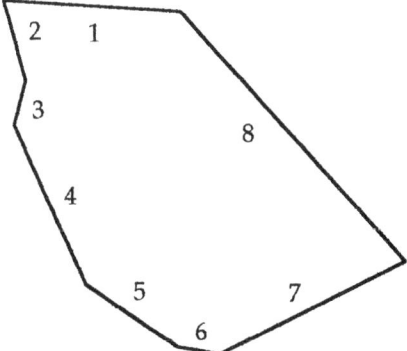

Beginning at a bounded red oak standing by the side of a little spring that runs into Catoctin Creek.

Lucky Hit
Samuel Baker
IC N, 16
surveyed 17 September 1792
50 acres

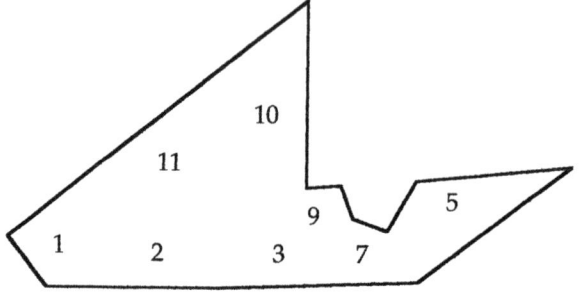

Beginning at the end of the fourth line of a tract of land surveyed for Andrew Bash called Bird's Bill.

Locust Valley
Frederick County
Unpatented Certificate 368, 1-25-4-83
Thomas Van Swearingen
surveyed 30 July 1790
384 acres

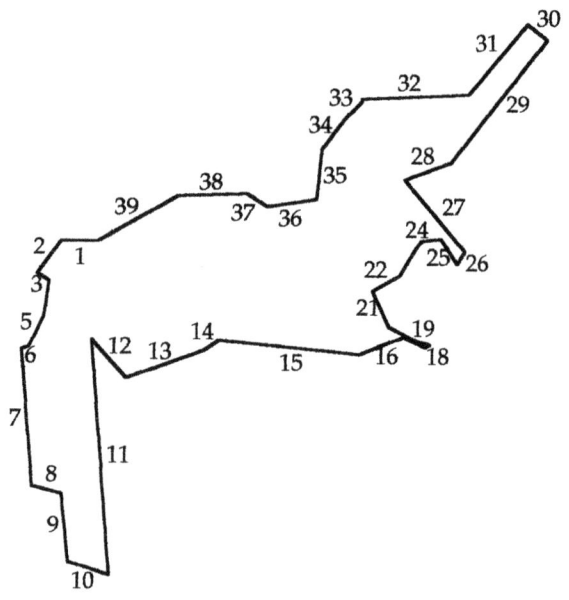

Beginning at a large rock marked TVS standing near the head of a small spring and in a gap of the South Mountain.

Martitany
Jacob Knave
Y & S 8, 514-516
surveyed 23 December 1752
50 acres

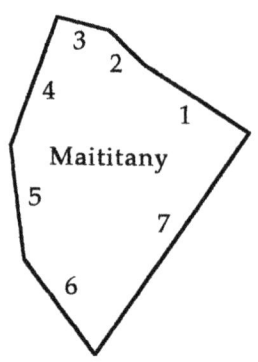

Beginning at a bounded white oak standing in the Hazel Branch a draft of Catoctin.

Mankine
Daniel Dulany and Walter Dulany
BC & GS 23, 363-364
surveyed 28 November 1741
231 acres

Beginning at a bounded red oak standing on a ridge near a small __ and near the main road.

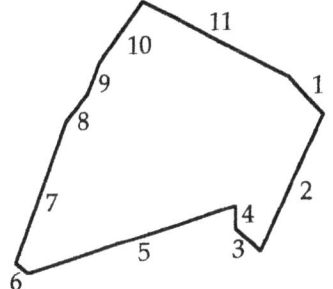

Martsome
Peter Baker
BC & GS 45, 27
surveyed 26 May 1763
50 acres

Beginning at a bounded white oak standing by the side of a branch falling from the end of the Short Hill Mountain down to Robert Turner's plantation being a draft of Little Antietam.

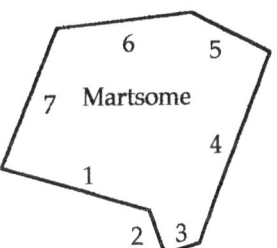

Mary's Cowpen
Casper Snavely
IC Q, 191
surveyed 6 April 1785
4 acres

Beginning at the end of the thirteenth line of a tract of land called Pile's Grove at a stone and running with said land reversed.

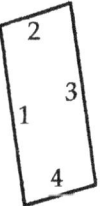

Miller's Hills
John Miller
IB G, 303-304
resurveyed 4 March 1813
180 acres

Beginning for the out lines of the whole at the end of the second line of a tract of land called Pile's Grove.

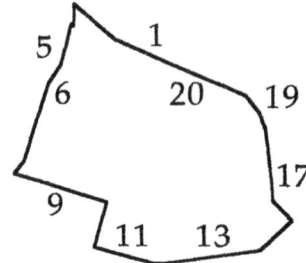

Mindall
Joseph Chapline
Y & S 7, 160
surveyed 12 December 1750
66 acres

Beginning at a bounded Spanish oak standing on a ridge about 100 yards from a little spring a draft of Catoctin Creek.

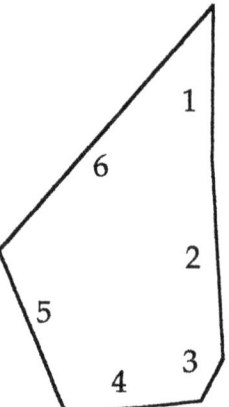

Mount Atlas
John Booth and Jonas Hogmire
IC M, 470-471
resurvey 19 December 1797
1072 and 1/2 acres

Beginning at the end of the third line of the Rsy on the Seven Mountains and running thence with said land reversed.

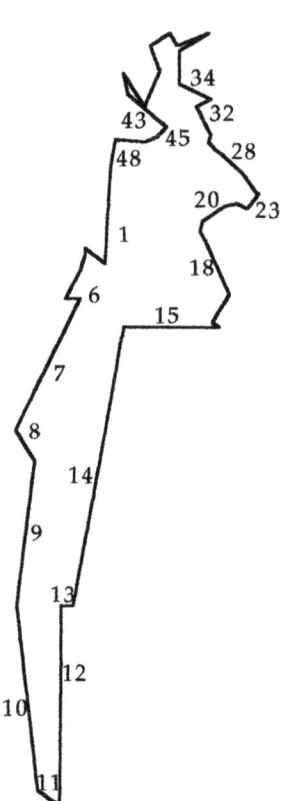

Mount Pleasant
Frederick Fox
IC H, 298
surveyed 10 January 1791
23 acres

Beginning at a rock stone marked at the north east end thus TV.

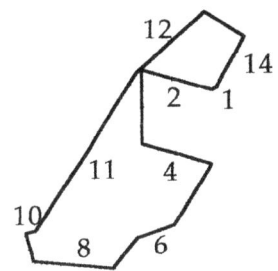

Mountain
John Baley
TI 3, 236-237
surveyed 27 September 1745
50 acres

Beginning at a bounded white oak tree standing on the side of an hill on the west side of Shanandore Mountain near the road that leads from Monocacy to Teague's Ferry running thence.

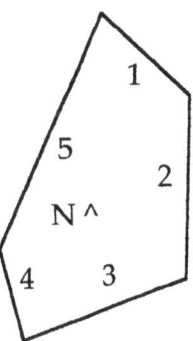

Nelson's Folly
Robert Turner
B, 336-338
recorded 5 March 1750
500 acres
surveyed 4 June 1734

Beginning at a bounded white oak standing on the south side of a draft of Antietam.

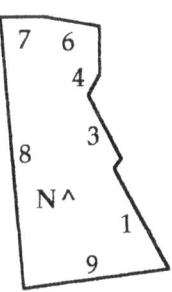

Newcomer's Purchase
John Mansberger
IC I, 713
resurveyed 5 January 1786
101 acres
A Resurvey on Fox's Last Shift

Beginning for the outlines of the rsy at the original beginning.

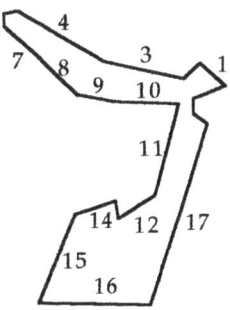

Nottingham
Isaac Brooke
BC & GS 7, 99-102
resurveyed 25 March 1753
550 acres

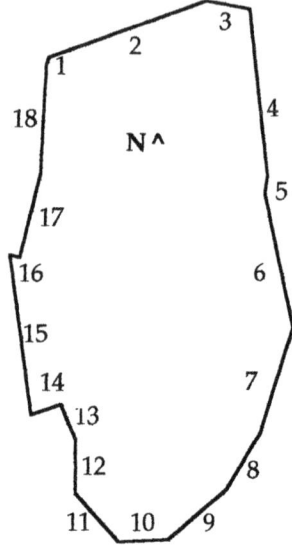

Beginning for the whole at a bounded black oak standing about one hundred and fifty yards from a branch of Little Antietam Creek it being the beginning tree of the original tract called Joyner's Fancy and the beginning tree of a tract of land called Charlemoont Pleasant taken up by Arthur Charlton and now in the possession of William Munsford and running thence with the first line of said Charlemount Pleasant.

Oxford
James Wardrop
BY & GS 5, 594
surveyed 9 August 1750
54 acres

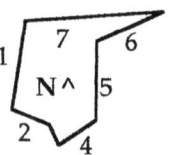

Beginning at a bounded black oak standing at the head of a valey that falls into a branch called John Crisles Spring Branch and about ten or fifteen yards of the Main Road that leads through Frederick Town by Robert Evans and on the north side of the said road.

Parks Hall
William Parks
AM 1, 236-7
9 April 1731
1550 acres

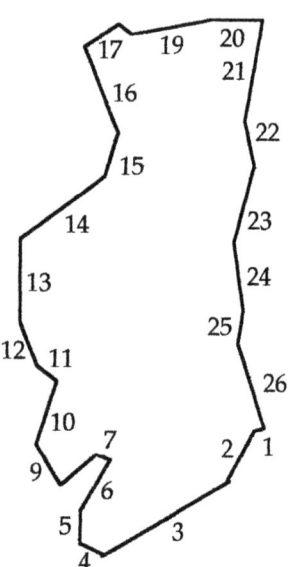

Beginning at a bounded white oak standing near the head of a spring on the west side of the second mountain not far from the road.

Pastures Green
William Good
IC B, 480-481
resurveyed 4 December 1784
290 acres
A resurvey of Mountain, Come by Chance, Killicrankey, Resurvey on Mount Pleasant, and Josiah's Bit.

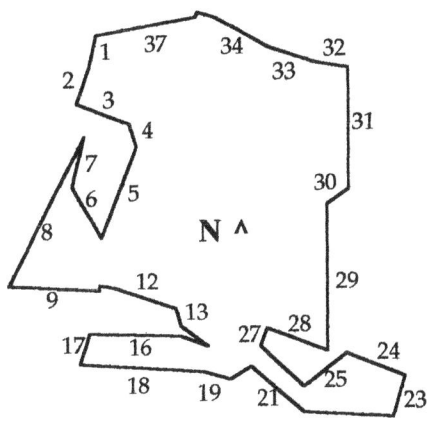

Beginning for the outlines of the whole by virtue of the before mentioned warrant at a stone standing at the end of thirty four perches in the third line of a tract of land called Pile's Grove and running thence with the second original.

Partnership
John Mansberger
IC K, 343-344
resurveyed 20 August 1794
685 acres
A resurvey of Newcomer's Purchase.

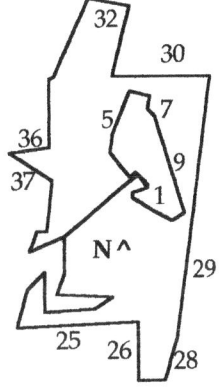

Beginning for the outlines of the rsy by virtue of the afsd warrant at a stone marked 1794 standing at the original beginning it being also the beginning tree of a tract of land called Swearingen's Disappointment.

Paul's Travels
Paul Rhodes
BC & GS 41, 4-5
surveyed 2 October 1769
40 acres

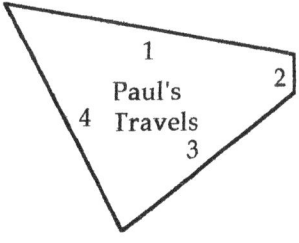

Beginning at a bounded white oak the beginning tree of a tract of land called Fellfoot.

Pegging Awl
Bartholomew Booker
BC & GS 41, 47
surveyed 12 May 1769
13 and 1/2 acres

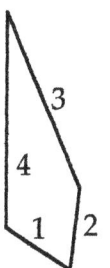

Beginning at a bounded white oak standing on the east side and near the South Mountain.

Maryland Hall of Records

Pickall
Bartholomew Booker
BC & GS 30, 214-216
resurveyed 3 February 1764
1224 acres

Beginning for the out lines of the whole by virtue of the before mentioned warrant at the beginning tree of a tract of land called John's Delight patented to James Wardrop which tree is a white oak standing by the side of the main road that leads from Frederick Town to Fort Frederick.

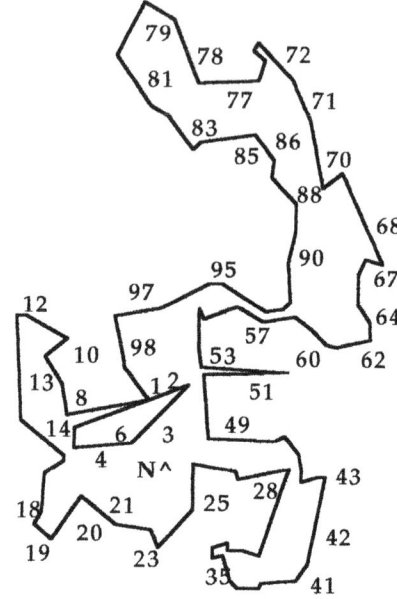

Pile's Grove
Richard Spriggs
EI 2, 478
14 August 1736
560 acres

Beginning at a bounded white oak standing near a small branch and near a large spring that makes into Antietam about half a mile above a road commonly called the wagon road.

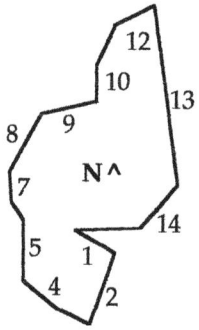

Peter's Neglect
Frederick Fox
JK T, 55-56
surveyed 1 May 1796
37 acres

Beginning at the end of the fifty third line of a tract of land called I Hope It Is Well Done granted Bartholomew Booker the twenty fifth day of September 1772.

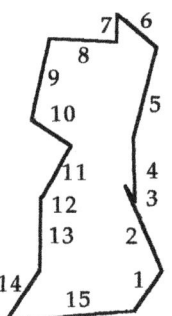

Poole's Delight Enlarged
Ashbury Sutton
GS 1, 65-66
resurveyed 4 September 1750
287 acres

Beginning at the original beginning tree of said Poole's Delight.

Raccoon
John Summer
BC & GS 45, 10-11
27 August 1770
253 acres

Beginning for the out lines thereof at the beginning tree of the original tract.

Racon
Jacob Hess (Hessing)
BC & GS 19, 310-311
10 April 1762
50 acres

Beginning at a bounded white oak standing on the south side of a road near the South Mountain.

Ram's Horn
Daniel Dulany, Esqr.
LG E, 346-348
surveyed 4 March 1739
494 acres

Begining at a bounded hickory standing on the west side of Abraham's Creek on the bank thereof being a draft of Potomac River and running thence.

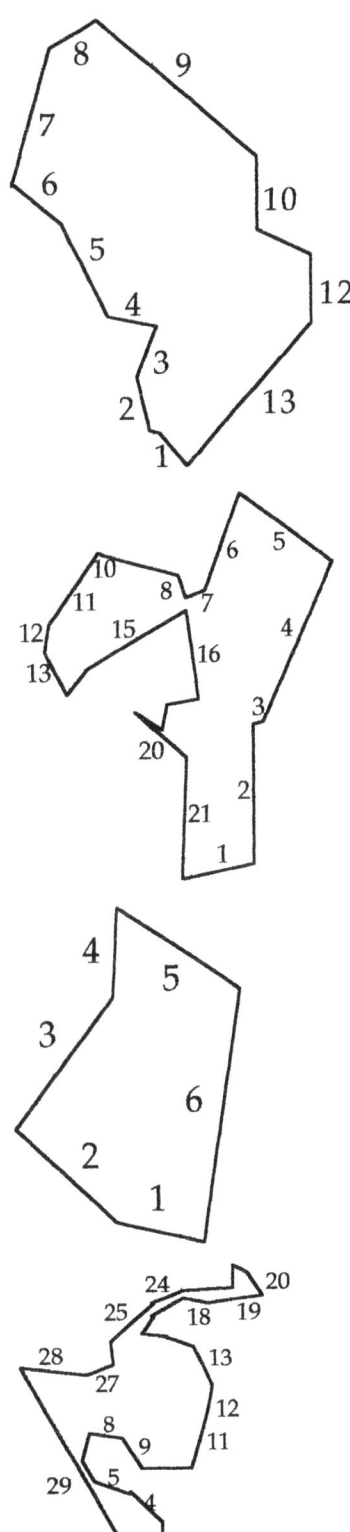

Maryland Hall of Records

Resurvey on Dearbought
James Wardrop
Y & S 7, 196-197
surveyed 18 September 1751
500 acres

Beginning at a bounded white oak it being the original beginning tree.

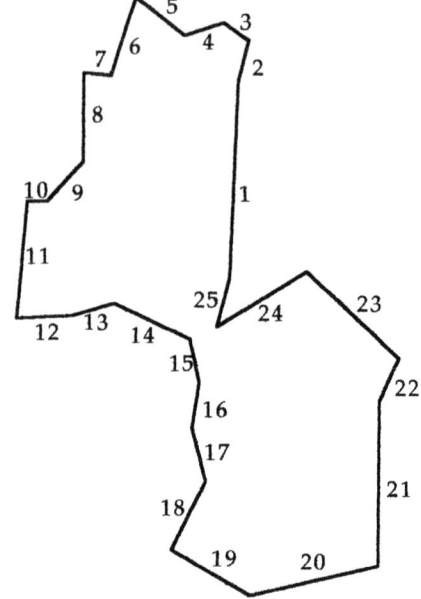

Resurvey on Exchange
Casper Shaff
BY & GS 4, 586-586
resurveyed 1 September 1751
275 acres

Begining at the original beginning tree.

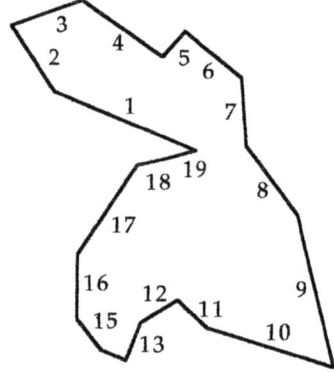

Resurvey on (The) Gap
Henry Beakley
IC N, 467-468
resurveyed 3 May 1798
219 and 1/2 acres

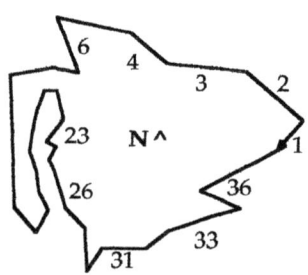

Resurvey on John's Delight
Maryland Historical Society
surveyed 20 April 1766
131 acres

Beginning for the outlines of the whole at the original beginning tree and running thence.

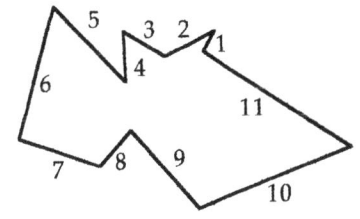

Resurvey on Learning, Addition to Learning, and part of the Resurvey on Learning
Jacob Flook
BC & GS 30, 225-226
resurveyed 22 May 1765
467 and 1/4 acres

Beginning for the out lines of the whole at the original beginning tree.

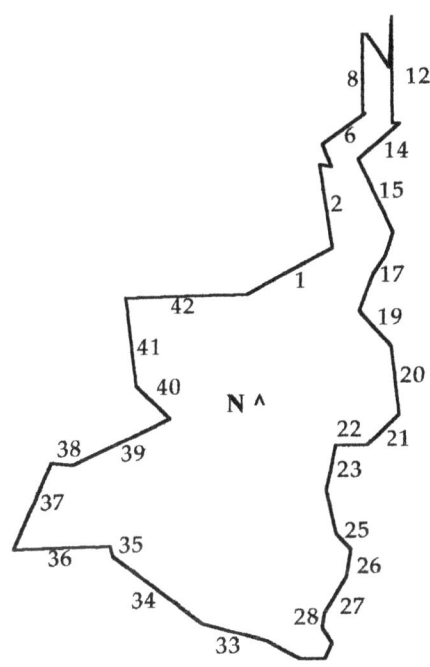

Resurvey on Tom's Gift
Joseph Chapline
BY & GS 28, 64-67
resurveyed 21 May 1764
1,012 acres

Beginning for the out lines of the whole by virtue of the before mentioned warrant at the original bounded tree.

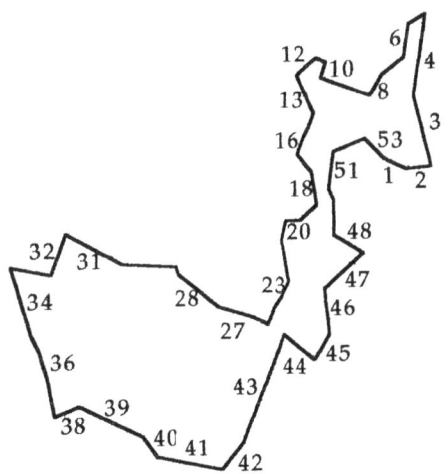

Resurvey of Roots Hill
Moses Chapline
BC & GS 14, 68-69
resurveyed 4 May 1759
300 acres

Beginning at the end of the first line of the said land called Roots Hills.

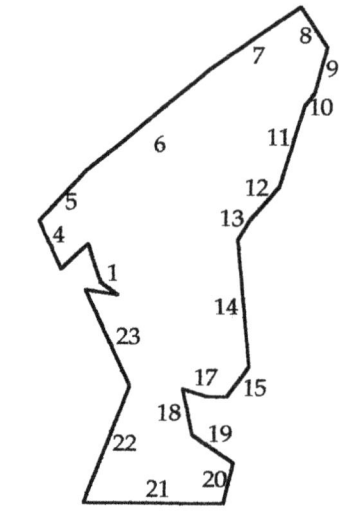

Resurvey on (The) Vineyard
William Stewart
assigned to Benjamin Tasker Sr and
Benjamin Tasker Jr
BC & GS 1, 164
resurveyed 10 September 1752
506 acres

Beginning at the original beginning tree.

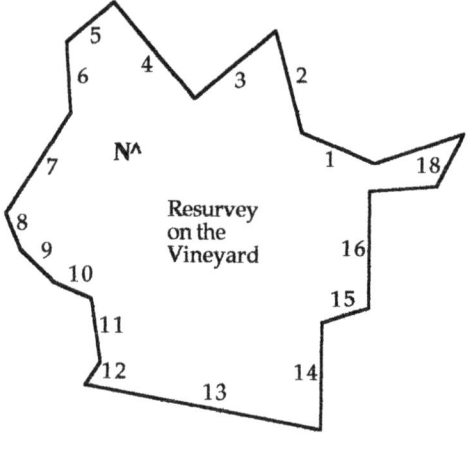

Resurvey on Watson's Welfare
Joseph Chapline
Y & S 7, 192
resurveyed 12 April 1751
260 acres

Beginning at the original beginning tree.

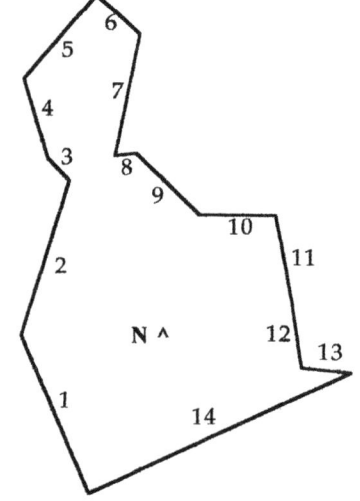

Resurvey on Oxford
Peter Beaver
BC & GS 50, 173-175
resurveyed 24 November 1774
252 and 1/2 acres

Beginning for the outlines thereof at the beginning tree of Oxford one of the original tracts.

Resurvey on Security
Jacob Hess
IC N, 6-7
resurveyed 11 September 1792
175 acres

Beginning for the outlines of the rsy by virtue of the afsd warrant at the original beginning it being a bounded white oak.

Resurvey on Seven Mountains
George Fidler
IC D, 91
resurveyed 14 Nov 1771
155 acres

Beginning for the outlines thereof at the end of the third line of the original.

Resurvey on Trembling
Michael Beigler
BC & GS 27, 392-393
resurveyed 10 July 1761
344 acres

Beginning at two bounded black oaks standing on a draft of Catoctin Creek they being the original beginning tree.

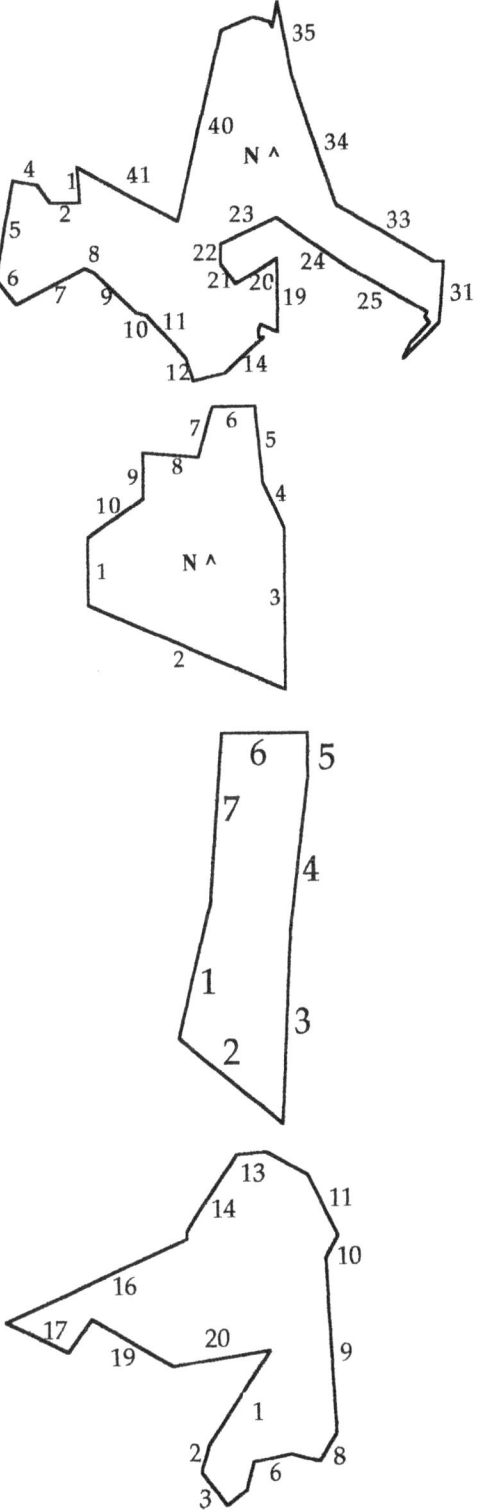

Maryland Hall of Records

Resurvey on Well Done
Moses Chapline
BC & GS 50, 15-18
resurveyed 1 February 1764
1822 acres

Beginning for the outlines of the whole by virtue of the before mentioned warrant at the beginning tree of the original.

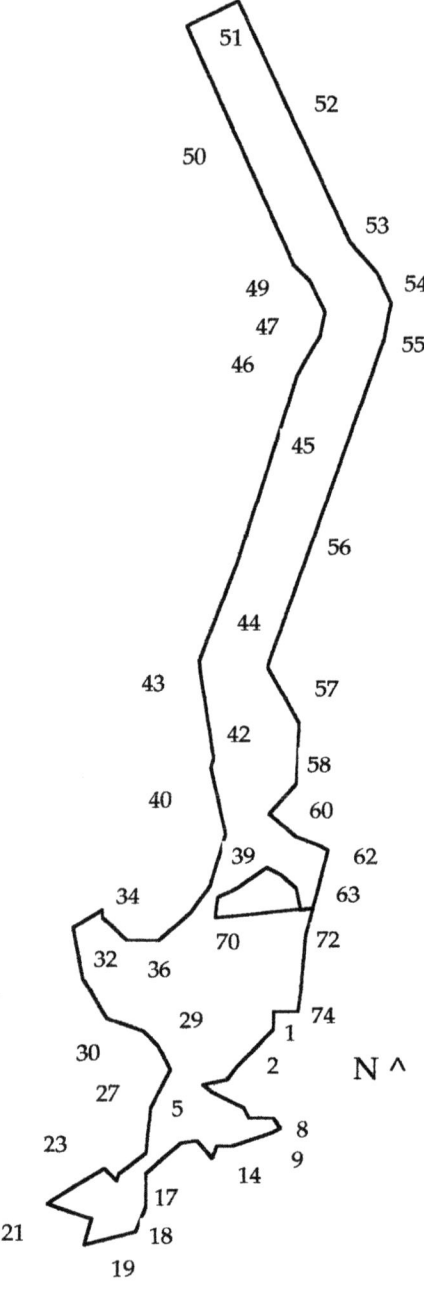

Resurvey on Well Done
Phillip Booker
BC & GS 47, 39-40
resurveyed 10 May 1771
332 acres

Beginning for the out lines thereof at the beginning tree of a tract of land called Grim's Fancy.

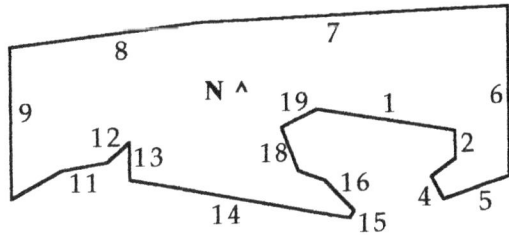

Resurvey on Whiskey Alley
Philip Keywhaughvor
BC & GS 32, 480-483
resurveyed 12 May 1762
567 acres

Beginning at a bounded white oak standing on the east side of Catoctin Creek it being the original beginning tree.

See FCLR WR-4-179, 13 Aug 1783, Jacob Keefour to Members and Trustees of the German Reformed Lutheran and Calvinist Congregations in and about Middle Town.

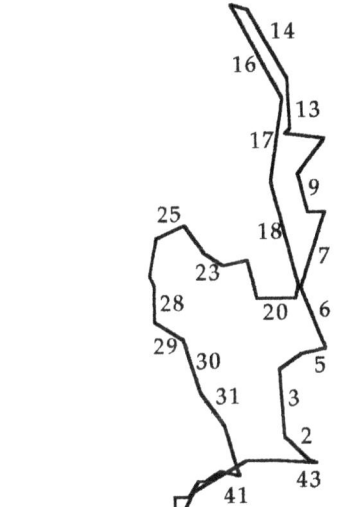

Resurvey of Wooden Platter
James Wardrop
BY & GS 1, 604-5
resurveyed 1 September 1748
327 acres

Beginning at the original bounded tree.

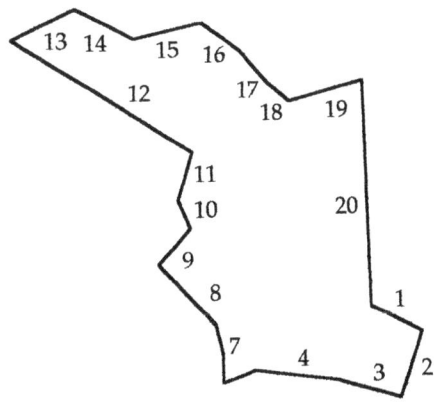

Security
Jacob Hess
IC N, 6-7
surveyed 10 May 1791
85 acres

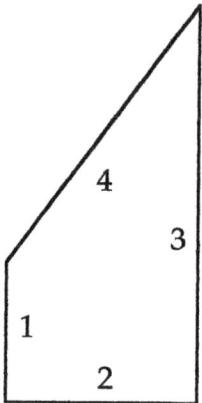

Beginning at a white oak marked on the body with twelve notches and on one of the roots extending eastward under the ground with three notches standing on the north side of the South Mountain about two hundred yards from the main road leading from Frederick Town to Sharpsburg on the south side thereof.

Showman's Purchase
Charles Beatty
IC R, 560-561
surveyed 15 May 1805
38 acres

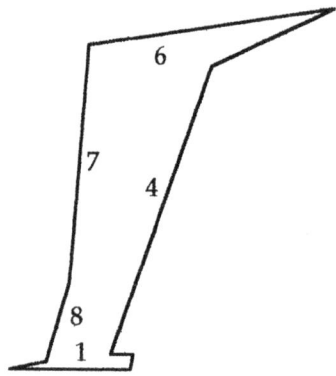

Beginning for the first parcel of the rsy by virtue of the afsd warrant at the original beginning.

Shettle
Daniel Dulany
Y & S, 105
9 September 1742
50 acres

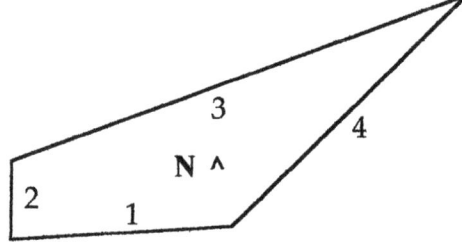

Beginning at a bounded white oak standing by the side of a branch a draft of Abrams Creek.

Small All
Bartholomew Booker
BC & GS 13, 193-194
surveyed 12 May 1759
25 acres

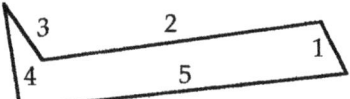

Beginning at the end of the twenty third line of the Rsy on Mendal l.

Small Ridge
Jacob Fulwiler
IC F, 307
surveyed 15 February 1785
11 June 1791
9 and 1/2 acres

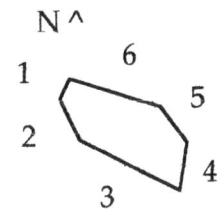

Beginning at a bounded white oak standing near the foot and on the east side of the South Mountain.

Smith's Hills
James Smith
PT 1, 261-263
17 April 1745
208 acres

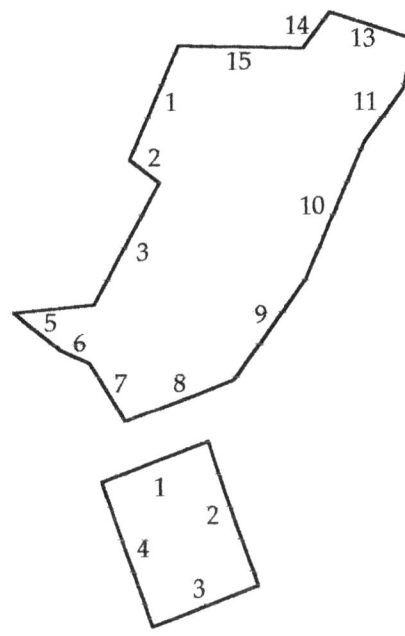

Beginning at a bounded white oak standing on the side of a hill within a quarter of a mile of the wagon road that crosses Antietam.

Stoney Ridge
Joseph Keepheart
BC & GS 37, 144-145
3 August 1768
5 acres

Beginning at a bounded white oak standing on the east side of Shanandore Mountain between the bridle road gap and the main wagon road gap that leads from Frederick Town to Sharpsburg.

Slusser's Choice
Peter Slusser
IC I, 99-100
resurveyed 20 October 1791
249 and 1/2 acres

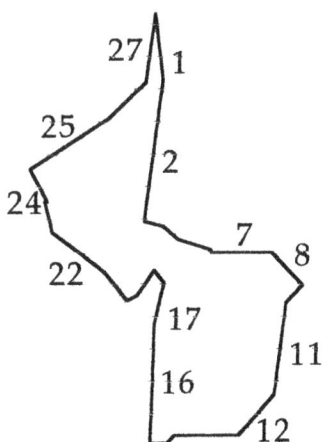

Beginning for the outlines of the whole by virute of the afsd warrant at the beginning tree of the land called Jerico.

Stoney Ridge
Ephraim Davis
BC & GS 27, 255-256
resurvey patent, 13 April 1765
73 & 3/4 acres

Beginning at the beginning tree of the said land called Tomkin's Green.

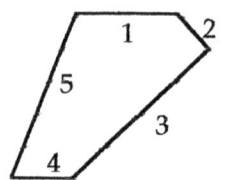

Strife
Andrew Grim
BC & GS 41 259-261
resurveyed 27 July 1770
982 acres

Beginning for the outlines thereof at the end of the nineteenth line of a tract of land called Park Hall and at the end of the 25th line of the original.

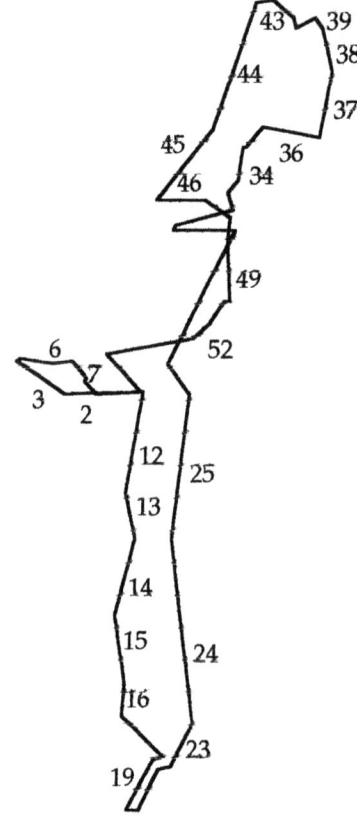

Swearingen's Disappointment
John Shaver
IC D, 326-327
surveyed 28 December 1782
100 acres

Beginning at the beginning tree of a tract of land called Fox's Last Shift granted to a certain Robert Smith.

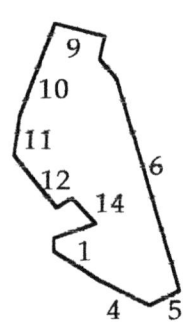

Turkey Ramble
Jacob Fulwiler
IC F, 306-307
1 June 1791
39 and 1/2 acres

Beginning at a bounded black oak tree the beginning of the Land of Gap.

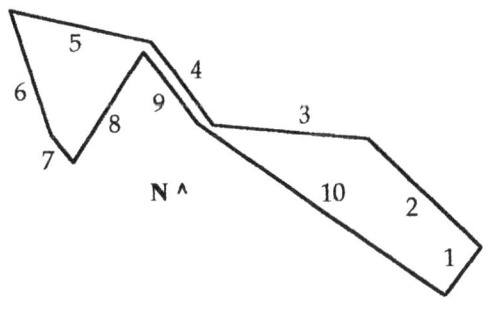

Turkeyfoot
Frederick Fox
IC G, 361
surveyed 13 March 1788
6 acres

Beginning at a bounded black oak tree standing on the east side of the South Mountain.

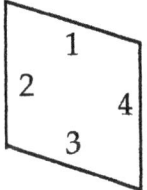

Turkey Plains
Catherine Knave
BC & GS 14, 14
14 November 1760
400 acres

Beginning at a bounded white oak it being the original beginning tree.

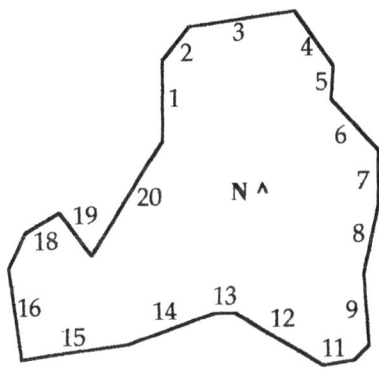

Uncle's Gift
Thomas Hawkins
BT & BY 3, 593
surveyed 30 September 1747
160 acres

Beginning at a bounded white oak standing by a small branch side that falls into Catoctin Creek it stands likewise near a tract of land called (The) Forest of Needwood belonging to John Hawkins.

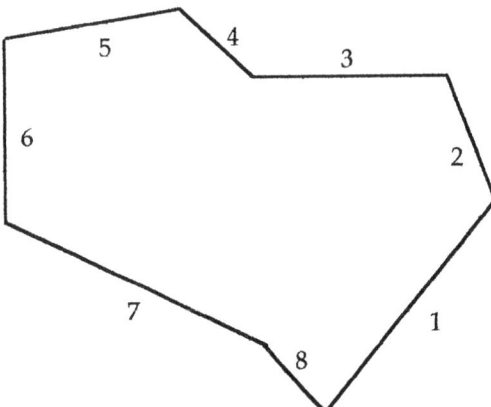

Vineyard
William Steuart
BC & GS 4, 181-183
surveyed 27 December 1739
154 acres

Beginning at a bounded red oak standing on the west side of Antietam Creek within ten poles of Conocoheague Road crosses the said creek.

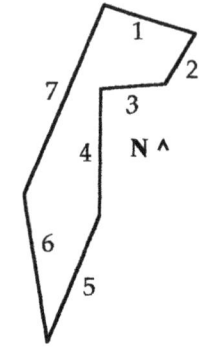

Volton's Seal
Moses Chapline
BC & GS 21, 484
surveyed 1 September 1761
97 acres

Beginning at the end of thirty four perches of the third line of Pile's Grove.

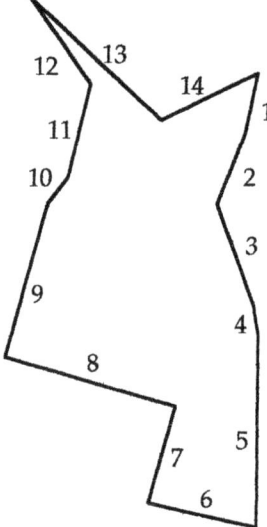

Watson's Welfare
Ewen McDonald
LG C, 576-577
29 June 1747
100 acres

Beginning at a bounded hickory tree standing on the east side of Catoctin Creek a draft of Potomac near a mile below the Great Road that leads from John Stull's Mill to the mouth of Monocacy.

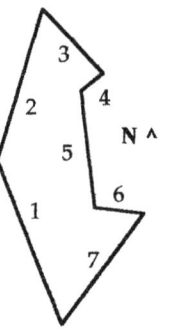

Well Done
Moses Chapline
BC & GS 14, 610-1
surveyed 1 September 1761
100 acres

Beginning at a bounded red oak standing near a little spring desending into Little Antietam on the west side of the South Mountain.

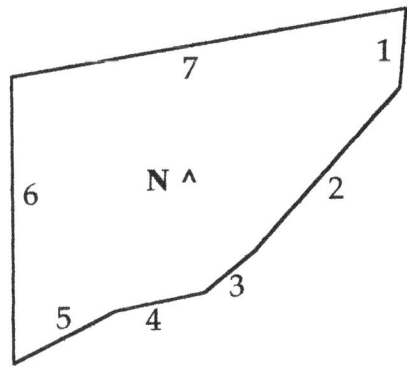

Wilyard's Lot
Duvall Wilyard
BC & GS 47, 234-235
surveyed 31 December 1765
100 acres

Beginning at four bounded gums standing at the foot of the Blue Ridge Mountain where the Bridle Road crosses the said mountain and about two or three perches to the north of the said road.

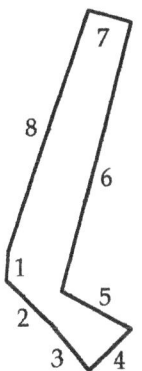

Wooden Platter
Daniel Dulany Esqr
TI 1, 486-487
surveyed 2 March 1742/3
100 acres

Beginning at a bounded white oak standing by the side of Abrams Creek.

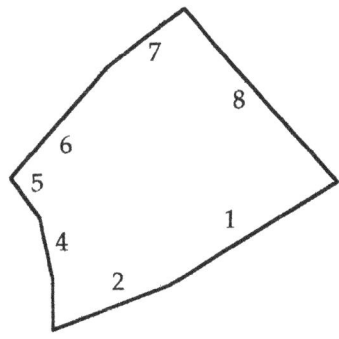

Maryland Hall of Records

Worse and Worse
John Teem (Team)
BC & GS 37, 218-219
surveyed 7 February 1766
41 and 1/2 acres

Beginning at a bounded white oak standing on the east side of the South Mountain and on the south side of the main road that leads from Frederick Town to Fort Frederick about forty perches from the said John Teem's dwelling house.

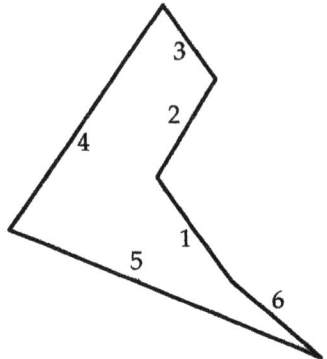

Youngest Brother
Conrad Young
BC & GS 40, 118
surveyed 1769
239 acres

Beginning for the outlines of the whole at the original beginning tree of a tract of land called Learning it being the beginning of the original tract called part of the Rsy on Learning.

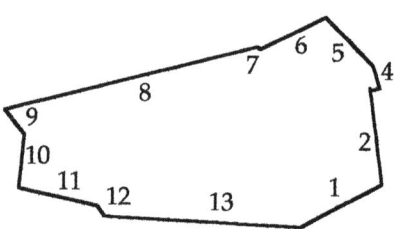

Antietam Works
John McPherson and John Brien
K U, 343-8
resurveyed 22 July 1808
9,548 and 3/8 acres

Beginning for the outline of the rsy by virtue of the afsd warrant at a stone marked A 1709 standing on the bank of Potomac River being the beginning of a tract called Boston then running up the river by and with it several meanders. Lines 110 through 118 and lines 130 through 135 were along the wagon road from Jacob Hess's Mill to Thomas Crampton's (Gap).

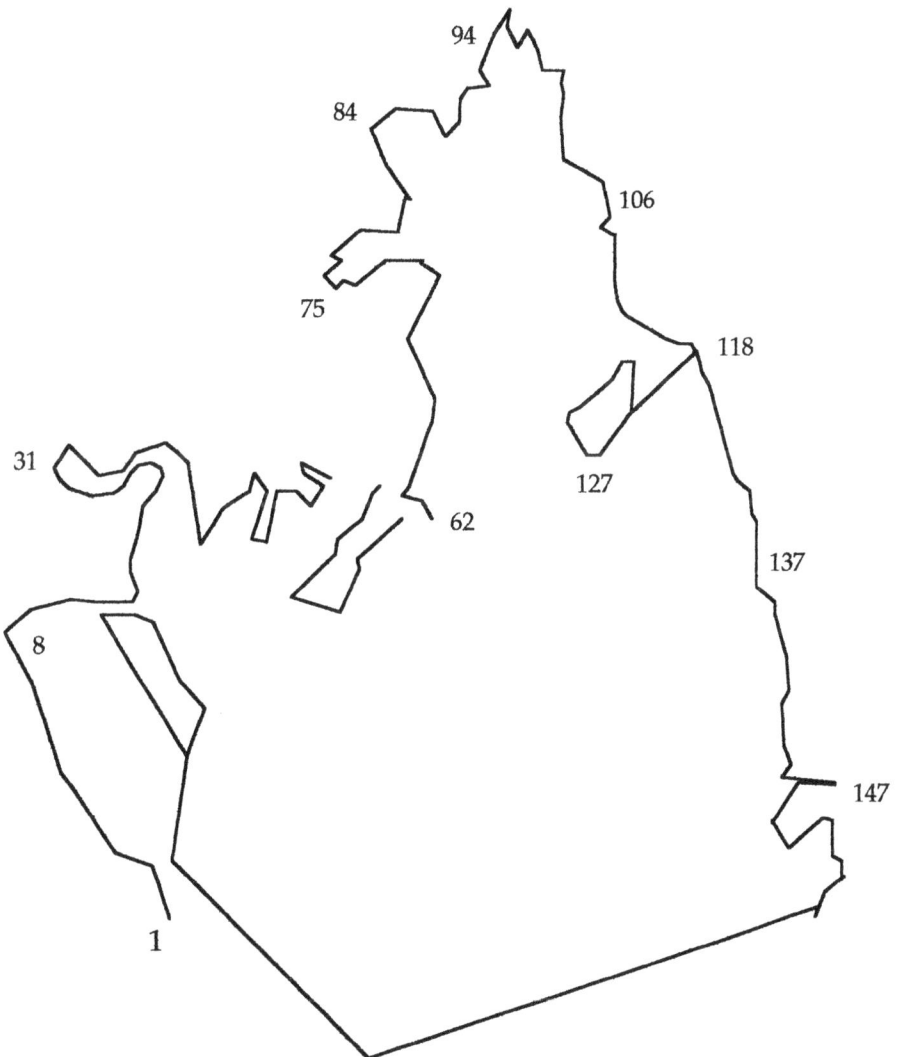

Fielderia Manor
Fielder Gannt
BC & GS 47, 1-12
resurveyed 18 May 1770
10,471 and 1/4 acres

Beginning for the outlines of the present rsy at the end of five hundred perches on the tenth course of a tract of land called Maryland granted unto Col. John Colvill of the colony of Virginia the said line being north sixty seven degrees east seven hundred perches which said course crosses the South or Blue Ridge Mountain.

The last lines of Fielderia Manor. These lines are near Crampton's Gap. Lines 638, 639, and 640 are along the perimeter of the Mountain tract at Crampton's Gap.

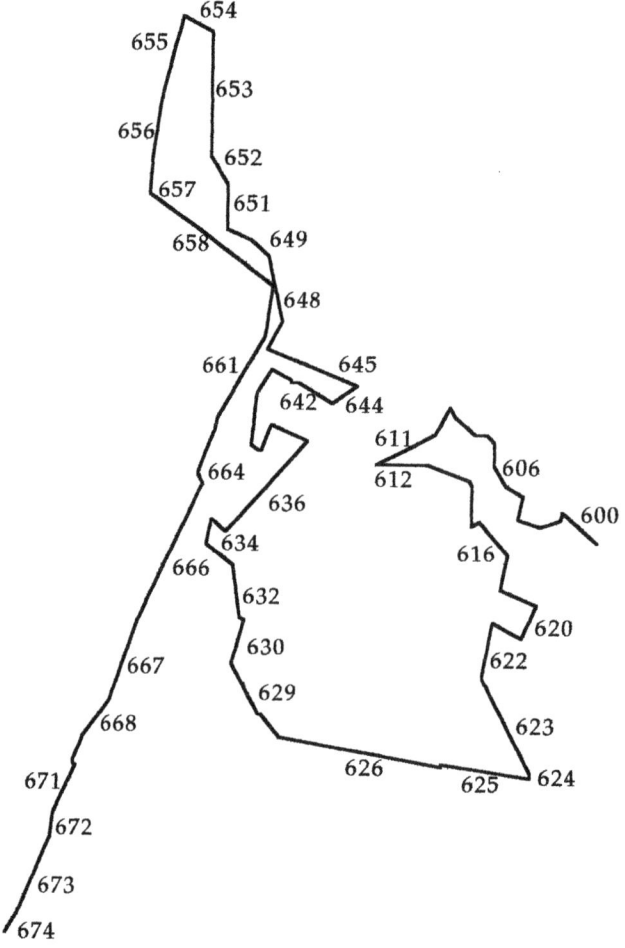

Keep Trieste
John Sample
BC & GS 19, 649-653
resurveyed 18 January 1764
10,202 acres

Beginning for the out lines of the whole by virtue of the before mentioned warrant at a bounded black oak standing at the end of the eighteenth line of a tract of land called Little I Thought It on the west hill side of the drain or run leading down to Potomac River opposite to Harper's Island to the westward of Elk Mountain about fifty or sixty perches from the river side.

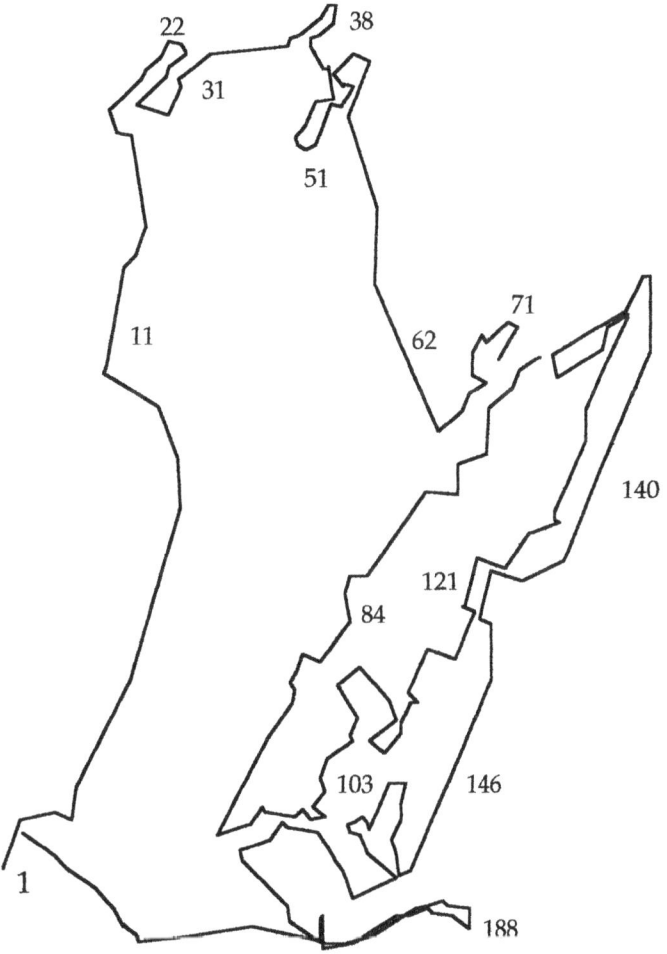

Maryland Hall of Records

Resurvey on Hills and Dales and the Vineyard
Joseph Chapline
BC & GS 45, 22-25
19 October 1763
2056 acres

Beginning for the outlines of the whole at a bounded white oak it being the beginning tree of a tract of land called Ward's Spring belonging to a certain William Reanolds.

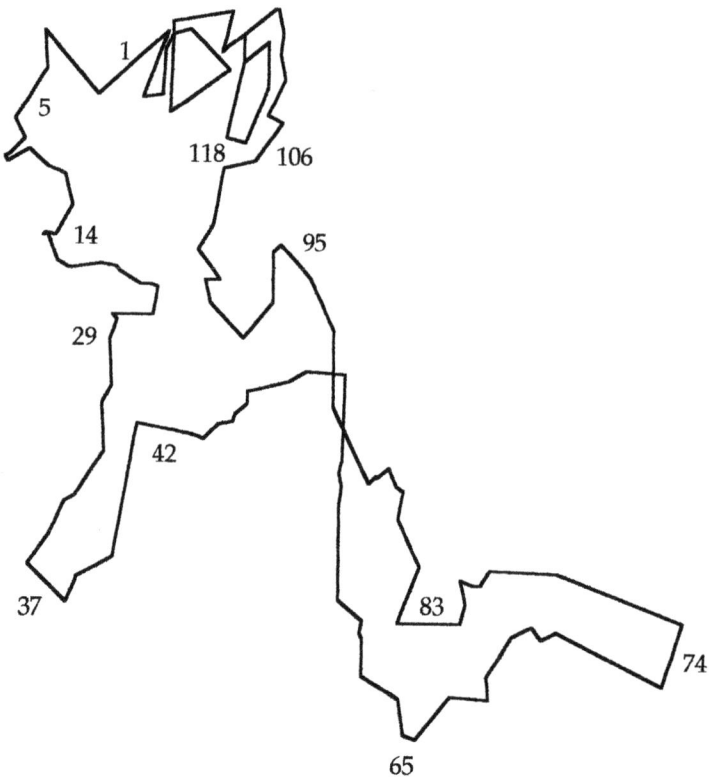

Frederick County Land Records

(FCLR)

Frederick County, Maryland

Surveys and Deeds

Note: Frederick County was part of Prince Georges County until 1748. Washington County was part of Frederick County until 1776.

Records appear in the following order:
From 1-1 to 999-999
From A-1 to Z-999
From AA-1 to ZZ-999
From AAA-1 to ZZZ-999

Frederick County Land Records

B-172
Thomas Whitaker to Nicholas Fink
Prevention
recorded 19 May 1750
50 acres

Beginning at a bounded white oak standing at the mouth of a run called Mill Run that falls into Catoctin Creek and running thence.

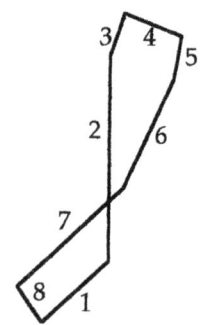

E-223
John Hepburn to Charles Carroll
Pile's Grove
recorded 9 July 1753
560 acres

Beginning at a bounded white oak standing near a small branch and near a large spring that makes into Antietam about half a mile above a road commonly called the wagon road and running thence.

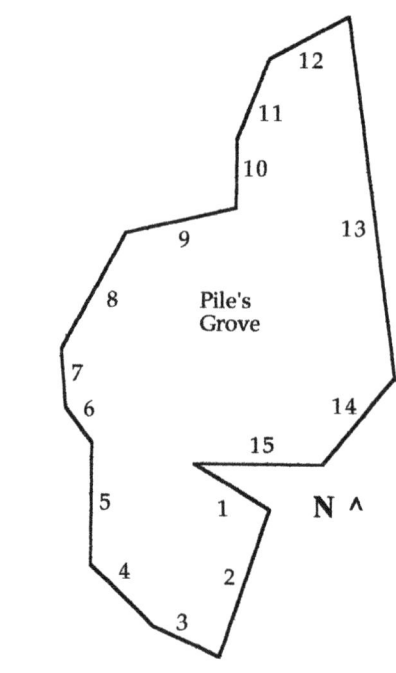

E-339
Joseph Chapline to Casper Shaff
(The) Exchange
recorded 11 December 1753
75 acres

Beginning at the beginning tree of the afsd tract of land called Exchange and running thence.

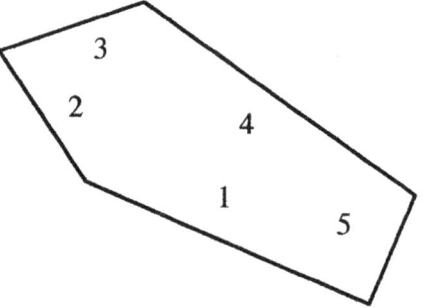

E-529
Moses Chapline Sr to James Smith
Three Springs
recorded 6 September 1754
739 acres

Begining at a bounded white oak being the original beginning tree of the afsd tract of land and running thence.

E-753
Richard Smith to Peter Beaver
Part of Christie's Folly
recorded 19 June 1755
100 acres

Part of a tract of land called Christie's Folly patented in that name of the afsd Richard Smith and beginning at the beginning tree of the afsd tract of land and running thence.

E-870
Joseph Chapline to James Fowler
Tick Neck
recorded 21 January 1755
54 acres

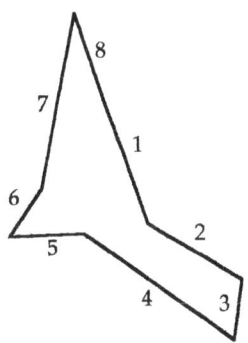

Beginning at the beginning tree of the afsd tract and running thence.

E-1026
Casper Shaff to Conrad Young
Part of Exchange
recorded 18 March 1756
125 acres

Part of a tract of land called Exchange lying in the county afsd according to the metes and bounds following beginning at a bounded black oak standing at the end of sixty two perches on the eighth line of said land called Exchange and running thence.

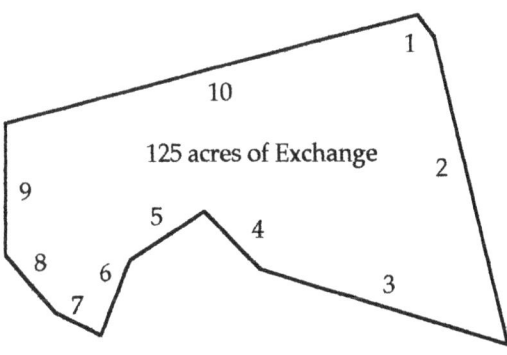

E-1049
Joseph Chapline to Andrew Arnold
Nazareth (Nazarih)
made 26 March 1756
100 acres

Beginning at the beginning tree of the afsd land and running thence.

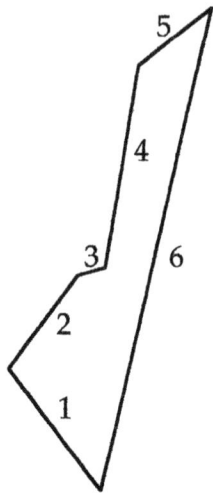

F-211
Joseph Chapline Sr to Peter Booker
Booker's Purchase
recorded 2 April 1757
60 acres
part of Little Good, Add to Little Good

Being part of two tracts of land the one called Little Good the other called the Add to Little Good beginning at the beginning tree of the afsd tract of land called Little Good and running thence.

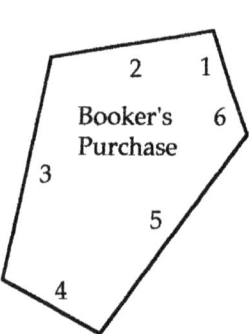

F-399-400
Moses Chapline Sr to Thomas Lane
Joyner's Fancy
recorded 4 March 1758
50 acres

Beginning at the beginning tree of the original tract and running thence.

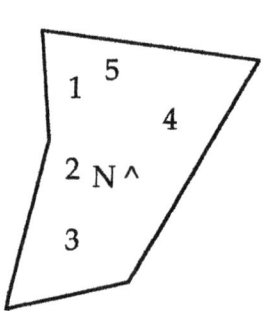

F-548 (mortgage)
John McEntire to John Henthorn
Smith's Choice
recorded 15 September 1758
50 acres

Beginning at the beginning tree of the afsd tract and running thence.

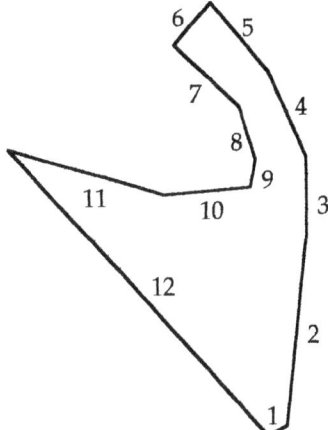

F-905
Christian Kemp to David Smith
Kemp's Long Meadow
recorded 19 December 1759
200 acres

Beginning at the end of the fifty third perch on the fifteenth course of said tract and running thence with the outlines.

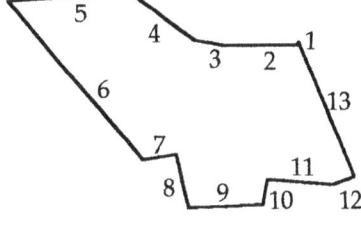

F-1020
Bartholomew Booker
to Christopher Everhart
Rsy on Mendall
recorded 14 June 1760
100 acres

Beginning at the end of three perches in the third line of the said Rsy on Mendall being the end of forty three in the north nineteen degrees east forty six perches line of a tract of land called the survey on Wooden Platter laid out for James Wardrop and running thence.

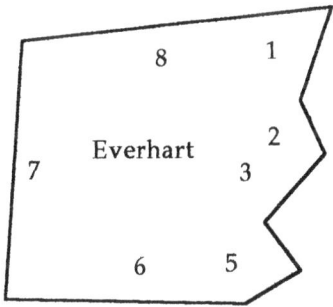

F-1023
Bartholomew Booker to George Yeaste
Rsy on Mendall
recorded 17 June 1760
52 Acres

Beginning at the beginning tree of the afsd tract and running thence.

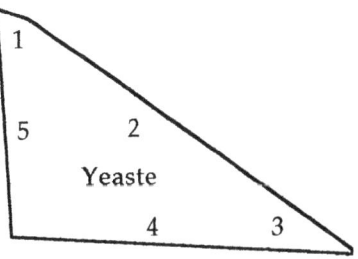

Frederick County Land Records

F-1064
Bartholomew Booker to George Shidler
Shidler's Dispute
recorded 28 June 1760
100 acres

Beginning tree of a tract of land laid out for James Wardrop in Curry's Gap it standing at the end of the twenty eighth line of the original tract of land called the Rsy on Mendall and running thence.

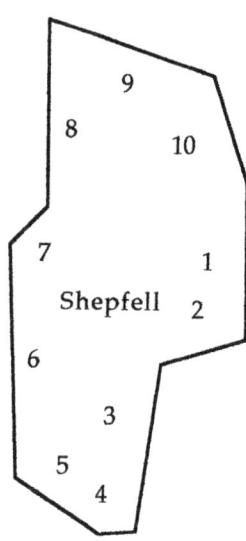

F-1077
Bartholomew Booker to Michael Shepfell
Rsy on Mendall
recorded 6 July 1760
100 acres

Beginning at a bounded red oak standing by the head of a little spring and near a road that leads from Bartholomew Booker's to Peter Beaver's and running thence.

F-1137
Joseph Chapline Sr to Martin Lyon
Lyon's Purchase, Rsy on (The) Grove, and Fellfoot Enlarged
20 October 1760
200 acres

Beginning at the end of twenty two perches in the ninth line of the original tract of land called (The) Grove and running thence.

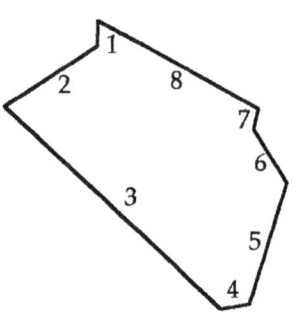

F-1137
Joseph Chapline Sr to Michael Thomas
Thomas's Purchase
20 October 1760
187 acres

Beginning at the end of the third line of the afsd tract of land called (The) Grove being the end of the last line of a tract of land called Nelson's Folly and running thence with said line reversed.

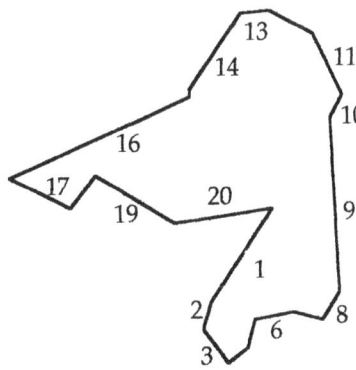

F-1198
James Spurgeon to Michael Beeghler
Rsy on Trembling
recorded 23 November 1760
226 acres

Beginning at two bounded black oaks standing on a draft of Catoctin they being the original beginning trees and running thence.

G-7, 621-626
Jacob Hess and others
Fellfoot Enlarged
recorded 19 March 1792
2100 acres

Beginning for the outlines of the whole tract at a bound white oak where is a stone now planted standing in the fork of Little Antietam it being the beginning tree of the original tract called Fellfoot.

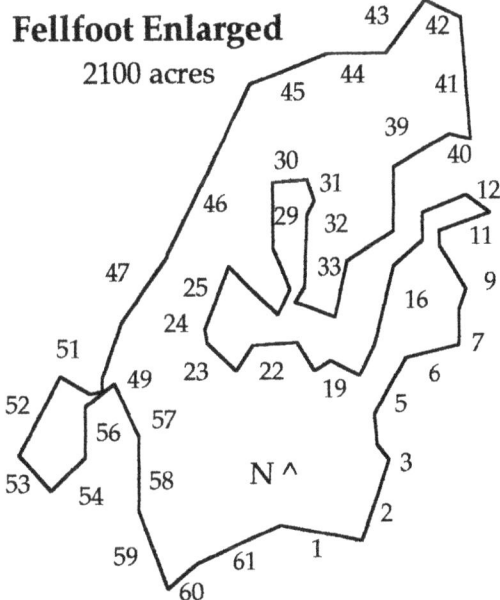

Fellfoot Enlarged
2100 acres

G-17
Michael Jesserong to Casper Shaff
Bubble (Boble)
recorded 4 June 1761
50 acres

Beginning at the beginning tree of a tract of land called the Exchange and running thence.

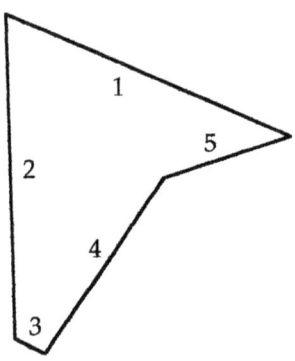

G-287
Thomas Crampton from John Shelton
Part of Parks Hall
recorded 18 Nov 1761
101 and 1/2 acres

Part of a tract of land called Parks Hall beginning at a marked white oak standing near the old Indian road and running thence.

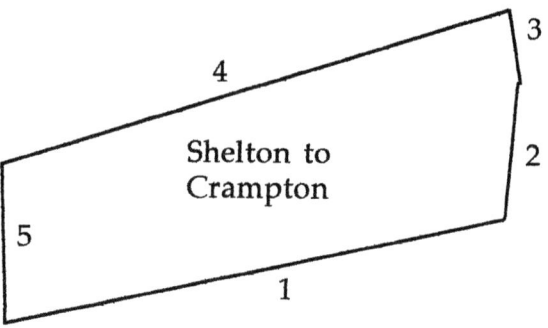

G-302
Moses Chapline Sr to Samuel Baker
Part of the Rsy on Roots Hill
recorded 21 Nov 1761
100 acres

Part of the Rsy on Roots Hell beginning at the end of fifty perches in the sixth line of the Rsy and running thence.

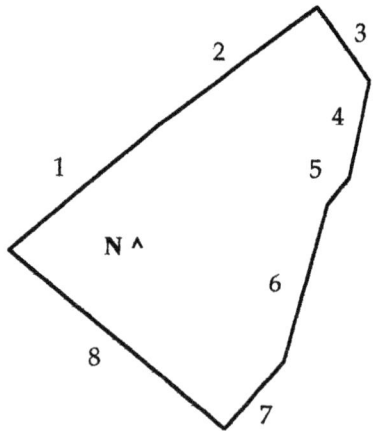

G-395
Thomas Hogg to John Harrison
Part of Parks Hall
recorded 19 Feb 1763
135 acre

Beginning at the end of the sixth line of the original tract of land called Parks Hall and running thence.

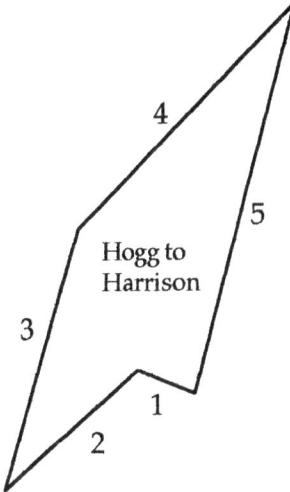

H-53
Thomas Hawkins to Elias Wilyard
Part of Uncle's Gift
recorded 28 Jun 1762
100+ acres

All that part or parcel of land being part of a tract of land called Uncle's Gift lying and being in the county and province a fsd beginning at the bounded white oak the beginning tree of the whole tract and running thence.

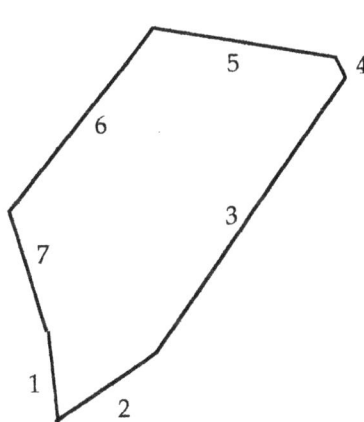

H-95
Greenberry Cheney to Jacob Funk
Hope Well
recorded 19 Aug 1762
100 acres

All that tract or parcell of land called Hope Well situate lying and being in Frederick County a fsd beginning at a bounded white oak standing at the head of a hallow that leads to Antietam Creek at Cox's Cabin running thence.

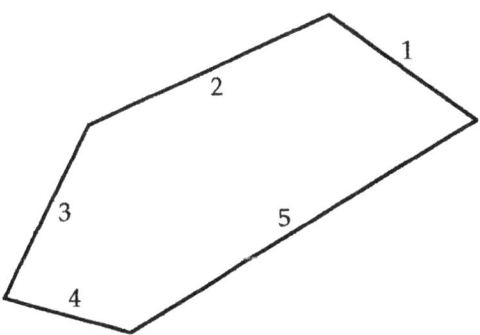

H-173
John Spurgeon to Adam Renninger
Spurgeon's Folly
recorded 2 October 1752
_0 acres

Begining at a bounded white oak standing near a draft of __ Run descending into Catoctin Creek running thence.

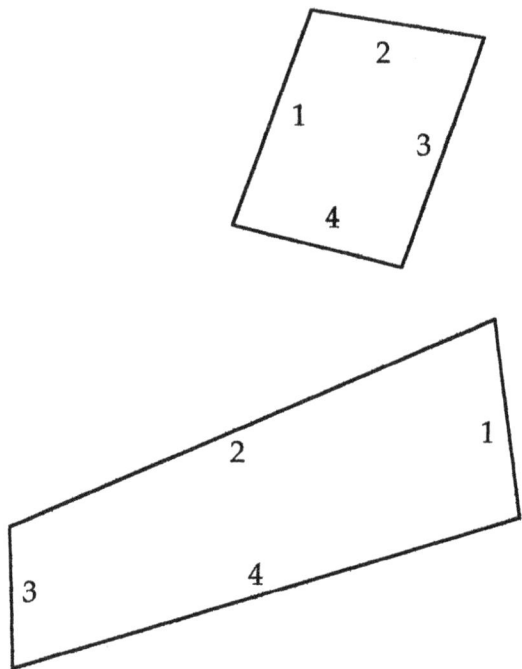

H-343
William B. Peddicord
to Thomas Crampton
Part of Parks Hall
recorded 21 March 1768
101 and 1/2 acres

All that tract or lot of land called Last Choice being part of a tract of land called Parks Hall which said lot doth begin at the end of eighty eight perches in the twenty fourth line or course of the said original tract of Parks Hall then reversing the said twenty fourth line and running thence.

H-448
George Robinett to John Huffer
Part of Parks Hall
recorded 20 May 1763
100 acres

All that part or parcel of land being part of a tract of land called Parks Hall beginning at the end of the twenty second line of Parks Hall and running thence.

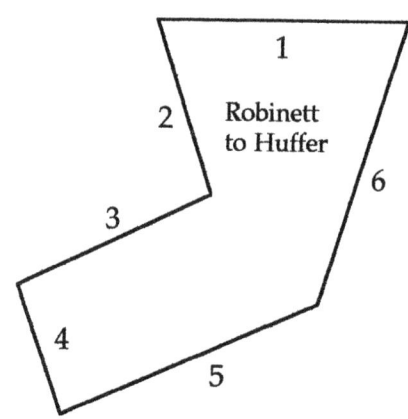

H-642
Samuel Magruder to Samuel Magruder, Jr
Part of The Forest
recorded 22 Oct 1763
150 acres

All that part of a certain tract of land lying in Frederick County on or near Catoctin Creek called The Forest contained within the metes and bounds following that is to say beginning at a bounded hickory it being the original beginning tree of the afsd land and running thence.

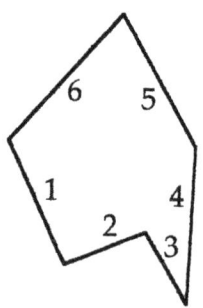

J-432
Nicholas Fink to John Shank
Goose Bill
recorded 3 May 1765
196 and 1/2 acres

Beginning at the end of thirteen perches in the second line of the said Goose Bill it being likewise the end of the second line of David Stottlemire's part of the said Goose Bill and running thence.

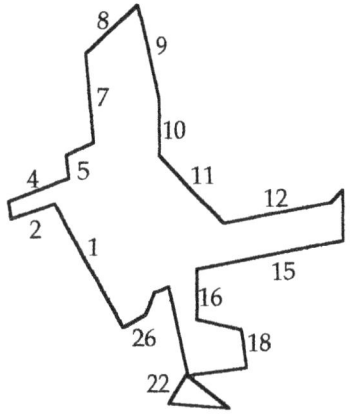

J-514-516
Joseph Ensor to Conrad Snabely
Hickory Tavern
2 June 1764
300 acres
Part of Fellfoot Enlarged

Beginning at the beginning tree of the said tract of land called Fellfoot Enlarged and running thence.

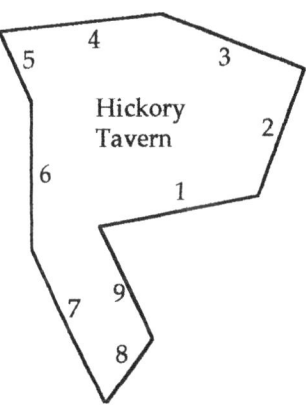

J-1086
John Tucker to Henry Neff
Cooperton
recorded 20 March 1765
100 acres

Beginning at the beginning tree of the afsd land which is a bounded white oak standing by the side of a small branch of broad run and draft of Abraham Creek and running thence.

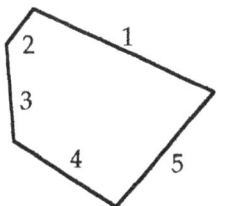

Frederick County Land Records

K-52
William Anderson to Andrew Grim
Part of Parks Hall
recorded 11 Oct 1765
50 acres

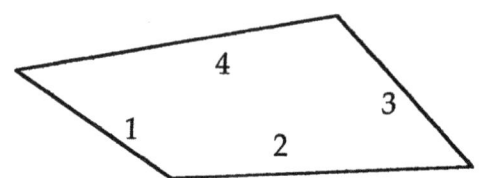

All that tract or parcel of land called William Anderson's part of Parks Hall situate lying and being in the county afsd and beginning at a bounded black oak standing in a swamp and at the end of the eighteenth line of said Parks Hall and running thence.

K-682
Thomas Hawkins to Daniel Arnold
I've Got It At Last, Mountain, Uncles' Gift
recorded 20 August 1766
100 acres

Beginning at a bounded white oak the beginning tree of the Rsy on Dawson's Purchase and running thence.

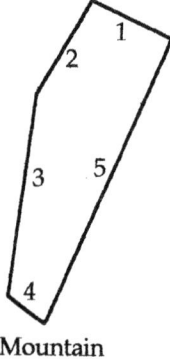
Mountain

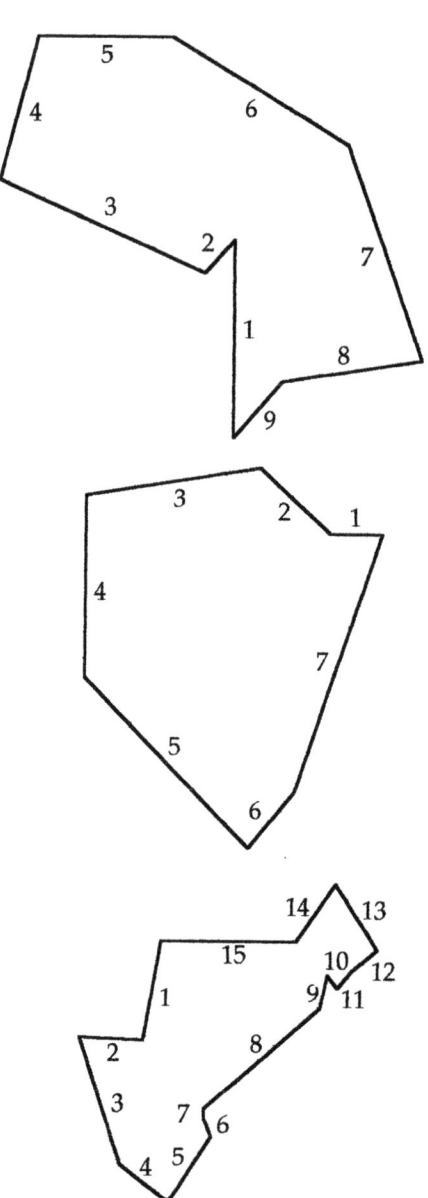

K-758
Mathias Ringer to Casper Shaff
Rsy on Chestnut Hill
recorded 2 October 1766
175 acres

Beginning at the original beginning tree and running thence.

K-917
Joseph Chapline to John Team (Teem)
(The) Gap
recorded 9 January 1767
50 acres

Beginning at the end of the third line of Wardrop's land called Curry's Old Place and running thence.

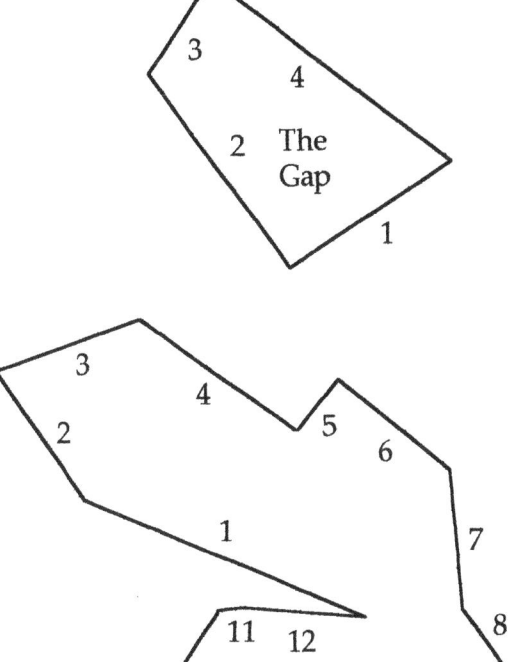

K-1373
Casper Shaff to Valentine Fidler
Fidler's Purchase
recorded _ June 1767
150 acres

Being part of a tract of land called the Rsy on Exchange lying and being in the county and province afsd beginning at the original beginning tree and running thence.

L-69
George Shidler to Bartholomew Booker
Shidler's Dispute
recorded the ? October 1767
100 acres

Beginning at the beginning tree of a tract of land laid out for James Wardrop in Curry's Gap it standing at the end of the twenty eighth line of the original tract and running thence.

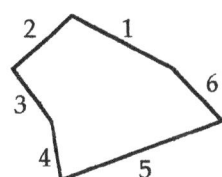

L-71
Bartholomew Booker to George Shidler
Long Dispute
recorded 16 October 1767
200 acres

Beginning at the beginning tree of a tract of land called John's Delight being the beginning tree of the said part called Shidler's Dispute.

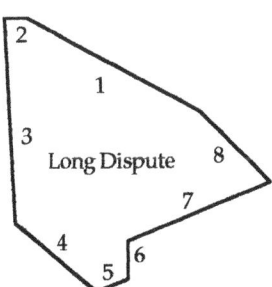

L-276
John Baley to Adam Teats
Mountain
recorded 31 March 1768
50 acres

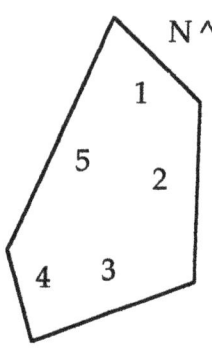

Beginning at a bounded white oak tree standing on the side of an hill on the west side of Shanandore Mountain near the road that leads from Monocacy to Teague's Ferry and running thence.

L-588
Philip Keywaughver to Nicholas Fink
Rsy on Whiskey Alley
recorded 28 November 1760
86 acres

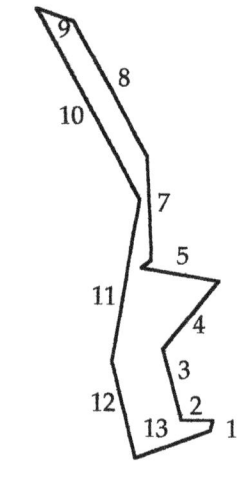

Beginning at the end of one hundred and thirty two perches in the seventh line of the whole tract and running thence with the out lines of the said Rsy on Whiskey Alley the twelve following courses (to wit).

L-649
Alexander Grim to George H. Coleman
Grim's Fancy
recorded 1 May 1770
50 acres

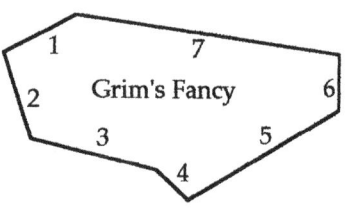

Beginning at a bounded black oak tree standing on the north side of the main road that leads from Frederick Town to Swearingen's Ferry and near to John Fox's house on the west side of the South Mountain and running thence.

M-450
James Piles to Henry Weaver
Chestnut Thickett
recorded 24 August 1769
21 acres

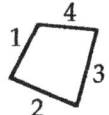

Beginning at a bounded hickory standing on the south side of the Blue Mountain and near the lower main road and running thence.

M-675
Henry Lighter to Peter Beaver
Rsy on Learning
recorded 12 December 1769
39 acres and 76 perches

Beginning at the end of the thirty eighth line of said rsy and running thence.

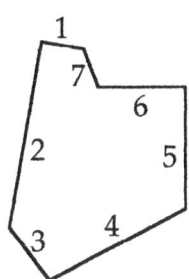

N-273
Josiah Wilson and Wadsworth Wilson
(The) Forest
recorded 20 Aug 1770
100 acres

All that part of a tract or parcel of land called The Forest lying and being in Frederick County in Province aforesaid beginning at the beginning tree a white oak of the said land and running thence.

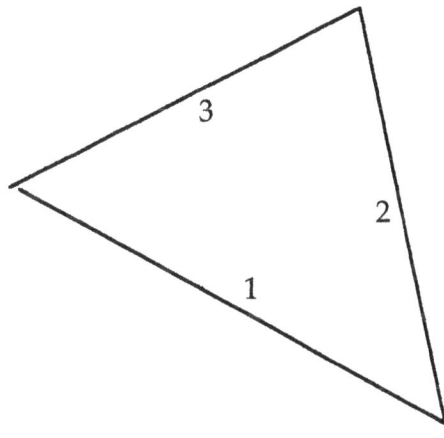

N-470
Daniel Arnold to Peter Miller
Part of I Have Got It At Last
and Part of Uncle's Gift
recorded 23 Nov 1770
13 acres and 85 perches

Part of a tract of land called I Have Got It At Last beginning at a locust post at the end of seventy two perches on the seventh line of said tract called I Have Got It At Last thence with said line or course.

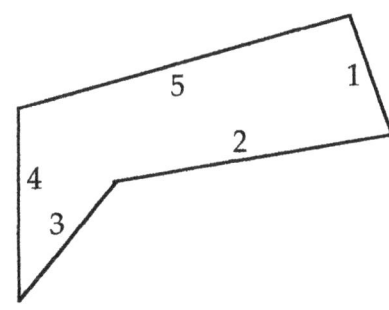

Frederick County Land Records

N-499
William B. Peddicord to Thomas Crampton
Part of Parks Hall
recorded 13 December 1770
101 and 1/2 acres

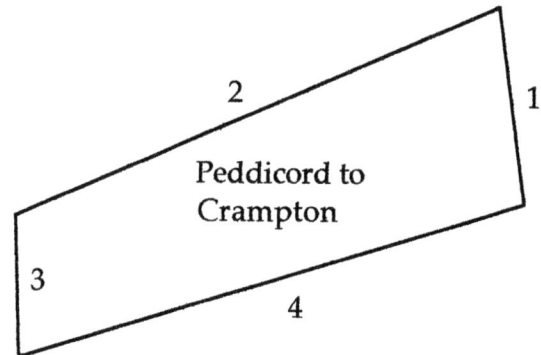

Part of a tract of resurveyed land on Park Hall but this part by conveyance is first called Last Choice beginning for said part at the end of eighty eight perches in the twenty fourth line of the whole rsy then reversing the said twenty fourth line and running thence.

N-517
Bartholomew Booker to Peter Beaver
Part of Pickall
recorded 15 December 1770
53 acres

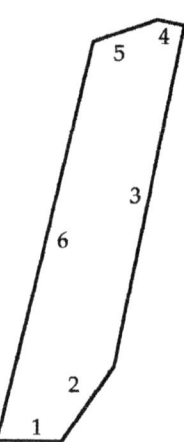

Part of a tract of land called Pickall situate lying and being in Frederick County aforesaid beginning at the end of thirty four perches on the fortieth course of the whole tract called Pickall and running thence.

N-560
Jacob Smith to Bartholomew Booker
Rsy on Mendall
recorded 23 January 1772
100 acres

Beginning at a bounded red oak standing by the head of __ Spring near a road that leads from Bartholomew Booker's to Peter Beaver's and running thence.

O-40
Daniel Dulany to Henry Butler
What Not
recorded 8 February 1772
50 acres

Beginning at a bounded chesnut tree standing at the foot of Shanandore Mountain on the east side thereof running thence.

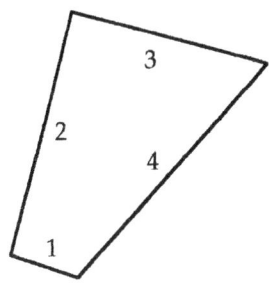

O-112
Casper Shaff to Peter Ruble
Shaff's Purchase
recorded 26 March 177_
93 acres

Beginning at a bounded white oak the beginning tree of a tract of land called Betty's Good Will and running thence.

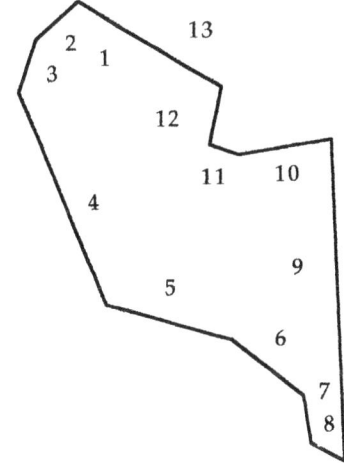

O-130
Wadsworth Wilson to Mathias Kershman
Part of (The) Forest
recorded 26 Mar 1773
100 acres

Beginning at the beginning tree a white oak of the said land and running thence.

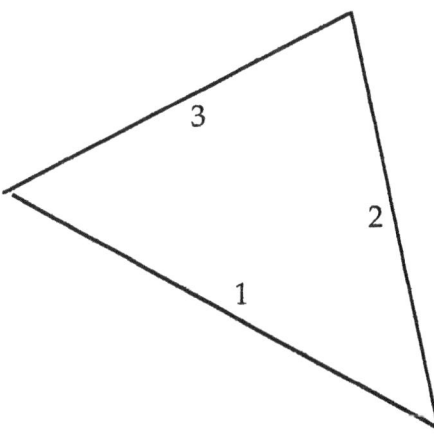

Frederick County Land Records

O-376
George Beall Jr to Michael Thomas
Penn's Disappointment
22 May 1761
80 acres

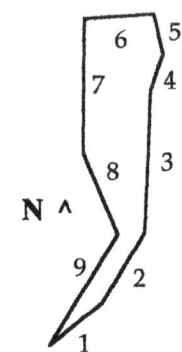

Beginning a a bounded white oak standing by a draft of Little Antietam commonly called the Dry Branch and about one hundred and fifty yards from a great spring and running thence.

O-540
Nicholas Fink to Thomas Welch
Goose Cap
recorded 2 September 1771
66 acres

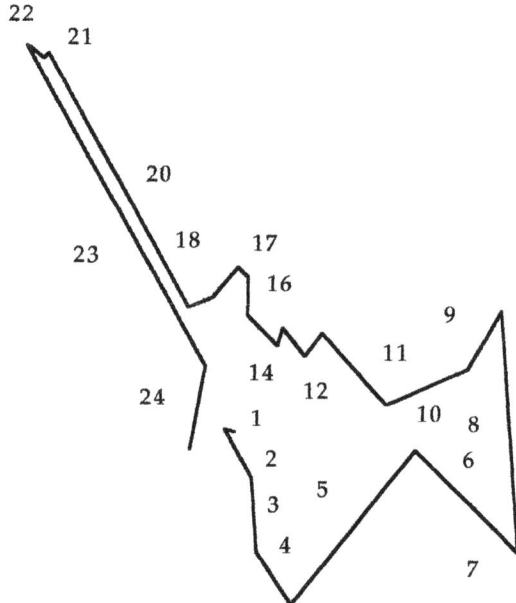

Beginning at a bounded Sycamore tree standing on the north west side of Mill Creek and about two perches from the said creek and running thence.

P-387
Daniel Dulany to Bartholomew Booker
Shettle
17 June 1772
50 acres

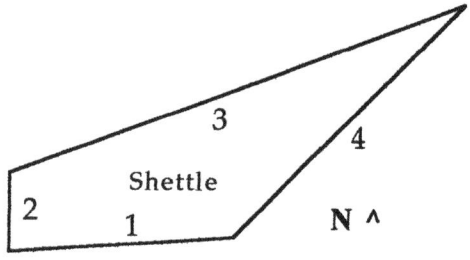

Beginning at the bounded white oak standing by the side of a branch a draft of Abrams Creek and running thence.

P-632
John Teem to Adam Coil
Worse and Worse
recorded 22 March 1773
41 and 1/2 acres

Beginning at a bounded white oak standing on the east side of the South Mountain and on the south side of the main road that leads from Frederick Town to Fort Frederick about forty perches from the said John Teems's dwelling house and running thence.

S-56
John Tucker to Adam Knouf
Honesty Best When Looked To
recorded 17 April 1773
206 acres

Beginning for the outlines thereof at the end of seventy two perches on the last line of the original of the afsd tract given as north twenty four degrees west one hundred and two perches line and running thence.

T-19
Bartholomew Booker to Peter Booker
Part of Resurvey on Mendall and
I Hope It Is Well Done
recorded 28 June 1773
87 and 1/2 acres

The two following tracts or parcels of land lying and being in the county afsd and contiguous to each other (viz!) 5 acres and 3/4 of an acre part of a tract of land called the Rsy on Mendall and 81 acres and 3/4 of an acre part of a tract of land called I Hope It Is Well Done beginning for the out lines of the whole at a bounded red oak the beginning tree of Jacob Smith's land and running thence.

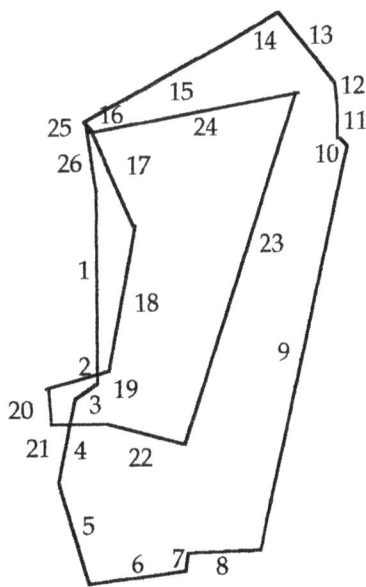

Frederick County Land Records

W-283
Joseph Keepheart to John Jacob Young
Stoney Ridge
recorded 24 November 1774
50 acres

Beginning at the end of the seventh line of the said tract of land called Stoney Ridge and running thence.

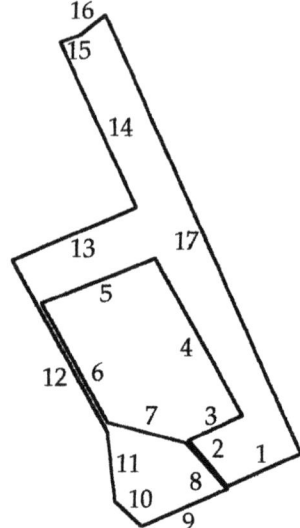

W-327
Joseph Keephart to Joseph Boyer
Stoney Ridge
recorded 20 November 1774
80 acres

Beginning at the end of the second line of the said tract of land called Stoney Ridge and running thence.

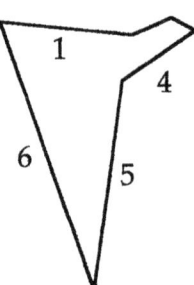

AF-9-541
David Arnold to George Alfred Townsend
recorded 20 December 1884
12 acres, 3 roods, and 17 square perches

(Note: The War Correspondents Memorial Arch stands on this tract.)

Beginning for the same at a marked white oak tree the end of the first line of the said deed from Ezra Slifer, Trustee, to David Mullendore and thence with the outlines thereof 4 courses and distances.

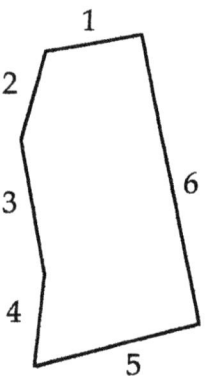

BD-1-286
Henry Balsell to Leonard Storm
Part of Rsy on Tom's Gift
recorded 20 March 1775
150 acres

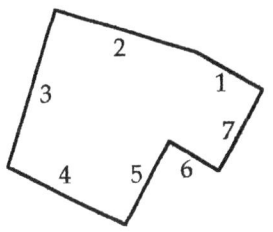

All that tract of land or farm situate lying and being in Frederick County afsd whereon the said Henry Balsell now lives commonly called and known by the name and part of the Rsy on Tom's Gift beginning at the end of the first line of Leonard Storm's part of the afsd rsy and running thence.

BD-1, 535-537
Moses Chapline Jr to
John Cary and Christopher Edelen
Rsy on Mt. Pleasant and Josiah's (Last) Bit
recorded 18 May 1775

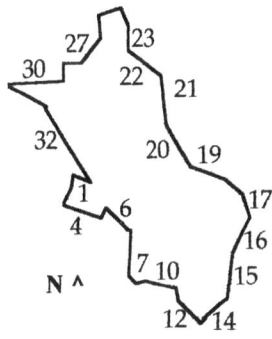

All the two following tracts (vizt) (The) Rsy on Mount Pleasant and Josiah's Bit - Except - 77 acres called Old Purchase which said Moses Chapline deeded to William Good the third day of March 1775 which will appear by said deed where and in what place said tract called Old Purchase effects the afsd two tracts of land then beginning for the afsd tract called the Rsy on Mount Pleasant at the end of the fourth line of the original and running thence.

CM-1-582
Vincent Sanner to Samuel Ausherman
Part of (The) Rsy on Exchange, Fidler's Purchase, Bubble, and Deeffer Snay
recorded 14 April 1868
194 and 1/2 acres

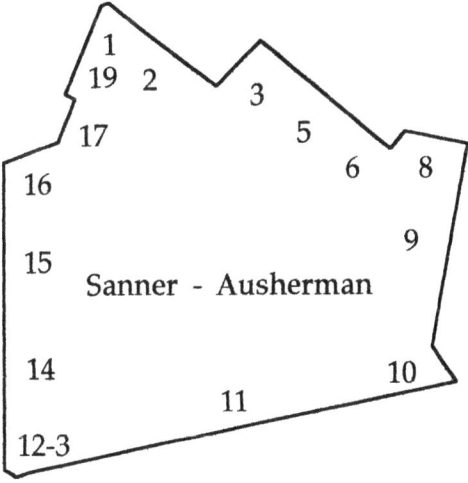

Part of a tract of land called Fidler's Purchase, part of a tract called The Rsy on Exchange, part of a tract called Bubble, and a tract called Deeffer Snay.

Beginning to include all the land hereby intended to be conveyed in one outline at a large planted stone standing at the end of the sixth line of the second piece of land described in the deed from Sidney Ringer and Jacob Everhart and wife to Vincent Sanner dated on the 3rd day of April 1833, and running thence according to the bearings of the lines on the 6th day of December 1867.

Frederick County Land Records

CM-2-381
Phillip and Lucinda Sheffer to
William H. Jones
Part of Flonham
recorded 6 October 1868
22 and 1/4 acres

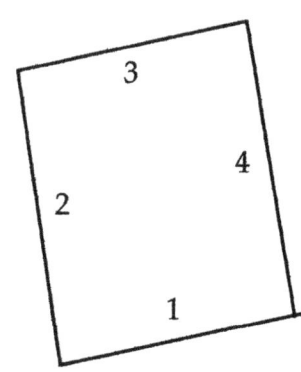

Part of a tract and parcel of land and premises lying and being in Frederick County and State afsd - being part of a tract of land called Flonhan beginning for the land hereby to be conveyed at the beginning of the original tract called Flonham as afsd and running thence two courses with the same.

CM-2-385
Daniel Beachley to William Jones
recorded 6 October 1868
12 and 3/4 acres and 14 perches

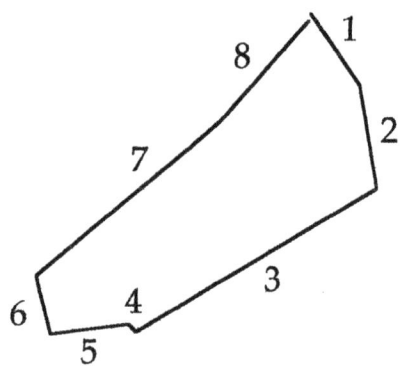

Beginning for the said part at a stone pile at the end of the fourth (4th) line of the deed from said Daniel Beachley and wife to Jonas Beachley for 9 1/2 acres and 4 per. bearing date 11 October 1860 and recorded in Liber B G F No 6 folios 217 and 218 one of the land records of Frederick County afsd and running thence with the third and fourth line of said reversed.

ES-5-252
Ezra Williard et al. to David Arnold
recorded 2 October 1832
169 and 1/4 acres excepting 1/2 acre

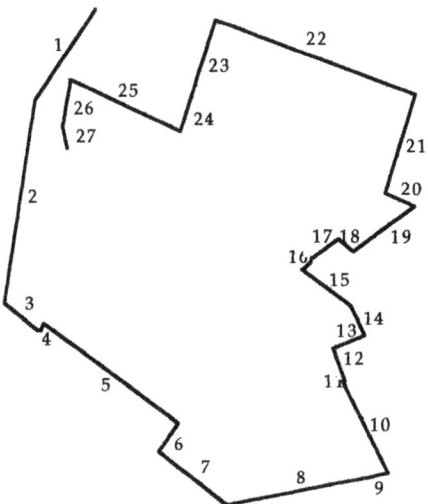

Beginning at a stone formerly planted in the public road leading through Burkettsville into Washington County at or near the end of the first line of the tract afsd called Gaver's Recovery it being also at the end of the 14th line of a tract of land called Miller's Farm resurveyed for Peter Miller 28 October 1804 and running thence by and with the outlines thereof reversed six courses correcting the lines.

JS-17, 504
Jacob Hutzel, Executor of Peter Hutzel,
to Jacob Hutzel
Long Dispute, Long Dispute Ended
2 Oct 1789
200 acres

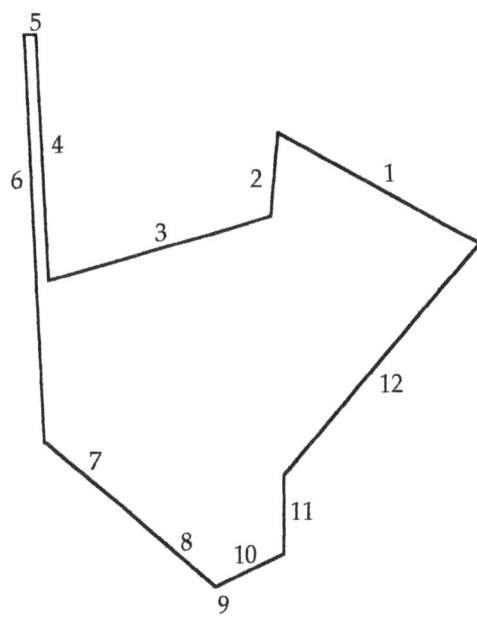

Beginning at a large stone formerly planted at the beginning of a tract of land called John's Delight being also the beginning of a tract of land called Pickall and running thence.

JS-25-372
Philip Sheffer to Henry Miller
Part of Flonham
recorded 6 July 1826
5 acres and 20 perches

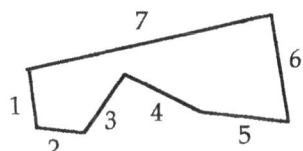

All that part of a tract of land called Flonham beginning at the end of the second line of the whole tract called Flonham and running thence with the second line of said land reversed.

JS-30-58-61
Jacob Routzong to George Routzong
Part of Fredericksburg and Add to Friendship
recorded 8 August 1828
68 acres

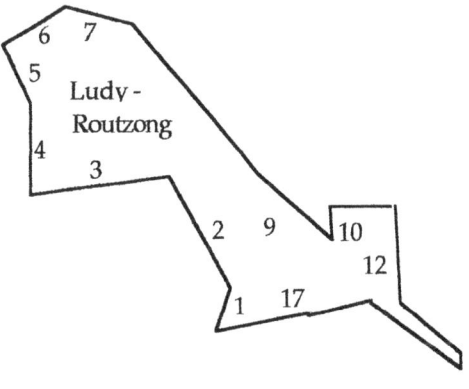

Part of the two following tracts of land to wit Fredericksburg and Add to Friendship. Beginning at the end of the first line of a tract of land called David's Will and reversing the said land three courses.

Frederick County Land Records

JS-38-194
Jacob Routzah to Henry Miller
Part of Fredericksburg and Add to Friendship
recorded 18 February 1832
68 acres

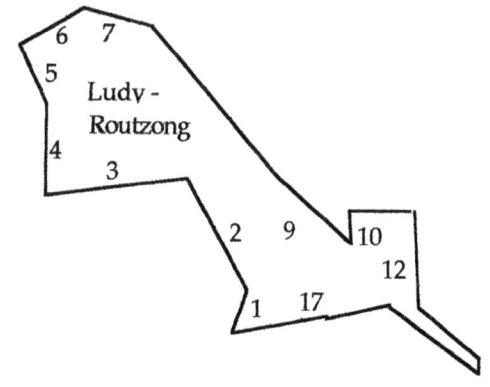

Being part of the following tract of land. To wit, Fredericksburg and Add to Friendship containing 67 acres of land more or less together with all and singular the buildings improvements and appurtenances thereunto.

JS-39-260
John Stemple et ux to George Baltzell
Watson's Welfare
recorded 5 July 1832
273 and 1/2 acres

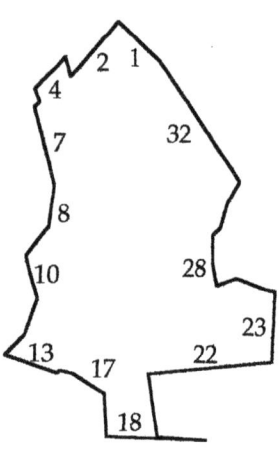

Beginning for the outlines thereof at a stone planted at the end of the sixth line of the afsd original tract of land called the Rsy on Watson's Welfare and also being the beginning of that tract of land called What Not it also being the end of the tenth line of John Young's land called I Wish There Was More and runing thence with the sixth and part of the fifth lines of said Watson's Welfare reversed by an allowance and correction of a half degree for variation.

JS-39-264-8
George Baltzell, Attorney, to Henry Miller
Part of Add to Friendship
recorded 5 July 1832
75 and 1/2 acres

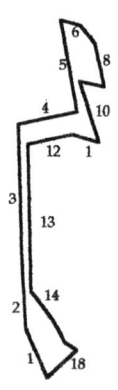

Part of a tract of land called Add to Friendship being principally in the county afsd and part thereof beginning and lying in Washington County and state afsd beginning for the same at the end of the 20 perches on the fifth line of the whole tract and running thence.

For the second part of said land called the Add to Friendship said part lying north of the turnpike road as afsd beginning for the same at a large __ being at the end of the third line of the original tract of land called Flonham and running thence with said line reversed.

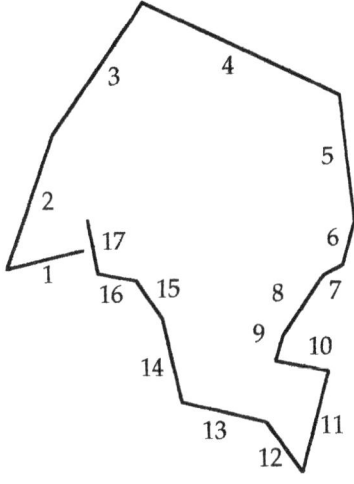

JS-44-393
Ezra Slifer, Trustee, to David Mullendore
recorded 18 November 1833
221 and 1/2 acres

Beginning for the same so as to embrace it all in one piece or survey at a bounded hickory it being the beginning tree of a tract of land called Chesnut Thicket granted James Piles July 8th 1757 and running thence.

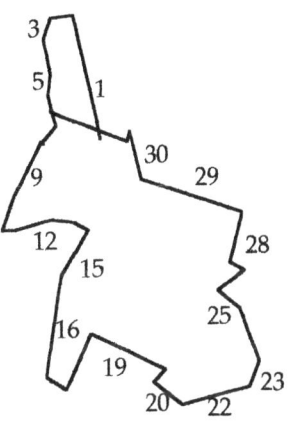

JS-42, 313-314
John Herring et al. to Mathias Flook
Part of Fredericksburg
recorded 28 January 1833
39 and 1/2 acres

All that part of a tract of land called Fredericksburg beginning at a bounded white oak tree it being the beginning tree of a track of land called Bowser's Addition and running thence with the outlines of Fredericksburg.

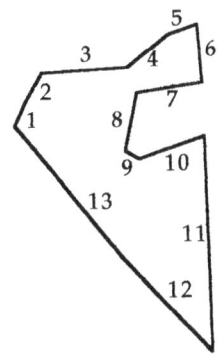

JS-42, 481
Sidney Ringer (widow of John Ringer)
to Vincent Sanner
Part of I Hope It Is Well Done, Pegging Awl, Turkeyfoot, Mount Pleasant, and Water Enough
recorded 15 May 1833
31 + acres; also 75 acres

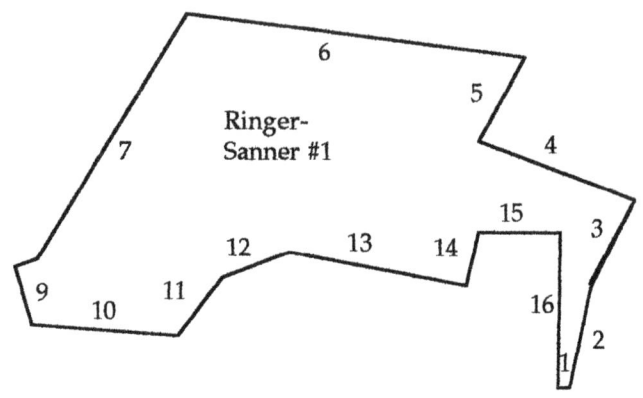

Part of a tract of land called I Hope It Is Well Done, part of a tract of land called Pegging Awl, part of Turkeyfoot, and part of Mount Pleasant. Beginning for the outlines of the whole at the end of forty perches on the seventh line of a tract of land called Water Enough and running thence.

Also part of a tract of land called Fidler's Purchase, part of a tract of land called the Rsy on Exchange, and part of a tract of land called Bubble. Beginning for the outlines of the whole at the original beginning tree of Exchange and running thence.

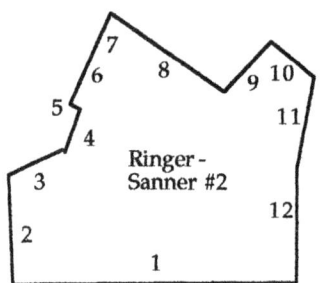

TG-6, 571
Hannah Beachley et al. to
John William Beachley
Part of Rsy on (The) Gap
recorded 27 January 1877
216 acres, also 7 acres and 30 perches

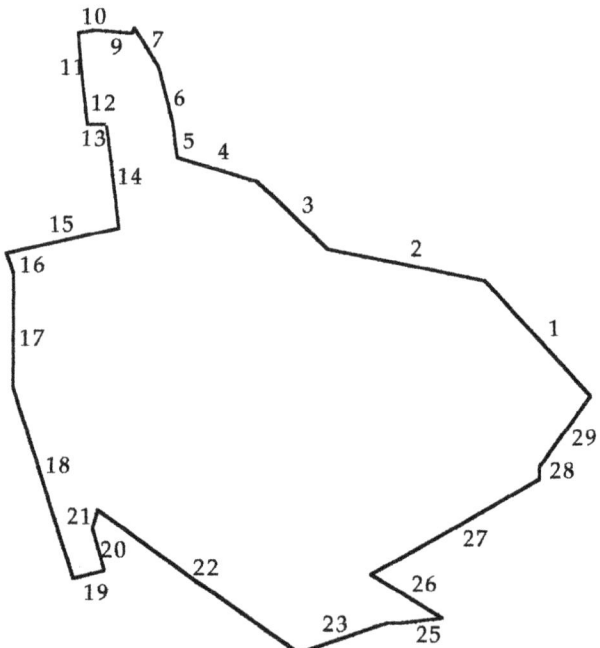

Beginning at a planted stone standing at the end of the first line of the whole tract called he Rsy on (The) Gap and running thence according to the bearings of the lines in the 26th day of October A. D. 1868 and with the outlines of said tract.

Also all that part of a tract of land called Flonham described as follows beginning at the beginning and running thence.

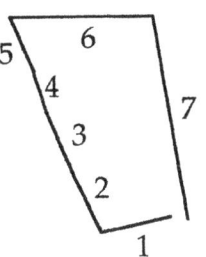

TG-8, 651
William H. and Catharine Jones
to John D. Flook
Part of Flonham and Remnant
recorded 16 January 1878
20 acres

Beginning to include both parts hereby conveyed at a stone pile on the west side of an old wagon road it being a corner of that part of Flonham sold by said Jones and wife to Daniel Beachley and reversing thence allowing two (2) degrees for variation.

(The "old wagon road" was undoubtedly the Main Road from Frederick to Fort Frederick.)

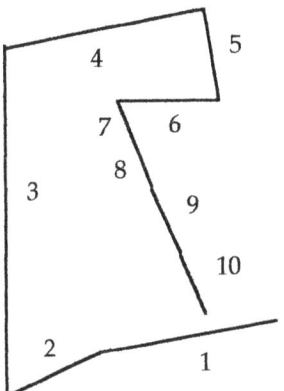

TG-9, 18
Joshua Flook and Jacob H. Flook, executors of John P. Flook, to Madeleine V. Dahlgren
Part of Flonham
recorded 23 February 1878
20 acres

Beginning to include both parts hereby conveyed at a stone pile on the west side of an old wagon road it being a corner of that part of Flonham sold by said Jones and wife to Daniel Beachley and running thence allowing two degrees for variation.

(Author: The "old wagon road" was undoubtedly the Main Road from Frederick to Fort Frederick.)

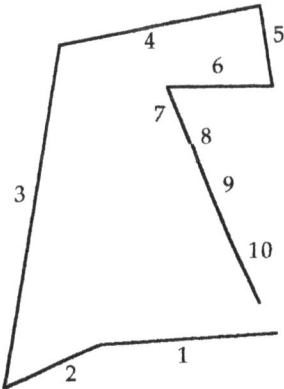

TG-9, 427
John W. Beachley and Marietta Beachley
to Madeleine V. Dahlgren
Part of Flonham and Rsy on (The) Gap
recorded 26 April 1898
38 acres, 3 roods, and 22 perches

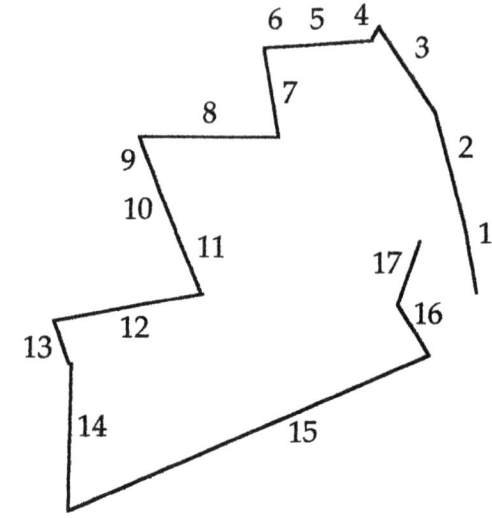

Being part of a tract of land called the Rsy on (The) Gap and part of a tract called Flonham both lying contiguous and embraced by the following metes and bounds, to wit: Beginning at a bounded white oak tree, standing on the east margin of the turnpike road leading from Frederick City to Boonsboro and at the end of the 4th line of said John W. Beachley's whole tract and running thence with the lines thereof the eight following courses and distances.

WR-3-224
Abraham Lemaster to C. Harshman
(The) Breeches
recorded 7 September 1782
26 and 1/2 acres

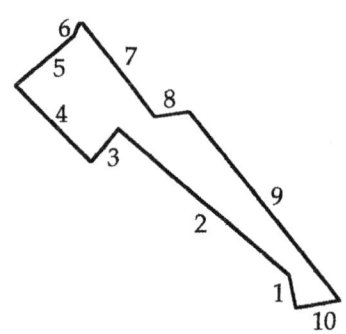

Beginning for said part at the end of sixteen perches on the eighteenth line of a tract of land called Hard To Find it being the original beginning of the said land and running thence.

WR 4, 531
Peter Beaver to Christian Kizer
Brayface
recorded 25 May 1784
40 acres

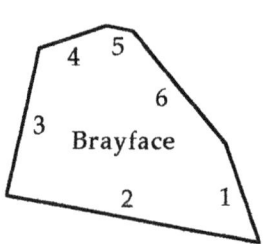

All that tract or parcel of land called Bray-face, which being part of the Rsy on Oxford. Beginning at the bounded tree of said Brayface, one of the original tracts, and running thence.

WR-6-135
Philip Marshall to Jacob Young
Part of Oxford
recorded 28 September 1785
100 acres

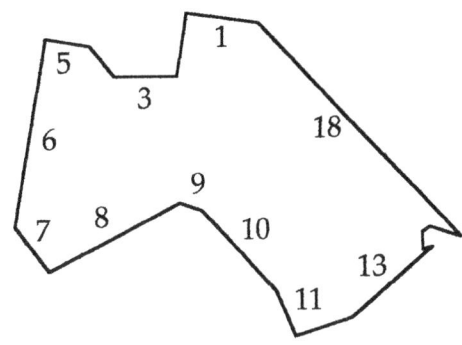

All that tract or part of a tract of land called Oxford situate lying and being in the county and state afsd beginning at a marked red oak the beginning tree of Peter Beaver's part of a tract of land called Pickall, and running thence.

WR-6, 169
Thomas and Fielder Gantt to Peter Gaver
Part of Fielderia Manor
recorded 12 November 1785
25 acres

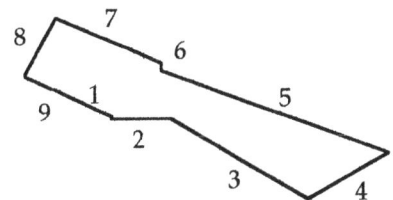

All that part of the afsd land conveyed to the said Thomas Gantt by the afsd deed lying and being in Frederick County afsd which is included within the following lines courses and distances to wit beginning at the end of the first line of a tract of land called The Mountain belonging to the said Peter Gaver.

WR-7
Bartholomew Booker to Frederick Fox
Part of I Hope It Is Well Done and
Pegging Awl
4 April 1787
92 acres

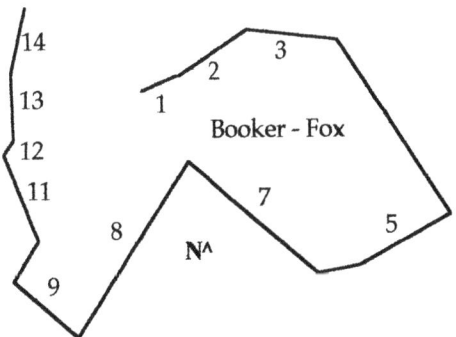

All that piece or parcel of land lying and being in county afsd part of I Hope It Is Well Done beginning for said part at a stone near the main road that leads from Middle Town to Sharpsburg and running thence.

Frederick County Land Records

WR-7-10
Peter Smeltzer to Henry Smith
Knave's Good Will
recorded 16 September 1786
50 acres

All that tract or parcel of land called Knave's Good Will lying and being in the county and state afsd and beginning for the afsd tract of land at a bounded red oak standing on the edge of a hill and running thence.

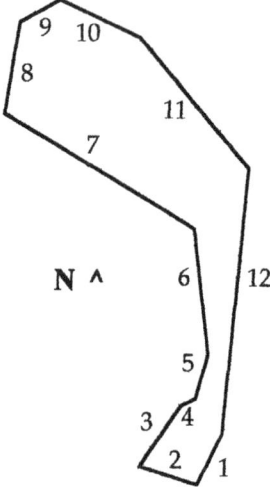

WR-7-33
Peter Beaver to Henry Lighter
Part of Christie's Folly
recorded 21 October 1786
9 acres and 1/2 acres

Part of a tract of land called Christie's Folly. Beginning at the beginning tree of a tract of land called Cool Spring and running thence.

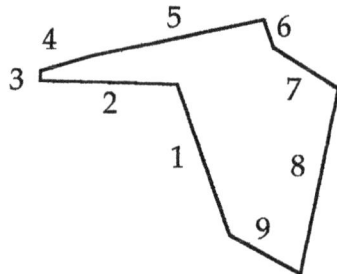

WR-7-34
Peter Beaver to Jacob Lawrence
Part of Christie's Folly
recorded 21 October 1786
19 and 1/4 acres

Being part of a tract of land called Christie's Folly beginning at the end of seventeen perches and a half-perch on the second line of said tract called Christie's Folly, and running thence.

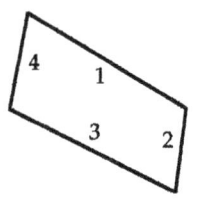

WR-7-48
George Fidler to Ludwick Layman
Part of Fidler's Purchase, Rsy on Exchange, and Bubble
recorded 18 November 1786
100 acres

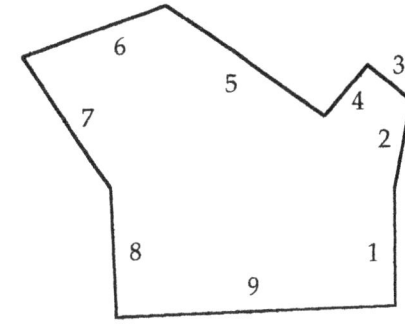

All that tract or parcel of land lying and being in Frederick County afsd called Fidler's Purchase being part of two tracts of land the one called the Rsy on Exchange and a tract called Bubble. Beginning for the outlines at the original beginning tree of Exchange and running thence.

WR-7-531
Joseph Kephart to Jacob Young
Rsy on Stoney Ridge
recorded 27 October 1787
50 acres

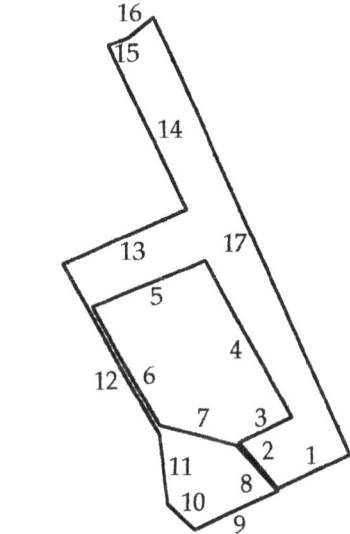

Being part of the Rsy on Stoney Ridge lying and being in the county and state afsd beginning at the end of the seventh line of the said rsy and running thence.

WR-8-632
Richard Butler to Jacob Fulwider
Goose Cap
recorded 16 September 1799
33 acres

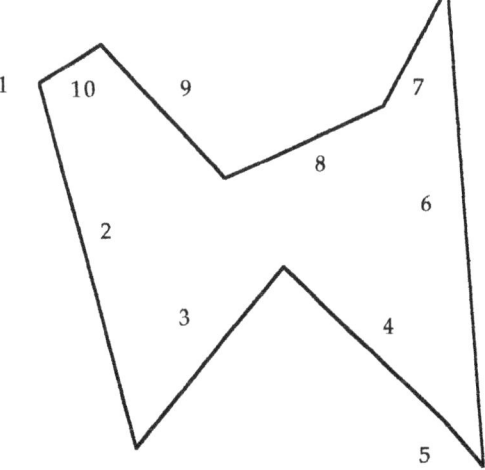

Beginning for said part at two small water Ash saplings standing on the westernmost bank or shore of Middle Creek a branch of Catoctin Creek about seven perches above the public road leading from Frederick Town to Hagers Town and on or very near to a line of part of the said land called Goose Cap __ by the said Thomas Welsh to David Stottlemyer and running thence.

Frederick County Land Records

WR-9-25
Peter Beaver to Henry Lighter
Part of Rsy on Oxford
recorded 11 April 1788
67 acres

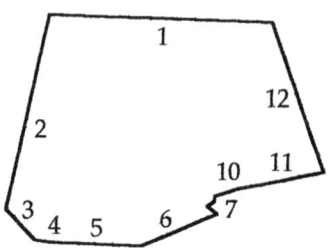

All the two following tracts or parcels of land being part of the Rsy on Oxford lying and being in the county aforesaid beginning for the first part at the end of forty three perches on the first line of a tract of land called Christie's Folly and running thence.

WR-9-607
Bartholomew Booker et al.
to Christian Koogle
Rsy on Wooden Platter
recorded _ February 1791
327 acres

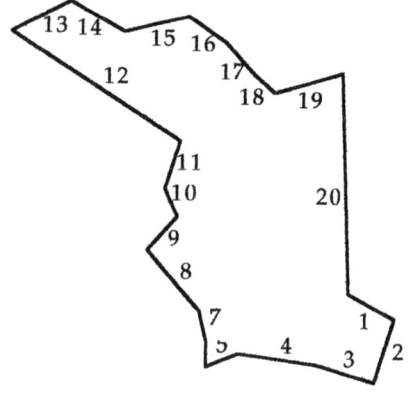

Beginning at the original beginning tree and running thence.

WR-12-56
Ludwick Layman to Peter Layman
Fidler's Purchase and Bubble (Boble)
recorded 14 November 1793
100 acres

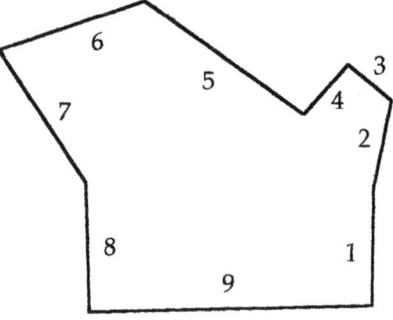

All the following tract or parcel of land called Fidler's Purchase lying and being in Frederick County afsd it being part of two tracts of land the one called the Rsy on Exchange and a tract called Bubble. Beginning at the original beginning tree of Exchange and running thence.

WR-12, 358-364
Bartholomew Booker Estate
Part of Pickall
recorded 19 April 1794
304 acres

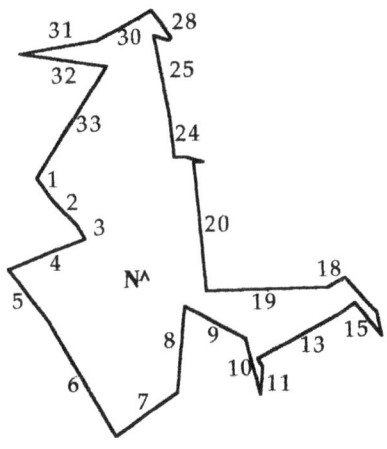

Lot Number One lying in the county and state afsd and being part of the five tracts of land herein before mentioned beginning at a bounded white oak tree bounded tree of a tract of land called John's Delight and running thence by and with the main road.

"on the road from Frederick Town to Williamsport and Hagerstown" (see F. Edward Wright, *Western Maryland Newspaper Abstracts 1786-1798* (Silver Spring, Md.: Family Line Publications, 1985), 1:14.)

WR-12, 367-368
Frederick Fox to Peter Hutzel
Part of Fredericksburg
recorded 23 April 1794
8 and 1/2 acres

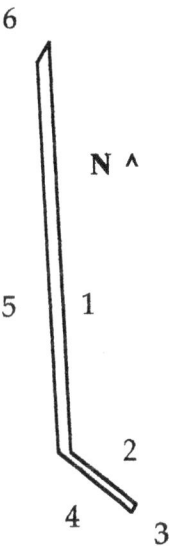

Part of a tract of land called Fredericksburg lying in Frederick County afsd beginning at the beginning of the afsd land called Fredericksburg and running therein with the outlines thereof.

WR-13-49
Jacob Smith Sr to Jacob Smith Jr
Part of (The) Rsy on Learning, Betty's Good Will, Rsy on Mendall, Pickall, I Hope It Is Well Done, and Exchange.
recorded 10 February 1795
10 acres

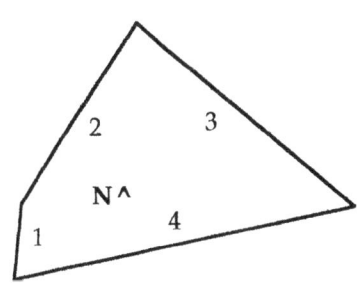

Also that tract or parcel of land lying in Frederick County afsd called Betty's Good Will beginning at a bounded white oak the original beginning tree and running thence.

Also one other tract or parcel of land lying in Frederick County afsd called a part of (The) Rsy on Mendall beginning at the end of the fourteenth line of the afsd tract of land called the Rsy on Mendall where it calls for the line of the afsd land called Betty's Good Will and running thence.

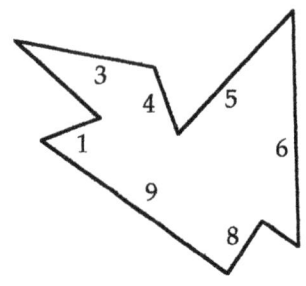

Also one other tract or parcel of land lying in Frederick County afsd called part of Pickall part of Mendall resurveyed and called I Hope It Is Well Done beginning at a bounded red oak standing at the end of a a line drawn south eleven degrees west twenty five perches from the beginning tree of Michael Smith's land called Last Shift and running by and with the lines between Jacob Smith and Michael Smith.

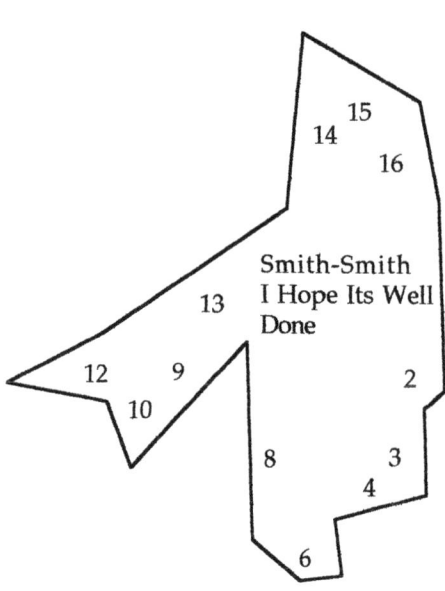

Also one other tract or parcel of land lying in the county afsd called Exchange beginning at the end of sixty nine perches on the second line of the original and running with said second line.

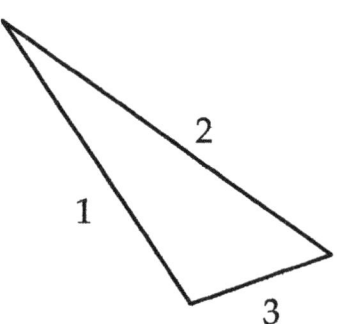

(**Author's Note:** The above portion of the Exchange tract was subject to a lawsuit between Joseph Chapline Jr and William William Chapline from about 1791 to 1801. The legal record in the MdHR mentions Frederick Fox.)

WR-13-621
Jacob Young to George Butt
Part of Rsy on Oxford and
I Hope It Is Well Done
recorded 7 November 1795
90 and 1/4 acres; also 4 and 1/4 acres

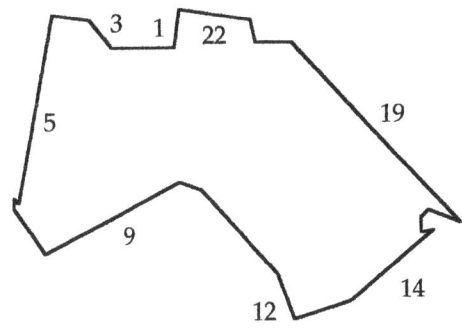

The two following tracts or parcels of land lying and being in Frederick County afsd part of a tract of land called (The) Rsy on Oxford beginning at the end of eleven perches on the fifth line of said Jacob Young's part of the afsd land conveyed him by Peter Beaver and running with the outlines thereof.

WR-17-158-9
Frederick Fox to George Methard
Part of Fredericksburg
21 April 1798
10 acres

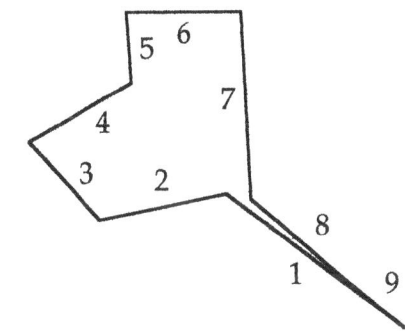

Beginning at a stone planted at the end of the third line of said land and running with it four courses.

WR-22-480
George Butt to Matthias Flook
Flook's Content, and Rsy on Oxford
date unknown
88 acres; also 4 and 1/4 acres

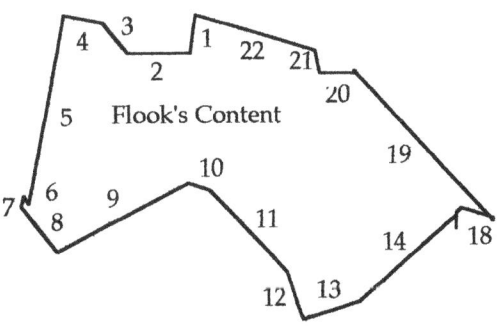

Beginning at the beginning of the said George Butt's part of a tract of land it being part of the Rsy on Oxford conveyed him by a certain Jacob Young of Conrad.

Frederick County Land Records

WR-26-569
Peter Gaver's heirs to Joshua Harley
Part of Mountain
recorded 11 April 1805
195 acres

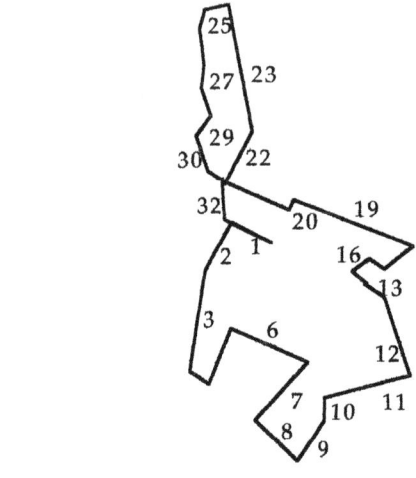

Beginning for the outlines thereof at a stone planted at the beginning of a tract of land originally called the Mountain marked B:M 1789 and running thence with said land.

WR-27-543
Peter Layman to George Fox
Rsy on Exchange, Bubble, and Mt. Pleasant
recorded 7 October 1805
100 acres, also 18 acres

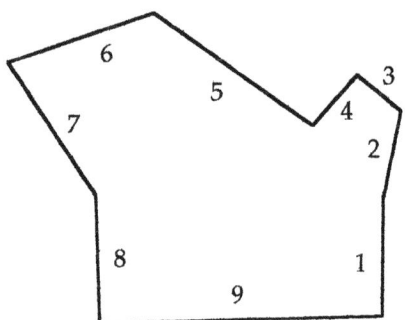

Fidler's Purchase it being part of two tract of land the one called the Rsy on Exchange and the other called Bubble beginning at the original beginning tree of Exchange and running thence.

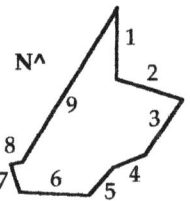

WR-31
George Fox to Frederick Fox
Mt. Pleasant
recorded 1 August 1807
18 acres

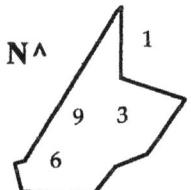

Part of a track of land called Mount Pleasant lying in Frederick County afsd beginning at the end of the second line of the whole tract and running with the outline thereof to the end of the eleventh line thereof to wit.

WR-31-478
George Methard to William Bottenberg
Part of Fredericksburg
recorded 12 September 1807
10 acres

The following piece or parcel of land lying and being in Frederick County afsd being part of a tract called Fredericksburg beginning at a stone planted at the end of the third line of said land and running with it four courses.

WR-32-26-8
Frederick Fox to Joseph Swearingen
Part of Fredericksburg
21 September 1807
30 acres

Beginning at the end of the 7th line of the whole tract afsd called Fredericksburg and running with the outline thereof according to the metes and bounds thereof to the end of the twentieth line of the whole tract afsd called Fredericksburg thence with a straight line to the beginning containing 30 acres of land more or less.

WR-32-28
Frederick Fox to John Ringer
Part of I Hope It Is Well Done, Pegging Awl, Turkeyfoot, and Mount Pleasant
recorded 7 October 1807
50 acres

Part of several tracts. I Hope It Is Well Done, Pegging Awl, Turkeyfoot, and Mount Pleasant, beginning at the beginning tree of said Pegging Awl and running with it.

WR-32-30
George Fox to John Ringer
Fidler's Purchase, Rsy on Exchange, and Bubble
recorded 7 October 1807
100 acres

That tract or parcel of land called Fidler's Purchase lying and being in Frederick County afsd and being part of two tracts of land the one called the Rsy on Exchange and the other called Bubble beginning at the original beginning tree of Exchange and running thence.

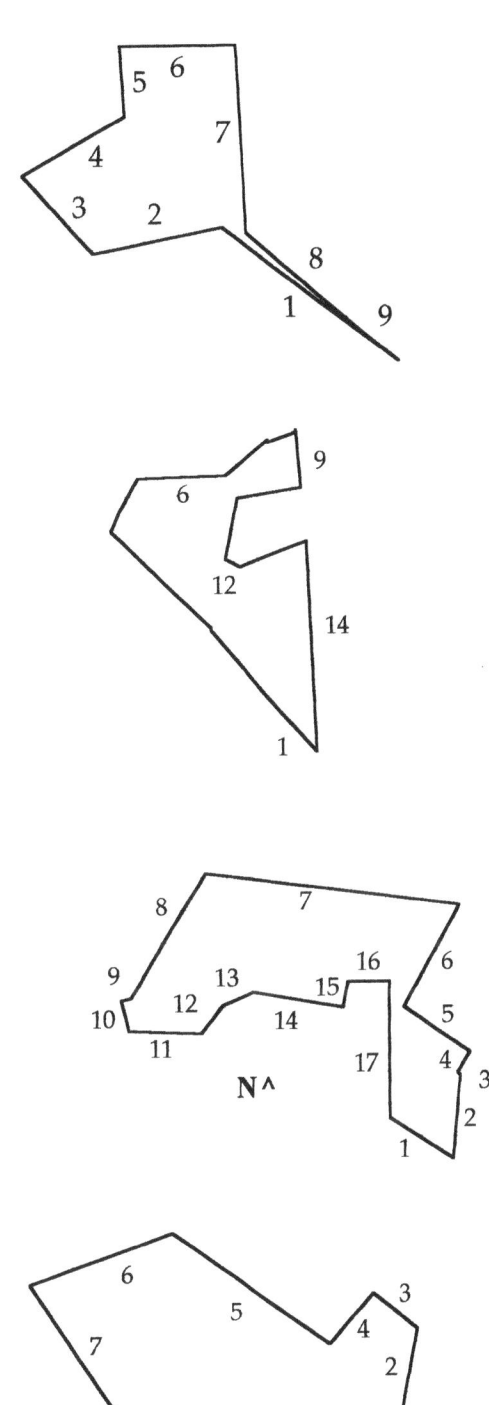

Frederick County Land Records

WR 32-63
Frederick Fox to Henry Ascherman
Part of I Hope It Is Well Done, Shettle, Exchange, Pegging Awl, Turkeyfoot, Mount Pleasant, and Peter's Neglect
recorded 14 October 1807
199 and 1/2 acres; also 19 acres

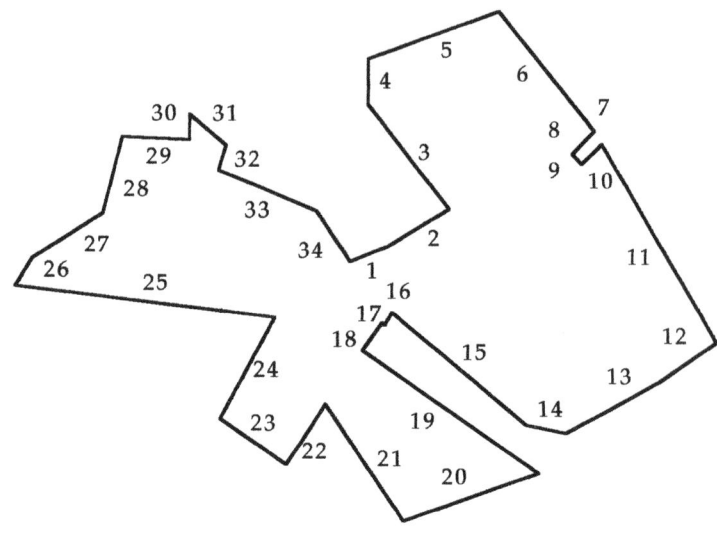

Being part of the several following tracts reduced into one entire tract to wit I Hope It Is Well Done, Shettle, Exchange, Pegging Awl, Turkeyfoot, Mount Pleasant and Peter's Neglect. Beginning at a stone planted near the main road leading to Sharpsburg and the beginning of Daniel Booker's land and running thence.

Also one other tract or parcel of land lying in the county afsd it being part of a tract called Fredericksburg beginning at the end of the fifth line of George Methard's part of said tract and running thence.

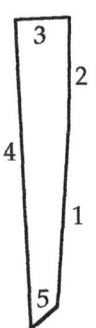

WR-32-225
Michael Miller to Jacob Smith
Part of I Hope It Is Well Done
recorded 30 December 1807
10 and 1/8 acres

Part of a tract of land called I Hope It Is Well Done and beginning at a stone planted at the end of the twentieth line of said Jacob Smith's land called Now I Know It and running with said line reverse.

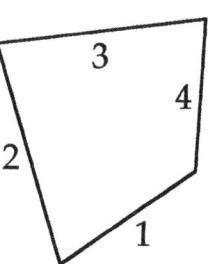

Line 1 - south 56 and 1/2 degrees west 36 perches to the middle of the main road leading to Boonsborough and with said road

Line 2 - north 16 and 1/2 degrees west 50 perches

WR-34-313
William Bottenberg to Peter Ludy
Part of Fredericksburg
recorded 4 February 1809
10 acres

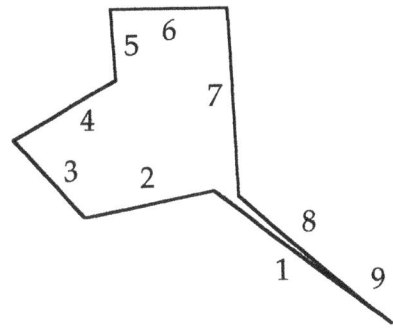

Part of a tract called Fredericksburg beginning at a stone planted at the end of the third line of said tract of land and running with it four courses.

WR-34-315
Joseph Swearingen to Peter Ludy
Part of Add to Friendship and Fredericksburg
recorded 16 February 1809
58 acres

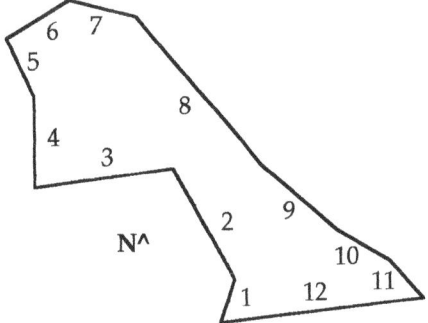

Part of the two following tracts to wit Fredericksburg and Add to Friendship beginning at the end of the first line of a tract of land called David's Will and reversing the said land three courses.

WR-36-85
Michael Miller to Jacob Smith
Part of Rsy on Mendall, Pickall, I Hope It Is Well Done, Shettle, and Martitany
recorded 26 December 1809
112 and 1/2 acres, excepting 10 and 1/8 acres; also 1/2 acre

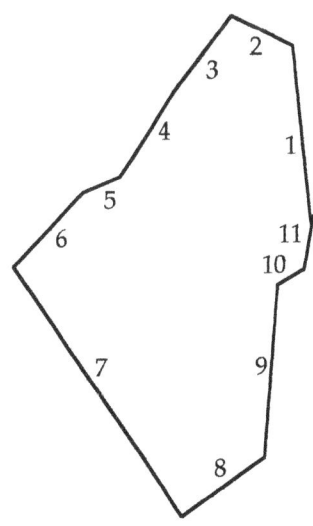

The first piece or parcel being part of several tracts to wit the Rsy on Mendall, Pickall, I Hope It Is Well Done, Shettle, and Martitany beginning at a stone planted at the end of the nineteenth line of John Routesawn's whole tract conveyed him by the exceutors of Bartholomew Booker deceased and running thence.

WR-40, 275-276
Alexander Grim to Joseph Garrott
Rsy on Grim's Delight
recorded 10 August 1811
200 acres

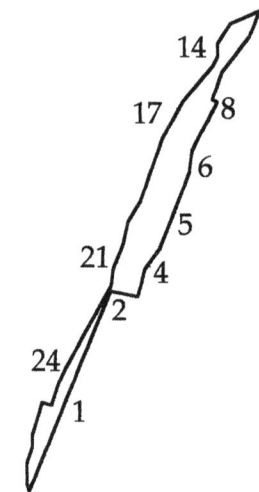

Being part of a tract of land called the Rsy on Grim's Delight beginning therefor at the end of three hundred and forty perches on the tenth line of a tract of land called the Rsy on Maryland it being also the beginning of a tract of land called The Mountain Side and running thence.

WR-42-550
Peter Ludy to Jacob Routzong
Part of Fredericksburg, Add to Friendship
recorded 9 July 1812
68 acres

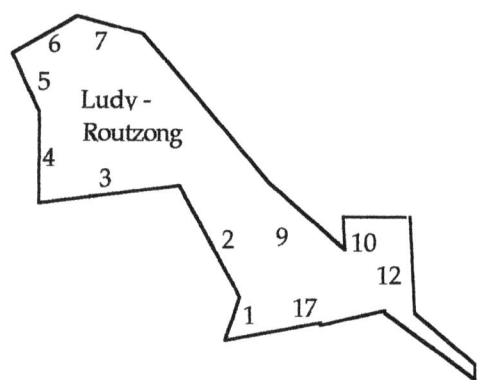

Part of the two following tracts of land (to wit) Fredericksburg and Add to Friendship. Beginning at the end of the first line of a tract of land called David's Will and reversing the said land three courses.

WR-42-550
Joel Keller to John Wise
Wise's Tract of Civil War fame
7 May 1858
4 and 3/4 acres

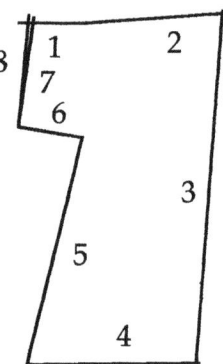

Excepting and reserving thereout a road through said land which is hereinafter more fully described. Beginning for said lot or parcel of land at a large chestnut tree standing on the north side of the Sharpsburg road and at the end of the 2nd line of the deed conveying said land to said Joel Keller and hereinafter more particularly referred to then with said road and the lines of said deed as follows to wit.

WR-46-312
Christian Baer to Jacob Routzong
Bowser's Addition
date unknown
10 acres

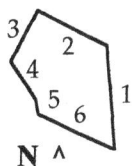

Beginning at a bounded white oak standing near the top of the South Mountain on the side of the main road leading from Frederick Town to Sharpsburg and running thence.

BFG-5, 516
John W. Derr, et al, to Adam Koogle
Part of Add to Friendship
recorded 25 April 1860
25 and 1/10 acres

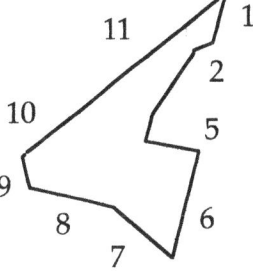

Part of a tract of land called Add to Friendship designated in a division of the real estate of Henry Miller deceased as lots No 1 and No 2 beginning to embrace both lots in one general outline at the end of the fifth line of 114 acres of said tract called Add to Friendship deeded the 31st day of May 1832 by George Baltzell, trustee, to Henry Miller and running thence by and with the outlines of the said 114 acres parcel eight courses and distances viz.

BGF-6, 216
Joel Keller to John Wise
Wise's Tract of Civil War fame
recorded 7 May 1858
4 and 3/4 acres

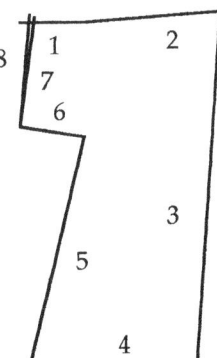

Beginning for said lot or parcel of land at a large chestnut tree standing on the north side of the Sharpsburg road and at the end of the 2nd line of the deed conveying said land to said Joel Keller and hereinafter more particularly referred to then with said road and the lines of said deed as follows to wit.

DSB-1, 397
Mary Sheffer, Trustee, to John W. Koogle
Part of Various Tracts
recorded 22 May 1867
23 acres

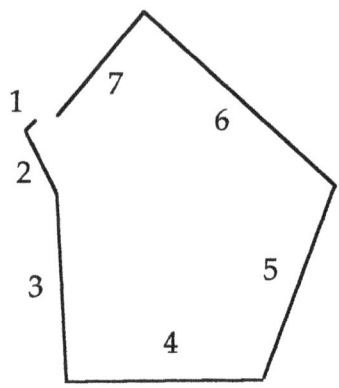

Being part of a tract of land called the Rsy on Mendall, part of a tract called Pickall, part of a tract called I Hope It Is Well Done, part of a tract called Shettle, and part of a tract called Martitany, or be it known by any other name or names whatever beginning for the same at a planted stone standing at the end of the fourth line of Michael Miller's deed to Jacob Smith dated in December 1809 for 112 1/2 acres, said stone being also the beginning of the deed from Jonas Smith to Jacob Lighter dated April 30 1835 for 15 5/8 acres and running thence according to the bearings of the lines on the 11th day of March 1867.

DSB-1, 398
George Routzahn to John W. Koogle
Part of Various Tracts
recorded 22 May 1867
16 and 1/4 acres, excepting 2 acres and 76 square perches

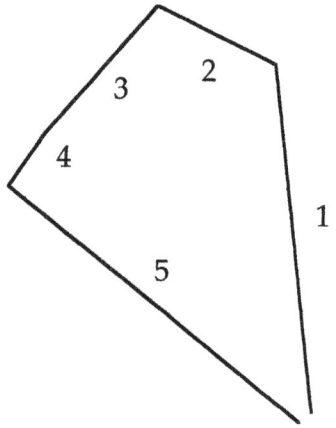

Being part of a tract of land called Pickall, part of a tract called the Rsy on Mendall, part of I Hope It Is Well Done, and part of a tract called Shettle, beginning for the outlines of the land hereby intended to be conveyed at the end of 4 perches on the first line in the deed from Michael Miller to Jacob Smith for 112 1/2 acres dated on or about the 2nd day of December 1809 and running thence with the outlines of said deed the four following courses and distances viz.

HGO-1-6
Henry Griffith
Hard to Find
surveyed 20 September 1784
38 acres

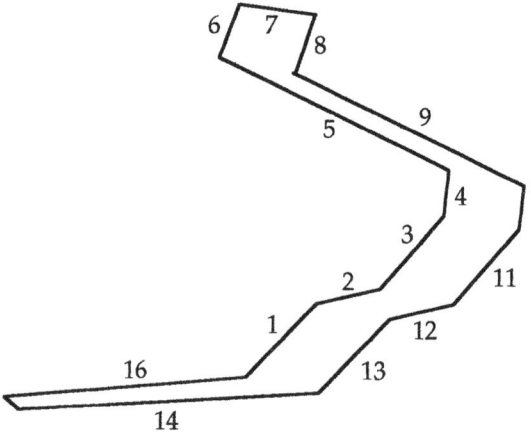

Beginning at the end of the twenty second line of a tract of land called (The) Meadow granted Thomas Johnson Esqr and running thence with said land.

HGO-1-9
Andrew Arnold
Stricker's Timber Land Enlarged
resurveyed 4 June 1792
284 acres

Beginning for the outlines of the whole at a stone planted at the end of the 2d line of the whole tract called the Rsy on Stricker's Timber Land and running thence with said land.

HGO-1-156
Frederick Fox
Fredericksburg
surveyed 6 July 1792
75 acres

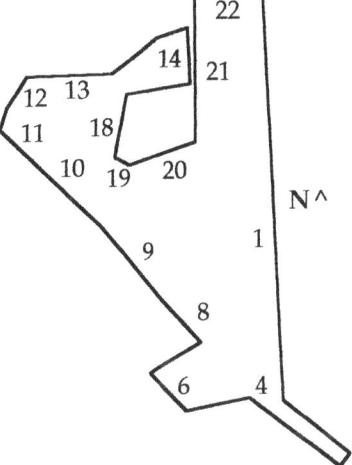

Beginning at the end of the 12th line of a tract of land called Pickall granted Bartholomew Booker on or about the 25th day of March 1766 and running thence.

HGO-1-359
James Clarke
(The) Forest of Needwood
surveyed 25 April 1789
275 acres

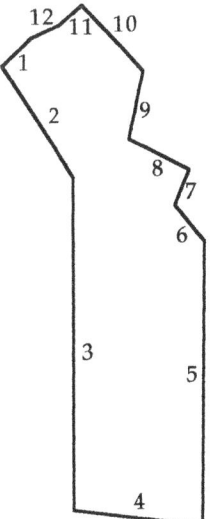

Beginning at the beginning of the whole tract called (The) Forest of Needwood running thence with the 1st line thereof.

Frederick County Land Records

HGO-1-396
Peter Miller
Miller's Purchase
resurveyed 26 November 1789
121 acres

Beginning for the outlines at a stone now planted at the end of the 2nd line of a tract of land called (The) Rsy on Dawson's Purchase and marked PM 1789 and running thence reverse of said line.

HGO-1-403
George Cost
Cost's Content
resurveyed 10 December 1789
369 acres

Beginning for the outlines thereof at a stone now planted at the end of 65 and 1/4 perches on the 4th line of the afsd original tract of land called (The) Forest and also north 32 west 3/4 perches from the bounded tree of a tract of land called the Rsy on Poole's Delight said stone is marked GCB 1789 and running thence with said land called (The) Forest.

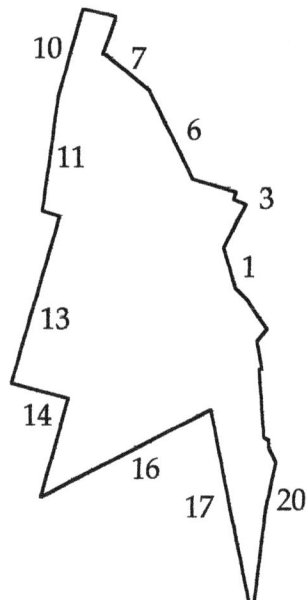

HGO-1-466
Andrew Smith
Neighbor's Content (Rsy on Middle Town)
resurveyed 25 November 1790
180 acres

Beginning for the outlines thereof at a bounded black oak the beginning tree of that original tract called Loving Brother it being the beginning tree of the afsd tract called Middle Town now resurveyed as an original beginning thence.

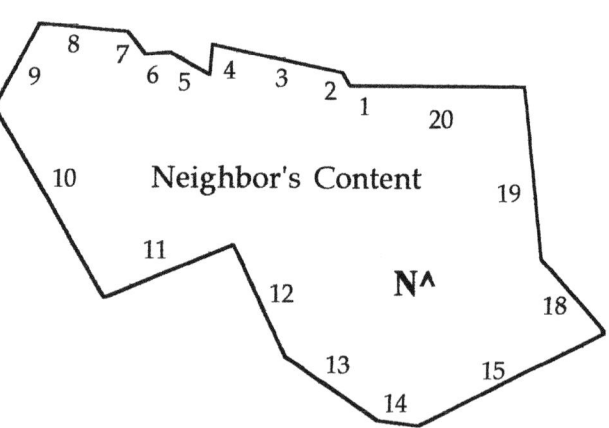

HGO-1-510
(The) Top of the Blue Ridge
Joseph Myers
recorded 26 March 1773
45 acres

Beginning for the outlines thereof at a stone planted at the end of the 11th and last line of a tract of land called Miller's Purchase and running thence with the given line of said land.

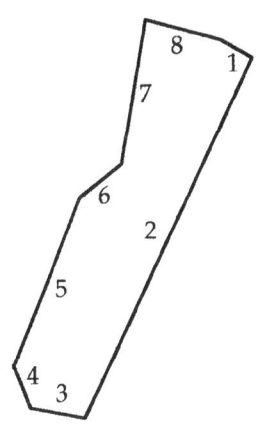

HGO-1-569
John Tucker to Henry Neff
Biegley's Displeasure
resurveyed 1 May 1792
222 acres

Beginning for the outlines of the 1st part at a bounded white oak it being the beginning tree of that original tract called Tick Neck and running thence with the given line reverse.

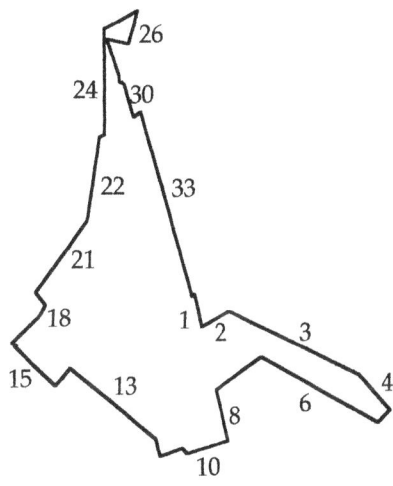

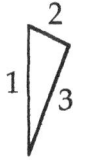

HGO-1-571
Jacob Smith
No Matter What
resurveyed 18 May 1792
210 acres

Beginning for the outlines thereof at a stone planted between 2 bound white oak they being the beginning tree of the whole tract called the Rsy on Learning, Add to Learning, and Part of the Rsy on Learning and running thence with said land 3 courses.

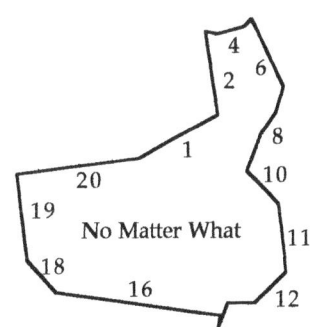

HGO-1-572
Jno Flook
(The) Blooming Month of May
resurveyed 18 May 1792
214 acres

Beginning for the outlines thereof at a large stone marked BS 1792 now planted at the end of the 23rd line of the whole tract called (The) Rsy on Learning, Add to Learning, and part of the Rsy on Learning and running thence with the dividing between Jno and Jacob Flooks.

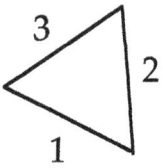

STH-267-367
George Alfred Townsend to
the United States of America
War Correspondents Memorial Arch
recorded 24 September 1904
28 and 1/8 square perches

Beginning at a point near the dividing line between Frederick and Washington Counties Maryland and in the middle of the road leading from Burkittsville to Gapland Station said point being south 10 degrees west 1 and 1/10 perches from a stone planted on the north side of said road and near the stone fence, and running thence with the middle of the road.

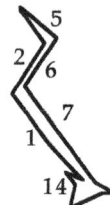

THO-1
Henry Beagley
It's Bad Enough
surveyed 15 April 1796
14 and 3/4 acres

Beginning at a bounded white oak tree the beginning of a tract of land called Worse and Worse and running with it three courses.

THO-1-38
George Darr
Bear Swamp Forrest
Surveyed 8 October 1795
319 acres

The original included in the rsy.

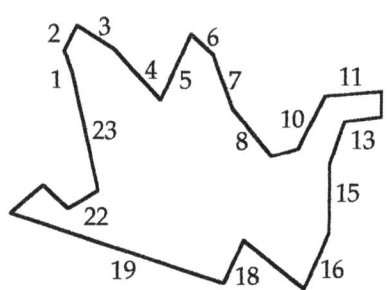

THO-1-38
George Scott
Rsy of Bear Swamp Forrest
resurveyed 8 October 1795
701 acres

Beginning at a large rock standing upright marked G S 1795 near a chesnut oak tree bounded with 12 notches and on the east side of the South Mountain and running thence.

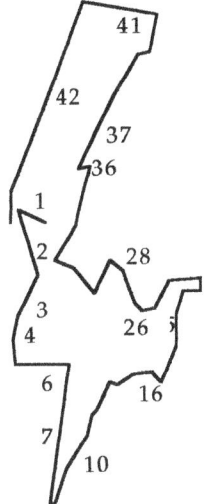

THO-1-90
Samuel Shoup
Chestnut Oak Ridge
surveyed 16 June 1796
138 acres

Beginning at a bounded chesnut oak tree standing about six perches from the fourth line of a tract of land called Joseph's Tricks and near the road leading to Lamb's improvement and running thence.

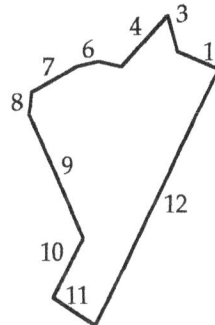

THO-1-103
Joseph Swearingen Esqr.
Mount Pelier
surveyed 8 November 1790
90 acres

Beginning at a bounded chesnut oak tree and running thence.

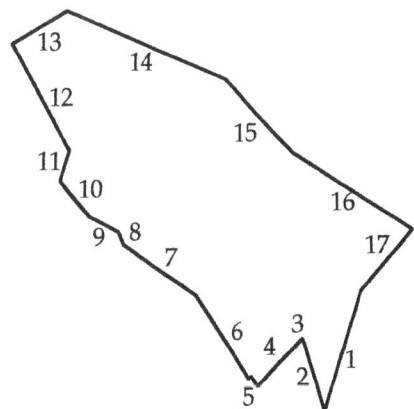

THO-1-116
John Miller
Miller's Timberland
surveyed 21 November 1797
16 acres

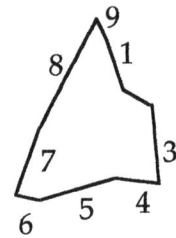

Beginning at the end of the 25th line of a tract of land called Gaver's Recovery resurveyed for Peter Gaver on or about the 8th day of December 1789 and running thence with said land the 3 following courses.

THO-1-188
We Could Not Agree
Henry Laydrat
resurveyed 18 July 1800
119 and 1/2 acres

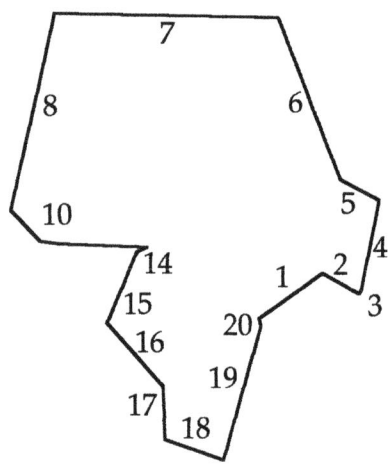

Beginning for the out lines thereof at a stone now planted at the end of the first line of that tract of land called Cool Spring granted James Wardrop May 17th 1750 for 75 acres and marked thus 1800 B. S. and running thence reverse of the said first line.

THO-1-194
Samuel Shoup
Cool Spring (A Resurvey)
resurveyed 18 January 1801
266 and 1/2 acres

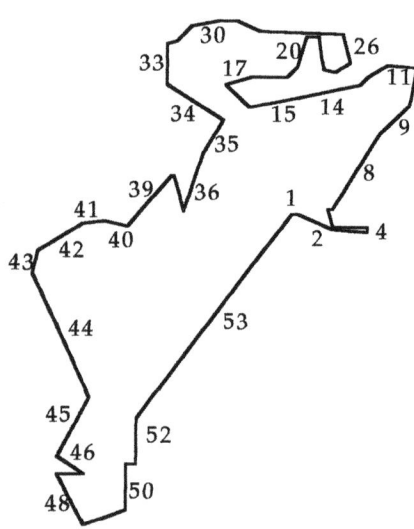

Beginning for the outlines of the whole resurvey made by virtue of the above mentioned warrant at the original beginning tree and running thence.

THO-1-220
Jacob Smith
Now I Know It
resurveyed 15 August 1803
198 acres

A Rsy of Betty's Good Will, Rsy on Learning, Part of the Rsy on Mendall, and I Hope It Is Well Done.

Said tree being the beginning of Bartholomew Booker's deed to Jacob Smith for 111 acres of land bearing date on the 4th April 1787 and running thence.

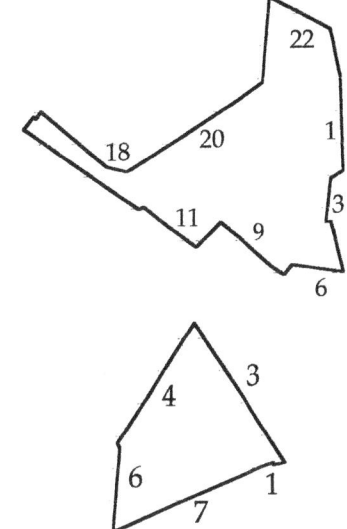

THO-1-238
Peter Miller
Miller's Farm
resurveyed 22 October 1804
360 acres

Beginning for the outlines thereof at a stone now planted and marked B:S P:M 1804 at the end of 65 perches on the 3rd line of that former original tract called Uncle's Gift granted Thomas Hawkins Sept 30th 1747 160 acres it being the beginning of the first mentioned of the above originals.

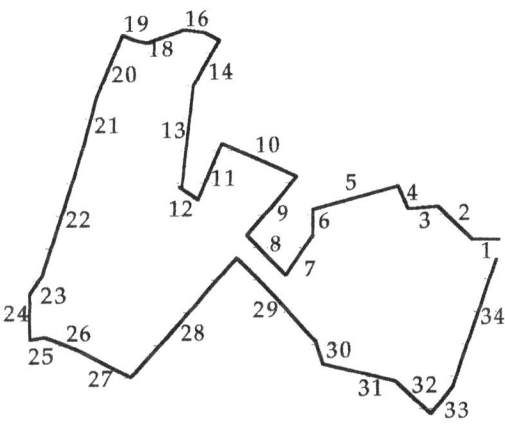

THO-1, 244
Elias Wilyard
Rsy on Part of Uncle's Gift
13 April 1804
177 acres

At the original place of beginning of Uncle's Gift a fsd which stone is marked 1747/B & S V G and running thence reverse of the given line of said origination.

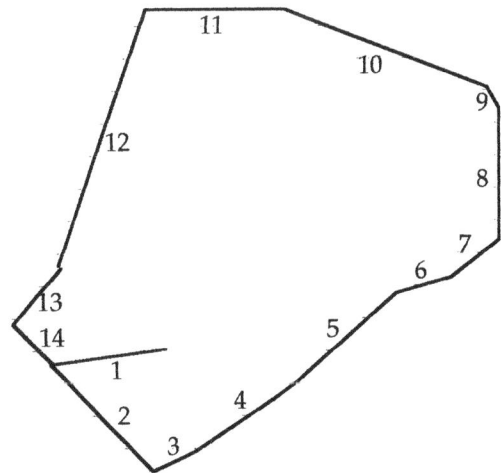

WBT-1, 100
Susan Miller, et al. to John Miller
Bowser's Addition and
Part of Add to Friendship
recorded 1 April 1845
13 and 1/4 acres

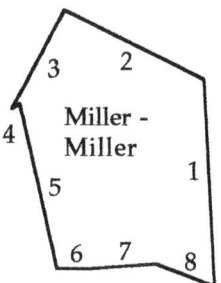

Bower's Addition and part of a tract called Add to Friendship lying and being in Frederick and Washington County and state afsd and included within the following courses and distance metes and bounds Beginning at a large white oak tree standing on the top of the South Mountain on the north side of the main road leading from Middletown to Sharpsburg and running thence.

WBT-6, 283
John Adam Main to Daniel Castle
Part of Pickall
recorded 8 October 1848
16 acres and 1/4 acre excepting thereout two acres

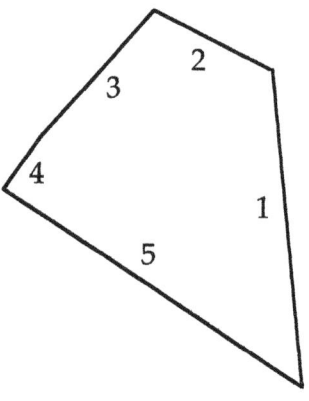

Part of a tract of land called "Pickall part of the Rsy Mendall part of I Hope It Is Well Done and part of Shettle Beginning for the outlines thereof at the end of four perches on the first line of Jacob Smith's deed as conveyed to him by Michael Miller on or about the 2nd day of December 1809 for 112 1/2 acres and running thence by and with the outlines of said deed the four following courses and distances viz.

WIP-9, 148
James W. and Mary Coffman to Jonas Gross
recorded 5 April 1889
6 and 1/2 acres

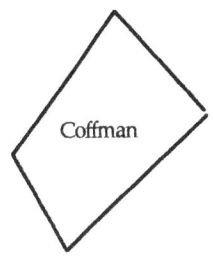

Beginning for the land hereby intended to be conveyed at a large chesnut tree standing at the end of 22 perches of the 2nd line of said land which was on the 22nd day of February 1828 deeded by Jacob Routzong to George Routzong for 68 acres and running thence with said second line.

WIP-9, 148
John W. Wise and Lana Wise, his wife,
to Jonas Gross
recorded 5 April 1889

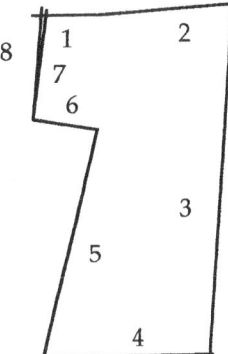

We the said John W. Wise and Lana Wise his wife do grant unto Jonas Gross of Frederick County in the state of Maryland all that lot and portion of ground situated in Frederick County Maryland and which is more particularly described in a deed from Joel Keller and wife to the said John Wise and Matilda Wise dated on the seventh day of May in the year 1858, reference to said deed being had for courses and distances will fully and at large appear, excepting and reserving hereunto a road as stated in said deed.

WIP-9, 148
George H. Kefauver to Jonas Gross
Part of Add to Friendship
13 February 1880
5 and 1/2 acres and 16 square perches

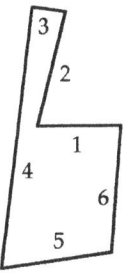

All that part of a tract of land called Fredericksburg it being part of the same land which was on the 4th day of May 1844, conveyed by Susan Miller and others to Joel Keller for eleven and a half acres. Beginning for the same at the place of the beginning of the deed from Susan Miller and others to the said Joel Keller and running thus with said lines.

(**Author's Note:** Although the deed refers to a tract named Fredericksburg, this parcel is part of Add to Friendship.)

Frederick County Land Records

WBT-10, 143
Susan Miller et al. to Daniel Beagley
recorded 21 April 1849
14 acres, 1 rood and 27 perches

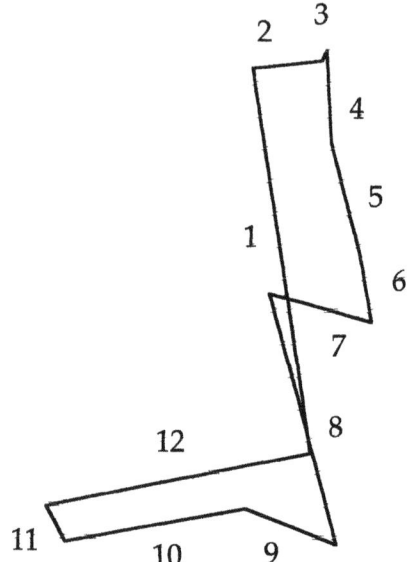

Beginning at the original beginning of a tract of land called Flonham and running thence by and with the given line of the said tract called Flonham with such allowance for variation as will agree with the former running thereof.

304-370
John N. Routzahn to Charles McC. Mathias
recorded 18 April 1913
16 acres and 9 square perches

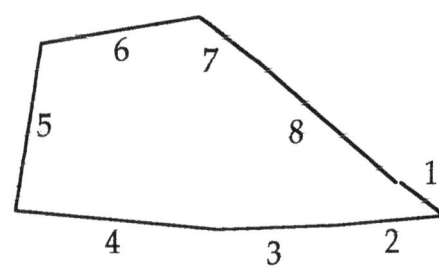

Beginning for the same at a stone planted at the end of the 5th line described in a deed from Vincent Sanner and Susan Sanner, his wife, to Samuel Ausherman, dated April 1, 1868, and recorded in Liber C. M. No. 1, folio 582, one of the land records of Frederick County, and running thence with the 6th line of said deed.

605-469
Stanley F. Young to
Richard B. and Helen B. Rudy
The Fox Inn
recorded 25 September 1958
173 acres, 1 rood, and 19 square perches

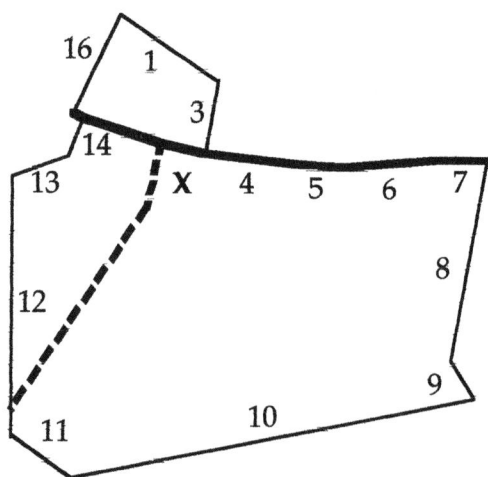

Beginning for the same at a stone standing at the beginning point of the deed from Vincent Sanner to Samuel Ausherman, dated April 1, 1868, and recorded in Liber C. M. No. 1, folio 582, one of the land records of the county afsd, and running thence.

Rsy on Mason's Folly
Tracey Collection Records

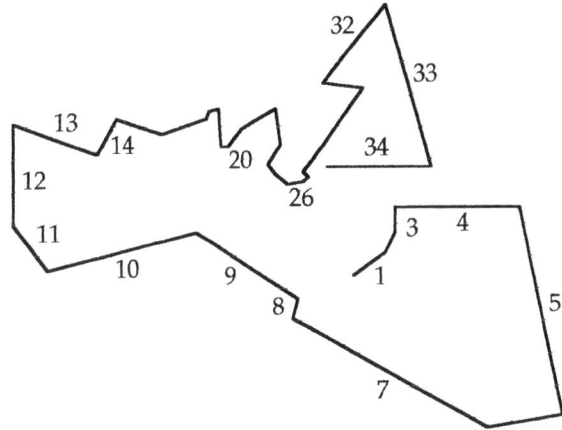

WIP-11, folios 8, 9, and 10
Jonas Gross to
Society of the Burnside Expedition
The Reno Monument
23 November 1889
40 feet square

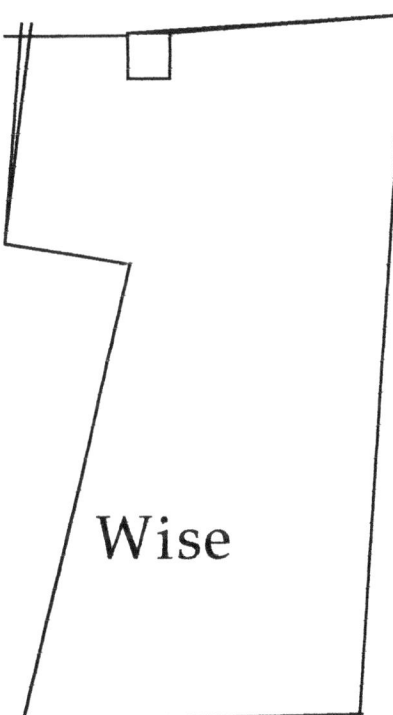

... all the following tract or parcel of land situated in the Middletown Election District in Frederick County in the State of Maryland along the Old Sharpsburg Road leading from Sharpsburg in Washington County in the state aforesaid to the pike near Middletown in said Frederick County said land being on the South Mountain, and fronting forty feet on said Old Sharpsburg Road and running back with uniform width at right angles to said road a distance of forty feet being a tract of land forty feet square upon which is now erected a monument in memory of General Reno said monument being near the center of said Lot of ground, said land being a part of the same land that was conveyed to said Jonas Gross by John W. Wise and wife by a deed dated the 9th day of June A. D. 1879 and recorded in Liber W I P No 9 folio 149 one of the land record books for said Frederick County, to which reference is hereby made, the north western corner of the land hereby conveyed being a distance of one hundred and seventeen feet (117 ft.) from the beginning point of the afsd deed and the north eastern corner of said Lot of ground being two hundred and twenty six feet from the end of the second line of said deed together with all and singular the rights ways privileges and appurtenances pertaining thereto ...

(**Author's Note:** See the Miller to Miller deed for Bowser's Addition and 3 and 1/2 acres of Add to Friendship for the tract adjacent the north side of the Wise Tract.)

Washington County Land Records

(WCLR)

Washington County, Maryland

Surveys and Deeds

Note: Frederick County was part of Prince Georges County until 1748. Washington County was part of Frederick County until 1776.

Listed in the following order:
From 1-1 to 9-9
From A-1 to Z-9
From AA-1 to ZZ-9
From AAA-1 to ZZZ-9

The following are the plotted land tracts from records in the Washington County Court House in Hagerstown, Maryland.

G-7, 621-626
Jacob Hess and others
Fellfoot Enlarged
recorded 19 March 1792
2100 acres

Beginning for the outlines of the whole tract at a bound white oak where is a stone now planted standing in the fork of Little Antietam it being the beginning tree of the original tract called Fellfoot.

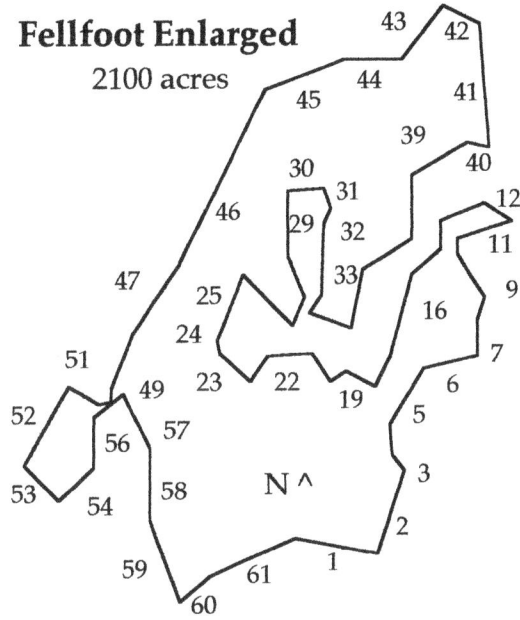

G-7, 621-626 (see above tract)
Conrad Snabley's Part of Fellfoot Enlarged

Begining for Conrad Snabley's part of said land being the part described on the plat no. 1 at the beginning of the whole tract.

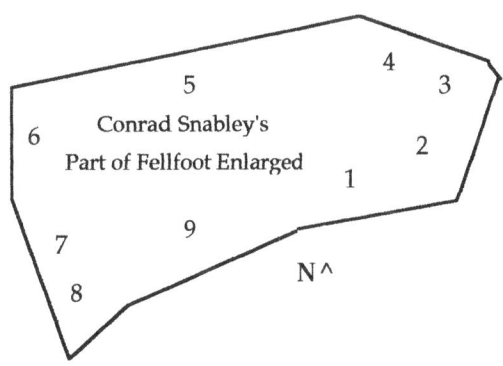

G-302
Moses Chapline Sr. to Samuel Baker
Part of the Rsy on Roots Hill
recorded 22 May 1761
100 acres

Part of the Rsy on Roots Hill beginning at the end of fifty perches in the sixth line of the resurvey.

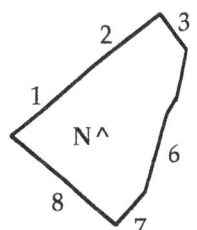

H-103
Lodowick Keedy to Henry Keedy
I Hope It Is So
recorded 19 February 1793
68 and 1/4 acre

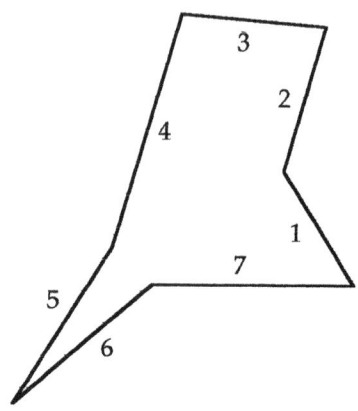

Begining at the end of twenty one perches in the ninth line of a tract of land called Park Hall.

O-376
George Beall Jr. to Michael Thomas
Penn's Dissappointment
recorded 22 May 1761
80 acres

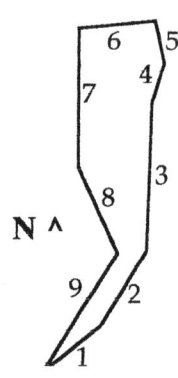

BD-1
Moses Chapline to William Good
Old Purchase
recorded 18 May 1775
77 acres

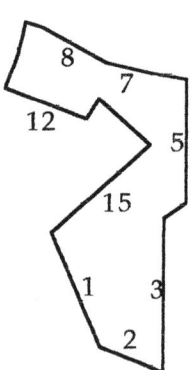

Part of that part of the Rsy on Mount Pleasant devised by Moses Chapline's will to his son Josiah Chapline situate lying and being in the county afsd and beginning at the end of the second line of a tract of land called Mountain.

(**Author's Note:** Lines 6 through 9 are along the wagon road.)

GG-29, 877-8
John Shafer to Henry Miller
Swearingen's Disappointment
recorded 21 May 1824
6 and 1/4 acres

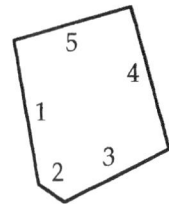

Beginning at a stone standing in a line formerly made as a division between John Shafer and Daniel Rench and at the end of a stone wall which has been put upon the division line between the afsd Henry Miller and Joseph Boyd and running thence along said stone wall.

II-431
John Booth and Jonas Hogmire to Henry Miller
Part of Partnership
recorded 29 May 1827
1 acre and 76 perches; also 92 perches

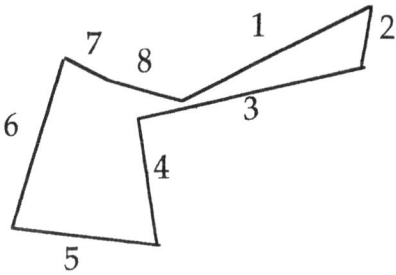

Being part of a tract of land called Partnership lying and being in the county and state afsd beginning for the first parcel in the center of the kitchen door of the said Henry Miller and running from the center of said door.

IN-6 51, 517-518
William Booth and Andrew Hogmire Trustees to William Miller
Part of Partnership
recorded 4 March 1852
11 and 1/4 acre

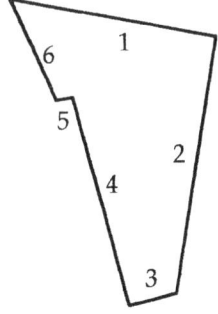

Beginning at a pile of stones at the end of the second line of Michael Gittles part of Partnership.

IN-7 52, 788-789
William Booth and Andrew Hogmire Trustees to George Strause
recorded 15 June 1853
9 and 3/4 acres and 15 square perches
Part of Partnership

Beginning at the end of the third line of the deed from Jacob Summers to John Booth and Jonas Hogmire for part of a tract of land called Raccoon and running from thence.

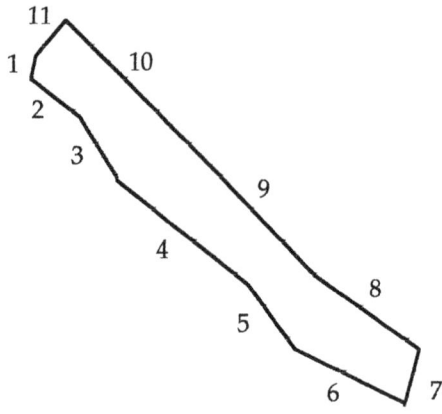

IN-9, 595
Henry Miller Estate to Edward L. Boteler
recorded 25 May 1855
40 acres
also Lot #5, 18 and 1/8 acres

Beginning for the same at a large stone at the north end of a stone wall a fence being a corner between the late Henry Miller and Daniel Gittle.

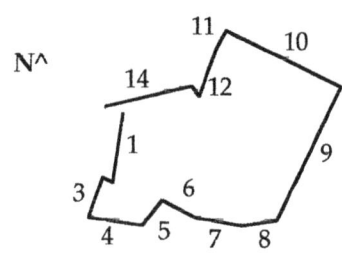

Also lot number No. 5 adjoining the Homestead being part of a tract of land called Add to Friendship.

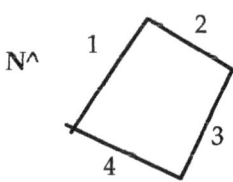

MM-33, 869-870
John Booth and Jonas Hogmire Trustees to Peter Gittle
Part of Partnership
recorded 21 January 1832
1/2 acres

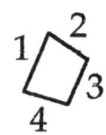

Beginning at a stone set up and planted on the north side of the turnpike road being at the end of the third line of the deed from John Booth and Jonas Hogmire to Michael Gittle for part of Partnership.

PP-33, 476-7
John Shafer to Daniel Zittle
Swearingen's Disappointment
recorded 11 December 183?4
15 acres and 1/2 acre

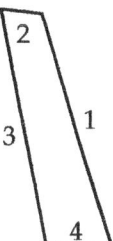

Beginning at a stake standing at the end of thirty one perches in the sixth line of the whole tract called Swearingen's Disappointment.

TG-12, 435
John and Harriet Murdock to Madeleine V. Dahlgren
Add to Friendship and Bowser's Addition
recorded 21 October 1879
19 acres, 3 roods, and 12 perches

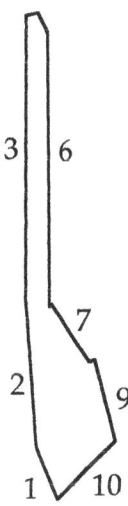

Washington County afsd and partly in Frederick County in the said state being part of two tracts called "Add to Friendship" and "Bowser's Addition." Beginning at the end of twenty perches on the fifth line fo the whole tract called "Add to Friendship" and running thence with the said line with an allowance of one and three quarter degrees for variation.

TT-39, 778-780
Joseph Boyd and Susan his wife to John Hutzell
Partnership , Swearingen's Disappointment
recorded 18 January 1839
1 acre and 19 perches, also 137 perches

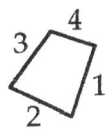

Beginning for the same hereby conveyed at a heap of stones near the south side of the turnpike it being the end of the last line except the closing one of the deed from John Booth and Jonas Hogmire to Henry Miller for part of Partnership.

Being part of a tract of land called Swearingen's Disappointment beginning for the part at a stone set up and planted near the end of thirty eight and one quarter perches on the fourth line of the whole tract of land called Swearingen's Disappointment and running thence with a stone fence.

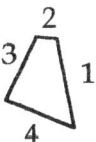

TT-39, 817-818
George Shafer and Jonathan Shafer to Michael Zittle
The) Vineyard - Swearingen's Disappointment
made 4 February 1839
13 acres and 9 perches
also 24 acres and 35 perches

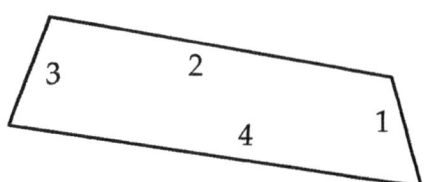

Beginning for the first of the said part of a tract of land called Swearingen's Disappointment at the end of one hundred and thirty five and one fourth perches in the sixth line of the said land called Swearingen's Disappointment, and running with the out lines of said land.

For the second part of a tract of land called The) Vineyard beginning at a stone at the end of nineteen perches in the second line of the whole tract called (The) Vineyard and running thence.

WW-41, 545-546
John Booth and Jonas Hogmire to John Hutzel
Part of Partnership
recorded 25 September 1840
125 perches

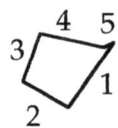

Beginning at the end of the third line of the deed from John Booth and Jonas Hogmire to Joseph Boyd for part of the afsd tract of land called Partnership and reversing that line.

WW-41, 630-632
John Booth and Jonas Hogmire to Andrew Hogmire
Partnership
recorded 10 November 1840
18 acres; also 8 acres

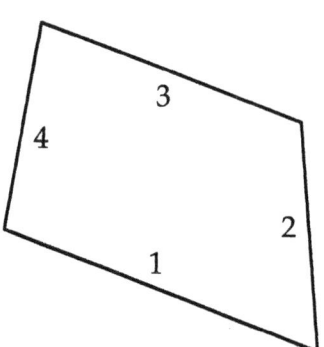

Beginning for the first part at a stone at the end of the north seventy degree ninety three perches line of the deed from John Booth and Jonas Hogmire to John Nicodemus and with it reversed.

GBO-77, 170
Jonas Speilman to Josiah Zittle
recorded 5 September 1878
21 and 3/4 acres; also 12 acres; also 1 acre

Beginning for one of said lots at a stone standing on the north seventy degrees west ninety three perches line of a deed from John Booth and Jonas Hogmire to John Nicodemus.

(**Author's Note:** Line number eight of this deed may have been along the last line, s 70 degrees east, of 1792 Road from Williamsport to Turner's Gap and the Frederick County line at the top of the mountain, 128 perches)

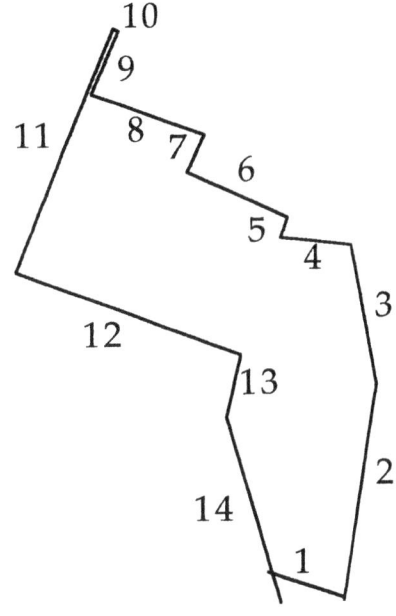

Beginning for the second of said lots or parcels of land at the end of the first line of Boons Forest and reversing said first line.

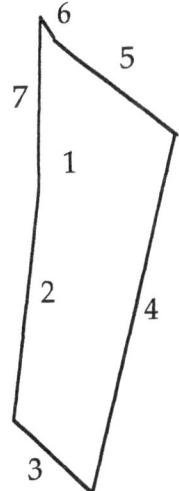

Beginning for the third of said lots at a stone pile at the end of the third line of William Miller's part of said land and reversing with the fourth line.

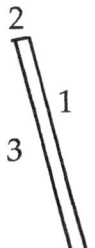

Washington County Land Records

GBO-81, 336-7
William Miller and Teresa Miller, his wife, to Madeleine V. Dahlgren
recorded 8 September 1881
11 and 1/4 acres

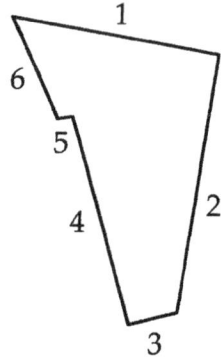

Beginning at a pile of stones at the end of the second line of Michael Zittles part of Partnership now deceased and reversing said line.

GBO-100, 618
Mauche H. Meline to Madeleine V. Dahlgren
recorded 18 July 1893
66 perches

Beginning at a heap of stones on the south west side of the turnpike road from Boonsboro to Frederick and at the end of two and a half perches on the second line of a deed from John Booth and Jonas Hogmire to John Hutzell for part of Partnership dated May 29 1840 and recorded in Liber WW folio 545 one of the land records of Washington County.

LBN-2, 133
Edward L. Boteler to George F. Smith
recorded 14 May 1867
60 acres

Partly in Washington and partly in Frederick County in the state of Maryland they being part of a tract of land called "Addition to Friendship," part of a tract called "Partnership," part of Swearingen's Disappointment," and part of a tract of land called "Flonham," beginning to include the several parts into one entire tract at a stake and pile of stones at the end of a line drawn north 77 east 40 and 3/10 perches from a large stone at the north end of a stone wall being the corner between the lands of the late Henry Miller and Daniel Gittle and running with that line reversed.

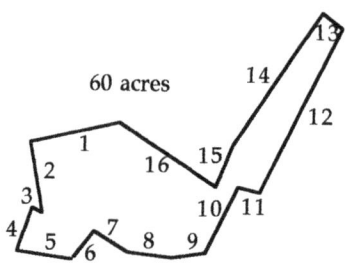

74-264
George F. Smith to Madeleine Dahlgren
19 April 1876
60 acres

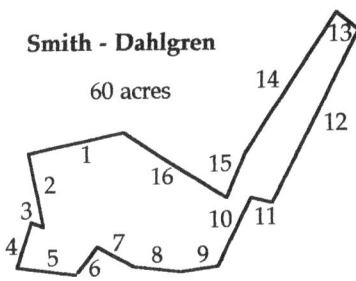

"Partnership" part of "Swearingen's Disappointment," and part of a tract called "Flonham" beginning to include the several parts hereby conveyed in one (?) tract at a stake and pile of stones at the end of a line drawn north 77 east 40 3/10 perches from a large stone standing at the north end of a stone wall being the corner between the lands presently belonging to Henry Miller and Daniel Zittle deceased and running with that line reversed.

77-287
Josiah Zittle and Seggrick Zittle, his wife, Mary Magdelena Zittle, and Elizabeth Zittle to Madeleine V. Dahlgren
recorded 19 September 1878
11 acres

Beginning for the same at a stone pile in the ridge of the mountain.

78-234
John Hutzell and Elizabeth Hutzell, his wife, to Madeleine V. Dahlgren
recorded 1 August 1879
10 and 1/8 acres

Beginning at a stone pile at the end of the first line of the first parcel of land mentioned and described in a deed from Joseph Boyd and wife to the said John Hutzell dated January 18th 1839 and recorded in Liber T T folio 778 per one of the land records of the said county.

(**Author's Note:** The last or 46th line of the Road from Williamsport to Turner's Gap in the South Mountain is south 70 degrees east, 128 perches to where it is supposed to intersect Frederick County line on the top of the mountain.)

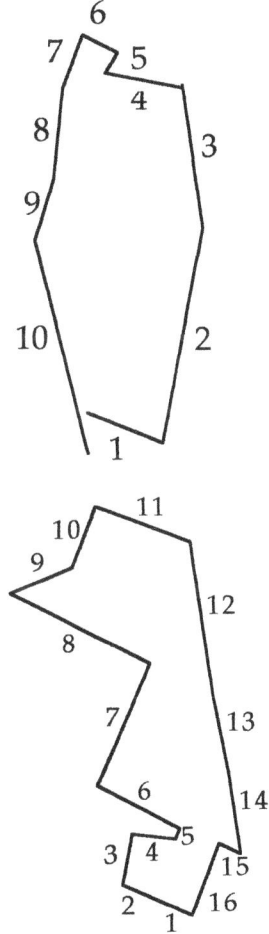

Washington County Land Records

172-524
St. Mary's Academy to Hewitt
recorded 28 September 1925
177 acres, 2 roods, and 14 square perches
The Mountain House at Turner's Gap

Beginning for the same at a stone on the ridge of the mountain.

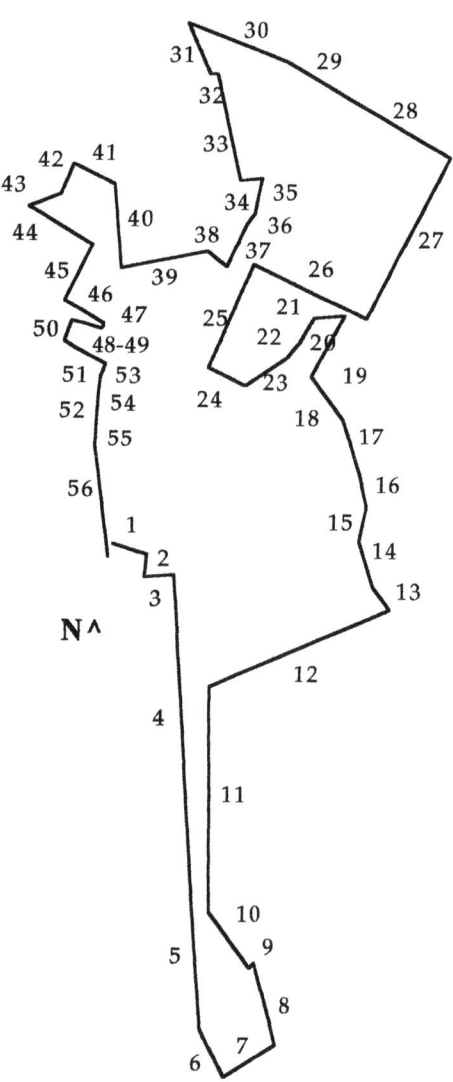

340-170-171
Ulrica Dahlgren Pierce
(widow of Washington City, District of Columbia)
to St. Mary's Academy, a body corporate of
Notre Dame, St. Joseph's County, Indiana
recorded 21 August 1922
The Mountain House at Turner's Gap

The preceeding conveyance is probably the same tract as that conveyed from St. Mary's to Hewit, as follows:

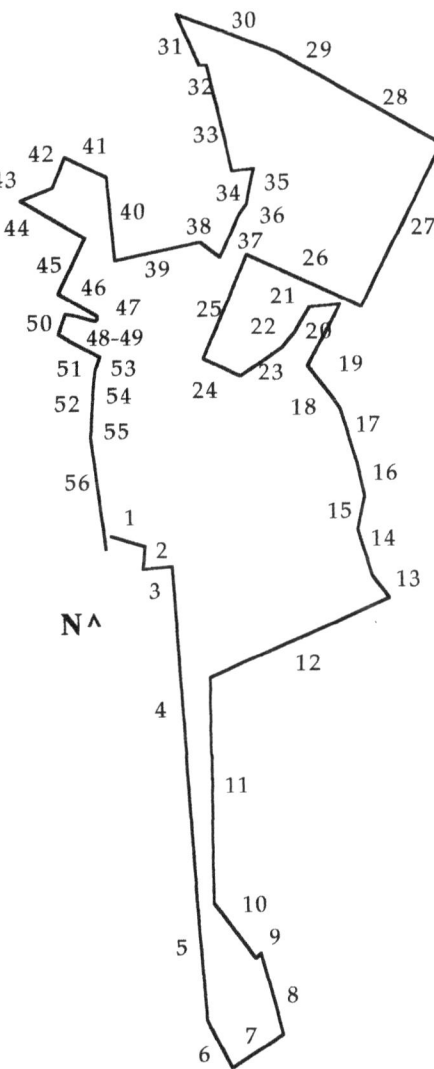

Washington County Land Records

Number Unknown
Elias Butter to Philip Laypole
made 23 August 1824
142 perches
Part of Foxes Last Shift

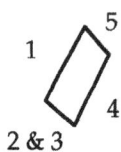

Lots or portions of ground laid out as a town or village on the north side of the South Mountain situated lying & being in the county and state afsd it being part of a tract of land called "Fox's Last Shift", and numbered 9 & 10. Beginning for them both at a stone standing one perch from the end of the 3rd line of Lot No. 8 and running thence.

Part IV

Historic Sites

on or near

The Battlefield of South Mountain

Traced through the Years

**The Reno Monument
The Fox Inn
The Reno School
The War Correspondents Memorial Arch
The Mountain House
The Ten Acres around the Dahlgren Chapel
and
The Moses Chapline Senior Cemetery**

Historic Sites

The Reno Monument

From Frederick Fox (1795) to the United States Government (1998)
Tract Name - Addition to Friendship

Reference	Date	Grantee of Deed	Acres
IC #P 672-3	9 May 1797	Frederick Fox - Addition to Friendship[1] (Friendship - 8 June 1795, Unpat. Cert. #238)	202
WR-32-26/8	21 Sep 1807	Joseph Swearingen from Frederick Fox - Addition to Friendship and 30 acres of Fredericksburg	202
WR-34-315	20 Aug 1808	Peter Ludy from Joseph Swearingen - part of Addition to Friendship and Fredericksburg	58
WR-42-550	9 Jul 1812	Jacob Routzong from Peter Ludy - part of Addition to Friendship and Fredericksburg	68[2]
JS-30-58/61	22 Feb 1828	Jacob Routzong to George Routzong - part of Addition to Friendship and Fredericksburg	68[3]
JS-38-194	18 Feb 1832	Henry Miller from Sheriff Peter Brengle - Writ of Fieri Facia issued against Jacob Routzah[4]	68
Will - Miller[5]	Date of Death	Estate of Henry Miller	68
Beneficiaries	Date of Death	Estate of Henry Miller	10 and 1/2
Unknown	7 May 1844	Joel Keller from Susan Miller et al.[6]	10 and 1/2
BGF-6-216	7 May 1858	John and Matilda Wise from Joel Keller	4 and 3/4
WIP-9-149	9 Jun 1879	Jonas Gross from John W. Wise	4 and 3/4
WIP 11	23 Nov 1889	Trustees, Society of the Burnside Expedition from folio. 8, 9, 10, Jonas Gross[7]	40 ft square
DHH-3-316	11 Sep 1898	United States Government	40 ft square

Fredericksburg Deeds Related to Preceeding Transfers

Reference	Date	Grantee of Deed	Acres
HGO-1-564/5	11 Jun 1792	Frederick Fox - survey of Fredericksburg	75
WR-17-158/9	21 Apr 1798	Frederick Fox to George Methard	10
WR-31-478	12 Sep 1807	George Methard to William Bottenberg	10
WR-34-313	11 Feb 1809	William Bottenberg to Peter Ludy	10

Historic Sites

The Wise tract, on which the Reno Monument stands, is contiguous to a 13 and 1/2 acre tract on the north side of the road, transferred from Susan Miller to John Miller, consisting of ten acres of Bowser's Addition and three and one-half acres of Addition to Friendship. See FCLR, WBT-1-100. Bowser's Addition,[8] "by the side of the wagon road leading from Sharpsburg to Frederick Town and on top of South Mountain," was surveyed in 1763. The Bowser's Addition tract offers proof the road through Fox's Gap crossed the mountain at the same point in 1763 as it does in 1998.

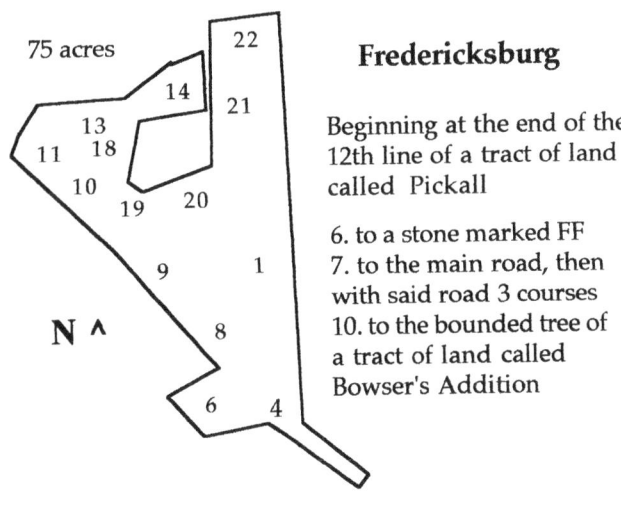

Fredericksburg

Beginning at the end of the 12th line of a tract of land called Pickall

6. to a stone marked FF
7. to the main road, then with said road 3 courses
10. to the bounded tree of a tract of land called Bowser's Addition

Fredericksburg of Frederick Fox

Historic Sites

Fox's Gap

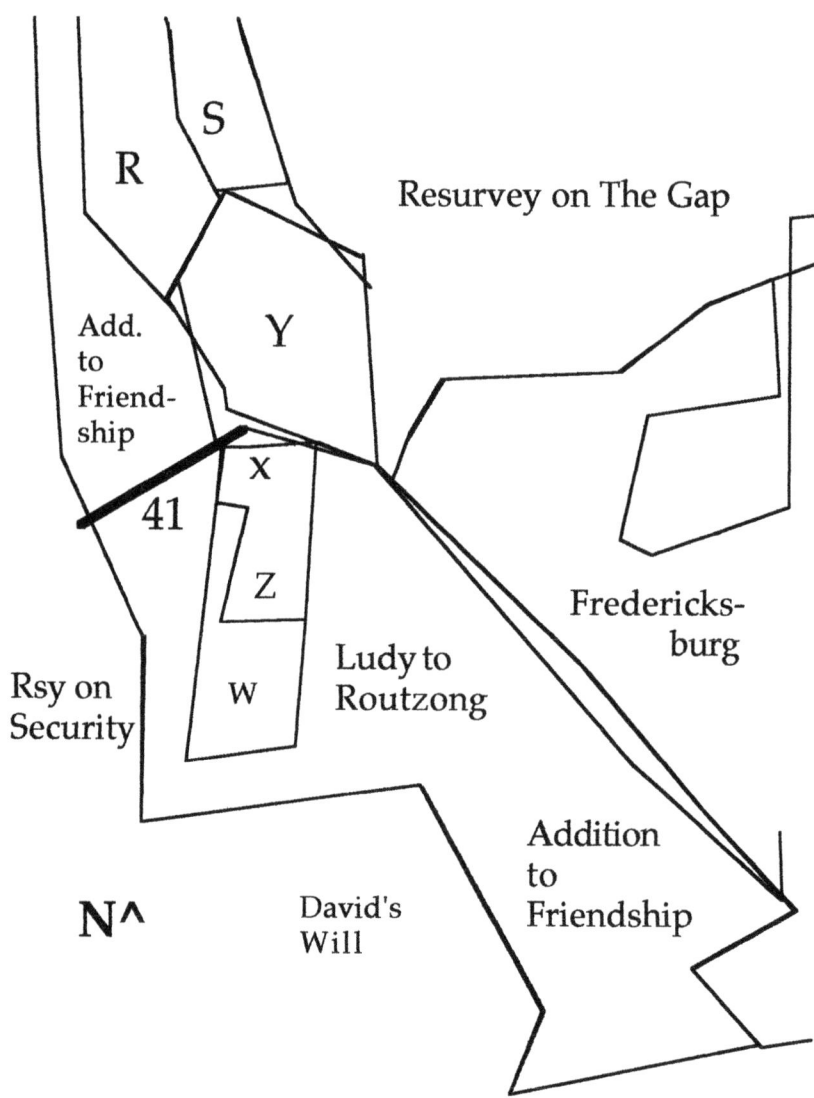

- **R** = The Resurvey on The Gap - Henry Beakley, MdHR, IC N, 467-468, special warrant, 16 Jul 1798.
- **S** = Apple Brandy - Jacob Fulwiler, MdHR, ID D, 75, surveyed 31 Oct 1791.
- **Z** = The Wise Tract of Civil War Fame - The Reno Monument stands on this tract - Joel Keller to John Wise, 7 May 1858, FCLR, WR-42-550.
- **X** = The Reno Monument - FCLR, WIP-11, 23 Nov 1889, Jonas Gross to Soc. of the Burnside Expedition.
- **W** = George H. Kefauver to Jonas Gross - 13 Feb 1880, FCLR, WIP-9-148.
- **Y** = Susan Miller et al. to John Miller - Bowser's Addition and three and one half acres of Addition to Friendship - FCLR, WBT-1-100.
- **41** = Last line of 1792 Map - *Road from Swearingen's Ferry to Fox's Gap* - MSA G1427-507, B5-1-3.

Historic Sites

Addition to Friendship
202 acres

Beginning at the end of the first line of a tract of land called David's Will

1. to the beginning of said land it being also the beginning of Friendship the present original

2. to the end of the last line of David's Will

3. to the 3rd line of Jacob Hess's Resurvey called Security

7. to the end of the 1st line of a tract of land called Flonham

8. to the bounded tree of said land

10. to the end of 21 perches on the 3rd line of said Flonham

12. to the end of the 7th line of a tract of land called Knave's Good Will

20. to the 14th line of a tract of land called Turkey Ramble

27. to the end of the 3rd line of a tract of land called Bowser's Addition

30. to the bounded tree of said Bowser's Addition it being the end of the tenth line of a tract of land called Friendship

34. to a rock marked FF

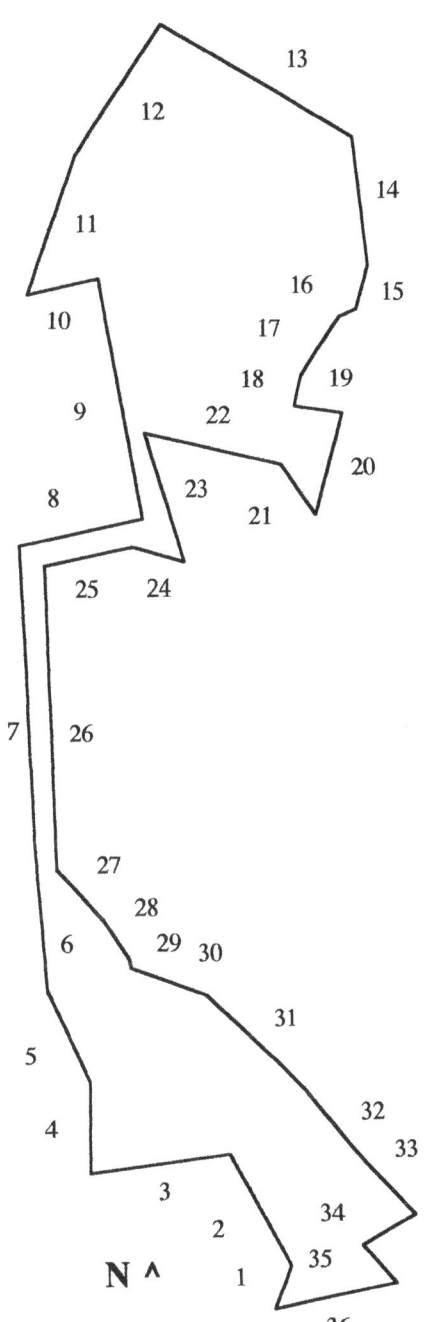

Addition to Friendship of Frederick Fox

Historic Sites

Footnotes - The Reno Monument

[1] Addition to Friendship was a resurvey obtained by Frederick Fox out of the western shore land office by a special warrant of proclamation to resurvey and affect the vacancy included in a resurvey made for him on the eighth day of June seventeen hundred and ninety five by the name of Friendship, the caution money for which had not been paid within the time limited by law. In pursuance whereof, a resurvey was made and a certificate thereof returned containing two hundred and two acres lying in the county aforesaid and called Addition to Friendship.

[2] Peter Ludy acquired 58 acres from Joseph Swearingen at the time he acquired 10 acres from William Bottenberg. See WR-34-315-317.

[3] This transfer was an attempt by Jacob Routzong to avoid confiscation of the property by the County Court. The sheriff confiscated the property under court order in 1832 and auctioned it to the highest bidder. The 1832 deed from Sheriff Brengle to Henry Miller indicates the court awarded a judgement on the first Monday of August 1827 against Jacob Routzong in favor of Peter Sower and Philip Hunslmen. The April 5, 1889, deed from James W. Coffman et ux to Jonas Gross, however, refers to the Jacob Routzong and George Routzong deed.

[4] The court voided the deed from Jacob Routzong to George Routzong and transferred the land to Henry Miller.

[5] No record of a will of Henry Miller was found. He probably died intestate.

[6] The heirs at law of Henry Miller were: Susan Miller, widow of Henry Miller; John W. Derr and Elizabeth Derr, his wife; John Miller and Susan Miller, his wife; Adam Koogle and Catharine Koogle, his wife; Phineas Williams and Ann Maria Williams, his wife; Joseph Nyman and Jane Rebecca Nyman, his wife; and Henrietta Miller.

[7] Jonas Gross recorded three deeds at 9:00 AM on April 5, 1889. WIP-9-148 from James W. Coffman et ux to Jonas Gross, 6 and 1/2 acres; WIP-9-148 from George H. Kefauver et ux to Jonas Gross, 5 and 1/2 acres; WIP-9-149 from John W. Wise et ux to Jonas Gross, 4 and 3/4 acres. The deeds to Jonas Gross from James W. and Mary Coffman and from George H. and Mary R. Kefauver both state they are part of a tract called Fredericksburg. The tracts probably became confused when Peter Ludy obtained 10 acres from William Bottenberg and 58 acres from Joseph Swearingen. These two tracts became part of one tract of 68 acres, containing portions of both Fredericksburg and Addition to Friendship. The deed to the United States government states, "said land (i. e. the 40 foot by 40 foot tract of the Reno Monument) being a part of the same land that was conveyed to said Jonas Gross by John W. Wise and wife by a deed dated the 9th day of June A. D. 1879, and recorded in Liber W I P No. 9, folio 149."

[8] MdHR 17,448, 1-23-4-2, Bowser's Addition, surveyed April 10, 1765, 10 acres. MdHR BC & GS #37, 138-9.

Historic Sites

The Fox Inn

From Daniel Dulany Sr (1742) to Helen Rudy (1998)
Tract Name - The Exchange

(**Note** - The 1808 Varle Map identifies the Fox Inn by the name "Ringer.")

Reference	Date	Grantee of Deed	Acres
MdHR, BC & GS #1, 177	5 Oct 1742	Daniel Dulany Esqr. - survey - The Exchange	100[1]
MdHR, BY & GS #1, 177	29 Apr 1749	assignment to Robert Evans - The Exchange	100[2]
MdHR, BY & GS #1, 177	20 May 1749	assignment to Joseph Chapline Sr - The Exchange	100
FCLR, E-339	11 Dec 1753	Casper Shaff - The Exchange	75
MdHR, BY & GS #4, 585-6	9 May 1754	Joseph Chapline [Sr] - Casper Shaff[3]	275[4]
MdHR, BC & GS #27, 578	29 Sep 1765	Daniel [Jr] and Walter Dulany - patent - The Exchange	100
FCLR, K-1373	9 Jul 1767	Valentine Fidler - Fidler's Purchase	150[5]
Probably inherited from his father.		George Fidler	150[6]
FCLR, WR-7-48	8 Nov 1786	Ludwick Layman	100[7]
FCLR, WR-12-56	14 Nov 1793	Peter Layman	100[8]
FCLR, WR-27-543	7 Oct 1805	George Fox	100[9]
FCLR, WR-32-30	25 Jul 1807	John Ringer	100[10]
FCLR, JS-42-481	15 May 1833	Vincent Sanner	75[11]
FCLR, CM-1-582	14 Apr 1868	Samuel Ausherman	194+[12]
FCLR, TG-3-298	10 May 1875	Eli Routzahn	192+
FCLR, AF-9-90	2 Apr 1884	Simon D. Routzahn	192+
FCLR, AF-9-91	2 Apr 1884	John H. Routzahn	192+
FCLR, 324/321	3 Apr 1918	Stanley J. Young	175+
FCLR, 388/316	21 Aug 1933	H. Noel Haller	175+
FCLR, 388/317	21 Aug 1933	Stanley F. Young	175+
FCLR, 605/469	25 Sep 1958	Richard and Helen Rudy	173+[13]

Historic Sites

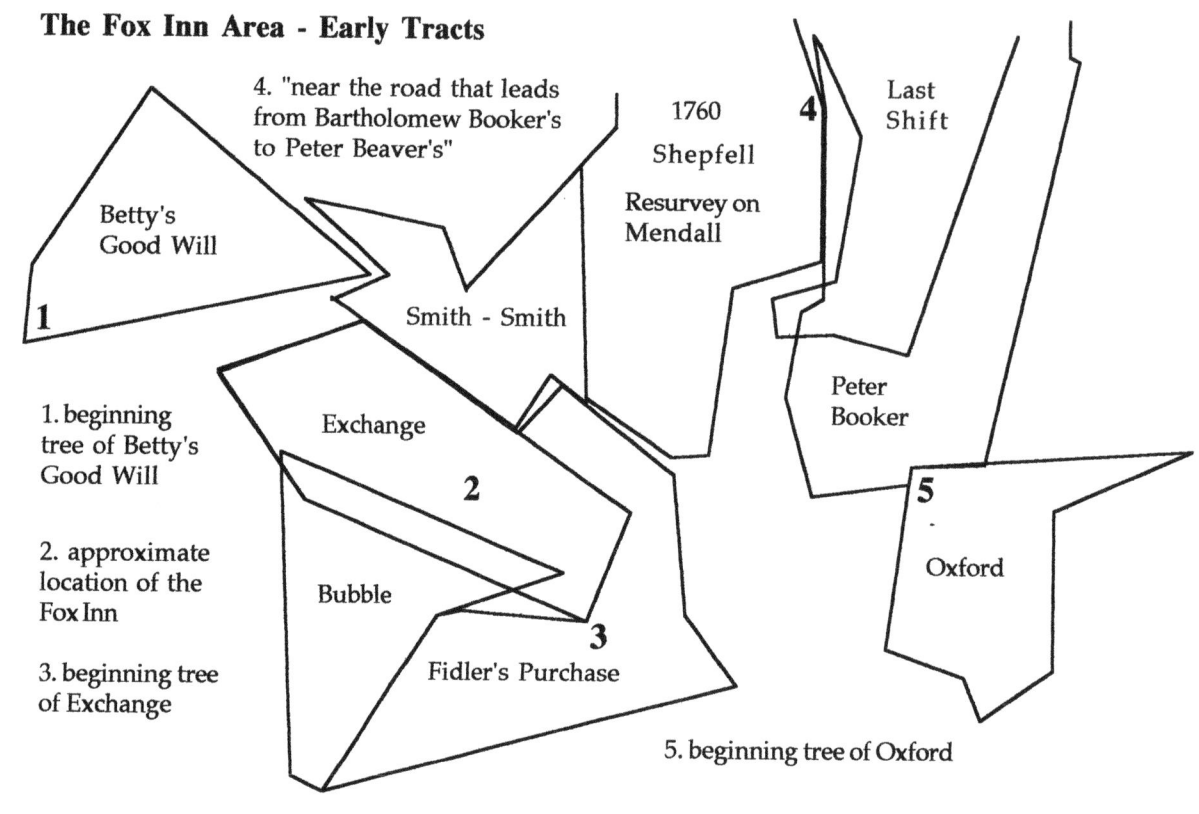

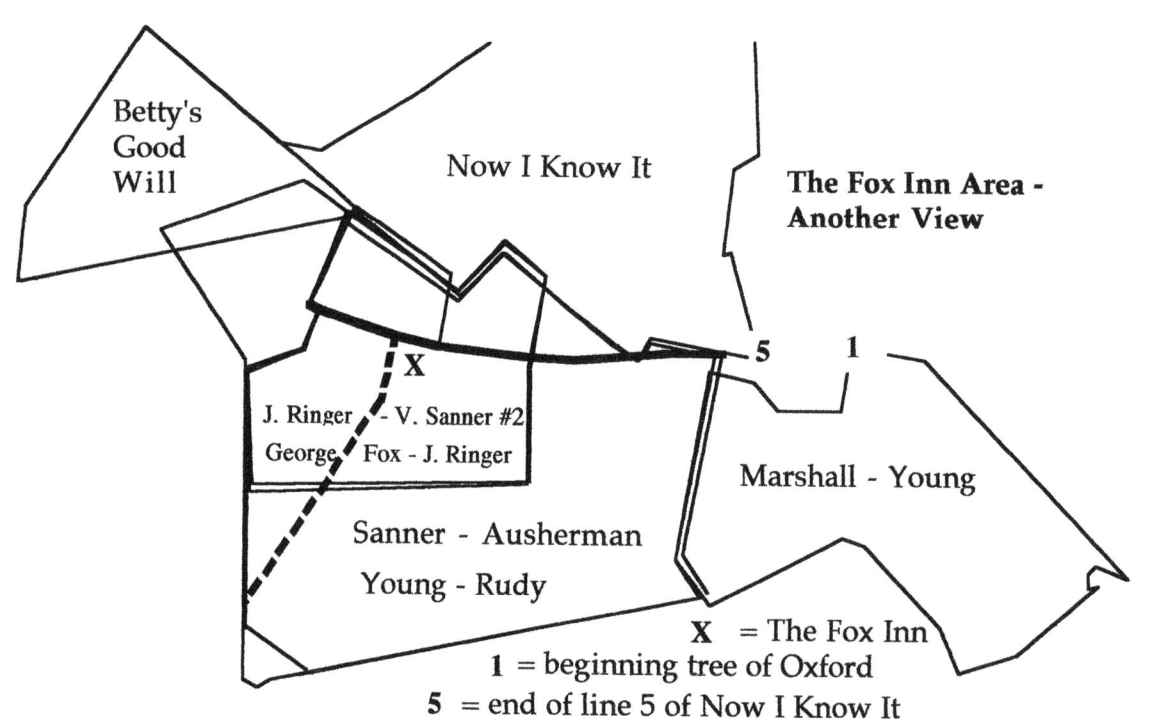

Footnotes - The Fox Inn

[1] Daniel Dulany Esqr., survey for The Exchange, Oct. 5, 1742, 100 acres. MdHR, BC & GS #27, 578.

[2] This tract was originally for 100 acres, but it actually contained only 75 acres. Also see MdHR, BY & GS #2, 239.

[3] FCLR, E-1026, sale to Conrad Young, March 18, 1756, 125 acres.

[4] See FCLR, G-17. Casper Shaff, a merchant, acquired Bubble (Boble), for 50 acres, from Michael Jesserong, an innholder, on June 4, 1761.

[5] Fidler also acquired Bubble (Boble) for 50 acres with this deed.

[6] George Fidler probably inherited the property on the death of Valentine Fidler.

[7] "Fidler's Purchase being part of two tracts of land the one called the Resurvey on Exchange and a tract called Bubble."

[8] "part of two tracts of land the one called The Resurvey on Exchange and the other called Bubble."

[9] "part of two tracts of land the one called the Resurvey on Exchange and the other called Bubble beginning at the original beginning tree of Exchange and running thence ... Also one other piece or parcel of land being part of a tract called Mount Pleasant." The Mt. Pleasant tract contained 18 acres.

[10] "Fidler's Purchase, being part of two tracts of land, the one called the Resurvey on Exchange and the other called Bubble."

[11] The deed is from Sidney Ringer, widow of John Ringer. The property was left to Sidney Ringer as a life estate. Daniel Ringer, son of John and Sidney, improperly transfered the property to Jacob Everhart Jr and his wife Eliza. The deed mentions Jacob Everhart Sr and Eliza his wife, Jacob Everhart Jr and Eliza L. Everhart, and the land tracts named Fidler's Purchase, the Resurvey on Exchange, and Bubble.

[12] "... part of a tract of land called Fidler's Purchase, part of a tract called The Resurvey on Exchange, part of a tract called Bubble and a tract called Deeffer Snay." Vincent Sanner acquired Deeffer Snay from George Routzahn.

[13] This tract is substantially the same as the tract sold by Vincent Sanner to Samuel Ausherman in 1868. Lines 4, 5, 6, 7, and 15 are along the Old Sharpsburg Road. The Fox Inn stands at approximately 35 perches directly west of the end of the third line of this tract at the intersection of Marker road (to Burkittsville) and the Old Sharpsburg Road.

Historic Sites

The Reno School along the Old Sharpsburg Road
From Bartholomew Booker (1764) to Edna I. Toms (1998)
Tract Name - Pickall

Reference	Date	Grantee of Deed	Area
MdHR BC & GS 30 pp. 214-216	3 Feb 1764	Bartholomew Booker, Patent for Pickall A resurvey on Mendall and Small All	1224 acres
FCLR L-71	16 Oct 1767	Bartholomew Booker to George Shidler, Long Dispute (Shidler's Dispute and part of Pickall)	200 acres
FCLR P-651	22 Mar 1773	George Shidler to Henry Smith, Long Dispute (Shidler's Dispute and part of Pickall)	200 acres
FCLR WR-8-662	20 Oct 1789	Henry Smith to Peter Hutzel, Long Dispute (Shidler's Dispute and part of Pickall)	200 acres
FCLR JS-17-504	7 Apr 1823	Ex of Peter Hutzel to Jacob Hutzel	160 acres
FCLR JS-19-6	1 Dec 1823	Jacob Hutzel to John Hutzel	160 acres
FCLR BFG-6-569	1 Apr 1861	John Hutzel Estate to Ezra Warenfeltz (Adam Hutzel, Samuel Hutzel, and Vincent Sanner, executors)	162 and 1/2 acres and 17 perches
FCLR BGF-6-680	7 May 1861	Ezra Warenfeltz to William J. Kepler and Anna M. Kepler, his wife	162 and 1/2 acres and 17 perches
FCLR BGF-7-561	30 Jun 1862	William J. Kepler and Anna M. Kepler, his wife, to John Mentzer and Martha E. Mentzer, his wife	3 acres and 66 perches
FCLR AF-11-311	27 Aug 1865	John Mentzer and Martha E. Mentzer, his wife, to County School Commissioners of Frederick County (the Reno School property)	1 acre
FCLR 368-32	25 Aug 1928	Board of Education to George L. Miller (the Reno School building became a private residence)	1 acre
FCLR 421-320	12 Sep 1939	Orpha M. Miller, widow of George L. Miller, to Everett Moser (Mount Reno School lot)	1 acre
FCLR 438-345	19 Apr 1943	Everett Moser to Murvil L. and Edna I. Toms (Reno School House lot)	1 acre, also 5 acres

Historic Sites

The War Correspondents Memorial Arch at Crampton's Gap

From Peter Gaver (1789) to the United States Government (1998)
Tract Name - Gaver's Recovery

Reference	Date	Grantee of Deed	Acres
MdHR BC & GS #47 pp. 1-12	18 May 1770	Fielder Gannt - Fielderia Manor[1] (25 acres of Fielderia Manor are part of the resurvey called Gaver's Recovery)	10,471 1/4
MdHR, IC #E pp. 702-704	8 Dec 1789	Peter Gaver - Gaver's Recovery[2]	197 acres
Estate of Peter Gaver	Death of Peter Gaver	Michael Bruner, Daniel Booker, John Cain, David Gaver, and others[3]	195 acres
FCLR, WR-26-569	11 Apr 1805	Joshua Harley	195 acres
Frederick County Equity HS-2-92	7 Mar 1831	Equity Case #945, Ezra Slifer, Trustee[4] (Joshua Harley Sr, a lunatic)	195+ acres
FCLR JS-44-393	1833	David Mullendore	220 1/2
(unrecorded)	about Sept 1835	Tilghman Biser and Mary Ann Biser, his wife	(unrecorded)
(see FCLR AF-9-541 for reference to the transfer from Mullendore to Biser)			
FCLR, ES-3-57, 58	12 Apr 1853	Ezra Williard and William Carroll, in trust[5]	All Real Estate In Trust
FCLR, ES-5-252	12 Apr 1853	David Arnold and John Arnold Jr.	168 3/4
No Deed	1856	From Trustees to William F. Gitings[6]	16 acres
No Deed	1856	From William F. Gitings to George W. Padget	16 acres
Estate of George Padget	Death of George Padget	Mary A. E. Koontz	16 acres
FCLR CM-7-381	6 May 1869	William M. Feaga, Collector	16 acres
FCLR CM-7-381	12 Oct 1871	David Arnold	16 acres
FCLR AF-9-541	15 Dec 1884	George Alfred Townsend[7]	12 acres, 3 roods, and 17 sq perches
FCLR STH-267-367	24 Sep 1904	United States Government[8]	28 1/8 square perches

215

Historic Sites

Footnotes - The War Correspondents Memorial Arch

[1] Fielderia originally on the 6th day of September anno domini 1763 granted unto the said Fielder Gannt for 8,151 acres.

[2] "Gaver's Recovery by resurvey made the 8th day of December 1789." "Nineteen and a half acres part of the resurvey on Dawson's Purchase originally on the fifth day of October seventeen hundred and fifty two granted Thomas Dawson for two hundred and fifteen and three quarters acres, eighty nine acres part of I Got It At Last originally on the fifth day of November seventeen hundred and fifty four granted Thomas Hawkins for one hundred acres, The Mountain originally on the nineteenth day of October seventeen hundred and sixty granted Thomas Hawkins for thirty acres, and twenty five acres part of a tract of land called Fielderia Manor originally on the fifteenth day of January seventeen hundred and seventy two granted Feilder Gannt for ten thousand four hundred and seventy one and a quarter acres."

[3] "Michael Brunner and Elizabeth Brunner, his wife, Daniel Booker and Catherine Booker, his wife, Samuel Gaver, John Cain and Mary Cain, his wife, Henry Beeler and Hannah Beeler, his wife, Jacob Parson and Huldak Parson, his wife, Gedion Gaver, David Gaver, Samuel Landis and Arsenith Landis, his wife, John Bizer and Lydia Bizer, his wife, all heirs and representatives of Peter Gaver deceased."

[4] ". . . by a decree of Frederick County Court setting as a Court of Equity bearing date the seventh day of March in the year one thousand eight hundred and thirty one the above named Ezra Slifer was appointed a trustee and authorized and empowered to sell and dispose of all the real estate of Joshua Harley Senr then a lunatic"

[5] "Tilghman Biser and his wife on the 12th day of April A. D. 1853 convey to Ezra Williard and a certain William Carroll said deed recorded in Liber E. S. Folio 252 etc one of the land records of Fred. County."

[6] ". . . said Trustees in execution of said trust about A. D. 1856 did sell said lot to William F. Gitings but did not give any deed for the same, though the purchase money was paid, and the said Gittings did about A. D. 1856, sell the same lot to one George W. Padget now deceased of the same county intestate, and whose sole child and heir is the said Mary A. E. Koontz and whereas after the death of said Padget intestate, said lot was sold at Public Sale for Taxes due thereon for the years 1866 and 7 by William A. Fenga, Tax Collector for the County aforesaid on the sixth day of May A. D. 1869 to the said David Arnold."

[7] "It being part of the same land which was conveyed to said George Alfred Townsend by a deed executed by David Arnold and his wife dated December 15, 1884, and which is recorded in Liber A. F. No 9 folio 541 one of the land records of Frederick County, Maryland."

[8] ". . . all that triangular tract or parcel of land lying in the forks of the road leading from the summit of South Mountain to Arnoldstown and Burkittsville respectively being in Frederick County state of Maryland and more particularly described, as beginning at a point near the dividing line between Frederick and Washington counties Maryland and in the middle of the road leading from Burkittsville to Gapland Station said point being south 10 degrees west 1 and 1/10 perches from a stone planted on the north side of said road and near the stone fence, and running thence with the middle of the road"

Historic Sites

The Mountain House at Turner's Gap
Philip Jacob Shafer (1770) to Russell and Judy Schwartz (1998)
Tract Name - Flonham

Reference	Date	Grantee of Deed	Area
MdHR BC & GS #47 pp. 496-497	27 Aug 1770	Philip Jacob Shafer[1] - Flonham surveyed 27 August 1770 patented 20 April 1774	36 acres
MdHR, Will Index GME-3-107	25/29 Dec 1795 will filed	Philip Sheffer II inherits entire tract from his father	36 acres
FCLR, JS-25-372	6 Jul 1826	Henry Miller, part of Flonham	5 acres
WCLR, IN-9-595	25 May 1855	Edward L. Boteler[2]	40 acres
WCLR, LBN-2-133	14 May 1867	George F. Smith[3]	60 acres
WCLR, 74-264	19 Apr 1876	Madeleine V. Dahlgren[4]	60 acres
Fred. Cty. Wills Liber J. K. W. No. 2 fol. 304	30 Nov 1890	Ulrica Dahlgren Pierce[5]	187 acres, 2 roods, and 14 square ps
WCLR, 163-294	31 May 1922	St. Mary's Academy[6]	187 acres, 2 roods, and 14 square ps
WCLR, 172-524	28 Sep 1925	Otho Hewitt, Charles M. Hewitt, and Robert W. Hewitt[7]	177 acres, 2 roods, and 14 square ps
WCLR, 173-576	30 Jan 1926	Charles M. Hewitt and Marie E. Hewitt	177 acres, 2 roods, and 14 square ps
WCLR, 225-494	2 Mar 1944	Charles M. Hewitt	177 acres, 2 roods, and 14 square ps
WCLR, 444-54	11 Sep 1944	E. Stuart Bushong, Trustee	177 acres, 2 roods, and 14 square ps
WCLR, 444-55	11 Sep 1944	Charles M. Hewitt and Edna E. Hewitt	177 acres, 2 roods, and 14 square ps
WCLR, 330-475	2 Dec 1957	Mitchell H. Dodson et ux[8]	3.7 acres
WCLR, 527-627	19 Jul 1971	Charles F. Reichmuth et ux[9]	3.7 acres
WCLR, 788-755	12 Jul 1985	Russell L. Schwartz et ux[10]	3.7 acres

Historic Sites

Flonham - From 1770 to 1842

Philip Jacob Shafer I surveys Flonham 27 August 1770, for 36 acres, and patents the tract 20 April 1774, 36 acres, MdHR BC & GS #44, 439-40. The will of Philip Jacob Shafer I probably is at the Maryland Archives, in German, not translated. See Will Index, GME-3-107. It was probably filed between December 25 and 29, 1795. The entire tract of Flonham must have been left to Philip Sheffer II.

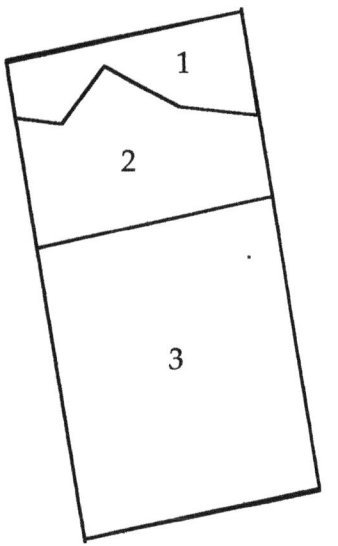

The three parts of Flonham in 1842:

1 - Philip Sheffer II to Henry Miller, 5 acres, 1826, FCLR, JS-25-372.

2 - Daniel Sheffer inherits from Philip Sheffer II in 1842, 8 and 3/4 acres. Tract number two is directly south of the Mountain House.

3 - Philip Sheffer III inherits from Philip Sheffer II in 1842, 22 and 1/4 acres.

The Mountain House is on the western portion of tract number one.

The Dahlgren Chapel is on, or very near, the eastern portion of tract number one.

Lot #2 above traced from Philip Sheffer II to Madeleine Vinton Dahlgren:

1. **Daniel Sheffer inherits the 8 and 3/4 acre tract from his father, Philip Sheffer II. The will of Philip Sheffer II, written in 1841, is found in GME-2-651.** "I also give to my son Philip 15 acres of mountain land lying on the south side of the Baltimore and Frederick Turnpike Road a land called Flonham ... the residue of my mountain land called as aforesaid Flonham lying on the south side of the turnpike aforesaid I give to my son Daniel and Philip jointly ..." Philip (III) and Daniel split their common portion, 7 and 1/4 acres to Philip (III) and 8 and 3/4 acres to Daniel.

2. **Mary Sheffer, Trustee, transfers the tract to John W. Koogle, FCLR, DSB-1, 397, recorded 22 May 1867.** "Part of a tract of land called Flonham of which Daniel Sheffer died seized and possessed situated on South Mountain in said county and immediately on the southwest side of the turnpike road leading from Middletown to Boonsborough and adjoining the lands of Daniel Beachley, William Jones, and others being and lying also **immediately south of the mountain house on said turnpike** and containing eight and three quarters acres of land."

3. **John W. Koogle transfers the tract to George P. Sheffer, FCLR, TG-3-396, recorded 1 Jun 1875.** "All those parts of tracts of land described in the deed from Mary Sheffer, trustee, to the said John W. Koogle bearing date on the 22nd day of April 1867, Liber D.S.B. No. 1, folio 397."

4. **George P. and Amanda D. Sheffer transfer the tract to Madeleine V. Dahlgren, FCLR, TG-5-194, recorded 25 Apr 1876.** "Being on the South Mountain in said county and **immediately on the south west side of the turnpike** road leading from Middletown to Boonsboro and adjoining the lands of Daniel Beachley, William Jones, **the Mountain House property on said Turnpike** and others, and containing eight and three quarters acres of land."

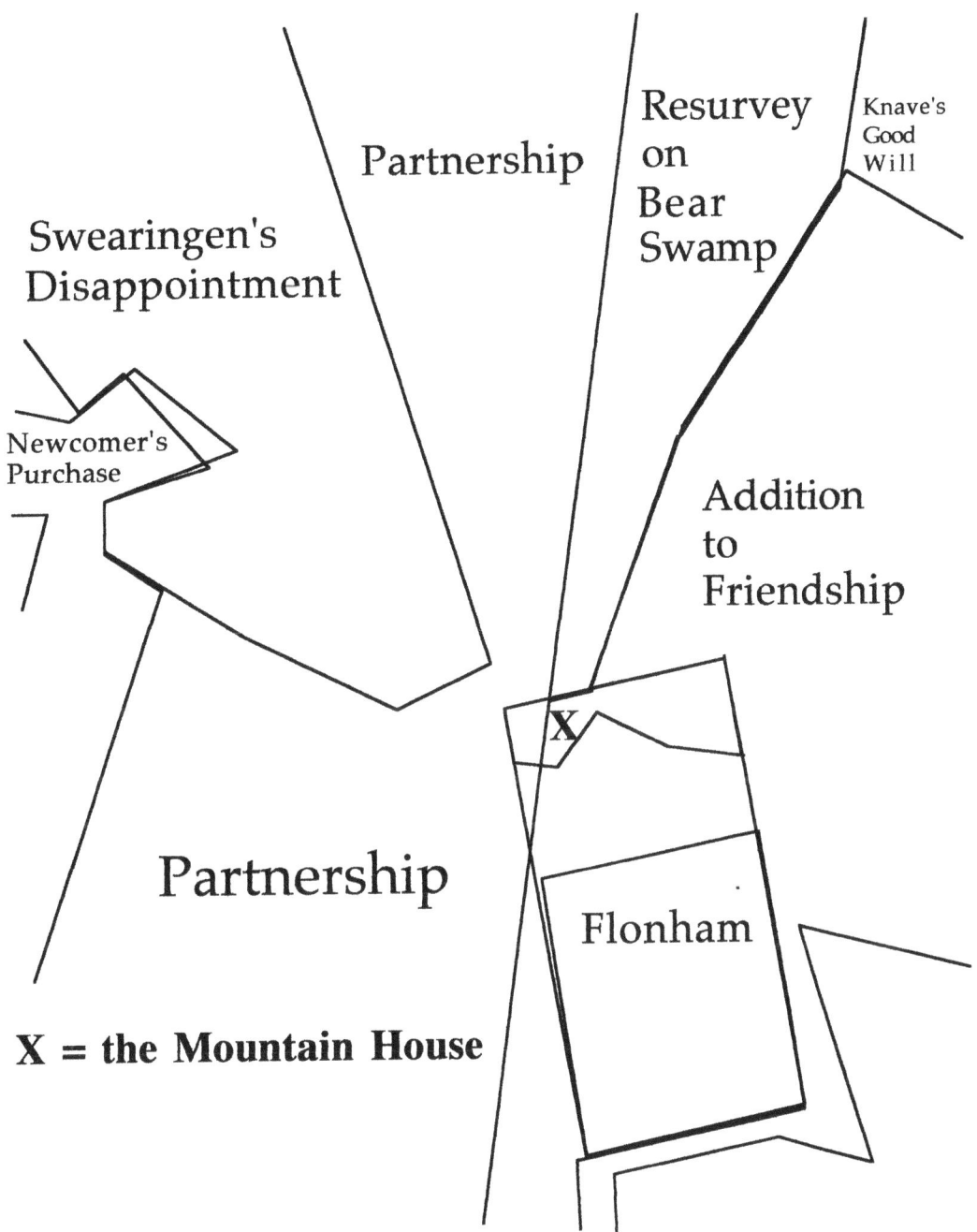

Tracts surrounding the Mountain House at Turner's Gap

Historic Sites

St. Mary's Academy of Notre Dame, St. Joseph's County, Indiana, to Charles M. Hewitt - 1925

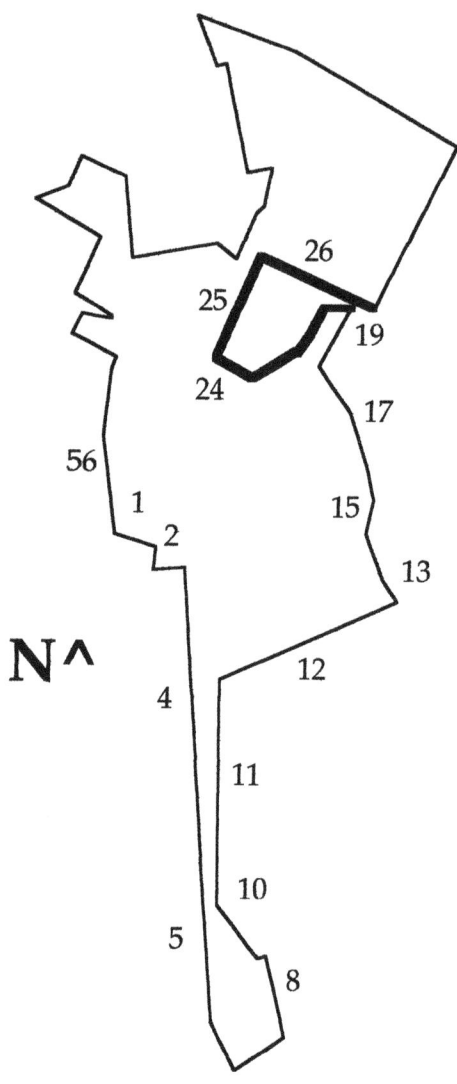

line 12   To the middle of the state road leading from Frederick to Hagerstown
line 15   To a white oak tree on the east side of the state road
line 19   Thence by lines now made to exclude the above mentioned 10 acres surrounding the chapel the 7 following courses
line 20   To a black oak tree on the west side of the public road
line 23   To the center line of the above mentioned state road

(**Note** - The public road is the Dahlgren road.)

Historic Sites

Footnotes - The Mountain House at Turner's Gap

[1] Philip Jacob Shafer, survey for Flonham, Aug. 27, 1770, 36 acres. MdHR, BC & BS #47, 496-7. Philip Jacob Shafer, patent for Flonham, April 20, 1774, 36 acres. MdHR, BC & GS #44, 439-40.

[2] This transfer was from the heirs of Henry Miller. This deed conveyed two parcels: the Homestead of 40 acres and Lot No. 5 consisting of 18 and 1/8 acres. The Mountain House is on the Homestead parcel. The first parcel being the Homestead belonging to the heirs of Henry Miller late of Washington County deceased being part of a tract of land called Addition to Friendship, part of a tract of land called Partnership, part of a tract of land called Swearingen's Disappointment, and part of a tract of land called Flonham or be it part of any other tract of land whatsoever. Between John W. Derr and Lizabeth Derr, his wife, John Miller and Susan Miller, his wife, Adam Koogle and Catharine Koogle, his wife, of Federick county and State of Maryland and Maria Williams Joseph Nuyman and Sara R. Nyman, his wife, and Henrietta Miller of Washington County and state of Maryland of the one part and Edwar L. Boteler of Washington County and state of Maryland of the other part.

[3] This transfer was from Edward L. and Prudence C. Boteler. This deed mentions the tracts of Addition to Friendship, Partnership, Swearingen's Disappointment, Flonham, and Knave's Good Will. It mentions "the Boonsboro and Middletown turnpike, north side of the public road leading from said turnpike to Daniel Rent's farm, and a stone wall. The deed indicates George Baltzell was an agent for Henry Miller. This deed indicates portions of the 60 acre tract lie on both sides of the turnpike road.

[4] This transfer was from George F. Smith. Part Addition to Friendship, part of Partnership, part of Swearingen's Disappointment, and part of Flonham. It identifies Madelein V. Dahlgren of Washington City in the District of Columbia, the Boonsboro and Middletown turnpike, north side of the public road leading from said turnpike to Daniel Rent's farm, and a stone wall. This tract contained 60 acres of land more or less it being the same land that Edward L. Boteler and wife conveyed to the said George F. Smith by deed bearing date March 27th 1867 and recorded in L B N No. 2, folio 133, one of the land records of Washington County.

[5] Will of Madeleine Sarah Vinton Dahlgren, recorded in Frederick County and also recorded in Washington County, Liber I, folio 357.

[6] Saint Mary's Academy of Notre Dame, St. Joseph's County, Indiana.

[7] "... SECOND. Deed from GEORGE F. SMITH TO MADELEINE V. DAHLGREN dated April 19th 1876 and recorded in Liber T. G. No. 5 Folio 708, one of the land records for Frederick County, it being also recorded in Liber No. 74 Folio 264, one of the land records for Washington County and containing 60 acres of land, more or less." Later, "ALSO EXCEPTING, 10 acres of land, upon which is located the Chapel, said 10 acres being part of the 60 acres more or less conveyed to MADELEINE VINTON DAHLGREN BY GEORGE F. SMITH by deed dated April 19, 1876, and recorded in Liber T. G. No 5, folio 708, one of the land records for Frederick County, it being the second of the above thirteen deeds."

[8] This deed created a 3.7 acre tract. The tract was "situate along the South side of U. S. Route No. 40A at the summit of Dahlgren Mountain, in District No. 6, Washington County, Maryland."

[9] "... situate along the south side of U. S. Route No. 40A at the summit of Dahlgren Mountain, in District No. 6, Washington County, Maryland."

[10] "... being situate along the south side of U. S. Route 40A at the summit of Dahlgren Mountain, in Election District No. 6, Washington County, Maryland."

Historic Sites

The Ten Acres around Dahlgren Memorial Chapel at Turner's Gap
From Frederick Fox (1795) to Vernon Hutzell (1942)
Tract Name - Addition to Friendship

Reference	Date	Grantee of Deed	Acres
MdHR, IC #P 672-3	9 May 1797	Frederick Fox - Addition to Friendship[1] (Friendship - 8 June 1795, Unpat. Cert. #238)	202
FCLR, WR-32-26/8	21 Sep 1807	Joseph Swearingen[2]	202 + 30
Will of Joseph Swearingen	Date of Death of Joseph Swearingen	Heirs of Joseph Swearingen[3]	189 1/2
FCLR, JS-39-260/4	5 Apr 1832	George Baltzell[4]	189 1/2
FCLR, JS-39-264/8	31 May 1832	Henry Miller[5]	189 1/2
None[6]	Date of Death of Henry Miller	Heirs at law of Henry Miller	189 1/2
WCLR, IN-9-595	25 May 1855	Edward L. Boteler[7]	40
WCLR, LBN-2-133	14 May 1867	George F. Smith[8]	60
WCLR, 74-264 Liber J. K. W.	19 Apr 1876	Madeleine V. Dahlgren[9]	60
Fred. Cty. Wills Liber J. K. W. No. ?, folio 304	Death of Madeleine V. Dahlgren	Ulrica Dahlgren Pierce[10]	177?
WCLR, 340-170-171	21 Aug 1922	St. Mary's Academy	177
FCLR, Liber No. 362 folio 314	10 Jan 1925	Ulrica Dahlgren Pierce[11]	10
Fred. Cty. Wills Liber G. E. S. No. 2, folios 63 etc	7 May 1925	Josiah Pierce, heir of Ulrica Dahlgren Pierce (Excepts land on which the Chapel stands)	9+?
FCLR, 433-241	27 Jan 1942	Vernon E. Hutzell (land around the Chapel)	9+

The listing of probable deeds for the Dahlgren Chapel itself appear on the following page.

Historic Sites

Probable Deeds for The Dahlgren Chapel

The direction and distances of the courses around the 10 acre tract on which the Dahlgren Chapel stands appear in the deed from Saint Mary's Academy to Ulrica Dahlgren Pierce dated 15 Jan 1925.

According to FCLR, JS-39-264/8, George Baltzell, Atty, to Henry Miller, recorded July 5, 1832, there were two portions of Addition to Friendship transferred to Henry Miller from George Baltzell. The first portion, consisting of 75 1/2 acres, was south of the turnpike and the second portion, consisting of 114 acres was north of the turnpike.

The Dahlgren Chapel is almost directly east of the Mountain House. The Chapel sits very close to the boundary line between Addition to Friendship and Flonham. While most of the ten acres around the Chapel is composed of the Addition to Friendship tract, the Chapel itself may sit on the northernmost portion of the Flonham tract. If that is true, then the one acre tract of land on which the Chapel now stands would begin with the following land records:

Reference	Date	Grantee of Deed	Acres
MdHR, BC & GS #47 pp. 496-497	27 Aug 1770	Philip Jacob Shafer[12] - Flonham surveyed 27 August 1770 patented 20 April 1774	36
FCLR, JS-25-372	6 Jul 1826	Henry Miller, Flonham	5

The sequence would continue with the acquisition of the 40 acre tract by Edward L. Boteler from the heirs of Henry Miller and continue through George F. Smith, Madeleine V. Dahlgren, Ulrica Dahlgren Pierce, St. Mary's Academy, Ulrica Dahlgren Pierce, and then

Frederick County Records of Wills Liber G. E. S. No. 2, folios 63 etc	7 May 1925	Josiah Pierce, heir of Ulrica Dahlgren Pierce[13] (Excepts land on which the Chapel stands.)	9+

It appears Josiah Pierce deeded the Chapel to someone else. The Josiah Pierce deed above appears to be the first deed to exclude the immediate 1 acre on which the Chapel stands.

The author believes the following deeds may be for the Chapel itself:

FCLR, 722-403	17 Apr 1965	Roy G. and Iona M. Routzahn	lots 1 and 2[14]
FCLR, Book 2114 page 0200	14 Jul 1995	Central Maryland Heritage League, Inc.	lots 1 and 2[15]
FCLR, Book 2186 page 0781	10 May 1996	United States of America	0.92 acre

The Central Maryland Heritage League, Inc. transferred the Chapel to the United States government in 1996.

Historic Sites

Footnotes - The Ten Acres around Dahlgren Memorial Chapel

[1] Addition to Friendship was a resurvey obtained by Frederick Fox out of the western shore land office by a special warrant of proclamation to resurvey and affect the vacancy included in a resurvey made for him on the eighth day of June seventeen hundred and ninety five by the name of Friendship, the caution money for which had not been paid within the time limited by law. In pursuance whereof a resurvey was made and a certificate thereof returned containing two hundred and two acres lying in the county aforesaid and called Addition to Friendship.

[2] This deed transfered all 202 acres of Addition to Friendship as well as 30 acres of Fredericksburg.

[3] The heirs of Joseph Swearingen were Joseph Van Swearingen, Eleanor (and John) Stemble, Elizabeth Swearingen, Marcia Swearingen, Margaret W. Swearingen, and Ruth D. Swearingen. Joseph Van Swearingen, son of Joseph Swearingen, appointed George Baltzell his attorney at law.

[4] Eleanor and her husband, John Stemble, sold the one sixth interest of Eleanor to attorney George Baltzell.

[5] This transfer consisted of two parts: Part One, "the first part of the whole tract aforesaid wherein before mentioned and lying south of the said turnpike road," consisted of 75 and 1/2 acres. Part Two, "the second tract of the aforesaid land called 'Addition to Friendship' lying north of the turnpike road," consisted of 114 acres. Henry Miller acquired a portion of Foxes Last Shift from Michael Easterday in 1824-1827. He acquired five acres of Flonham from Philip Shafer in 1824, deed WC JS-25-372. He acquired a portion of Swearingen's Dissapointment from John Shafer in 1824-1827.

[6] Henry Miller probably died intestate. There is no will of Henry Miller on record at either the Washington or Frederick County Courthouses.

[7] This transfer was from the heirs of Henry Miller. This deed conveyed two parcels: the "Homestead" of 40 acres and Lot No. 5 consisting of 18 and 1/8 acres. The Mountain House is on the "Homestead" parcel. "The first parcel being the "Homestead" belonging to the heirs of Henry Miller late of Washington County deceased being part of a tract of land called Addition to Friendship, part of a tract of land called Partnership, part of a tract of land called Swearingen's Disappointment, and part of a tract of land called Flonham or be it part of any other tract of land whatsoever." "Between John W. Derr and Lizabeth Derr, his wife, John Miller and Susan Miller, his wife, Adam Koogle and Catharine Koogle, his wife, of Federick County and state of Maryland and Maria Williams, Joseph Nuyman, and Sara R. Nyman, his wife, and Henrietta Miller of Washington County and state of Maryland of the one part and Edward L. Boteler of Washington County and state of Maryland of the other part."

[8] This transfer was from Edward L. and Prudence C. Boteler. The deed mentions the tracts of Addition to Friendship, Partnership, Swearingen's Disappointment, Flonham, and Knave's Good Will. It mentions "the Boonsboro and Middletown turnpike," "north side of the public road leading from said turnpike to Daniel Rents farm," and "a stone wall." The deed indicates George Baltzell was an agent for Henry Miller. This deed indicates portions of the 60 acre tract lie on both sides of the turnpike road.

[9] This transfer was from George F. Smith. "Being part of a tract of land called Addition to Friendship, part of Partnership, part of Swearingen's Disappointment, and part of a tract called Flonham." It identifies "Madelein V. Dahlgren of Washington City in the District of Columbia," "the Boonsboro and Middletown turnpike," "north side of the public road leading from said turnpike to Daniel Rents farm," and "a stone wall." This tract contained "60 acres of land more or less it being the same land that Edward L. Boteler and wife conveyed to the said George F. Smith by deed bearing date March 27th 1867 and recorded in L B N No. 2, folio 133, one of the land records of Washington County."

[10] "...last will and testament of her mother, Madeline Sarah Vinton Dahlgren, as recorded in Liber J. K. W. No. 2, folio 304, etc., one of the will records for Frederick County, also recorded in Liber No. 1, folio 357, one of the will records for Washington County."

[11] Will of Madeleine Sarah Vinton Dahlgren, recorded in Frederick County and also recorded in Washington County, Liber I, folio 357.

Historic Sites

12 Philip Jacob Shafer, survey for Flonham, Aug. 27, 1770, 36 acres. MdHR, BC & BS #47, 496-7. Philip Jacob Shafer, patent for Flonham, April 20, 1774, 36 acres. MdHR, BC & GS #44, 439-40.

13 "said real estate containing ten (10) acres, more or less, save and excepting thereout and therefrom all that small lot situated in the southwest corner of said real estate and bordering 76.5 feet on the north side of the state road from Frederick to Hagerstown, Maryland, and running in a northerly direction on the west side thereof along the lands of Charles Hewitt 156 feet and having a width of 48 feet on the north side thereof and running 143 feet and 6 inches from the north side thereof to the Frederick and Hagerstown state road, and on which said reserved lot of ground is a stone memorial chapel erected by my grandmother, Madeleine Sarah Vinton Dahlgren."

14 "being lots Nos. 1 and 2 of an unrecorded Plan of Lots for Mrs. Edna E. Hewitt, Top of Dahlgren Mountain, prepared by J. H. Seibert, County Surveyor, on June 18, 1960"

15 "being lots Nos. 1 and 2 of an unrecorded Plan of Lots for Mrs. Edna E. Hewitt, Top of Dahlgren Mountain, prepared by J. H. Seibert, County Surveyor, on June 18, 1960"

Historic Sites

The Moses Chapline Senior Cemetery

The Moses Chapline Senior Cemetery was on property owned by Merwin Sims in 1996, about two miles west of Fox's Gap along the Old Sharpsburg Road. The cemetery is about one-fourth of a mile north of the Old Sharpsburg Road. The author at one time visited the cemetery with Mr. Sims and Doug Bast. See *Drums Along the Antietam* by John W. Schildt for a brief discussion of the cemetery. Also see, *Chaplines from Maryland and Virginia* by Maria J. Liggett Dare.

The following land tract information may provide the reader with the ability to trace the land records related to the cemetery:

Rsy on Mt. Pleasant   MdHR: IB #D-226   Jacob Snyder   198 acres   25 April 1814

Near Keedysville. A Resurvey on Part of the Resurvey on Mt. Pleasant 21 Jul 1757 by Moses Chapline for 471 acres; A Resurvey on Part of the Resurvey on Well Done 25 Oct 1774 by William Good for 1822 acres; A Resurvey on Josiah's (Last) Bit 20 Apr 1786 by William Good for 67 acres; A Resurvey on Remnant 16 Jun 1791 by Michael Fackler for 8 and 1/4 acres. Near Jacob Snyder's Mill. The Michael Fackler tract may contain the Moses Chapline Sr. family cemetery.

Moses Senior was a brother of the founder of Sharpsburg, Joseph Chapline Senior. The grave of Joseph Chapline Senior is about 100 feet into the cemetery that is directly across the street from the Antietam National Battlefield Cemetery in Sharpsburg.

War Correspondents Memorial Arch   **Photo by Susanne Flowers - 1998**

Photo by Susanne Flowers - about 1993 **The Fox Inn**

The Wise House U.S. Military History Institute - Carlisle, PA

Photo by Susanne Flowers - 1993   **The Reno Monument**

The Reno School Building   Photo by Susanne Flowers - 1997

Photo by Susanne Flowers - 1998   **The Dahlgren Chapel**

The Old South Mountain Inn   Photo by Susanne Flowers - 1998

Part V

Supplemental Material

Occupations of Residents along the Old Sharpsburg Road in the 1700s

Kodak Photo CD-Rom Computer Disc - "Fox's Gap in Maryland"

Biographical Listing of Some Early Land Owners of the Area

Occupations of Residents along the Old Sharpsburg Road in the 1700s

Land tract records give valuable insight into the economy along the Old Sharpsburg Road in the 1700s. By reviewing these one can determine the occupations of numerous residents along or near the road. The records indicate most of the individuals living there in the 1700s probably made their living as farmers. Many also worked, at least part time, in various skilled trades.

The various crafts practiced along the Old Sharpsburg Road imply there were enough travelers on the road to support such trades. Therefore, the route must have been an important thoroughfare and the economy along the road must have been vibrant. The following identifies the land tracts along or near the Old Sharpsburg Road (from Shepherdstown, Virginia, through Sharpsburg and Fox's Gap to Middletown, Maryland) that give the occupation of the tract owner. The chronological date that someone first occupied the various properties is given.

James Smith patented Smith's Hills for 208 acres on 17 April 1745. The tract had its "beginning at a bounded white oak standing on the side of a hill within a quarter of a mile of the wagon road that crosses Antietam". The Smith's Hills tract was not far from the Burnside Bridge on the south side of the Battlefield of Antietam. The patent states ". . . the certificate of survey aforesaid and the land and premises therein mentioned unto a certain James Smith of Prince Georges County planter . . ." Today the tract is in Washington County which was part of Frederick County until 1776. In addition, Frederick County was part of Prince Georges County until 1748.

A tract named Shettle was in the area of the present town of Bolivar, about one mile northeast of Fox's Gap. Daniel Dulany Esquire patented the tract on 9 September 1742 for 50 acres. ". . . that I Daniel Dulany within named in consideration of thirty one pounds fifteen shillings and six pence current money secured to be paid to me by Robert Marks of Frederick County shoemaker have assigned and transfered and hereby assigns set over and transfer unto him the said Robert Marks the land within mentioned . . ." Robert Marks probably was one of the earliest settlers within a mile or so of what became Fox's Gap. Traffic along the route of the Old Sharpsburg Road apparently justified the presence of a shoemaker by about 1742.

One of the most significant early deeds identifies Richard Smith as an innholder. Court records identify Richard Smith as living on the Great Road to Conococheague. ". . . between Richd Smith of Frederick County in the province of Maryland innholder of the one part and Peter Beaver of the same county and province aforesaid of the other part . . . for and in consideration of the sum of forty six pounds current money . . ." The year 1755 is the earliest point in time at which we can identify an innkeeper along the Old Sharpsburg Road between Shepherdstown and Middletown. The presence of an inn may be the best indicator of numerous travelers along the road.

Many craftsmen owned tracts along the Old Sharpsburg Road by 1770. One important tract owner was Casper Shaff, a merchant. Casper acquired The Exchange tract on which the Fox Inn stands. Casper made a resurvey on The Exchange tract. ". . . between Casper Shaff of Frederick County and province of Maryland merchant of the one part and Conrad Young of said county and province farmer of the other part witnesseth that the said Casper Shaff for and in consideration of the sum of forty pounds current money of Maryland . . ."

Grim's Fancy was one half mile west of Fox's Gap and along the Old Sharpsburg Road. The tract record is significant. It identifies John Fox's house and the road from Swearingen's Ferry to Frederick Town. ". . . between Philip Booker of Frederick County and province of Maryland farmer of the one part and Geo. Common of said County and province blacksmith of the other part . . ."

John Fox settled at Fox's Gap by no later than 1760. No land records for him exist, except for tracts in Sharpsburg. Perhaps John Fox was a squatter and never owned land at Fox's Gap. His will indicates he owned skin dressing tools. Daniel Gebhart Fox, in *The Fox Genealogy*, describes John Fox as a tanner by trade. The house of John Fox probably was near the site of the Reno Monument at Fox's Gap. The parcel of land on which the Reno Monument stands was part of a tract named Addition to Friendship that was patented by Frederick Fox.

The Birely Tannery Report may be of interest to those who seek additional information about the tannery craft of John Fox [Archaeological Data Recovery at the Birely Tannery (18FR575) City of Frederick, Maryland, prepared by M.A.A.R. Associates, Inc. of Newark, Delaware, 1991]. The Birely Tannery began operation in Frederick, Maryland, in the 1760s and remained in business until the 1920s!

A tract named Bubble (Boble) was just south of the Fox Inn and the Exchange tract acquired by Casper Shaff. A transfer in 1761 between Casper Shaff and Michael Jesserang identifies Jesserang as an innholder. "... made this fifth day of May in the year of our lord one thousand seven hundred and sixty one between Michael Jesserang of Frederick Town in Frederick County and province of Maryland innholder of the one part and Casper Shaff of same place merchant of the other part . . . in consideration of the sum of fourteen pounds ten shillings current money of Maryland . . ."

A tract named the Resurvey on Chestnut Hill identifies Matthias Ringer as a farmer and Casper Shaff as a merchant. "... between Matthias Ringer of Frederick County and province of Maryland farmer of the one part and Casper Shaff of the same place merchant of the other part witnesseth that the said Matthias Ringer for and in consideration of the sum of twenty pounds current money of Maryland . . ." The Resurvey on Chestnut Hill tract is about a mile south of the Fox Inn and along the road to Burkittsville and Crampton's Gap.

The Resurvey on Whiskey Alley tract was north of Middletown and near the fork of the Old Hagerstown Road and the Old Sharpsburg Road at the Catoctin Creek. "... between Philip Keywaughver of Frederick County and province of Maryland farmer of the one part and Nicholas Finck of the county and province aforesaid taylor of the other . . . for and in consideration of the sum of eighteen pounds current money . . ."

The Resurvey on Learning tract was south of the Fox Inn. A small portion of the tract came up near the Old Sharpsburg Road east of the Fox Inn. Henry Lighter (Leiter) was a wheelwright. He purchased part of the Resurvey on Learning tract. A daughter of Frederick Fox married a son of Henry Lighter (Leiter). "... between Henry Lighter of Hamshire County in the province of Virginia, wheelwright of the one part and Peter Beaver of the same county and province aforesaid farmer of the other part . . ."

The Goose Cap tract was at the fork of the Old Hagerstown and Old Sharpsburg Roads at the Catoctin Creek, about one mile north of Middletown. "... between Nichs Fink of Frederick County in the province of Maryland taylor of the one part and Ths Welch of same county and province aforesaid surveyor of the other part . . . for and in consideration of the sum of ninety nine pounds current and lawful money of Maryland . . ."

Shaff's Purchase was immediately west of the Fox Inn tract. "... between Casper Shaff of Frederick Town in Frederick County and province of Maryland of the one part and Peter Ruble of Frederick County and province aforesaid clocksmith of the other part witnesseth . . ."

The Brayface tract was northeast of the Fox Inn. "... between Peter Beaver of Frederick County and State of Maryland farmer of the one part: and Christian Kyser of the same county and state aforesaid miller of the other part . . . All that tract or parcel of land called Brayface, which being part of the Resurvey on Oxford Resurvey on Oxford. Beginning at the bounded tree of said Brayface, one of the original tracts, and running thence . . ."

The review of the preceding land records indicates the people living along the Old Sharpsburg Road in the 1700s were industrious and free-market oriented. It seems evident that they were able to unite in a common cause to oppose the British by the mid 1770s.

Fox's Gap in Maryland

Kodak Photo CD-Rom Computer Disc

A copy of this computer disc is at:

>Washington County Free Library
>Western Maryland Room
>100 South Potomac Street
>Hagerstown, MD 21740

An partial version of the disc is at:

>Family History Library
>35 N. West Temple
>Salt Lake City, Utah 84103

At the time of the publication of this book, a copy of the disc may be obtained for the price of duplication, postage, and handling, by writing:

>The Society of the Descendants of Frederick Fox of Fox's Gap in Maryland
>c/o Curtis L. Older
>618 Tryon Place
>Gastonia, N. C. 28054

The following is a partial list of items included on the disc:

Maps:

The Winslow Map of 1736. "A Plan of the upper Part of Patomack River called Cohongoroot Survey'd in the year 1736.

Fry and Jefferson Map of 1751, 1755, and 1775.

1755 French version of Fry and Jefferson Map; Robert de Vaugondy, Gilles. Shows Virginia, Maryland, and "De La War counties." The photo on this disc is a close-up view of a portion of the map.

1794 Dennis Griffith Map of Maryland. Map of the State of Maryland.

1808 Varle Map. Both a complete map and a close-up of portion of the map for the area of the Battlefield of South Mountain are on the disc.

Map of the Battlefield of South Mountain. South Mountain showing the postitions of the forces of the United States and the enemy during the battle fought by the Army of the Potomac Sept. 14, 1862.

1995 Map of Western Maryland. Maryland Dept. of Transportation. base map copyright-State Highway Administration.

Fox's Gap, east side, 1995, and Fox's Gap, west side, 1995. Maryland Dept. of Transportation. base map copyright-State Highway Administration.

Land tracts in the area of Boonsboro, Maryland. Courtesy of Doug Bast of the Boonesborough Museum of History, Boonsboro, Maryland. The map was not included in this book because the print quality was not sharp enough to be read easily.

Kodak Photo CD-Rom Disc

Historical Sites:

Ft. Frederick, Maryland (probably 1995). Photo courtesy of Allan Powell of Hagerstown.
Wise Farmhouse at Fox's Gap. Photograph about 1885. U. S. Military History Institute, Carlisle, Pennsylvania.
The Fox Inn, owned by George Fox, a son of Frederick Fox, from 1805 to 1807. Photo by Susanne F. Flowers, 1992.

Historical Markers:

State Roads Commission Marker. General Edward Braddock. This marker is on the square in Sharpsburg, Maryland. Photo by Susanne Flowers, 1992.
Society of Colonial Wars and Maryland Historical Society Marker. General Edward Braddock. This marker is near the front of the Maryland State Police Barrack B in Frederick on Route 40 (Patrick Street). Photo by Allan Powell, 1995.
The Boulder at Braddock Spring. Along the Braddock route of 1755. Photo by Susanne F. Flowers, 1995.
Maryland Bicentennial Commission and Maryland Historical Society Marker. Swearingen's Ferry and Pack Horse Ford. This marker is at the Rumsey Bridge on the Potomac River at Shepherdstown. Photo by Susanne Flowers, 1992.
Sign about General Braddock. State Police Barrack B, Patrick Street, Route 40, Frederick, Maryland. Photo by Susanne F. Flowers, 1992.
17th Michigan Memorial at Fox's Gap. Photo by Susanne F. Flowers, 1992.
The Reno Monument at Fox's Gap. Photo by Susanne F. Flowers, 1992.

Drawings:

The Battle of South Mountain, Md. Library of Congress. b/w lithograph by Endicott & Co., c1864 by Joseph J. Joel, drawn on stone by A. A. Fasel. LC-USZ62-12926. Sunday, Sept. 14, 1862. The Glorious charge of the 23rd & 12th Ohio volunteers (Col. Scammon) against the 23rd & 12th North Carolina, under the rebel Gen. Garland who was killed in the charge.

Fox Tombstones:

Frederick Fox	**John Liter**
Susannah (Schutt) (Young) Fox	**Elizabeth (Fox) Liter**
George Fox	**George Mettard**
Elizabeth Ann (Link) Fox	**Christiana (Fox) Mettard**
Daniel Booker Fox	**Jacob Benner**
Susannah (Christman) Fox	**Mary Magdalene (Fox) Benner**

Fox Family

A Gun of Frederick Fox. The gun was given to Robert H. Fox by Daniel Gebhart Fox, author of *The Fox Genealogy*. Photo taken about 1993 by Curtis L. Older at the home of Robert H. Fox in Cincinnati, Ohio.

Retouched photo of Daniel Booker Fox, a son of Frederick Fox. Photo probably taken about 1860. Photo courtesy of Robert H. Fox of Cincinnati, Ohio.

Biographical Listing

Booker, Bartholomew (Probably born in 1720 and died in 1791 or 1792.)[1] was aged "71 years or thereabouts" on December 26, 1790.[2] Bartholomew and Peter Booker arrived in Philadelphia on September 3, 1739, on the Loyal Judith from Rotterdam.[3] Robert H. Fox of Cincinnati indicates the first land record for Bartholomew was August 1748 for 100 acres of land in Lancaster [now Franklin] county, Pennsylvania.

Bartholomew was in the Fox's Gap area by 1754, when he acquired a tract named Mendall (Mindall) from Joseph Chapline Sr. Bartholomew owned Pickall, patented February 22, 1764, a tract stretching from the forks of the roads at the Catoctin Creek just north of Middletown all the way to Orr's and Fox's Gaps.

Bartholomew married Margaret and they were the parents of 14 children. Bartholomew was the father-in-law of Frederick Fox. According to Robert H. Fox of Cincinnati, Ohio, a desk belonging to Bartholomew Booker passed to his widow, Margaret, who died in 1796,[4] and then to Frederick Fox. Robert viewed the desk in the 1930s when he visited Daniel Gebhart Fox, author of *The Fox Genealogy*, who owned the desk at that time.

Carroll, Charles The name Charles Carroll is well known in Maryland History. An article by Calvin E. Schildknecht identifies eight Charles Carrolls of record in Maryland.[5]

The first Charles Carroll (1660-1720) was Attorney General and Land Agent of Lord Baltimore.[6] He gradually rose to the position of proprietary agent held by Darnall. He was a leading Catholic layman in the province, a lawyer and man of wealth, long connected with the Calverts while they were still Catholics. "It was in connection with the trial of his nephew that Charles Carroll produced a commission from the proprietor which gave him surprisingly large powers."[7]

A Dr. Charles Carroll of Annapolis lived from 1691 to 1755. His son lived from 1723 to 1783 and was Barrister of Annapolis. Dr. Charles Carroll was the owner of Fellowship, a land tract at Boonsboro, in 1753.

A Charles Carroll acquired Pile Grove, northwest of Fox's Gap, on July 9, 1753, from John Hepburn. He probably lived from 1703 to 1783. He was known as Charles Carroll of Annapolis but was also sometimes known as Charles, the Landowner. He was the son of the first Charles Carroll of note in Maryland.

Cressap, Thomas (c. 1702 - c. 1790), emigrated from Yorkshire, England, at the age of fifteen and married at the age of thirty near Havre de Grace, Maryland.[8] He moved about 1742 to a farm near Old Town. He called the farm "Shipton," after the place of his nativity in England. It was on the north fork, a few miles above the north and south branches of the Potomac. Here he acquired a large landed estate.

He renewed his intimacy with Washington, who always had confidence in him. Employed in 1748 by the Ohio Company, with the aid of an Indian named Nemacolin, he marked the road to their territory, which was the same route pursued by Braddock in his ill-fated expedition. He visited England at the age of 70, and whilst in London was commissioned by Lord Baltimore to run the western line of Maryland, in order to ascertain which of the two branches of the Potomac was in reality the fountain head of the stream. He was commissary for the Maryland troops.[9]

Dulany Sr., Daniel (1685 - Dec. 5, 1753), lawyer, descended from a medieval Irish family, the O'Dulaneys; he was born in Queen's County, Ireland, in the year 1685. He arrived at Port Tobacco, Md. about the year 1703 and was admitted to the bar of Charles County in 1709. Having served for twenty years in the popular branch of the Legislative Assembly, he was sworn into the Governor's Council on September 25, 1742, and was a member of that body until his death in Annapolis eleven years later. He was married three times.[10]

Dulany Jr., Daniel (June 28, 1722 - Mar. 17, 1797), lawyer, was born in Annapolis, Md., the son of Daniel Dulany Sr and his wife Rebecca (1696 - 1737). Educated in England at Eton College and at Clare Hall, Cambridge University, he studied law at the Middle Temple, and was admitted to the bar in Maryland in 1747. Two years later he married Rebecca Tasker, daughter of Benjamin Tasker, who was a member of the Governor's Council and the proprietor's agent and receiver general.

Biographical Listing

In 1751 Frederick County elected Dulany one of its representatives in the popular branch of the Maryland Legislative Assembly. He was commissary general from 1759 to 1761 and secretary of the province from 1761 to 1774. His forceful arguments ranked foremost among the political writings of the period and were freely drawn upon by William Pitt when speaking for repeal of the Stamp Act. Having opposed radical factions from the beginning of his public career, he manifested no sympathy for the Revolution and at its outbreak retired to Hunting Ridge, near Baltimore. He resided there as a Loyalist, except during a brief visit to England, until 1781, when nearly all of his property was confiscated and he moved to Baltimore, where he died.[11]

Fox, Frederick (May 10, 1751 - Feb. 27, 1837), was born at Hesse-Cassel, Germany.[12] He was a farmer[13] and probably a tavern owner or innkeeper[14] and married Catharine Booker (1748 - Nov. 1, 1800),[15] oldest daughter of Bartholomew and Margaret Booker,[16] on March 1, 1773.[17] Father of Christiana, Rose, Mary Magdalena, George, Daniel Booker, Joseph, and Elizabeth.[18]

Frederick was a member of Joseph Chapline's Company of Militia, probably between 1775 and 1777,[19] and he signed the Patriot's Oath of Fidelity and Support in 1778.[20] He served as a drummer in the Lieutenant Colonel's Company of the 10th Regiment, Pennsylvania Continental Line, from April 22, 1777, to January 1, 1781.[21] Fox survived the winter encampment at Valley Forge[22] and probably fought in the battles of Brandywine, Paoli "Massacre," Germantown, and Monmouth.

A religious man, he served as an elder in the Zion Lutheran Church of Middletown, Md., from September 26, 1787, to November 21, 1790.[23] Sometime between 1800 and 1807 Frederick Fox married Susannah (Schutt) Young (Apr. 19, 1754 - Nov. 13, 1831), a widow. Mrs. Young's former husband was accidently killed while hunting deer.[24] They moved to western Ohio in late 1807. ". . . of short and rather stout build, and wore his hair in the olden time cue style."[25] He played the violin, according to Robert H. Fox of Cincinnati, Ohio. Fox died near Miamisburg, Ohio and was buried at the St. John or Gebhart Church, Miamisburg, on the northeast side of the church yard.[26]

Fox, George (Mar. 10, 1781 - June 14, 1847)[27] was the oldest son of Frederick Fox and a great, great, great grandfather of the author.[28] Records of the Zion Lutheran Church of Middletown indicate he was a member of that church.[29] He married Elizabeth Ann Link (Jan. 28, 1784 - Mar. 9, 1872) of Shepherdstown, on Aug. 9, 1807.[30] She was the daughter of John Adam Link II and Jane Ogle.[31] John Adam Link II was a grandson of Johan Jacob Link, an ancestor of Dwight D. Eisenhower.[32] Jane Ogle, daughter of Alexander Ogle, was a descendant of John Ogle of Delaware.[33]

Fox, John Frederick (? - 1784), is the person for whom Fox's Gap in Maryland is named. John and his wife, Christiana, were the parents of Daniel, Frederick, Magdelin, Michael,[34] and Rachel.[35] John Fox was a skin-dresser by trade.[36] Christiana Fox died Aug. 6, 1812, probably in Sharpsburg.[37]

It is possible John Fox and his family settled in the Pennsylvania German community or elsewhere before coming to Maryland. The name of John Fox appears in the Moses Chapline Sr. Administration Account papers submitted by the executors of the estate, bearing a date of June 19, 1766.[38] John Fox acquired lots in Sharpsburg in 1767.[39]

There is no land record for any tract John Fox acquired at Fox's Gap or in the area of Fox's Gap. A land record for a tract called Grims Fancy, one-half mile west of Fox's Gap and owned by Alexander Grim, confirms the location of John Fox's house to be in the area of Fox's Gap between 1764 and 1769. The Grims Fancy land record indicates John Fox's house was along the Main Road from Swearingen's Ferry to Frederick Town. Frederick Fox, not John, patented the land in the area of Fox's Gap.

The middle name of John Fox is not known with certainty. The middle name stated here is from Appendix No. 1 of *The Fox Genealogy*. Johan Frederich Fuchs and his wife Christiana arrived at the port of Philadelphia on the ship Anderson, Captain Hugh Campbell, September 27, 1752.[40] John Fox appeared in the state house in Philadelphia the day of his arrival and "took and subscribed the usual Qualifications."[41]

Ogle, Samuel (c. 1702 - May 3, 1752), colonial governor of Maryland,[42] was born in Northumberland County, England, where the Ogle family had become prominent as early as the eleventh century.

While in England he served with the British Army, and by the time of his departure for America in 1731, he had advanced to the rank of Captain of Cavalry. After his arrival in Annapolis in December 1731, he assumed office as Lieutenant

Governor of Maryland, a position he held until December of 1732. Ogle also served as Lieutenant Governor from July 1733 to August 1742, and from March 1747 until his death.

In 1741 he married Anne, the daughter of Benjamin Tasker, through whom he came into possession of "Belair," an estate of 3,600 acres in Prince George's County twenty miles west of Annapolis. Brother of Thomas and perhaps others. Father of Anne (died young), Samuel (died young), Benjamin (who was governor of Maryland from 1798 to 1801), Mary and Mellora.

Ogle defended Maryland's interests during a "border war" with Pennsylvania in 1736-37, a skirmish resulting from a boundary dispute between the two colonies. While still in office, Ogle died in Annapolis, Maryland, on May 3, 1752.[43]

Sharpe, Horatio (Nov. 15, 1718 - Nov. 9, 1790), Governor of colonial Maryland, was born near Hull, Yorkshire, England, one of a large and celebrated family.[44] Some historians credit him with first suggesting the Stamp Act; it is certain that in 1754 in a communication to Lord Baltimore he outlined concisely a plan that is a prototype of the famous act (Archives, post, VI, 99). Especially charged to determine the boundaries of his province, he set men at work surveying the line in dispute with Virginia and by 1760 arrived at an agreement that resulted in the establishment of Mason and Dixon line.

Commissioned as Captain of Marines in 1745; he was later promoted to Lt. Col. of Foot in the West Indies. Appointed Lt. Gov. of Maryland, he arrived in the province in August 1753 to assume that office. He served as Commander-in-Chief of troops raised "to defend the frontiers of Virginia and the neighboring colonies and to repel the unjustifiable invasion and encroachments of the French, on the river Ohio." He was then replaced by General Braddock as commander in 1755. In June 1769, replaced as Governor by Robert Eden, Sharpe retired to "Whitehall," his country estate near Annapolis. In 1773 he returned to England, where he remained until his death on November 9, 1790.[45]

Swearingen, Thomas (The Elder of the Ferry) (1708 - 1760), owned a ferry which began operation in early 1755 near the site of the present Rumsey Bridge at Shepherdstown. It operated until 1849.[46] Two brothers in Maryland, Thomas and Van Swearingen, crossed the Potomac River and settled on the banks of the Virginia side in the 1740s.

"Van Swearingen and his brother Thomas Swearingen and his son Thomas (son of Thomas the Elder) were prominent early settlers and played a big part in the settlement and development of the area from north of Shepherdstown to the Hard Scrabble (Jones Mill) area of present Berkeley County. Thomas Swearingen the Elder established a ferry that operated on the Potomac River just north of Mecklenburg in 1755 at what became known as Bellevue. The original dwelling on the place, known as the Hip Roof House built in 1760 by Thomas the Elder, was located on a 478 acre land grant from Lord Fairfax in 1750 and joined the 210 acre tract his brother Van had purchased from Richard Morgan."[47]

Tasker Sr., Benjamin Son of Captain Thomas Tasker, Benjamin Tasker was President of the Council of Maryland for thirty-two years, and as such was acting Governor of the Province from the death of Governor Ogle, May 3, 1752, until the arrival of Governor Horatio Sharpe, August 10, 1753.[48] He and Charles Carroll (signer of the Declaration of Independence) were the delegates from the Province to the famous Albany Convention of 1754. He was on the Committee appointed to draw up a Constituion for a perpetual Confederacy.

He married Anne, daughter of the Hon. Wm. Bladen, Commissary-General of the Province. They had five children, one son and four daughters. Rebecca married Daniel Dulaney, Counsellor of Maryland in 1776. Anne Tasker married Governor Samuel Ogle of Maryland. The tomb of Governor Benjamin Tasker is at Annapolis, Md.

Wardrop, James (? - 1760), was a member of the Ohio Company who owned many land tracts in the Fox's Gap area from 1750 to 1760. "A wealthy merchant originally from Virginia who lived at Marlborough in lower Prince George's County, Maryland." "Although 'of Upper Marlboro,' Wardrop wrote his will in New York City. It was probated in Prince George's County in 1760, and in it he named his wife Lettice and his brother-in-law Alexander Symmer as executors. He devised to a nephew houses belonging to his father in Edinburgh, Scotland, and to his wife all his real estate in America."[49]

Footnotes - Biographical Listing

[1] Daniel Gebhart Fox, *The Fox Genealogy including the Metherd, Benner and Leiter Descendants.* (n.p., 1914), 13.

[2] FCLR, WR 9-607, Agreement regarding Resurvey on Wooden Platter, deposition of Bartholomew Booker.

[3] Strassburger, Ralph Beaver, *Pennsylvania German Pioneers*, ed. by William John Hinke, (Baltimore: Genealogical Publishing Co., 1966), 269. Lists 71 - 73 B. Loyal Judith, 3 Sept. 1739, Capt. Paynter, "Peter Bucher, Bardoll Bucher."

[4] Frederick County, Maryland, Register of Wills Records, GM-3-126, will of Margaret Book (Booker). Witnesses to the will included Joseph Chapline Jr, Catharine Fox, and two names in German.

[5] Calvin E. Schildknecht. "Which Charles Carroll?" *The News*, Frederick, Maryland, April 4, 1990. Also see Edward C. Papenfuse et al., *Biographical Dictionary of the Maryland Legislature, 1635 - 1789*, 2 vols. (Baltimore and London: The Johns Hopkins University Press, 1982), 1:193-9.

[6] Herbert L. Osgood. *The American Colonies in the eighteenth century*, 4 vols. (Gloucester, Mass.: P. Smith, 1958), 2:192, 201-2 and 3:6-8, 10, 25.

[7] Osgood, *American Colonies in the Eighteenth Century*, 3:6. Osgood cites Maryland Archives, 30:375.

[8] Papenfuse, *Biographical Dictionary*, 1:244-5.

[9] T. J. C. Williams and Folger McKinsey, *History of Frederick County* 2 vols. (Baltimore: Regional Publishing Company, 1967), 1:31.

[10] Papenfuse, *Biographical Dictionary*, 1:284-6. Also see Aubrey C. Land, *The Dulanys of Maryland* (Baltimore: Maryland Historical Society, 1955).

[11] Papenfuse, *Biographical Dictionary*, 1:286-7. Also see Land, *Dulanys of Maryland*.

[12] Fox, *Fox Genealogy*, 12.

[13] FCLR, WR-19-206, Mortgage from Christian Benner to Frederick Fox, recorded April 11, 1799, Shaff's Purchase and Mount Sinai. "Between Christian Benner Sr of Frederick County, farmer, of the one part; and Frederick Fox of the same county, farmer, of the other part."

[14] Lemoine Cree, *A Brief History of the South Mountain House* (Boonsboro, Md.: Dodson, 1963); *Ohio D.A.R. Soldiers' Rosters*, 2 vols., 1:146; and Fox, *Fox Genealogy*, 13-4.

[15] Frederick S. Weiser, ed., Maryland German Church Records Vol. 2, *Zion Lutheran Church 1781-1826* (Manchester, Md.: Noodle-Doosey Press, 1987), 77. The Death Register of Zion Lutheran Church indicates "Catarin, wife of Friedrich Fuchs, bur. 4 Nov. 1800. Heb. 4:9."

[16] Frederick County, Maryland, Register of Wills Records, GM-2-431, will of Bartholomew Booker, Oct. 21, 1791.

[17] *Ohio D.A.R. Soldiers' Rosters*, 2 vols., 1:146.

[18] Will of Frederick Fox, Will Book C, Case #1444, Montgomery County, Ohio. Dec. 10, 1833. Mary and Elizabeth, daughters of Frederick Fox, are mentioned in the will of Margaret Booker.

[19] S. Eugene Clements and F. Edward Wright, *The Maryland Militia in the Revolutionary War* (Silver Spring, Md.: Family Line Publications, 1987), 241. Maryland Historical Society Records for Washington County. Militia Lists of Daus. of Founders and Patriots.

[20] Washington County, Maryland, Patriot's Oath, March Court, 1778. Sharpsburg Hundred, March 2, 1778, Christopher Cruss's Returns.

[21] National Archives, card numbers 37404176, 4837, 37188278, and 39144421; National Society of the Daughters of the American Revolution. 17th Report, *Pierce's Register*, #67913. Also see Pennsylvania Archives, Series 5, 3:487, 529, 533, and 572.

22 The author is a member of The Society of the Descendants of Washington's Army at Valley Forge.

23 Weiser, *Zion Lutheran Church 1781-1826*, Maryland German Church Records 2:4.

24 Fox, *Fox Genealogy*, 15.

25 Fox, *Fox Genealogy*, 18.

26 Ohio D.A.R. Soldiers' Rosters, 1:146.

27 Warren County Genealogical Society, Lebanon, Ohio, estate papers of George Fox.

28 Curtis L. Older, *Documentation Related to Frederick Fox including material on his Descendants* (unpublished manuscript).

29 Frederick S. Weiser, ed., *Zion Lutheran Church 1781-1826*, Maryland German Church Records Vol. 2, (Manchester, Md.: Noodle-Doosey Press, 1987), 25. "Samuel, son of Jacob and Magdelena Benner was born April 14, 1801. Baptised June 21, 1801. Sponsored by George Fox, a single person." (Mary) Magdelena Benner was the daughter of Frederick Fox and a sister of George.

30 Jefferson County, West Virginia, Marriage Records, 1807, page 286.

31 *Index to Marriage Licenses, Frederick County, 1778-1810*, married April 14, 1783.

32 Paxson Link, *The Link Family* (Paris, Illinois: [s.l.], 1951).

33 Francis Hamilton Hibbard, assisted by Stephen Parks, *The English origin of John Ogle, first of the name in Delaware* (Pittsburgh: n.p., 1967); Sir Henry Asgill Ogle, *Ogle and Bothal* (Newcastle-upon-Tyne: Andrew Reid & Company, 1902). Alexander Ogle, father of Jane Ogle, provided wheat and flour from his mills to the Maryland troops during the American Revolution. See Maryland State Papers, Series A, MdHR, 6636-23-29/7 1/7/5 and related papers. John Adam Link I, the grandfather of Elizabeth Ann Link (Fox), was a patriot during the American Revolution. "In the first Liberty Bond drive he purchased $800.00 worth of certificates." He received payment for bacon in 1778 from William Beatty, an officer in the Maryland Militia. See Maryland State Papers, Series A, MdHR 4586-15 1/6/4/18. John Adam Link II, the father of Elizabeth Ann Link (Fox), was an officer during the American Revolution in the Frederick County, Maryland, Militia. See *The Link Family* by Paxson Link.

34 Clements and Wright, *Maryland Militia in the Revolutionary War*, 241. Michael Fox, a brother of Frederick, also was a member of Joseph Chapline's Militia Company.

35 Will of John Fox, Book A Liber 102, Washington County, Maryland. Jan. 17, 1784.

36 Fox, *Fox Genealogy*, 12.

37 Letter from Jacob Reel to Michael and Frederick Fox, dated at Sharpsburg, Aug. 9, 1812, from a copy obtained from Robert H. Fox of Cinicinnati, Ohio. "The following letter received and forwarded from Lebanon, Warren County, Ohio, Sept. 8, 1812, addressed to Msrs. Fredric(k) and Michael Fox, Franklin Township, Warren Co. Ohio."

38 Frederick County, Maryland, the account of Joseph and Jennett Chapline, executors of Moses Chapline late of Frederick County deceased.

39 See WCLR, K-703, K-1231, J-1400, K-1278, and K-1279 in the years 1766 to 1769.

40 I. Daniel Rupp, *Thirty-Thousand Names of Immigrants* (Baltimore: Genealogical Publishing Co., 1971), 280-1.

41 R. B. Strassburger and W. J. Hinke, *Pennsylvania German Pioneers, Lists of Arrivals* (Norristown, Pa.: Pennsylvania German Society, 1934), 488-9.

42 Papenfuse, *Biographical Dictionary*, 2:618-9.

43 Sir Henry Asgill Ogle, *Ogle und Bothal* (Newcastle-upon-Tyne, England, 1902). DAB.

44 Papenfuse, *Biographical Dictionary*, 2:726-8.

45 Lady [Matilda Ridout] Edgar, *A Colonial Governor in Maryland: Horatio Sharpe and his Times, 1753-1773* (New York: Longmans, Green, and Co., 1912).

Biographical Listing

[46] Maryland Historical Society marker at Rumsey Bridge, Shepherdstown, West Virginia.

[47] Berkeley County Historical Society, *The Berkeley Journal* Issue Thirteen, 1989, 9-21.

[48] Papenfuse, *Biographical Dictionary*, 2:799-801.

[49] Grace L. Tracey and John P. Dern, *Pioneers of Old Monocacy* (Baltimore: Genealogical Publishing Company, 1987), 44. Prince George's County Wills, 1:520, probated August 20, 1760.

Bibliography

Contemporary Sources

American State Papers: 1, *Miscellaneous.*

Andersen, Patricia Abelard. "Jacob Fluck of Middletown, Frederick County, Maryland, and his Flook and Fluke Descendants." *National Genealogical Society Quarterly,* September 1984, Volume 72, Number 3, 163.

Browne, William H. et al., eds. *Archives of Maryland.* Baltimore: Maryland Historical Society, 1888.

Browne, William Hand, ed. *Letters to Governor Horatio Sharpe.* Archives of Maryland. Vol. 30. Baltimore: Maryland Historical Society, 1911.

Browne, William Hand, ed. *Correspondence of Governor Horatio Sharpe, 1753-1771.* Archives of Maryland. Vols. 6, 9, 14, 31. Baltimore: Maryland Historical Society, 1888-1911.

Clements, S. Eugene and Wright, F. Edward. *The Maryland Militia in the Revolutionary War.* Silver Spring, Md.: Family Line Publications, 1987.

Dare, Maria J. Liggett. *Chaplines from Maryland and Virginia.* Washington, D.C.: The Franklin Print, 1902.

Davis, George B., Perry, Leslie J., and Kirkley, Joseph W. *Atlas to Accompany the Official Records of the Union and Confederate Armies.* Washington: Government Printing Office, 1891-5.

Eshleman, Esq., H. Frank. *Lancaster County Historical Society Papers,* "The Great Conestoga Road," Volume XII, No. 6 (June 5, 1908), pp. 215-232.

Evans, Lewis. *Geographical, historical, political, philosophical and mechanical essays, the first containing an analysis of a general map of the middle British colonies in America, and of the country of the confederate Indians; a description of the face of the country; the boundaries of the confederates; and the maritime and inland navigations of the several rivers and lakes contained therein.* Philadelphia: Franklin and Hall, 1755.

Fox, Daniel Gebhart. *The Fox Genealogy including the Metherd, Benner, and Leiter Descendants.* N.p., 1924.

Fry, Joshua. *The Fry and Jefferson map of Virginia and Maryland; facsimiles of the 1754 and 1794 printings with an index.* 2nd ed. Charlottesville: University Press of Virginia, 1966.

Green, Karen Mauer. *The Maryland Gazette 1727-1761 Genealogical and Historical Abstracts.* Galveston: The Frontier Press, 1989.

Hazard, Samuel, et al., ed. *Pennsylvania Archives.* 138 vols. to date. Philadelphia and Harrisburg: The State, 1644-.

Hening, William Waller, ed. *Hening's Statutes at Large of Virginia.* 13 vol. Richmond: Samuel Pleasants, 1809-23.

Hinke, William J., transl. "Report of the Journey of Francis Louis Michel October 2, 1701, to December 1, 1702." *Virginia Magazine of History and Biography.* 24:1-43, 113-141, 275-303.

Laws, Documents and Judicial Decisions, Relating to The Baltimore and Fredericktown, York and Reisterstown, Cumberland and Boonsborough Turnpike Road Companies. Baltimore: John D. Toy, 1841.

Link, Paxson. *The Link Family.* Paris, Illinois: n.p., 1951.

Mathews, Edward Bennett. *The Maps and Map-Makers of Maryland.* Baltimore: The Johns Hopkins Press, October, 1898.

Ogle, Sir Henry Asgill. *Ogle and Bothal.* Newcastle-upon-Tyne: Andrew Reid & Company, 1902.

Older, Curtis L. *The Braddock Expedition and Fox's Gap in Maryland.* Westminster, Md: Family Line Publications, 1995.

Older, Curtis L. *Documentation Related to Frederick Fox, including material on his descendants.* Self-published, 1996.

Older, Curtis L. *The Land Tracts of Fox's Gap, including material on Crampton's, Orr's, and Turner's Gaps - Long Version.* (Also known as, *The Land Tracts of the Battlefield of South Mountain - Long Version*) Self-published, 1996.

Bibliography

Papenfuse, Edward C. and Coale III, Joseph M. *The Hammond-Harwood House Atlas of Historical Maps of Maryland, 1608-1908*. Baltimore & London: The Johns Hopkins University Press, 1982.

Papenfuse, Edward C. et al. *Biographical Dictionary of the Maryland Legislature, 1635-1789*. 2 vols. Baltimore: The Johns Hopkins University Press, 1982.

Reese, Timothy. *Maryland Genealogical Society Bulletin*, "Coming Home: The Deardorff Family in Burkeittsville, Frederick County, Maryland 1769-1803," Volume 29, No. 3 (Summer, 1988), pp. 252-266.

Rice, Millard M. *New Facts and Old Families*. Redwood City, California: Monocacy Book Company, 1976.

Rice, Millard M. *This Was the Life excerpts from the judgment records of Frederick County, Md. 1748-1765*. Redwood City, California: Monocacy Book Company, 1979.

Rupp, I. Daniel. *Thirty-Thousand Names of Immigrants*. Baltimore: Genealogical Publishing Co., 1971.

Stevens, Henry M. *Lewis Evans, His Map of the British Middle Colonies in America, A Comparative Account of 18 Different Editions Published between 1755 and 1814*. London: n.p., 1920.

Strassburger, Ralph Beaver. *Pennsylvania German Pioneers*. ed. by William John Hinke. Baltimore: Genealogical Publishing Co., 1966.

Tracey, Grace L. and Dern, John P. *Pioneers of Old Monocacy*. Baltimore: Genealogical Publishing Company, 1987.

United States War Department. *The War of the Rebellion: A Compilation of the Official Records of the Union and Confederate Armies*. 70 vols. Washington, D.C.: U.S. Government, 1880-1891.

Weiser, Frederick S., ed. *Maryland German Church Records*. Manchester, Md.: Noodle-Doosey Press, 1987.

Wright, F. Edward. *Western Maryland Newspaper Abstracts 1786-1798*. Silver Spring, Md.: Family Line Publications, 1985.

Secondary Sources

Barron, Lee and Barbara. *The History of Sharpsburg, Maryland*. Sharpsburg, Md.: Barrons, 1972.

Bast, Doug. "William, George Boone Lay Out Boone's Berry." *Maryland Cracker Barrel, Inc.* Volume 20, No. 6. Boonsboro, Maryland.

Cox, Jacob D. *Military Reminiscences of the Civil War*. 2 vols. New York: Charles Scribner's Sons, 1900.

Cree, Lemoine. *A Brief History of South Mountain House*. Boonsboro, Md.: Dodson, 1963.

Cunz, Dieter. *The Maryland Germans, a History*. Princeton: Princeton University Press, 1948.

Dandridge, Mrs. Danske. *Historic Shepherdstown*. Charlottesville: Michie, c1910.

Drake, Julia A. and Orndorff, James R. *From Mill Wheel to Plowshare*. Cedar Rapids, Iowa: The Torch Press, 1938. Reprinted by the Maryland Historical Society, 1971.

Edgar, Lady [Matilda Ridout]. *A Colonial Governor in Maryland: Horatio Sharpe and His Times, 1753-1773*. New York: Longmans, Green, and Co., 1912.

Fiske, John. *Old Virginia and Her Neighbors*. Boston: Houghton Mifflin Co., 1900.

Fox, Robert H. *Middletown Valley Register*, Aug. 19, 1932.

Frassanito, William A. *Antietam: The Photographic Legacy of America's Bloodiest Day*. New York: Scribner's, 1978.

Gibson, John, ed. *History of York Co., Pennsylvania*. Baltimore: Genealogical Publishing Company, 1975.

Hamilton, J. G. de Roulhac, ed. *The Papers of Randolph Abbot Shotwell*. Raleigh: N. C. Historical Commission, 1929.

Hays, Helen Ashe. *The Antietam and Its Bridges*. New York: The Knickerbocker Press, 1910.

Hill, Jr., Daniel Harvey. *Bethel to Sharpsburg*. 2 vols. Raleigh: Edwards & Broughton Co., 1926.

Hotchkiss, Jedediah. *Make Me a Map of the Valley, The Civil War Journal of Stonewall Jackson's Topographer*. Archie P. McDonald, ed. Dallas: Southern Methodist Press, 1973.

Johnson, Allen and Malone, Dumas. *Dictionary of American Biography*. New York: Charles Scribner's Sons, 1927.

Land, Aubrey C. Land. *The Dulanys of Maryland*. Baltimore: Maryland Historical Society, 1955.

Maryland Geological Survey. *Report on the Highways of Maryland.* Baltimore: The Johns Hopkins Press, 1899.

McSherry, James. *History of Maryland.* Baltimore: Baltimore Book Co., 1904.

Mish, Mary V. *Jonathan Hager, Founder.* Hagerstown, Md.: Hagerstown Bookbinding & Printing Co., 1937.

Nead, Daniel Wunderlich. *The Pennsylvania-German in the Settlement of Maryland.* Lancaster, Pa.: The Pennsylvania-German Society, 1914.

"The Old National Pike," *Harper's New Monthly Magazine.* Vol. LIX, 1879.

Osgood, Herbert L. *The American Colonies in the Eighteenth Century.* 4 vols. Gloucester, Mass.: P. Smith, 1958.

Rhoderick Jr., George C. *The Early History of Middletown, Maryland.* Middletown Valley Historical Society.

Rouse Jr., Parke. *The Great Wagon Road.* New York: McGraw-Hill Company, 1973.

Scharf, J. Thomas. *History of Western Maryland.* 2 vols. Baltimore: Regional Publishing Co., 1968.

Schildknecht, Calvin E. "Which Charles Carroll?" *The News.* Frederick, Maryland, April 4, 1990.

Schildt, John W. *Drums Along the Antietam.* Parson, W.Va.: McClain, 1972.

State Roads Commission of Maryland. *A History of Road Building in Maryland.* 1958.

Stevens, Henry M. *Lewis Evans, His Map of the British Middle Colonies in America, A Comparative Account of 18 Different Editions Published between 1755 and 1814.* London:n.p., 1920.

Williams, Byron L. *The Old South Mountain Inn, An Informal History.* Shippensburg, Pa.: Beidel Printing House, 1990.

Williams, T. J. C. and McKinsey, Folger. *History of Washington County, Maryland.* Baltimore: Regional Publishing Company, 1967.

Index

Index entries appear in alphabetical sequence. The index lists tract names, names of individuals, reference numbers for tracts, and other information that appears in this book.

The page number or numbers on which the Maryland Archive reference number will be found is (are) listed to the right of each index entry.

Maryland Archives Example: BC & GS 41, 4-5   119

The above tract record may be found in the Maryland Archives under BC & GS 41 on pages 4 and 5. The tract may be found in this book at page number 119.

Frederick County Example: AF-9-541   158

The above tract record may be found in the Frederick County Land Records under AF 9 on page 541. The tract may be found in this book at page number 158.

Washington County Example: IN-6 51, 517-518   195

The above tract record may be found in the Washington County Land Records under IN-6 51 on pages 517-518. The tract may be found in this book at page number 195.

1755 Frye and Jefferson Map 42
1791 Map of Road from Hagerstown to Newcomber's Mill 54
1794 Dennis Griffith Map of Maryland 42
1808 Varle Map 54
1840 Maryland map 54
304-370 190
605-469 190
74-264 201
77-287 201
78-234 201
Abrams (Abraham's) Creek 106, 109, 121, 128, 133, 149, 156
Add to Friendship 35, 40, 41, 46, 52, 98, 161, 162, 163, 178, 179, 191, 196, 197, 200
Add to Little Good 142
Add to Tom's Gift 98
AF-9-541 158
Aldredge, Solomon 112

allowance for variation 41, 165, 190, 197
AM 1, 236-7 118
AM 1, 365-366 107
AM 1, 375-376 107
American Revolution 41
Anderson, William 150
angle of four degrees 51
Annapolis 46, 50
Antietam Creek 32, 41, 43, 48, 113, 117, 120, 132, 140, 147
Antietam Hundred 45
Antietam Works 135
Apple Brandy 35, 52, 98, 99
Arnold Jr., John George 47
Arnold, Andrew 105, 142, 181
Arnold, Daniel 150, 153
Arnold, David 158, 160
Arnold, John George 49, 109
Artisans Street at Williamsport 33

Ascherman, Henry 176
Ashbough 99
Asherman (Ausherman), Samuel 43, 159, 190
Aulabaugh's land 34
B D, 228-229 101
B, 336-338 117
B-172 140
Bad Enough 99
Badham's Refuse 100
Baer, Christian 179
Bainbridge, Peter 44
Baker (Pecker), Peter 115
Baker, Samuel 32, 114, 146, 193
Baker, Tilghman 99
Bakersville 41, 44
Baley, John 117, 152
Balsell, Henry 159
Baltimore 46
Baltimore and Frederick Town Turnpike
    Company 51, 52
Baltzell, George 50, 52, 53, 162, 179
Barron Hill 54
Bash, Andrew 32, 114
Battle of South Mountain 53
BC & GS 1, 164 124
BC & GS 1, 173-174 102
BC & GS 1, 330 100
BC & GS 12, 92-3 100
BC & GS 13, 193-194 128
BC & GS 14, 14 131
BC & GS 14, 18-19 105
BC & GS 14, 19-21 111
BC & GS 14, 610-1 133
BC & GS 14, 68-69 124
BC & GS 14, 86-87 110
BC & GS 19, 310-311 121
BC & GS 19, 649-653 137
BC & GS 2, 112-3 105
BC & GS 21, 484 132
BC & GS 22, 89-90 113
BC & GS 23, 363-364 115
BC & GS 24, 270 108
BC & GS 27, 236-237 109
BC & GS 27, 255-256 130
BC & GS 27, 331 108
BC & GS 27, 392-393 125
BC & GS 27, 396 104
BC & GS 27, 578 106
BC & GS 30, 214-216 120
BC & GS 30, 225-226 123
BC & GS 30, 259-261 102
BC & GS 32, 480-483 127

BC & GS 37, 144-145 129
BC & GS 37, 218-219 134
BC & GS 4, 181-183 132
BC & GS 4, 195-196 100
BC & GS 40, 114 109
BC & GS 40, 118 134
BC & GS 41 259-261 130
BC & GS 41, 4-5 119
BC & GS 41, 47 119
BC & GS 41, 473 112
BC & GS 44, 439-440 107
BC & GS 45, 10-11 121
BC & GS 45, 22-25 138
BC & GS 45, 27 115
BC & GS 47, 1-12 136
BC & GS 47, 234-235 133
BC & GS 47, 31-33 110
BC & GS 47, 39-40 127
BC & GS 47, 455 99
BC & GS 5, 163-164 113
BC & GS 50, 15-18 126
BC & GS 50, 173-175 125
BC & GS 51, 252-253 104
BC & GS 7, 99-102 118
BC & GS 9, 405-406 102
BD-1 194
BD-1, 535-537 159
BD-1-286 159
Beachley, Daniel 160, 165
Beachley, Hannah 164
Beachley, John W. 164, 166
Beachley, Jonas 160
Beachley, Marietta 166
Beagley, Daniel 52, 53, 190
Beakley (Beagley), Henry 122, 184
Beall Jr., George 156, 194
Beam's Purchase 100
Beam, Jacob 100
Bear Swamp Forrest 184
Beatty, Charles 128
Beaver Creek 33, 47, 48
Beaver, Peter 44, 50, 125, 141, 153, 154, 166,
    167, 168, 170, 173
beds of the present roads 51
Beeghler (Beigler), Michael 125, 145
Betty's Good Will 43, 100, 155, 171, 172, 187
BFG-5, 516 179
BGF-6, 216 179
Biegley's Displeasure 183
Bird's Bill 114
block-houses 46, 47
Blooming Month of May 184

Index

Blooming Plains 101
Bloomsbury 101
Blue Mountain 152
Blue Ridge (South Mountain) 50, 54
Boble (Bubble) 43, 146, 159, 164, 169, 170, 174, 175
Bolivar 54
Booke's tavern 34
Booker's Purchase 142
Booker's Rsy on Well Done 42
Booker, Bartholomew 48, 50, 110, 119, 120, 128, 143, 144, 151, 154, 156, 157, 167, 170, 171, 177, 181, 187
Booker, Daniel 176
Booker, Margaret 48
Booker, Peter 142, 157
Booker, Phillip 127
Boon's Forest 199
Boon's land 34
Boonsboro 45
Booth's bridge on Antietam Creek 33
Booth, John 116, 195, 196, 197, 198, 199, 200
Booth, William 195, 196
Boston 135
Boteler, Edward L. 196, 200
Bottenberg, William 175, 177
Bowser's Addition 36, 41, 163, 179, 191, 197
Bowser, David 40, 41, 104
Boyd, Joseph 195, 197, 198, 201
Boyer, Joseph 158
Braddock Expedition 44, 51, 54
Braddock Road 46, 49, 52
Braddock's Gap 54
Braddock, General 41
Brayface (Bray-face) 166
Breeches 166
bridge 44
bridge on Antietam Creek 33
bridge over Catoctin Creek north of Middletown 42
bridge over Monocacy 52
bridle road 133
bridle road gap 129
Brien, John 135
Bringle, Lawrence 52
Brooke, Isaac 118
Bruner, Elias 40
Bubble (Boble) 43, 146, 159, 164, 169, 170, 174, 175
Bullskin 41
Bumgardner's Mill 54
Burger, John 43, 101, 103

Burnside (or Lower) Bridge 41
Burrell's Disappointment 100, 105
Butler, Henry 155
Butler, Richard 169
Butt, George 173
Butter, Elias 204
BY & GS 1, 604-5 127
BY & GS 1, 610 106
BY & GS 1, 611-612 103
BY & GS 28, 64-67 123
BY & GS 3, 427-428 113
BY & GS 4, 467-468 113
BY & GS 4, 536-537 112
BY & GS 4, 586-586 122
BY & GS 5, 59 112
BY & GS 5, 594 118
BY & GS 5, 607-609 101
BY & GS 5, 608-609 103
Cabin Branch 104
Carey's (Curry's) Old Place 48
Carroll, Charles 106, 140
Cary, John 159
Castle, Daniel 188
Catoctin Creek 43, 44, 50, 51, 98, 104, 106, 107, 113, 114, 116, 125, 127, 132, 140, 145, 148, 169
certificate #368 114
Chapel, Dahlgren 35
Chapline Jr., Joseph 172
Chapline Jr., Moses 159
Chapline Sr., Joseph 142
Chapline Sr., Moses 42, 141, 142, 146, 193, 194
Chapline's Ill Will 101
Chapline's Mill 49
Chapline, Joseph 48, 99, 100, 101, 102, 108, 116, 123, 124, 138, 140, 141, 142, 144, 145, 151
Chapline, Josiah 194
Chapline, Moses 47, 112, 124, 126, 132, 133, 194
Chapline, William William 172
Charlemount Pleasant 45, 102, 118
Charlton, Arthur 118
Cheney, Greenberry 147
Chesnut Thicket 152, 163
Chestnut Oak Ridge 185
Christie's Folly 102, 170
Christie, James 44
Civil War 40
Clarke, James 181
Clear Spring 46
CM-1-582 159

Index

CM-2-381 160
CM-2-385 160
Coffman, James W. and Mary 189
Coil, Adam 157
Coleman, George H. 152
Colvill, John 136
Come by Chance 119
Conestoga 42
Conococheague (Williamsport) 41
Conococheague Road from Frederick 43, 45, 107, 132
Contentment 54, 101, 102
Cool Spring 40, 43, 103, 168, 186
Cool Spring Rsy 40, 186
Cooperton 149
Cornucopia 103
Cost's Content 182
Cost, George 182
county line 32
court minutes 49
Cox's Cabin 147
Crampton's Gap 44, 136
Crampton, Thomas 44, 146, 154
Cuckold's (Cuckhold's) Horns 49, 103
Curry's Branch 48, 112
Curry's Gap 45, 47, 48, 112, 144, 151
Curry's Old Place 48, 108, 151
D D, 75 98
Dahlgren Chapel 46
Dahlgren, Madeleine V. 53, 165, 166, 197, 200, 201
Daniel's Race Ground 36, 104
David's Will 36, 40, 98, 104, 161, 177, 178
Davis, Ephraim 130
Dawson's Purchase 104
Dawson, Thomas 104
Deeffer Snay 43, 104, 159
Delemere 48
Dennis Griffith Map of Maryland 42
Derr, John W. 53, 179
Devil's Backbone bridge 48
Dick, James 47
Discontent 105
Domer's Hill 32
door, kitchen 195
Dorsey's Risk (Risque) 105
Dorsey, Edward 44, 105
Dr. Neal 47
Dr. Tracey 54
Dry Branch 156
DSB-1, 397 180
DSB-1, 398 180

Dulany, Daniel 41, 106, 109, 111, 115, 121, 128, 133, 155, 156
Dulany, Walter 106, 115
Dunbar's Regiment 41, 54
Dunbar's Run 52
E-223 140
E-339 140
E-753 141
E-870 141
Ebenezer 105
Edelen, Christopher 159
EI 2, 478 120
EI 2, 623-624 106
Elk (Ridge) Mountain 100, 137
Elk Hill 105
Ensor, Joseph 149
ES-5-252 160
Evans, Robert 42, 43, 49, 98, 100, 103, 106
Everhart, Christopher 143
Everhart, Jacob 159
Exchange 43, 106, 113, 140, 146, 164, 170, 171, 172, 174, 175, 176
F-1020 143
F-1023 143
F-1077 144
F-1137 144, 145
F-1198 145
F-211 142
F-399-400 142
F-548 (mortgage) 143
F-905 143
Fellfoot 41, 42, 106, 119, 145, 193
Fellfoot Enlarged 42, 43, 144, 145, 149, 193
Fellowship 106
Feltygrove's 54
fence, stone 184
ferry house 31
Ferry Landing 42
Fidler's Purchase 151, 159, 164, 170, 174, 175
Fidler, George 125, 169
Fidler, Valentine 151
Fielderia Manor 136
Fink, Nicholas 50, 109, 140, 149, 152, 156
Fink, Philip 44
Flonham 35, 36, 46, 48, 52, 107, 165, 190, 200, 201
Flook's Content 173
Flook, Barbara 99
Flook, Jacob 123, 184
Flook, Jacob H. 165
Flook, Jno 184
Flook, John P. 165

Index

Flook, Joshua 165
Flook, Mathias 163, 173
Flowers, Susanne 48
Fockler, Adam 101
foot of Shanandore (South) Mountain 155
ford, pack horse 44
Forest 42, 44, 45, 50, 107, 148, 153, 182
Forest of Needwood 131, 181
fork of Little Antietam 106, 145
fork of Old Sharpsburg and Old Hagerstown Roads 50
fork of the roads 49
fork of Turnpike and Old Sharpsburg Road 38
fort 46, 47
Fowler, James 141
Fox Genealogy, The 41
Fox Inn 43, 44, 51, 190
Fox's Gap 31, 32, 35, 40, 42
Fox's Last Shift 36, 47, 48, 49, 108, 117, 130
Fox, Daniel G. 40
Fox, Frederick 40, 46, 48, 53, 98, 117, 120, 131, 167, 171, 173, 174, 175, 176, 181
Fox, George 54, 174, 175
Fox, John 40, 109, 152
Fox, John George 41
Frederick County court minutes 47
Fredericksburg 36, 40, 41, 104, 161, 162, 163, 171, 176, 177, 181, 189
French and Indian War 46
Frye and Jefferson Map 42
Ft. Cumberland 41, 46
Ft. Frederick 46, 47, 49
Fulwiler, Jacob 35, 52, 98, 129, 131, 169
Funk, Jacob 147
G-287 146
G-302 146, 193
G-395 147
G-7, 621-626 145, 193
Gaming Alley 54
Gantt, Thomas and Fielder 136, 167
Gap 35, 48, 108, 151
gap of the South Mountain 114
gap, bridal road 45, 129
Gap, Curry's 45, 47, 48
gap, main wagon road 45, 129
Garrison, Frederick 113
Garrott, Joseph 178
Gaver's Recovery 108, 160, 186
Gaver, Peter 108, 167, 174, 186
GBO-100, 618 200
GBO-77, 170 199
General Braddock 41

General Reno 191
German Monocacy Road 42
German Reformed Church 53
German Reformed Lutheran and Calvinist Congregations about Middletown 50
GG-29, 877-8 195
GGB 2, 141-142 100
Gittle (Zittle), Daniel 196, 197, 200, 201
Gittle (Zittle), Elizabeth 201
Gittle (Zittle), Josiah 199, 201
Gittle (Zittle), Mary Magdelena 201
Gittle (Zittle), Michael 195, 196, 198, 200
Gittle (Zittle), Peter 196
Gittle (Zittle), Seggrick 201
Good Hope 108
Good, William 31, 112, 119, 159, 194
Goose Bill 149
Goose Cap 50, 156, 169
Gordon's Purchase 109
Gordon, George 109
Governor Edward Lloyd 52
Governor Sharp 41, 49
Great Philadelphia Wagon Road 42
Great Road from Frederick to Hagerstown 50
Great Road to Conococheague from Frederick 44
Great Wagon Road to Philadelphia 42
Griffith, Henry 180
Grim (Trim), Alexander 109
Grim's Fancy 36, 40, 42, 45, 109, 127, 152
Grim, Alexander 152, 178
Grim, Andrew 130, 150
Grimes Run 104
Grimes, Edward 43
Grindstone Branch 109
Gross, Jonas 40, 189, 191
Grove 144, 145
GS 1, 209-211 98
GS 1, 45-46 106
GS 1, 65-66 121
H-103 194
H-173 148
H-343 148
H-448 148
H-53 147
H-642 148
H-95 147
Hager Sr., Jonathan 53
Hagerstown 53, 54
Hamburg Pass 54
Hard To Find 166, 180
Harley, Joshua 174

Harper's Ferry 45
Harper's Island 137
Harrison, John 147
Harshman, C. 166
Harsman, Christian 105
Hawkins, John 131
Hawkins, Thomas 131, 147, 150, 187
Hazel Branch 114
Henthorn, John 143
Hepburn, John 140
Herring, John 163
Hess (Hessing), Jacob 121, 125, 128, 145, 193
Hewitt 202
Hewitt, Charles M. 35, 53
HGO-1-156 181
HGO-1-359 181
HGO-1-396 182
HGO-1-403 182
HGO-1-466 182
HGO-1-510 183
HGO-1-569 183
HGO-1-571 183
HGO-1-572 184
HGO-1-6 180
HGO-1-9 181
Hickory Tavern 149
Highway 68 48
Hill Jr., Daniel Harvey 54
Historical Society of Carroll County 41
Hitt (or Upper) Bridge 49
Hog Yard 49, 109
Hogg, Thomas 147
Hogmire, Andrew 195, 196, 198
Hogmire, Conrad 54
Hogmire, Jonas 34, 116, 195, 196, 197, 198, 199, 200
Holmes, Joseph 47
Homestead 196
Honesty Best When Looked To 157
Hope Well 147
Horse Neck 110
House of Representatives of the U. S. 52
Houser, Isaac 49
Huffer, John 148
Hutzel, Jacob 161
Hutzel, Peter 161, 171
Hutzell, Elizabeth 201
Hutzell, John 197, 198, 200, 201
I Hope It Is So 110, 194
I Hope It Is Well Done 38, 43, 110, 120, 157, 164, 167, 171, 172, 173, 175, 176, 177, 180, 187, 188

I Wish There Was More 50, 162
I've Got It At Last 150
IB G, 303-304 116
IC A, 495 111
IC B, 301 111
IC B, 480-481 112, 119
IC B, 703-704 101
IC D, 326-327 130
IC D, 91 125
IC E 702-704 108
IC F, 306-307 131
IC F, 307 129
IC G, 361 131
IC H, 298 117
IC H, 301 110
IC I, 570-571 103, 108
IC I, 713 117
IC I, 99-100 105, 111, 129
IC K, 288 104
IC K, 343-344 119
IC L, 455 110
IC M, 470-471 116
IC N, 16 114
IC N, 188-189 105
IC N, 191 99
IC N, 467-468 122
IC N, 6-7 125, 128
IC P, 672-673 98
IC Q, 191 115
IC R, 560-561 128
II-431 195
IN-6 51, 517-518 195
IN-9, 595 196
Indian road 44, 146
innholder 44
Interstate 70 54
It's Bad Enough 48, 110, 184
Ives Folly 111
J-1086 149
J-514-516 149
Jacob's Broom (Brune) 45, 103, 111
Jerico 102, 129
Jerico Hills 111
Jesserong, Michael 146
JK T, 55-56 120
John Crisles Spring Branch 42, 118
John George's road 49
John's Delight 36, 47, 48, 112, 120, 151, 161, 171
John's Lot 54
Johnson, Thomas 180
Jones, William H. and Catharine 160, 165
Joseph's Tricks 185

Index

Josiah's (Last) Bit 42, 112, 119, 159
Joyner's Fancy 118, 142
JS-17, 504 161
JS-25-372 161
JS-30-58-61 161
JS-38-194 162
JS-39-260 162
JS-39-264-8 162
JS-42, 313-314 163
JS-42, 481 164
JS-44-393 163
K U, 343-8 135
K-1373 151
K-52 150
K-682 150
K-758 150
K-917 151
Keedy, Henry 194
Keedy, Lodowick 110, 194
Keedysville 43
Keefour, Jacob 50
Keep Trieste 137
Keephart (Keepheart) (Kephart), Joseph
    129, 158, 169
Kefauver, George H. 189
Keller, Joel 178, 179, 189
Kelly's Purchase 112
Kelly, Thomas 112
Kemp's Long Meadow 143
Kemp, Christian 143
Kershman, Mathias 155
Keywhaughvor (Keywaughver), Philip
    127, 152
Killicrankee 112, 119
kitchen door 195
Kizer's Lowden 47, 49, 113
Kizer, Christian 166
Knave's Good Will 168
Knave, Catherine 131
Knave, Jacob 114
Knouf, Adam 157
Koogle, Adam 53, 157
Koogle, Christian 170
Koogle, John W. 38, 180
Koogle, W. 38
L-276 152
L-588 152
L-649 152
L-69 151
L-71 151
Lancaster (in Pennsylvania) 42
Land of Gap 131

Lane, Thomas 142
Lannafield 45, 99, 111
Last Choice 148, 154
last lines of Fielderia Manor 136
Last Shift 172
Lawrence, Jacob 168
lawsuit 172
Layman, Ludwick 169, 170
Layman, Peter 170, 174
Laypole, Philip 204
LB C, 196-8 104
LBN-2, 133 200
Learning 113, 134
Leiter (Lighter), Henry 153, 168, 170
Leiter (Lighter), Jacob 180
Lemaster, Abraham 166
LG B, 1-2 109
LG C, 576-577 132
LG E, 346-348 121
LG E, 397 109
Lighter (Leiter), Henry 153, 168, 170
Lighter (Leiter), Jacob 180
Little Antietam Creek 45, 102, 106, 109,
    115, 118, 133, 156, 193
Little Beaver Creek 48
Little I Thought It 137
Little Meadow 44, 113
Lloyd, Governor Edward 52
Locust Valley 114
Long Dispute (Ended) 36, 48, 151, 161
lot 1 171
lot 5 196
lot 8 204
lots 1 and 2 179
Loving Brother 113, 182
Lower (or Burnside) Bridge 41
lower main road 152
Ludy, Peter 41, 177, 178
Lyon's Purchase 144
Lyon, Martin 144
Magrudar, John 107
Magruder, Samuel 44, 102, 148
main road 40, 115, 171
main road from Fox's towards
    Sharpsburg 104
main road from Frederick to Ft. Frederick
    36, 38, 45, 46, 48, 107, 108, 113, 120,
    134, 157
main road from Frederick to Sharpsburg
    42, 128, 179
main road from Frederick to Swearingen's
    Ferry 109, 152

main road from Middletown to Sharpsburg 43, 167, 188
main road from Williamsport to Frederick 51
main road gap 45
main road through Frederick 42
main road through Frederick by Robert Evans 118
main road to Boonsboro 38
main road to Sharpsburg 176
main wagon road gap 129
Main, John Adam 188
Major Ogles 54
Mansberger, John 48, 52, 117, 119
map drawn by Arthur Tracey 43
map of road from Hagerstown to Newcomer's Mill 54
map of road from Swearingen's Ferry to Fox's Gap 41
map, Post 42
market house in Hagerstown (Elizabethtown) 54
Marshall, Philip 167
Martitany 38, 114, 177, 180
Martsome (at Mousetown) 45, 115
Mary's Cowpen 115
Maryland (land tract) 136
Maryland Historical Society 123
Mathias, Charles McC. 190
McDonald, Ewen 132
McEntire, John 143
McPherson, John 135
Meadow 180
Mecklenburg 41
Meline, Mauche H. 200
Mendall (Mindall) 110, 116
Methard, George 173, 175, 176
Middle Creek 169
Middle Spring 109
Middle Town 182
Middletown 42, 50
Middletown Election District 191
Mill Creek 50, 156
Mill Run 50
Miller to Miller deed 191
Miller's Farm 160, 187
Miller's Hills 42, 116
Miller's Purchase 182, 183
Miller's Timberland 186
Miller, Henry 52, 53, 161, 162, 179, 195, 196, 197, 200, 201
Miller, John 40, 116, 186, 188
Miller, Michael 38, 176, 177, 180, 188

Miller, Peter 153, 160, 182, 187
Miller, Susan 40, 52, 53, 188, 189, 190
Miller, Teresa 200
Miller, William 195, 199, 200
Mindall (Mendall) 110, 116
Monocacy 41, 107
Monocacy Creek 50
Monocacy Road 42
Monocacy Town 43
Mountain 41, 42, 108, 112, 117, 119, 150, 152, 167, 174, 194
Mountain House 35, 45, 46, 52, 202, 203
Mountain Side 178
Mousetown 45
mouth of Antietam Creek 45
mouth of Mill Run 140
Mt. Atlas 42, 116
Mt. Pelier 185
Mt. Pleasant 42, 54, 117, 164, 174, 175, 176
Mt. Tabor Church 54
Mullendore, David 158, 163
Munsford, William 118
Murdock, John and Harriet 197
Murdock, William 47
N-273 153
N-470 153
N-517 154
N-560 154
Nazareth (Nazarih) 142
Neff, Henry 149, 183
Neighbor's Content (Rsy on Middle Town) 182
Nelson's Folly 45, 106, 117, 145
Nelson, Paul David 41
new road 47
Newcomer's Purchase 48, 117
Nicodemus, Conrad 34
Nicodemus, John 198, 199
No Matter What 183
North Mountain 47
Notre Dame 203
Nottingham 118
Now I Know It 43, 176, 187
O-112 155
O-130 155
O-376 156, 194
O-40 155
O-540 156
Ogle, Samuel 45, 102
Ogles, Major 54
Old Hagerstown Road 49, 50, 54
old Indian road 44, 146

251

Index

Old National Pike 46, 47, 54
Old Purchase 42, 159, 194
Old Sharpsburg Road 36, 41, 43, 49, 50, 191
Old South Mountain Inn 46
old wagon road (Frederick to Ft. Frederick) 165
Opequon (in Virginia) 42
Orendorff's Bridge 31, 32
Orr's Gap 44, 54
Orr, John 54
overseers for the road 49
Owings, Robert 43
Oxford 42, 43, 118, 125
P-387 156
P-632 157
pack horse ford 44
Parks Hall 44, 110, 118, 130, 194
Parks, William 118
part of Add to Friendship 162, 177, 179, 189
part of Christie's Folly 141, 168
part of Exchange 141
part of Fidler's Purchase 169
part of Fielderia Manor 167
part of Flonham 160, 161, 165, 166
part of Flonham and Remnant 165
part of Fox's Last Shift 204
part of Fredericksburg 161, 162, 163, 171, 173, 175, 177, 178
part of I Have Got It At Last 153
part of I Hope It Is Well Done 167, 176
part of Little Good 142
part of Mendall (Mindall) rsy 172
part of Mountain 174
part of Oxford 167
part of Parks Hall 146, 147, 148, 150, 154
Part of Partnership 195, 196
part of Pickall 154, 171, 172
part of Rsy on Exchange 159
part of Rsy on Learning 171
part of Rsy on Mendall (Mindall) 157, 172, 177
part of Rsy on Oxford 170, 173
part of Rsy on Roots Hill 146, 193
part of Rsy on The Gap 164
part of Rsy on Tom's Gift 159
part of The Forest 148, 155
part of Uncle's Gift 147, 153
Partnership 52, 119, 195, 197, 198, 200, 201
Pastures Green 42, 119
Paul's Travels 119
Peagley, Henry 110
Pecker (Baker), Peter 115

Peddicord, William B. 148, 154
Pegging Awl 43, 119, 164, 167, 175, 176
Penn's Disappointment 156, 194
Peter's Neglect 120, 176
Phillip's Cabin 104
Pickall 38, 43, 47, 154, 161, 167, 171, 177, 180, 181
Pierce, Ulrica Dahlgren 203
Pike, Old National 46, 47, 54
Pile's Grove 42, 100, 115, 116, 119, 120, 132, 140
Piles, James 152, 163
Poole's Delight 121
Poole's Delight Enlarged 121
Poplar Spring 100
Post Map 42
Potomac Ferry 49
Potomac River 107, 113, 121, 132, 135
Poulis (Powlis), Henry 103, 111
PP-33, 476-7 197
Prevention 50, 140
Prince Georges County Court 43
PT 1, 261-263 129
public house 44
public road through Burkettsville into Washington County 160
Punch Spring 106
Raccoon 49, 121, 196
Racon 36, 49, 121
Ram's Horn(s) 49, 103, 121
Reanolds, William 138
Red Hill 32
Rench, Daniel 195
Renninger, Adam 148
Reno Monument 35, 40, 191
Reno, General 191
Rhodes, Henry 49
Rhodes, Paul 119
Rice, Millard M. 50
ridge of the mountain 201, 202
Ridout, John 111
Ringer, John 50, 53, 54, 164, 175
Ringer, Mathias 150
Ringer, Sidney 159, 164
Ringold's Manor 33
road 118, 171, 178, 189
road by Robert Evans 49
road commonly called the wagon road 42, 106, 120, 140
road from Bartholomew Booker's to Peter Beaver's 50, 144, 154
road from Boonsboro to Frederick 200

road from Burkittsville to Gapland Station 184
road from Conestoga to Opequon 42, 107
road from Cumberland, Maryland, to Ohio 52
road from Elizabethtown (Hagerstown) to Newcomber's Mill 54
road from Fox's towards Sharpsburg 104
road from Frederick through Fox's Gap to Sharpsburg 101
road from Frederick to Ft. Frederick 36, 38, 45, 46, 48, 107, 108, 113, 120, 134, 157
road from Frederick to Hagerstown 50, 53, 169
road from Frederick to Sharpsburg 42, 128, 129, 179
road from Frederick to Stull's Mill (Hagerstown) 49, 54
road from Frederick to Swearingen's Ferry 109, 152
road from Frederick to Williamsport and Hagerstown 48, 171
road from Ft. Frederick to Ft. Cumberland 49
road from Funkstown to Turner's Gap 33
road from Isaac Houser's to Chapline's Mill 113
road from John Stull's Mill to the mouth of Monocacy 50, 132
road from Middletown to Sharpsburg 43, 167, 188
road from Monocacy to Conococheague (Williamsport) 43
road from Monocacy to John Stull's mill 53
road from Monocacy to Teague's Ferry 117, 152
road from Shafer's Mill to Turner's Gap 33
road from Sharpsburg to Frederick 40
road from Sharpsburg to Hagerstown 44
road from Stull's Mill 113
road from Stull's Mill to Conococheague (Williamsport) 54
road from Stull's Mill to Robert Turner's 99
road from Stull's Mill to the Monocacy 54
road from Swearingen's Ferry to Fox's Gap 41
road from Teague's Ferry to Monocacy Town 100
road from Volgamot's (Wohlgemuth's) to Stull's 54
road from Williamsport to Frederick 51
road from Williamsport to Turner's Gap 33, 199, 201

road near the South Mountain 121
road that goes to Stull's Mill 44
road through Burkettsville into Washington County 160
road through Fox's Gap 35
road through Frederick 42, 103
road through Frederick by Robert Evans 118
road to Annapolis 50
road to Conococheague (Williamsport) from Frederick 43, 44
road to Lamb's improvement 185
road to Opequon (in Virginia) 42
road to Philadelphia (in Pennsylvania) 42
road to Sharpsburg 176
road to Swearingen's Ferry and to mouth of Conococheague 44
road, bridal 45, 133
road, Great Philadelphia Wagon 42
road, Indian 44
road, John George's 49
road, lower main 152
road, main 40, 115
road, new 47
road, Old Hagerstown 49, 50, 54
road, old Indian 44, 146
road, Old Sharpsburg 36, 41, 43, 49, 50, 191
road, old wagon (Frederick to Ft. Frederick) 165
road, overseers 49
roads, beds of the present 51
Robinett, George 148
rock marked G S 1795 185
Roots Hills 124
Ross, David 105
Route 40 54
Routes 68 and 56 46
Routesawn, John 177
Routzah, Jacob 162
Routzah, John 53
Routzahn, George 38, 180
Routzahn, John N. 190
Routzong, George 161, 189
Routzong, Jacob 41, 161, 178, 179, 189
Rsy of Bear Swamp Forrest 185
Rsy of Mendall (Mindall) 110, 128, 188
Rsy of Roots Hill 124
Rsy of Security 42
Rsy of Wooden Platter 127
Rsy on Chestnut Hill 150
Rsy on Cool Spring 36
Rsy on Dawson's Purchase 150, 182

Index

Rsy on Exchange 43, 104, 122, 151, 159, 164, 169, 170, 174, 175
Rsy on Grim's Delight 178
Rsy on Hills and Dales and Vineyard 43, 138
Rsy on Learning 43, 134, 153, 187
Rsy on Learning, Add to Learning, and part of the Rsy on Learning 123, 183, 184
Rsy on Maryland 178
Rsy on Mason's Folly 191
Rsy on Mendall (Mindall) 38, 43, 50, 143, 144, 154, 171, 180, 187
Rsy on Middle Town (Neighbor's Content) 182
Rsy on Mt. Pleasant 42, 112, 119, 159, 194
Rsy on Oxford 125, 166, 173
Rsy on Park Hall 154
Rsy on Poole's Delight 182
Rsy on Security 42, 125
Rsy on Seven Mountains 125
Rsy on Stoney Ridge 169
Rsy on Stricker's Timberland 105, 181
Rsy on the Add to Pile's Delight 99
Rsy on The Gap 48, 53, 122, 166
Rsy on The Vineyard 124
Rsy on Tom's Gift 123
Rsy on Trembling 125, 145
Rsy on Watson's Welfare 124, 162
Rsy on Well Done 36, 126
Rsy on Whiskey Alley 50, 99, 127, 152
Rsy on Wooden Platter 170
Ruble, Peter 155
Rudy, Richard B. and Helen B. 190
Rumsey Bridge 42
Russell, Jacob 32
S-56 157
Sample, John 137
Sanner, Susan 190
Sanner, Vincent 43, 159, 164, 190
Schley, John 52
Schwartz, Russell and Judy 46
Scott's land 33
Scott, George 103, 185
Security 42, 128
Shafer, George 198
Shafer, John 195, 197
Shafer, Jonathan 198
Shafer, Philip Jacob 35, 53, 107
Shaff's Purchase 155
Shaff, Casper 50, 122, 140, 141, 146, 150, 151, 155
Shanandore Mountain (South Mountain) 43, 45, 48, 50, 100, 107, 152

Shank, John 149
Sharp, Governor 41, 49
Sharpsburg 42
Sharpsburg road 178, 179
Sharpsburg square 31, 32
Shaver (Shafer), John 130
Sheffer, Mary 38, 180
Sheffer, Phillip 53, 161
Sheffer, Phillip and Lucinda 160
Shelton, John 44, 146
Shepfell, Michael 51, 144
Shepherd's Ferry 41
Shepherd's ford 42
Shepherdstown 41, 42, 44, 49
Shettle 36, 38, 128, 156, 176, 177, 180, 188
Shidler's Dispute 36, 48, 144, 151
Shidler, George 144, 151
Short Hill Mountain 45, 115
Shotwell, Randolph Abott 53
Shoup, Samuel 40, 185, 186
Shuey, John 101
Simms, Iagnatious 33
Slifer, Ezra 158, 163
Slusser's Choice 129
Slusser, Peter 105, 111, 129
Small All 128
small branch 120, 131
Small Ridge 129
small run 112
Smeltzer, Adam 104
Smeltzer, Peter 111, 168
Smith Jr., Jacob 171
Smith Sr., Jacob 50, 171
Smith's Choice 111, 143
Smith's Hills 129
Smith's shop 32
Smith, Andrew 182
Smith, David 143
Smith, George F. 200, 201
Smith, Henry 168
Smith, Jacob 38, 154, 157, 172, 176, 177, 180, 183, 187, 188
Smith, James 47, 129, 141
Smith, Jonas 180
Smith, Joseph 44, 47
Smith, Michael 172
Smith, Richard 44, 102, 141
Smith, Robert 108, 130
Smithfield 50
Smithsburg 47
Snabely, Conrad 149, 193
Snavely, Casper 115

Snavely, Conrad 31, 32, 42
Snyder, Jacob 101
Society of the Burnside Expedition 191
Society of the Descendants of Frederick Fox
	of Fox's Gap in Maryland 233
South Mountain (Shanandore Mountain) 100,
	107, 204
South Mountain Inn, Old 46
Speilman, Jonas 199
Sprigg, Osborn 107
Spriggs, Edward 99
Spriggs, Richard 120
spring 100, 102, 106, 107, 109, 112, 114, 116,
	118, 120, 140, 154, 156
Spurgeon's Folly 148
Spurgeon, James 145
Spurgeon, John 148
square in Sharpsburg 31, 32
St. Mary's Academy of Notre Dame 53, 202,
	203
State Roads Commission 46
Stemple, John 162
Stewart (Steuart), William 124, 132
STH-267-367 184
stone fence 184, 197
stone marked 1747/B & S V G 187
stone marked 1794 119
stone marked 1800 B. S. 186
stone marked A 1709 135
stone marked at north east end TV 117
stone marked B:M 1789 108, 174
stone marked B:S P:M 1804 187
stone marked BP 101
stone marked BS 1792 184
stone marked GC B 1789 182
stone marked I B 100
stone marked PM 1789 182
stone wall 195, 196, 200, 201
Stoner, Stephen 52
Stoney Ridge 45, 129, 130, 158
Storm, Leonard 159
Stottlemire (Stottlemyer), David 149, 169
Strause, George 196
Stricker's Timberland Enlarged 181
Strife 130
Stull, John 54
subscriptions for stock 53
Sultiner, George 113
Summer's land 34
Summers, Jacob 196
Summers, John 52, 113, 121
Supply Bill of 1756 46

Sutton, Ashbury 121
Swearingen's 197
Swearingen's Disappointment 36, 52, 119,
	130, 195, 197, 198, 200, 201
Swearingen's Ferry 31, 32, 41, 42
Swearingen, Joseph 53, 175, 177, 185
Swearingen, Thomas 106, 114
T-19 157
Taneytown 42
Tasker Sr. (and Jr.), Benjamin 43, 124
tavern 44
Taylor, Michael 33
Teagues Creek 41
Teagues Ferry 41, 43
Team (Teem), John 35, 48, 134, 151, 157
Teats, Adam 152
Terms Stool 54
TG-6, 571 164
TG-8, 651 165
TG-9, 18 165
The Blooming Month of May 184
The Breeches 166
The Exchange 140
The Forest 44, 45, 50, 153, 182
The Forest of Needwood 131
The Gap 35, 36, 48, 108, 151
The Grove 144, 145
The Meadow 180
The Mountain 167
The Mountain Side 178
The Uncle's Gift 131
The Vineyard 43, 132, 198
The Wooden Platter 133
THO-1 184
THO-1, 244 187
THO-1-103 185
THO-1-116 186
THO-1-188 186
THO-1-194 186
THO-1-220 187
THO-1-238 187
THO-1-38 184, 185
THO-1-90 185
Thomas's Purchase 145
Thomas, Michael 145, 156, 194
three notches 128
Three Springs 141
TI 1, 486-487 133
TI 3, 236-237 117
Tick Neck 141, 183
Tomer's (or Domer's) Hill 32
Tomkin's Green 130

Index

Tomlinson, Joseph 47
Top of the Blue Ridge 183
top of the mountain 199
top of the South Mountain 32, 34, 98, 179, 188
town or village 204
Townsend, George Alfred 158, 184
Tracey and Dern 43
Tracey Collection 43, 47, 191
Tracey, Arthur 47
Travis Cabin Branch 100
TT-39, 778-780 197
Tucker, John 110, 149, 157, 183
Turkey Plains 131
Turkey Ramble 48, 131
Turkeyfoot 131, 164, 175, 176
Turner's Gap 34, 35, 40, 202, 203
Turner, Robert 45, 49, 51, 102, 106, 111, 113, 115, 117
turnpike road 35, 45, 48, 51, 52, 53, 196, 197, 200
turnpike road from Frederick to Boonsboro 163, 166
twelve notches 128
U. S. Senate 52
Ulrick, Henry 104
Uncle's Gift 131, 147, 150, 187
United States of America 184
unpatented certificate #368 114
Upper (or Hitt) Bridge 49
VanLear, Wm 34
Varle Map 50, 54
Varle, Charles 54
Vineyard 43, 132, 198
Volgamot's (Wohlgemuth's) 54
Volgamot, Joseph 47
Volton's (Vultan's) Seal 112, 132
W-283 158
W-327 158
wagon road 194
wagon road from Conestoga (in Pennsylvania) to Opequon (in Virginia) 42, 107
wagon road from Sharpsburg to Frederick 40
wagon road from Stull's Mill 113
wagon road from Teague's Ferry to Monocacy Town 100
wagon road gap 129
wagon road that crosses Antietam 129
wagon road through Frederick Town 103
wagon road to Philadelphia 42
wagon road to Stull's Mill 44
Walker, Thomas 44, 105, 113

Wampler, Lewis 52
War Correspondents Memorial Arch 158, 184
Ward's Spring 138
Wardrop, James 40, 47, 101, 103, 108, 112, 118, 120, 122, 127, 143, 144, 151, 186
Washington County Court House 48
Washington, George 41
Water Enough 164
Watson's Welfare 132, 162
WBT-10, 143 190
WBT-6, 283 188
We Could Not Agree 186
Weaver, Henry 152
Welch (Welsh), Thomas 50, 156, 169
What Not 50, 155, 162
Whiskey Alley 50
Whitaker, Mark and Thomas 49, 50, 140
Williams, Byron L. 46
Williams, Otho Holland 33
Williamson, James 100
Williamsport (Conocoheague) 41
Williard, Ezra 160
Wilson, Josiah 153
Wilson, Wadsworth 153, 155
Wilyard's Lot 45
Wilyard, Duvall 133
Wilyard, Elias 147, 187
Winchester (in Virginia) 42
Winder, Daniel 54
WIP-9, 148 189
Wise's tract 178, 179, 191
Wise, John 40, 178, 179
Wise, John W. 189, 191
Wise, Lana 189
Wise, Matilda 189
Wohlgemuth's (Volgamot's) mill 54
Wolstenholme, Daniel 47
Wooden Platter 42, 133, 143
Woodsborough 42
Worse and Worse 35, 36, 47, 48, 110, 134, 157, 184
WR 32-63 176
WR 4, 531 166
WR-12, 358-364 171
WR-12, 367-368 171
WR-12-56 170
WR-13-49 171
WR-13-621 173
WR-17-158-9 173
WR-22-480 173
WR-26-569 174
WR-27-543 174

WR-3-224 166
WR-31 174
WR-31-478 175
WR-32-225 176
WR-32-26-8 175
WR-32-28 175
WR-32-30 175
WR-34-313 177
WR-34-315 177
WR-36-85 177
WR-40, 275-276 178
WR-42-550 178
WR-6, 169 167
WR-7 167
WR-7-10 168
WR-7-33 168
WR-7-34 168
WR-7-48 169
WR-7-531 169
WR-8-632 169
WR-9-25 170
WR-9-607 170
WW-41, 545-546 198
WW-41, 630-632 198
Wyand, Jeffery 54
Y & S 6, 327-329 99
Y & S 7, 160 116
Y & S 7, 192 124
Y & S 7, 196-197 122
Y & S 8, 514-516 114
Y & S, 105 128
Yeaste, George 143
York (in Pennsylvania) 42
Young, Conrad 134, 141
Young, Jacob 167, 169, 173
Young, John 162
Young, John Jacob 158
Young, Stanley F. 190
Youngest Brother 134
Zittle (Gittle), Daniel 196, 197, 200, 201
Zittle (Gittle), Elizabeth 201
Zittle (Gittle), Josiah 199, 201
Zittle (Gittle), Mary Magdelena 201
Zittle (Gittle), Michael 195, 196, 198, 200
Zittle (Gittle), Peter 196
Zittle (Gittle), Seggrick 201

About the Author

Curtis L. Older was born in Danville, Illinois, in 1947. He served as a Spanish interpreter in the United States Navy from 1969 to 1973. He earned a Bachelor of Science in Accounting from Millikin University in Decatur, Illinois, in 1969, and a Master of Science in Accountancy from Northern Illinois University in DeKalb, Illinois, in 1974. He worked in public accounting and taught accounting at several universities from 1974 to 1990.

Since 1990, Curt, as he is known, has worked as a computer programmer and has devoted considerable time to the study of Fox's Gap in Maryland. His interests include studying the American Civil War, the American Revolution, and the concept of freedom as it relates to economic development. He is descended from Frederick Fox of Fox's Gap in Maryland as follows: George Fox, John L. Fox, Daniel Alexander Fox, Ethel Belle (Fox) Gouty, and Mavis Lorene (Gouty) Older.

The author at the grave of
Frederick Fox of Fox's Gap in Maryland
Gebhart Cemetery, Miamisburg, Ohio
Photo by Rachael Lynn Older
May 1998

www.ingramcontent.com/pod-product-compliance
Ingram Content Group UK Ltd.
Pitfield, Milton Keynes, MK11 3LW, UK
UKHW051301180426
11947UKWH00020B/1832